GOD DAY BY DAY

FOLLOWING THE WEEKDAY LECTIONARY

VOLUME THREE

ORDINARY TIME:

LUKE

COMMENTARY ON THE TEXTS

SPIRITUAL REFLECTIONS * SUGGESTED PRAYERS

MARCEL BASTIN · GHISLAIN PINCKERS · MICHEL TEHEUX
TRANSLATED BY ROBERT R. BARR

Paulist Press ● New York/New Jersey

Library of Congress Cataloging In Publication Data

(Revised for vol. 3)

Bastin, Marcel.
   God day by day.

      Translation of: Dieu pour chaque jour.
      Vol. 2 has bibliography: p. 450–451.
      Vol. 3 translated by Robert R. Barr.
      Contents: v. 1. Lent and the Easter season —
v. 2. Ordinary time: Matthew — v. 3. Ordinary time:
Luke.
      1. Church year—Prayer-books and devotions—
English.   2. Devotional calendars—Catholic Church.
3. Bible—Liturgical lessons, English.   4. Catholic
Church—Liturgy.   I. Pinckers, Ghislain.   II. Teheux,
Michel.   III. Title.

BX2170.L4B3713   1984   242'.3   84-60391
ISBN 0-8091-2642-7 (pbk. : v. 1)
ISBN 0-8091-2643-5 (pbk. : v. 2)

Published by Paulist Press
997 Macarthur Blvd.
Mahwah, New Jersey 07430

Printed and bound in the United States of America

CONTENTS

This volume is the third in a series that covers the entire weekday lectionary. There have been many books of commentary, suggestions and prayers for the Sundays of the three-year cycle. There was still a need, however, of a similar aid for the days of the corresponding weeks; this need has been met here.

The structure and organization of each volume is simple. The order of the weekdays has been followed, with groupings according to the liturgical seasons or to other coherent units, each of which opens with an introductory statement.

For each day there are three sections:

1. A short commentary on the readings and psalm. Here a professional scripture scholar derives a substantial, clear and coherent message from the sacred texts.

2. Spiritual reflections for use in personal meditation, homily preparation, or other individual and collective purposes outside of Mass.

3. Suggested prayers, offered as ways of prolonging meditation through (for example) thanksgiving or for use during the day. These prayers are characterized by biblical language.

The commentaries, suggestions and prayers are not meant, of course, to replace the texts and prayers of the liturgy itself. On the contrary, by helping to prepare for the liturgy and to prolong it outside of Mass, they aim to be at the service of the liturgical action proper. The following pages, springing as they do from the eucharistic liturgy, have for their purpose the sanctification of each day, and to this end they offer a message that will bring to light the spiritual benefits of that privileged liturgical action.

The Publisher

THE FIVE VOLUMES OF THE SERIES

Vol. 1: Lent and the Easter Season
Vol. 2: Ordinary Time: Matthew
Vol. 3: Ordinary Time: Luke
Vol. 4: Advent and Christmas; the Sanctoral Cycle
Vol. 5: Ordinary Time: Mark

N.B. These volumes are based on the ministry and experience of the parish of Saint-Denis in Liège. A very large congregation comes daily to this church, which is located in a section of the city devoted exclusively to trade, administration, and leisure-time activities. A constantly shifting community has thus been formed. This is another face of the church that may be glimpsed in the following pages.

INTRODUCTION

The aims and possible uses of this work have already been explained in the first volume (Lent and the Easter Season).

This third volume covers Weeks 22–34 of Ordinary Time in both uneven and even years. The division we have chosen for Ordinary Time is based on the reading of the three synoptic Gospels. Volume 3, therefore, covers the weeks in which the Gospel According to Matthew is read.

The exegesis of the gospel (which is read in both uneven and even years) is given under the heading of "Uneven Years." For the even years we simply refer the reader to the correct page in the uneven years.

We have remained faithful to the general principle that governs the entire work: to set the two readings side by side and use each to shed light on the other, at least whenever this is possible. In the case of certain particularly important books, however, we have prioritized their continuous reading.

Readers who prefer to link their daily reflection to a continuous commentary on the gospel will find a table at the end of the book which will refer them to the uneven, and the even, years.

UNEVEN YEARS

ORDINARY TIME
WEEKS 22-34

Gospel According to Saint Luke
First Letter to the Thessalonians
Letter to the Colossians
First Letter to Timothy
Ezra, Haggai, Zechariah, Nehemiah, Baruch, Jonah, Malachi, Joel
Letter to the Romans
Wisdom
First Book of Maccabees
Daniel

The third gospel has a special flavor. It is perhaps the easiest of the synoptic gospels to appreciate today. Would this be because it grafts the proclamation of faith, and the novelty of the revelation manifested in Jesus Christ, to the common longing of all human beings and the common values underlying that universal hope? Luke addresses pagans, and this is surely one of the reasons why his message stirs its special echo in this heart of ours so concerned with contemporary questions. But another reason why we find Luke a gospel for our times is that it shows us the face of God that constitutes the Christian revolution, the Christian "conversion." Well has the Gospel According to Luke been called the gospel of mercy. God is another sort of God here, a God with different traits from the ones with which we spontaneously sketch our own image of God.

A comparison of this gospel with the readings from the letters of Paul is instructive in this regard. The only thing Paul has to impart to the young communities he has founded is this novelty of Christian faith and the revolution it begets in the lives of believers. Luke preaches a new word of grace, and the novelty of a life turned topsy-turvy by the infinite mercy of a God who would bestow himself on human beings, the novelty of a faith secured by no other bond than a promise tendered and received.

The prophets of the exile manifest the same astonished reaction to a seemingly preposterous message, a message upside-down and backwards. Hope will have the last word! Nor do we mean, by hope, a "hope" kept up "for what it's worth" throughout the random vagaries of history that might

3

give it the lie at any moment. No, this hope is a steadfast one, because, with all believers of all times, we have but a humble testimony to offer: we declare that God has come among us. God makes our trial his own, and now our exile is transformed. The gospel has been proclaimed, and we come home—home to the promised land.

READING AND UNDERSTANDING LUKE

Luke, Evangelist of the Spirit

No one questions the fact that Luke wrote for non-Jews. But do we grasp the implications of this fact? The pagans inject something totally, radically new into the life of the primitive church. The religious culture of the Jews is completely foreign to them. How can they be told of the Messiah, for example, when they have never entertained messianic expectations?

We are scarcely surprised, then, to see the evangelist initiate a new pedagogical method. He does not begin with the proclamation of Jesus Christ. Or if he does, he does so in terms of the human values already cultivated by his pagan audience. He even exhorts his addressees to live their values in depth. After all, he knows these values to be the vessels of the breath of the Spirit, and thus just so many stepping-stones to a proclamation of the Good News.

For, we see, the Spirit is the principal personage of the Third Gospel. Luke's Christians know nothing of the traditions of Jewish religious history. They are acquainted with the Christian communities, however, and this experience has been a challenge to them even before their conversion. Now they are full-fledged members of these communities. Thanks to the witness of men and women who live by the Spirit, they have become Christians. If there is any message that Luke seeks to transmit, it is that the Spirit by which the church lives is precisely the Spirit by which Jesus has lived. Christians and Jesus are one another's contemporaries. They live by the same Spirit. And this will be Luke's starting point. Using an inductive method, the evangelist begins with facts available to his readers, and leads them to Christ Jesus before they are aware of it. The Third Gospel, then, can only be read in tandem with the Acts of the Apostles.

The activity of the Spirit is underscored from the outset. In the annunciation, the Spirit is present to stand warranty for the New Creation unfolding in the Virgin's womb. He is present in Jesus' baptism, too, and in the inaugural discourse at Nazareth, guaranteeing the authenticity of the message issuing from the young prophet's lips. After all, the word of Jesus' proclamation is an astounding one. It is a message of grace for all women and men. God loves everyone! Is there any likelihood that such a message will be heard? Luke has too much experience of mission not to propose a response to a question which is this basic for the church. As Paul's companion on the apostle's great missionary journeys, Luke has observed the favorable impact of the word of Jesus on the Gentiles. For him, then, the future is secure: the word of grace will not return without having borne fruit. [CF. J. Radermackers and P. Bossuyt, *Jésus, Parole de la Grace selon saint Luc*, Bruxelles, 1982.]

The Holy Face

A face. What an encounter! Surprising, mysterious. Dare to be gripped by its presence, its glance, and—what a miracle!

A face has but one thing by which to invite us to an encounter: the strength of its presence. The only means it has of manifesting itself is to present itself, to offer itself. The only meaning a face has for me is its meaning for my life. Its appearance in my life has no need of long discourses to demonstrate that it launches a revolution. Let a face come into my life and suddenly I have a taste for living.

Jesus is the holy Face of God, the icon and image of the invisible God. In this human being, we believe, our entire adventure with God is concentrated. In the traits of this person's life, God shows us that he does not refuse to bear human dreams in his arms, and that even now he is transfiguring our hopes into eternal reality. In Christ, a frontier has been crossed. We are in a new land. The hidden face of things has been revealed to us. We have become "capable of eternity."

We must fulfill God's word. That is, we must carry it towards ultimate consequences, allow it to become reality, unfold its hidden potential, thrust its dynamism to the maximum. A face is beautiful not only as an object of contemplation—museums are filled with "beautiful faces"—but because it begets encounter. It engenders a relationship. It creates something new. A face is made for caresses, for kisses. Then no one will ever exhaust its richness. A face can become a portrait only if it dies.

From now till everlasting, God has bound the face of his Son to the visage of humanity. Jesus, Icon of God, will never be an adorable portrait. The holy Face will always be modeled in the living traits of a humanity transfigured by God's own tenderness.

■

Only-begotten One of the Father, Jesus Christ,
in your face we contemplate
the glory with which you shone
in the bosom of God before all ages.

You who dwell among us,
O Word full of every grace,
teach us truth,
transform us into your image.

To you be glory, Holy Father,
as to your Son be praise,
with the Spirit, the Comforter,
always and everywhere, to everlasting ages.

MONDAY OF THE 22ND WEEK

THIS PERSON CALLED JESUS

1 Thessalonians 4:13-17: Paul broaches a question with which the first Christians are most deeply concerned. As we know, the first generation of Christians—Paul included—firmly expected Christ's imminent return. Of course, they did not know the date of that return. So they were anxious as to the fate of any Christians who would have died before the moment of this Parousia. What was ultimately at stake here was the resurrection of the body. This was a special problem for the Greeks, who stubbornly resisted any notion of survival after death. Paul bases his response on Christ's resurrection, and places a great deal of emphasis on the divine power that has raised Jesus from the dead. After all, it is this same might that will raise Christians who will have died.

As for the description of the meeting of believers with their Lord, Paul borrows the images from the most traditional apocalyptic of the time. He refers to a teaching of Christ, which may have been part of the whole teaching of Jesus that Paul has received concerning the end of the ages, or may simply be a product of post-resurrection Christian reflection under the guidance of the Spirit.

Psalm 96 is one of the hymnic psalms, placed here because of its theophanic elements, which are suggestive of Christ's return.

Luke 4:16-30: Jesus' inaugural discourse at Nazareth? Why not? Jesus enters the synagogue at Nazareth, takes up the book of the scriptures, and pronounces his commentary on the prophet Isaiah. But in the background we can make out the figures of Paul preaching to the Jews of the synagogue, and Stephen provoking with his discourse the wrath of members of the Sanhedrin.

Indeed, underlying the whole of Luke's gospel is Acts, that compendium of the entire missionary experience.

Seized by the spirit of his baptism, Jesus addresses the Jews for the first time. For the first time a message of grace issues from his lips. He rereads his mission in light of Isaiah: yes, he has been sent to proclaim the Year of Jubilee, the age of the Lord's favors, the moment of deliverance for the earth and all humanity. That the message is one of grace is set in relief by Jesus' conscious omission of the prophet's threatening finale: ". . . a day of vindication by our God . . ." (Is 61:2). The Year of Jubilee is the Year of the Great Pardon.

But Jesus' life will bear witness to the fact that one is never a prophet in one's own country. To the people of Nazareth, the son of the carpenter is too familiar. They will be blind to the New Human Being in him, unreachable by the One bearing the mark of the Spirit. And so, as past experience shows, there is nothing for it but to leave the synagogue and carry the word to the pagans—to the widow of Zarephath, to the leper of Syria.

■

"Jesus came to Nazareth where he had been reared. . . ." His name was Jesus of Nazareth. And the first apostles proclaimed this. They would make it very clear to their audience that the person of whom they spoke was none other than "Jesus Christ the Nazorean whom you crucified and whom God has raised from the dead" (Acts 4:10).

"He shall be called a Nazorean" (Mt 2:3). We believe, not in an idea, but in a human being—a particular individual in time and space. We proclaim a reality of our history, not a notion of some kind—not mere mystical experiences, then, and still less an ideology, but an event, an occurrence among a particular number of men and women who were transformed by it into witnesses and heralds of the Word.

Jesus is not a myth. He is an individual human being, someone who lived in a temporal context, in a sociological environment. With his roots in a particular locale, and stemming from a particular lineage, he belonged to a family. Together with other persons he studied the Bible. He worked as a carpenter, who at that time was a sort of jack-of-all-trades. He had friends of all kinds. He entered into disputes with representatives of the official religion and of various sects. He spoke, acted, and lived in the midst of one particular people, espousing their faith and their customs, learning their language, sharing their psychology.

Jesus is a fact. Our Christianity would be false if we failed to take account of the "fleshly" truth of that fact. Were we to ignore this truth, we would fail to appreciate the density of the incarnation. Jesus is not just any human being, but a particular human being. Surely here we have the reason for the questions asked at Nazareth when the evangelist Luke, opening his account, presents us with a portrait of Jesus. "Incarnation," just in itself, fails to do justice to the content of these three words: Jesus of Nazareth. The scandal arises when two assertions are coupled: Jesus is from Nazareth; and it is Jesus who opens the book of the scriptures in the synagogue, reads the passage from Isaiah, and declares: "Today this scripture passage is fulfilled in your hearing."

In this human being, we believe, the whole human adventure with God is concentrated. It is he who is the pinnacle and the totality of revelation. "Today this scripture passage is fulfilled," Jesus cries. Today his declaration is eternal, for it remains the ongoing challenge of this remarkable person named Jesus. We believe not only in a great human being, an admirable hero of our humanity—we assert that this great human being is God's "last word."

"Today this scripture passage is fulfilled. . . ." The encounter is accomplished today. It is in the banality of our everyday life that we are challenged by our faith. Now the grandeur of our humdrum lives is unveiled for us: here in the lowly "today" of ordinary life, we meet God. After all, we meet God whenever we are confronted with the revelation of this human Jesus and we respond by saying: "To whom shall we go? You have the words of eternal life." Only these words will utter the totality of the mystery.

■

Today is your word fulfilled:
your Word, your only-begotten, touches our heart
and every day becomes the day of salvation.
Be blessed, God of the word that is promise:
may our fleeting "today" grow to be an eternity—
the eternity of the everlasting encounter.

TUESDAY OF THE 22ND WEEK

THE WAGER
1 Thessalonians 5:1–6, 9–11: Like Jesus, Paul does not judge it useful to enter upon disquisitions as to "specific times and moments." But he insists that the Day of the Lord will be sudden. The Lord will come when people least expect it.

Actually, does he not come every day?

This passage contains no threat, but it is intended as an admonition. Paul is appealing for watchfulness. Christians must know that they belong to light and not darkness. The path they tread leads to life, not to death. God's will is a will of salvation. "God has not destined us for wrath but for acquiring salvation through our Lord Jesus Christ," and this applies to the living and dead alike.

Psalm 27 combines an individual lament (vv. 7–14) with a royal psalm of trust (vv. 1–6). Its character as a royal psalm clearly appears in verse 4, since the "contemplation of the loveliness of the temple of God"—keeping watch over the sanctuary of Yahweh—is an eminently royal task. Today this vigilance is to be recommended to all Christians. Besides, there is a new temple to watch over and guard: the church.

Luke 4:31–37 tells of a day at Capernaum, the locale par excellence of Jesus' activity. At first glance this typical day would seem to differ but little from the one described in Mark 1:21–44. We have a healing in the synagogue on the sabbath, and we have the "implosion" of God into the life of a person stunned by the distance that divides him from the divinity. But while Mark emphasizes the novelty of Jesus' teaching (Mk 1:27), Luke insists on its nature as an event. The exorcism becomes a *dâbâr*—a bewildering, challenging word.

■

People were thunderstruck by Jesus' teaching. A human being rises up in the name of God and the world is set on its ear—literally "converted," turned around, turned upside-down. The old world is gone. A new world is already born! Of course, what we see in the gospel is a world, not upside-down, but right-side-out. After all, human beings are not made to be possessed by someone else, to be dispossessed of themselves, demeaned, bound hand and foot by forces beyond their control. In the eternal will of God the Creator, men and women are made to live erect and free, with their eyes turned to heaven.

Jesus' challenge pierced the sufferer to the heart. Jesus speaks—and is—the Word that holds life in its bosom. His are the cries we hear, from time to time, that strike us with all their force, in radical protest of our petty narrowness, and dare us to emerge from ourselves.

Today, new sages write: "No, we shall no longer bear human dreams in our arms, for we know them vain, and we know our impotence. But the demand abides, and this will be our care and concern: to make the maddest, most senseless of wagers—that human beings can change into the thing that is most profound within them" (Bernard-Henri Lévy).

Today the only sign God gives us is the transformation of women and men into what is deepest within them. Is this not what we call salvation? Is it not "the maddest of wagers"? And yet God makes that wager. "Come out of him."

Do we realize?—this sign is ourselves. Under the guidance of the Spirit we form the church of Jesus Christ. "You are not in the dark . . . so that the day might catch you off guard, like a thief. No, all of you are children of light and of the day. . . . God has . . . destined us . . . for acquiring salvation through our Lord Jesus Christ." Bond for a wager— we? Yes, this is what we are when, on the strength of our faith in the words of the savior, we begin to relish the exhilaration of snatching ourselves from the grasp of the enslaving powers of our age to become disciples of the freedom of the gospel. This is what we are when, cost what it may, we want to be artisans of peace; when, without despair but without naiveté, we bear witness to hope, and to a future that is genuinely possible; when, despite our divisions, and the world's separatisms, we gather around one Word and one Bread.

"All began saying to one another: 'What is there about his speech?' " God does not let human dreams slip from his arms. Even now he is making them daily realities.

■

You speak and you act.
Creative God,
>*renew the face of the earth*
>*and we shall be saved.*

See the overpowering evils that possess us!
"Come out of him."
May your word deliver us.
>*Lord, have mercy on us.*

How many sufferings bring us to the brink of despair!
"Come out of him."
May your word be our future.
>*O Christ, have mercy on us.*

Sin engulfs us still.
"Come out of him."
May your word be our forgiveness.
>*Holy One of God, have mercy on us.*

TO SPEAK OF FAITH

Colossians 1:1–8: The church at Colossae is beset with the same problems as at Ephesus, in the sense that, here too, the community is beginning to feel the lethal influence of the Gnostic doctrines. We recall that Gnosticism was a speculative movement resting on a dualistic view of the universe, reaching its apogee in the course of the second century A.D., when it had spread throughout the Jewish and pagan worlds alike. By now the danger is such that in the beginning of his letter, Paul is moved to confirm, by his apostolic authority, the preaching of his disciple Epaphras, a native Colossian and the founder of the community. The letter likewise testifies to the prudence with which the apostle approaches a church that he has not himself built: his first words are in praise of the Colossians' faith and hope, both founded on the Good News.

Are we certain of the Pauline authorship of this letter? As with the Letter to the Ephesians, opinions are divided, especially since Colossians bears resemblances to letters of different dates. For example, the Gnostic threat conjures up a milieu impregnated by Pauline thought but belonging to the post-apostolic generation, while the christological reflection of Colossians is close to the Adamological themes of the Letter to the Romans.

Psalm 52 belongs to the group of psalms known as psalms of thanksgiving. Verse 10 recalls the trust that has led the faithful into Yahweh's presence, and verse 11 actually introduces thanksgiving.

Luke 4:38–44: Paul welcomed "all who came to him. . . . He preached the reign of God and taught about the Lord Jesus Christ" (Acts 28:30–31). "To other towns I must announce the good news of the reign of God, because that is why I was sent" (Lk 4:43). Luke underscores the continuity he has discovered between the preaching of Jesus and Paul. For example, he relates the experience of the Hellenistic communities to the Jesus event. After all, for Luke there is no distinction between the time of the church and that of Jesus, since the same Spirit is at work in both.

We hear of another cure, that of Simon's mother-in-law, who thereupon takes her place at the head of the list of all who will soon be placing themselves at the service of the young community. Finally, Jesus works a great number of cures and exorcisms at the hour of sunset, recalling the disappearance of the sun at the moment of his death (Lk 23:44).

The first words addressed by Paul to the Colossians are: ". . . We have heard of your faith. . . ."! Believing is an act, not a pious feeling. It is the same with faith as with love: only in their exercise do we discover what they are. The ultimate justification of faith is its simple existence. The truth of faith is experienced only in exercising it, in living it: I know that faith makes sense because it gives my life a meaning, it undergirds my actions, it liberates my thought, it affirms my taste for life. Love has no need of long discourses in order to demonstrate its importance: it is enough that it be a source of joy, pleasure, gift, and life. Faith consists in deeds of faith. Faith is the glory of believers. Perhaps we forget that "believer" comes from a verb in the present tense and the active voice! Faith can only be active and "now." The Good News is revealed when the blind see, the lame walk, and the deaf hear. The gospel is written in the active voice. There is no such thing as a "non-practicing Christian."

Faith is a practice because it is modeled on Jesus—Jesus the Savior. Jesus is not just someone I see before me, beckoning me to follow him. Jesus is actually within me. Therefore when I live according to his invitation to follow him I can say that I am "living in the faith." Suddenly "I live, now not I, but Christ lives in me!" It is because Jesus is within me, in truth and in word, that I can live his word and act in accordance with his truth. It is because he is within me as the source of life that, even now, his life quickens my heart, my mind, and my deeds.

We thank God for your faith! We bless God not for your merits or your good works, we grant no certificate of a moral life, we give out no stars for good behavior. When we bless God on your account, it is because of what God accomplishes within you. As a liturgical prayer so well says: "To offer you our praise, we can but point to your own gifts." A reciprocal relationship obtains between the act of believing and the fruits of faith. After all, the beginning and end of faith are one and the same: the encounter with God.

■

Increase our faith:
    only this prayer can be heard.
God our Father,
    be blessed for what you have accomplished in our lives even now.
And be blessed even now
    for what your grace will accomplish still.

A Gospel Written for Both Jews and Gentiles (5:1–9:17)

The Acts of the Apostles report the development of the first Christian mission. Generally speaking, Christian preachers addressed the Jews first. Then, because of the mistrust, indeed the open hostility, encountered in the synagogues, they turned to the pagans. Thus the church quickly gathered converts from both milieus, Jewish and pagan, and now these two elements had to learn to live together.

The presence of two distinct religious traditions precluded addressing them both in a single word or in a single form. Thus, to do justice to the religious aspirations of each tradition, the one word of God had to be diversified. Luke's interesting demonstration of this diversification begins in chapter five. Two figures emerge, each symbolizing one of the communities. First we have Peter, fisher of the Sea of Galilee. The word Jesus addresses to him shows him the seriousness of his sin, along with the holiness of the One speaking with him. In Peter we somehow feel the mysterious presence of the great Jewish prophets, Isaiah and the rest. But we are also aware of the people of a covenant, called to hope when Yahweh blessed Abraham and his posterity, and called to witness with the bestowal of the law of Sinai. Today, however, it is the whole church, the new Israel, that is called with Peter to live the law of the Beatitudes, in light of the great messianic themes (5:1–6:49).

After Simon, Jesus addresses the Roman centurion (7:1–10). Here, however, we have neither call nor witness. On the contrary, the centurion is sent back where he came from. And yet something has changed. Henceforth his life has a meaning. He knows that it has been signed by the Spirit. He knows that he must take the zeal he shows for his sick slave and develop it to the maximum. It is Jesus who has made him aware of all that—or rather the Risen One, the individual who has restored a son to his mother on the road to Naim (7:11–17) and given a prostitute of the town a second chance by showing her how much more her heart is worth than her way of life (7:36–50).

Jewish and pagan converts are thus both sprung from a Word that, while one and the same for both groups, is diversified in form. Now a question arises in each group. This Jesus—who is he? And that question resounds in the hearts both of those who have already bestowed their faith (8:21), and of those who yet stand aloof (9:9). Who is this Jesus, who sends the Twelve on their mission (9:1–6)? Why does he convoke a gathering in the desert? What manner of meal can this be (9:10–17)?

CATCH AND BE CAUGHT

Colossians 1:9-14: Paul's prayer echoes difficulties that have arisen in the Church of Colossae. The trouble is so severe that Epaphras has decided to call on the apostle. The unity of the church community is threatened by the appearance of Gnostic tendencies in its midst. One of the ploys of Gnosticism was to dangle before Christian eyes the shimmering lure of a higher knowledge of the "mysteries," a special, exclusive knowledge, to complement mere faith in Christ, and exalt its possessors above the simple faithful. And so we are not surprised at the polemical tone of Paul's prayer: ". . . We have been . . . asking that you may attain full knowledge *(epiqno-sis)* of his will through perfect wisdom and spiritual insight."

For Paul, the Gnostic ambition to attain a higher knowledge was both superfluous and perverse. It was superfluous because it ignored the fact that the cross of Christ, which is the one source of salvation, had already brought believers out of the realm of darkness into the reign of light. It was perverse because it surreptitiously stripped the cross of all its value. And finally, with the Gnostics begins the long line of those who, throughout church history, have made salvation dependent on personal effort when it is first and foremost a divine gift.

Of course, we must not conclude, from Paul's onslaught, that he regards "works" as superfluous. No, deeds are not without value. On the contrary, the apostle strives precisely to correct the Gnostic tendency to exalt knowledge over the practical life. For Paul, true wisdom must engender good works.

Psalm 98 is a hymn, and is placed here in response to the Pauline invitation to render thanks.

Luke 5:1-11: In leaving us his accounts of Simon's encounter with Jesus, and the Roman centurion's intervention on behalf of his slave (7:1-10), Luke offers us a remarkable illustration of two "manners of being," two ways of taking a position vis-à-vis God's word. He does so in order to accommodate the particular sensitivity of Hellenistic churches, such as that of Antioch, in Syria, where Jews and pagans were making each other's acquaintance and developing a mutual appreciation.

Simon represents Israel, the Israel of the covenant, defined by its obedience to the law of Sinai. Thrice Jesus calls, and thrice Simon is challenged. First Jesus requests the hospitality of his boat. Then he dares him to cast his nets, in utter disregard of the failure of the night's toil. Finally, Jesus reveals to Peter, in the latter's sinfulness, the chronic faithlessness of the people to whom he belonged. Now this triple call will make its way into Simon's heart, along with the blessing of which they are the vessel—just as did Yahweh's words to Abraham of old. Now these three "words" will converge in a sending, a mission like that of an Israel of yore called to bear witness to its God. And the disciple obeys. He will "catch men."

■

Jesus' friends had struggled all night through, and returned in frustration. Now suddenly Jesus invites them to go once more to the deep and cast their nets. And the catch is beyond all belief. The nets begin to snap. Throughout all the centuries to come Christians will hear of the "miraculous catch of fish." And this could have been the whole story. What happened next day could have been something else. But Jesus pursues his point: "From now on you will be catching men." The image is striking, and the unusual event becomes a parable. That morning, Jesus unveiled the mission of the church.

Catching human beings. And fierce is the competition along the shores! Sects, gurus, ideologies dangle the bait under the noses of masses of men and women swept hither and yon in the tumultuous currents of a life with no recognizable meaning. Is the church, then, just one competitive fishing concern among many?

"From now on you will be catching men." But human beings can be caught like prisoners, or they can be caught like lovers! "From now on you will be catching men." Yes, but the church can only cast its nets in the fashion of its Lord. It has caught people, yes. It has called them, yes, but without deceiving them. It has enlightened them with its truth, but has not manipulated them. It has fortified them with its spirit, but without doing them violence. Yes, Jesus catches people. But he catches them that they may have joy. He sets them free. Jesus catches people that they may be "taken with" him. Jesus catches people that they may fall in love with him.

Henceforth the church has the mission of broadcasting the Word to all the winds, that men and women may be seduced by that glance that awakens them to life and freedom. "From now on. . . ," Jesus says. Start now. Now you are on your way. Your starting point is this experience. Here is where you begin, and not only in the temporal sense—from this moment forward—but in the causal sense as well. You begin your mission precisely in virtue of the experience you have now had. The church has been seduced, but it refuses to play seducer. Pressure, slogans, rote, have no place in mission. The vocation of the church is not to snare people in its nets; the task of the church is not to "have" persons, possess them—the church touches only those who have seen their freedom awakened, aroused, raised to life again. It is out of the freedom of a converted heart awakening to self-abandonment that the cry bursts forth, "Thou knowest that I love thee"! Only lovers are caught in nets that plunge them into the liberty of life.

■

You have seduced us, God of tenderness,
*   by your care for us.*
Your love has become a passion
*   for revealing to us your project:*
*   to catch us in the nets of your loving-kindness.*
Grant that we may abandon ourselves to just such a passion.
*   Give us to know the joy of being loved forever.*

FRIDAY OF THE 22ND WEEK

ORIGIN AND GOAL OF FAITH

Colossians 1:15–20: What is the apostle's motivation for inserting a christological hymn at this point? We can deduce the reason from his insistence on the role of Christ in creation. "In him," writes Paul, "everything . . . was created, things visible and invisible . . ." (cf. Jn 1:3). The latter Joannine verse envisages the heavenly beings, angelic or astral powers exalted by the Gnostics above the material universe for its governance. The Pauline hymn too, then, appears as a well-deserved attack on the Gnostic heresy.

Divided into two parallel strophes, Paul's hymn celebrates the universal supremacy of Christ. On the one hand Christ is the image of the invisible God. On the other, he is a "beginning" of something, a "head" of something. Here it is obviously the church, as the source of salvation, that Paul has in mind. Once these two foundational propositions have been made, the apostle fleshes them out, details them, with a stylistic interplay of gradations and parallelisms. Christ, he tells his audience, is the image of the invisible God in his capacity as the firstborn of creation. He holds his "preeminence and consecration" in virtue of having participated in all creation. In like manner he is principal and head of life, since he is the first to have been raised from the dead: "It pleased God to make absolute fullness reside in him, and, by

17

means of him, to reconcile everything in his person . . . making peace through the blood of his cross."

Thus the christology of the poem focuses primarily on Christ's action, his "work," which renders the firstborn Christ the one and only source of salvation. Flying in the face of Gnostic speculation, the hymn asserts first of all that only Christ, as co-creator, can reveal God—a declaration worth its weight in gold in the presence of a heresy that insisted on God's invisibility and then concerned itself with manifesting him to human beings. Second, however, the poem also emphasizes the redemptive value of the cross. Thanks to the cross, all things, in heaven and on earth, have been reconciled.

Psalm 100:3 takes up the themes of the hymn and invites us to acknowledge in Christ the image of the invisible God.

Luke 5:33–39: A bit jumbled by the lectionary, the sequence (Lk 5:12–6:49) recalls the three great themes of the messianic preaching. Verse 32 sums these up: "I have not come to invite the self-righteous to a change of heart, but sinners." Jesus then concretizes this appeal for reconciliation in the invitations he addresses to tax collectors and other sinners to take their places with him at table (5:29–32). The repast to which they are invited is an offer both of forgiveness and of a communion in friendship and living—as is suggested by the two miracle accounts immediately preceding: the cleansing of the leper, now readmitted to the body social (5:12–16), and the healing of the paralytic after his reconciliation with God (5:17–26).

When all is said and done, what Jesus preaches is the unexpected. But who will lend an ear to the word of so bewildering a God? This message is too like a wine that has not been sufficiently aged: it will be disagreeable to the palate, and some will prefer to return to their routine.

■

A face is surprising. A face is mysterious. True, if you look at it "right up close," you only make out skin, lashes, and so forth. But if you let yourself be "taken" by the presence of that face, challenged by its glance—ah, then, what a marvel! What an encounter!

Some did violence to Jesus' face. They saw only a Nazarene, a killjoy, a public danger. To torture him was sport, and himself an object of ridicule, with his face all covered with blood and spittle. Truly here was an object of rejection. But others followed Jesus, fascinated by his mystery, and these found a reign of light and peace. Paul has discovered a language for designating the inexpressible: this poem, sung by the community. "Christ is the image of the invisible God. . . ."

Like Father, like Son. In the face of the Son, we are certain to know the unapproachable Father, and we begin, in love, the inexhaustible exploration that will penetrate the mysteries of God.

The Letter to the Colossians will open out upon two perspectives. First: the well-beloved Son appears to us here as the one who has given himself up for us completely in being handed over to death. Then must not his Father, too, consist of consummate, overflowing gift? Second: it is Christ who delivers us from all of our debts, from our enslavement to laws, from the imperialism of all manner of servitude. Then will not his Father be the font of all peace? In the contemplation of Jesus Christ, all of the false images of an authoritarian, crushing, legalistic God go up in smoke. No, we are attracted by love. As image of the invisible God, and perfect reflection of his glory, Jesus is the only route of access to that God. "Whoever has seen me has seen the Father" (Jn 14:9).

But this revelation does not come to us from without. Christ is not a mere ambassador with a message. He *is* the very message. When Jesus speaks to us of God, his word wells up from within ourselves. For he is not only the image of the invisible God, he is Head of the Body, as well. And if we are believers, it is surely only because he, firstborn from the dead, believes in us. "I am the vine, and you are the branches." At the origin and terminus of faith is Christ—and Christ alone, for God has willed that in him all things have their total fulfillment.

■

We have contemplated the face of your Son,
     the features of your own visage, O invisible God.
In his words, we have recognized
     the Word you pronounce from all eternity,
     O God whose name cannot be discovered.
Be blessed, then—for Jesus, the origin of our faith,
     and for the Spirit, who guides that faith
     to its goal and consummation.
All honor and glory be yours.

RECONCILIATION

Colossians 1:21–23: "You yourselves were once alienated from him. . . ." In bygone days, even you were strangers to God. In a few quick phrases, Paul evokes the Colossians' situation before their conversion to Christianity. Soon, as in the Letter to the Ephesians (chap. 3), he will be speaking of the "mystery"—God's manner of implementing his salvific will. For the apostle, this design of God's is especially manifested in the reconciliation of Jews and pagans, who up until now have been divided in every way. Paul also emphasizes the work of Christ, and exhorts his addressees not to abandon the hope engendered in them by the proclamation of the gospel.

To act in this way is to place our trust in God—the invitation of *Psalm 54.*

Luke 6:1–5: According to Luke's version, the sabbath during which the disciples had been picking a little grain was no ordinary one, but the "second sabbath of the first month"—around harvest time, when the Law forbade eating the firstfruits of the grain. Still Jesus' reaction is consistent with his messianic preaching. Because the Bridegroom is with them, the disciples' act takes on a symbolic meaning. It expresses the arrival of the messianic sabbath, which abolishes fasts and does away with old structures. Is not the bread the disciples eat the Bread of Life?

■

A frontier has been crossed. "You . . . were once alienated. . . ." Strangers to yourselves, you were helpless to respond to your desires or dreams in any real way, unable to invest your freedom with action, incapable of understanding your future and making a beginning of it. Strangers to others, you could only regard them as competitors and enemies. Thus you were incapable of establishing ties of genuine solidarity. Strangers to God, you could only regard him as an almighty Master, the implacable guardian of the good order of the world.

"You . . . were once alienated from him. . . . But now Christ has achieved reconciliation for you. . . ." Now you are reconciled with yourselves. Now you acknowledge that you are more than your past: you are capable of a future. You are more than your failures: you are capable of conversion. You are more than your lack of understanding: you are capable of an unsuspected identity. You are reconciled with others, in the revelation that you are one another's sisters and brothers, beneficiaries of the same grace, born of one tenderness, members of one

Body: for you have become capable of loving one another. You are reconciled with God; for now you have the opportunity to correspond to his will, by abandoning yourselves to his mercy in the certitude that you are loved, without hesitation and without retreat: for you have become capable of being daughters and sons of God.

A frontier has been crossed in Christ. Now you are capable of living the gospel! Then be not deterred from the hope that you have received. Do not subject yourselves once more to the slavery of fear, which would have you doubt yourselves, or the fatalism that would make you say: "Why bother?" Do not subject yourselves once more to the slavery of the realism that destroys dreams, the cold lucidity that puts all enthusiasm to sleep. Do not fly to the refuge of your well-defended territories, all secure behind the battlements of your own prisons, lolling in your privileged lives, sacrificing your duties to the maintenance of your rights. Do not allow yourselves to be deterred from this new hope of yours by shutting God up within your own confines and setting earth at odds with heaven. This would be but to submit anew to the yoke of a law of death, when, in Christ, you have tasted life.

■

Father of us all,
to those who have the heart of the poor
    you offer the wealth of your reign.
Prepare us to hear your Word of grace.
May it be the source of our oneness
    and the strength of the people born of your mercy.
God, our Father,
receive our praise, through your Son, in the Spirit.

■

In bestowing upon us the Spirit of your Son,
you have begotten us to a new life.
God, our Father,
may this newness be the cause of our hope,
    and your benevolence the source of our peace.

■

Fruit of our earth and our toil,
    this bread has become the sacrament of your grace.

21

Lord, our God,
you welcome us as guests in your house.
Now that we are no longer strangers to you,
may this communion blossom into joy
in the everlastingness of your presence.

MONDAY OF THE 23RD WEEK

TO FULFILL THE WORD

Colossians 1:24–2:3: One of Paul's major concerns with respect to the
Christians of Colossae appears in verse 25 of the reading: ". . . the
commission God gave me to preach among you his word in its fullness. . . ."
Not having founded the church of Colossae, or even visited it as yet, the
apostle is well aware that he must justify his ministry to his addressees. This
ministry, he says, consists in "completing the proclamation of God's word"—
plē-rō-sai ton logon tou Theou, "fulfilling the word of God," or "filling up the
word of God," filling that word to the full. Thus Paul identifies his mission as
that of completing the preaching of Epaphras, and in this manner leading the
Colossians to the perfection of Christian faith.

Paul's commission, entrusted to him by God, is all the more urgent in view of
Gnosticism's infiltration of the church. Once more Paul denounces the Gnostic
perversity: he speaks of the "mystery"—a technical term denoting the divine
economy of salvation which, once upon a time, lay hidden from human eyes,
but which now has been revealed. The Letter to the Ephesians places a great
deal of emphasis on the fact that the reconciliation of Jews and pagans in one
church has brought this revelation to its fullness. Paul is making the same
point here in Colossians: Christ is in the midst of the pagan nations. And so,
confronted with Gnostic thought, which reserved to a small number of the
"perfect" a knowledge that could be attained only through severe ascetical
practices, Paul presents instead a revelation he claims as universal and given
by Christ.

Paul likewise insists that his ministry is one of suffering. He is offering the
Colossians yet another reason why they should welcome him. He has not
preached to them, it is true. But he has suffered for them.

Then he says: "In my own flesh I fill up what is lacking in the sufferings of
Christ for the sake of his body, the church." What can he mean by that?
Surely not that there is anything "missing" in Christ's suffering. His
insistence, in this very letter, on Christ as the only savior precludes that
possibility. No, Paul's "suffering" has a very precise meaning here. He has

---

chosen terminology reminiscent of the Old Testament, where "suffering" designates the sufferings of God's people, especially the tribulations of the just. These sufferings, these tribulations, were to signal the inauguration of the messianic age. Thus Paul's suffering is to be understood in the sense of a "communion" in the trials of Christ, who suffered for the church before any of his followers were required to do so.

Psalm 62 invites the sufferer to trust in God.

Luke 6:6–11: In Acts, Peter says to the Jews: "Thus may a season of refreshment be granted you by the Lord when he sends you Jesus, already designated as your Messiah. Jesus must remain in heaven until the time of universal restoration which God spoke of long ago through his holy prophets" (Acts 3:20–21). "Refreshment" and "restoration" are expressions calculated to remind Peter's audience that the age of the Christ is the age of the transformation of human existence. By now the messianic age has come to be understood as the age of the new human being, the re-created universe. As an illustration we have the healing of the paralytic who, one sabbath day, recovered the use of his "right hand," representing his faculties of action. Thus the sabbath appears as a day of grace, the day of the restoration of the entire universe: the Great Sabbath.

■

". . . The commission God gave me to preach among you his word in its fullness. . . ." This is the mission of the apostle, this is the vocation of the church.

To "preach among you his word in its fullness"—or, as the original Greek would have it, to "fill up," to "fulfill" God's word, to bring it to its fullness—means to take up God's word and proclaim it. It means unveiling the hidden mystery, lifting the veil of the hidden face of things, revealing the other side of the cloth—showing the "right side" of the cloth that has been so patiently woven by all of the seeking, the striving, the hopes, and the frustrations of human beings down through the millenia. The church's vocation is to bestow on men and women an openness to meaning, and hence an openness to hope. To "fulfill" the word is to proclaim it, then, and to proclaim it in such a way as to render it effective.

To fulfill the word means to proclaim it—but not as an added meaning, as if it were somehow external to the world. Have we meditated sufficiently on the meaning of the word, "fulfill"? To fulfill means to bring something to its intended or destined outcome, to lead something to its materialization, its actualization. It means to unfurl or spread out all of the potential of some hidden dynamism. It means to take something dynamic and thrust it to its furthest limit. Mission, as God actualized it "in the beginning" through his creative Word—then as it took flesh in the people of Israel—then as it was lived by Jesus—and now as the church ought to be living it—does not consist in transplanting women and men into a society where they will find salvation in rites, or in a particular system of thought.

Our vocation, then, is to "fulfill" the word—to reveal the hidden place where, even now, the whole of reality is God's own universe.

This revelation can be made only if its mediators, the believer and the church, thrust themselves deep into the heart of reality—all reality: word, thought, love, culture, civilization. No genuine believer will be found elsewhere. No church will strike its roots elsewhere. Our purpose in this insertion, this rooting? Not to take Jesus and place him where he is not—but to show, and to declare, that he is everywhere, even now.

■

Fulfill your work in us,
O Lord our God.
May your spirit unveil to us the hidden meaning of things,
and may our life shine with the light of your Word.
Be blessed even now,
for the fulfillment of your promise
and the consummation of our history,
to endless ages.

TUESDAY OF THE 23RD WEEK

IN CHRIST

Colossians 2:6–15: Speaking most solemnly now, Paul contrasts the fullness of Christ with the emptiness of the Gnostic pretensions. We might say that he does so by describing two "churches." The "church" used by the Gnostics as a lure to entice the Colossians is as empty as the so-called philosophy on which they seek to erect it. This philosophy is based on "speculations upon the world of angelic powers, demoniacal practices and a certain recourse to legal observances."

The church can continue to be authentic only if it faithfully preserves the face of the Lord, transmitted by the apostolic preaching: not "a mythic being inserted into the angelic hierarchies, but the one crucified and risen, the one preached by the apostles." Only the church, which has received its being from God, can claim to hold in its bosom the fullness of the divinity. This is the case with the Colossians who, from their baptism onward, have professed their faith in the power of the God who has raised Jesus from the dead. With Christ they have let themselves be placed in the tomb. With him they have risen. Thus they have no obligation toward the Mosaic law or the Gnostic ordinances, from which God delivered them when he nailed the bill of their indemnification to the cross of Christ.

Psalm 145, one of the hymnic psalms, praises the God who has raised Jesus and delivered the Colossians.

Luke 6:12–19: Suddenly we see a great number of disciples, a swarm of people pressing around Jesus—for all the world as if there were some complicity between Jesus and this throng seeking to touch him. We thrill at this image of the intimacy between Yahweh and Israel. But there is more than Israel here! There are folk from Tyre, from Sidon. The people of God have taken on a universal dimension.

Twelve Jews are chosen to be apostles, heralds of the Reign, witnesses of the Good News. There is continuity, then, between the old Israel and the new. Are not both chosen to be salt for the earth and light to the world? Are not both established to challenge the certitudes into which individuals and societies so readily flee for refuge? Jesus has chosen these twelve individuals after a long night spent in prayer.

■

"In Christ the fullness of deity resides in bodily form." The obvious focal point of this extraordinarily vigorous passage is the expression, "in bodily form." Suddenly all the spiritualisms of a false piety, all the idealisms of an unenlightened faith, lie in smithereens.

To be sure, Christ, Son of God from everlasting, enjoys the fullness of the divinity from all eternity. We made this profession of faith in the liturgy last Friday, at the beginning of the passage from this same letter of Paul: "Christ is the image of the invisible God. . . . In him everything . . . was created. . . . All were created through him. . . . In him everything continues in being." But how could we have access to this icon of God except through the element of God rendered visible in this humanity of his, here become the very humanity of God? God is a human

---

being now. The Son of God has become flesh. Henceforth and forever more, it will be in this "flesh," this humanity, that we shall find our God.

The words of Paul to the Christians of Colossus—scarcely any philosophers—ring with a realism no philosopher dared dream of. We are actually incorporated into this human body of God, as so many cells in the organism of which he is the head. Let us not imagine that we are dealing with metaphor here. Far from it. This is a real body—yours joined to that of God-become-a-human-being. The resurrection is the sign of this truth. In the risen Christ, human nature itself wins glory. After all, it is Jesus' body that is raised—the body of a human being, marked with the scars of his life, the wounds of his passion, his joys and his pains, his long journeys and his human toil, and having the good scent of Galilee and Judea about it. This is the body that is raised—the one belonging to God.

Under the pretext of your quest for God, you have sought to dissociate religion from earthly realities. You have relegated the latter to a profane history. The former, then, would be a mere superaddition to the vanities of earth. Reject this breach. It destroys the work of Christ.

Henceforth all human reality will be the way to God. There will never be another. The human being, that last, supreme fruit of the long evolution of a ripening world, discovers, exploits, subdues, humanizes the forces of nature, century by century, over the course of all the millenia of a continuous history. And in humanizing nature, men and women humanize themselves, becoming the image of God the creator. It is by way of this slow childbirth that the recapitulation of all things in Christ, the head of the body, is accomplished. "All things are yours, you are Christ's, Christ is God's." Undreamed-of grandeur of the world! Place of the advent of God! Unhoped-for vocation of women and men: to be co-creator with God! Wedding announcement between heaven and earth! Nothing human will ever be foreign to God. For in Christ, God has pitched his tent among us.

What God has joined together, let no one put asunder. The world is yours, and God's. And you will be God's by living in this world and consecrating it.

■

Be praised, God, creator of all things!
Be sung by stars and luminaries,
    by moon and sun,
        by the birds of heaven and the fishes of the sea!
Be blessed

by the fruits of the earth
and the animals that live on it,
the flowers that enchant it
and the springs that refresh it!
May young and old do honor to your name:
may they rejoice your heart
and bless your greatness!

For the design of your loving-kindness,
God of heaven and earth, be blessed!
From the first day,
you have made for us what is good.
It is our happiness that you desire.

What are we, women and men,
that you should care for us,
we children of Adam,
that you should make of us the sovereigns of creation?
For all the many honors you do us,
God, our Father, be blessed!

Be praised for the loveliest of the children of Adam,
Jesus, your Son from all eternity!
In him, you reveal your project
and fulfill your love.
Here is the One after your own heart,
the new Adam.
Here is the one who will be loyal to your designs.
In him your creation finds its destiny,
and through him all things give you glory.
In him our earth leaps forward to eternity,
for through him all things are swept up
into an immense body a-building,
body saved, body transfigured, body risen!
By him who is the Fullness of your Grace,
this eldest Child of a new world,
O God our creator, we praise you!

Possible . . .

Blessed . . . ! Woe . . . ! The obvious is a shambles now. All our reckonings have been in error. Men and women thought their game so well in hand, their felicity assured! But God has just reshuffled the cards. He opens up a new perspective altogether.

"May the word dwell in your hearts!" Paul's wish is a "recommendation," in both senses of the word. It recommends our person, as one might recommend someone for employment, citing the quality that will be ours from this moment forward: the Word dwells in our hearts. But it also recommends in the sense of advising, pleading, supplicating: "Have the sentiments of Christ!" Faith is profession, and pleading; attestation, and appeal. For us, to live is Christ. This is our dignity, and this is our project.

Blessed, woe . . . ! In the ebb and flow of our faith, in its certitudes and doubts, certitude carries the day. We know to whom we have given our faith. Thanks to the mercy of God, it will forevermore be possible to believe that human suffering and unhappiness, our cries of revolt and the faith we cling to despite life's vicissitudes, are swept up in the light of Christ that streams from the cross of Jesus. God loves us, this light tells. He has created us for happiness. God must love us, if he fashions our happiness. His love has but one sign to hold before the eyes of our faith: the joy of that faith. Love will never be aught but deeds of love. The future will have but one reality: the possible, become reality indeed.

■

Blessed be you, God, Father of Jesus Christ:
you have made your Son to be the first Living One.
In him you have reconciled us with life.
Praised be your Name:
your loving-kindness is warranty for our happiness,
and your grace is our deliverance.
You do not abandon us to our despair,
and your promise is our guarantee that a future is possible.
Since to live, for us, is Christ,
may the peace that he has inaugurated
be our heritage today,
and may the hope that he stirs

be the gift that you make to every human being
   at the appointed time.
In expectation of that happy day
   when our happiness will be manifested forever,
God, sovereign of all life, we bless you!

BLESSED?

Colossians 3:1–11: Having reminded the Christians of Colossus that, in their baptism they die and rise in Christ, Paul draws some conclusions. Thanks to the indwelling of the Spirit, Christians live a wholly renewed life. Baptism has shaped them to Christ, the image of God and the new Adam. Therefore they form the new human race, a race that transcends all distinctions of religion, culture, and class.

Once more Christ is the center of the Pauline argumentation. Christ is the only way to holiness. The Colossians should be concerned with realities from on high, "things above"—that is, they should concern themselves with the "new life revealed in Christ Jesus." As we see, Paul's polemic with Gnosticism has lost none of its momentum. The apostle tells of the "new man, one who grows in knowledge as he is formed anew in the image of his Creator." Likewise he speaks of "things of earth"—the Gnostic means of sanctification. We are not very far from the Letter to the Galatians here, where Paul condemns the Law. Once you have tasted Christ, you will never want to go back to substitutes.

By the choice of its verses, *Psalm 145* directs our praise towards the Lord Jesus.

Luke 6:20–26: "The rich he has sent empty away" (Lk 1:53). The Beatitudes have a paschal flavor. They are in the spirit of Yahweh's revelation to the Jews when he has snatched them from their slavery in Egypt. The preaching of the prophets always stressed God's preference for the little. When the prophets announced the coming of the Messiah, they always took care to represent him as the herald and defender of human dignity. From that time forward, the God of the Bible has stood as the last wall of defense against the injustice and rapacity of the great. The poor are those who have no hope left but God.

Now we see why no materialistic reading of the Bible, any more than a moralistic one, can quite figure out what to do with the Beatitudes. In Jesus' socioreligious context, the "poor" include both those thrust out of the way of salvation by the arrogance of the Pharisees, and those crushed by the strength of the mighty.

Furthermore the Beatitudes do not shut human beings up within a closed universe. The gift of the Reign does not mean that men and women have no more to do. On the contrary, Beatitudes and woes alike place human beings squarely before the demands of that Reign. They make room for freedom. "Love your enemies," Jesus says, immediately after proclaiming the Beatitudes. In other words, it is our task to be the incarnation of what the Beatitudes assert.

■

"By the time you're forty, you find out that people aren't happy." This admission, that of Péguy, dates from 1913—a year when the world still knew the euphoria of *la belle époque*, the lovely, wonderful years. Today, unfortunately, we seem to be more precocious. It does not take us that long to make Péguy's observation.

Or still worse: have we not become such strangers to happiness that we no longer even wonder if we are happy? The anxieties that spring from our crises only sharpen the everlasting question: What is it all worth? Where is my life headed?

A painful uncertainty grips us. We are caught in the vise of a mortal doubt. "What good is life?" Blind, unjust fate, unhappiness, poverty, death, failure, threaten us at every turn. "What a wretched life!" we cry to God. Nor is our cry a blasphemous one. The Book of Job and the Psalms are filled with the same agonized outbursts. Our cry is the cry of men and women brought low by a surfeit of adversity. We are drowning in anguish and nausea. People know that they are not happy!

"Happy!" No, you are not damned by God! On the contrary, God holds you in his heart. The Lord is God of the poor and defender of the oppressed. Once more Jesus whips the rug out from under common sense. To poor shepherds of Bethlehem, to fisher folk gathered in the springtime countryside of Galilee, to the young Christian communities sprung up in the deep, dark heart of the Mediterranean cities, to the church of today, he cries: "Salvation is for you!" He congratulates the poor and bewails the fate of the rich!

Blessed . . . ! Woe . . . ! The obvious is a shambles now. All our reckonings have been in error. Men and women thought their game so well in hand, their felicity assured! But God has just reshuffled the cards. He opens up a new perspective altogether. For it is Jesus who is poor. See, he is abandoned, he is sentenced unjustly. The royal way? He has traversed it already. The road to happiness? He has walked it all the way. And his footprints point toward Golgotha: that madness, that scandal, for human beings—that road to Easter! "If Christ is not risen, then our faith is in vain."

The happy and the unhappy? Seek not to reformulate the happiness of the poor in terms of this earth. Say not, "Who laughs last laughs best"! No need to contort your mind until we can regard the poverty of the poor, their humiliations, their tears, as happiness. No, these are the opposite of happiness. We need seek only to join Jesus on the royal way of the cross, which is the road to Easter. People are not happy. We know that. But the gospel assures us that everything is upside down now. Suddenly we have been swung out of "this world" and dropped on the farther shore. Behold the madness of the cross. Behold the scandal of Easter. Behold the power of very Life in our hands, for the Word is become our eucharist.

■

Happy they who set their hopes on you!
Happy they who risk their lives
*   on the strength of their faith in your word!*
God our Father,
your will for us is life beyond all measure,
*   heaped up and overflowing,*
*   beyond our wildest dreams.*
May the law of the gospel
*   be our happiness today*
till our joy be full to overflowing,
*   in the gladness of the everlasting ages.*

■

God of tenderness and love,
*   ever and again you renew your covenant with us.*
Change our hesitations to a trust renewed,
*   our fears to a hope purified.*
Through the indwelling of your Spirit,
*   may our ordinary words*
*   become hymns of praise,*
that we may glorify you in Jesus Christ.

■

In this Eucharist, O God of love,
*   you seal your promises to us—*
*   the promises of the Beatitudes.*

31

For your Son is the consolation of the weeping,
    the vision of pure hearts,
    the heritage of the meek,
    and the hope of those who suffer persecution.
Renew our faith: may we find the strength
    to enter upon this adventure of grace,
    in which Jesus himself is to be our happiness
    for endless ages.

THURSDAY OF THE 23RD WEEK

LET THE WORD DWELL IN YOU

Colossians 3:12–17: Five virtues, five vices: we hear the language of a world common to late Judaism and Greek philosophy. As he customarily does in the latter part of his letters, Paul exhorts his addressees to translate into terms of their own comportment the life they have received in baptism. The most precious gift is charity, the apostle reminds his hearers—the bond of perfection that sums up all virtues and gathers Christians into one people, the new Israel—"God's chosen ones, holy and beloved."

By way of response to the apostle's invitation, as well as to mark the conclusion of his Letter to the Colossians, *Psalm 150* invites us to lift our voices in a mighty cry of praise.

Luke 6:27–38: "If you love those who love you, what reward (*misthos*) will you have?" writes Matthew (5:46). In Luke, on the other hand, we hear: "If you love those who love you, what credit (*charis*) is that to you?" The difference in vocabulary between Matthew and Luke is one of the characteristics of this part of those gospels. Matthew speaks in juridical terms. Luke delves into the very heart of God. Then let us ask ourselves indeed: What is the origin of the credit, the recognition, that Christians are promised? If they love only those who love them, if they lend only to borrowers who pay their debts, they are still within the narrow horizon of human relations. But if they love their enemies, then they live by the very spirit of God: they testify to the grace dwelling within them, the divine favor with which they are invested.

Christians are merciful, even as their Father is merciful. If we compare verses 31, 36, and 38, we see that the first invites the disciples to behave toward others as they would have others behave toward them. This alone implies considerable progress with respect to the rule of the ancients, which enjoined forbearance from what one would *not* wish to see another do. But we are still in the realm of reciprocity. On the other hand, to show mercy (v. 36) is to behave as God behaves. Now one is both aware of, and living by, God's grace, which is always bestowed gratuitously—spilled forth in "good measure, pressed down, shaken together, running over . . ." (v. 38). We abandon the rule of tit for tat. We adopt that of profusion.

■

"Let the word of Christ, rich as it is, dwell in you." And Paul's Letter to the Colossians is ended. He has contemplated the mystery of Jesus, that pinnacle of creation and perfect icon of God. Now, in a thrilling compendium, he invites his hearers to live the logic of the mystery revealed: "Because you are God's chosen ones . . . clothe yourselves with heartfelt mercy. . . ." With good reason will spiritual tradition speak of the "imitation of Jesus."

Elsewhere (cf. Rom 11:17–24), Paul uses an image calculated to afford us access to this mystery in great depth. He tells the Romans they have been grafted onto Christ.

We know how a graft is made. First there must be two wounds, one on the trunk, the other on the branch. Second, these two wounds must come in contact with each other. And we have the whole mystery. Here is a wounded God, whose most visible lesion is the cross of Jesus. And there is a wound in us—the wound of our desire and our prayer. Here are two hearts, a life-giving one, and one in quest of happiness.

No one has forgotten the wild parable of life and death that unfolded before the eyes of all the world when, for the first time in history, the heart of one human being was grafted onto another, and a fragment of the hope of human beings everywhere hung in the balance.[1] A year's struggle later, Blaiberg died—and the stupefying fact came to light that, during that whole time, not for one moment had his entire organism, from his brain to the least of his cells, given up the fight to reject the foreign heart on which its survival depended. The resourcefulness of the organism in its—ultimately successful—suicidal efforts was simply astonishing.

"Let the word . . . dwell in you!" Paul's wish is a "recommendation," in both senses of the word. It recommends our person, as one might recommend someone for employment, citing the quality that will be ours from this moment forward: the Word dwells in our hearts. Unlike Blaiberg, God will not reject us before the graft has "taken." Each morning the graft is new. But Paul also "recommends" something to us in the sense of advice or counsel. Earnestly he beseeches us: "Have in you the sentiments of Christ." The only purpose, the only meaning of this graft is to make it possible for us to live. For us, from now on, to live is Christ.

■

May your word, God our Father,
*   make our lives fruitful.*
Give us the sentiments of your Son.
Clothe our hearts in tenderness and goodness,
*   meekness and patience.*
Grant us to be faithful to Jesus' commandment:
*   may we love as he has loved us.*

FRIDAY OF THE 23RD WEEK

LOVING-KINDNESS

1 Timothy 1:1–2, 12–14: The authenticity of the "pastoral" letters raises the same problems as do Ephesians and Colossians. Here too we find a writer confronted with a Gnostic threat that calls for a stronger church organization. It has been suggested that a secretary of Paul may have taken it upon himself to compose what he regarded as his teacher's spiritual legacy and testament.

Chapter one expresses the apostle's wonder and gratitude. All that he is he owes Christ, who has placed his trust in him despite his past and the persecutions he has inflicted on the church.

Psalm 16, often regarded as a kind of lamentation, expresses the psalmist's trust, which is unshakable, he claims, if he has God at his side.

Luke 6:39–42: Once again Jesus addresses the disciples. He has just shown them that true perfection consists in mercy. Now he puts them on their guard against false teachers—so eager to rush to the rescue of those with specks in their eye, but having a heart bereft of all kindness and benevolence. They are blind. They are the eternal Pharisees, whose vain quest for perfection renders them utterly pitiless.

■

"Every student when he has finished his studies will be on a par with his teacher"! Behold the dynamism of the Christian life. Christians live "as

---

God"—that famous little evangelical "as." Christians are Christic by nature, having chosen Jesus as teacher and ruler of their lives. Today's gospel invites us to look upon the world and others with the same loving regard that Jesus directs upon them. Be benevolent. Be persons of "loving-kindness."

The eyes are a mirror of the world. For some, reality is nothing but sadness. Lamentation is the order of the day. All goes ill, and the "yes, buts . . ." sap all one's reasons to hope. The world mimics our glance. It takes on the hue of our regard. Be benevolent. Be kind and loving to others. They are less evil than you think. Love the best part of them: in the worst of miscreants is a reflection, albeit a hidden one, of the fire God has kindled in each and every one of us. You have a calling to hope. Your vocation is to hope in the human being. Come what may, Christians may not allow themselves to pillory their brothers and sisters on the gibbet of judgment or shut them up in the prison of condemnation. Believe in people! Be women and men dedicated to mercy. Exercise loving-kindness toward yourselves, as well. Regard yourselves with less severity. If you happen to be in a "bad humor" about something, look at the "humorous" side, instead. You have not uttered your last word, either! Exercise loving-kindness, benevolence, toward the world. Be not eternal malcontents. Live, and enjoy life. Be *bons vivants*. God was the first to marvel at the works that spilled from his hands in the first days of the universe.

If I am a person of benevolence, of "loving-kindness," must I make excuses for people, or be indifferent or naive with regard to their failings and errors? Far from it. Benevolence? Words have a meaning! "Benevolence" contains two roots, *bene* and *volens*. Be persons of "good will," think of others, wish them genuinely well, will their happiness. But this also means the will to correct them when they nurture illusions, when they espouse false values, and strive after a chimerical "happiness"! Let your highest value be the good of others—their genuine good. This alone will be your happiness. Any other "happiness" you may chance upon will itself prove ephemeral, deceitful. Benevolence means taking responsibility for the happiness of others—loving-kindness indeed.

A number of years ago, a French newspaper spearheaded its new advertising campaign with an arresting slogan: "Others see it all in solemn black. We see reasons to hope." We might say the same of Christian benevolence. Love is patient. It excuses all things, it forgives all things, because it takes God's mercy as its model. Christian loving-kindness does not mean looking at the world through rose-colored glasses. Christian benevolence is implicitly theological: our "reasons to hope" are grounded in the very being of God, who is a patient God, and in his grace, which will never fail.

■

God of infinite patience,
  be our teacher:
  teach us to love as you alone can love.
Give us a heart of mercy
  and reasons to hope
  that this time of ours is destined to overflow
  into everlasting happiness.

SATURDAY OF THE 23RD WEEK

YOU ARE MY ROCK, MY FORTRESS

1 Timothy 1:15–17: Using the solemn formula which we shall hear twice more in this letter, as in the other pastoral letters (1 Tim 3:1, 4:9; 2 Tim 2:11; Tit 3:8), the apostle invites the reader to reflect on the deed of Christ in his own regard. Well indeed does "the case of Paul" illustrate God's generosity toward human kind. "A blasphemer, a persecutor, a man filled with arrogance" has been called to the ministry by Christ Jesus!

Psalm 113 responds to the doxology of 1 Timothy 17: "To the King of ages, the immortal, the invisible, the only God, be honor and glory forever and ever! Amen."

Luke 6:43–49: Jesus has urged us to mistrust false teachers. But how are we to distinguish the false from the true? We judge a tree by its fruits. When a person's heart is good, when it lives by divine grace and beats in rhythm with mercy, it is a treasury from which its depositor can draw only good.

So many greet Jesus with the title of "Lord," while failing to observe what this "Lord" commands. And so Jesus concludes his discourse by recalling the judgment to come. Here is a language that will be understandable to Luke's readers. Just as the Jews have been judged on the basis of their observance of the commandments, so Christians will have to answer for any noncompliance with the law of mercy. Do they live in reliance on their strength alone? Or do they trust in God?

36

■

I know in whom I have placed my faith! Here, when all is said and done,
is why we must believe. There is no other reason for us to posit the act
of faith than this humble interior conviction: "You are the rock of our
life! To whom could we go? You have the words of life!" Nothing can
persuade us to believe but this hidden, interior conviction: apart from
Christ we can do nothing!

Our faith ebbs and flows. It is serene certitude, and it is doubt, humbly
accepted. We all have had experience of both. Snuffed out by trial and
suffering, toil, pleasure, or sheer negligence, faith can drop off to sleep,
grow pale, and cease to shape our lives. But we know perfectly well that,
in our lives, as in the life of the world, faith can be the driving force of
our most radical commitments. Our faith can be an awakening to
freedom, the courage of our fidelities, the rock on which we build our
dwelling.

How many men and women, seeing so much anguish and suffering, so
much hate and inhumanity, so much misery, hunger, oppression, and war
all over the face of the earth—in other words, seeing what everyone
sees—nevertheless believe that God has dominion even over forces such
as these! How many human beings, faced with the experience of so many
false teachers seeking control of their lives—the hostility, aggression,
prejudice, and jealousy, the conventions and the systems, and above all,
the manifold forms of human selfishness—in other words, faced with
the same experience as everyone else—nonetheless believe that Jesus is
Lord! Are there not women and men who, despite the common
experience of uncertainty and inadequacy, doubt and rebelliousness,
arrogance and inertia, in their own thought, will, and sensibility, believe
nonetheless that the Spirit of God can determine that thought, that will,
and that sensibility? Blow storm, rage wind, nothing will be able to
separate us from the love we have been shown. In our faith's ebb and
flow, certitude wins out over doubt. After all, we know to whom we have
given our faith. And with the psalmist we can give thanks: My rock, my
fortress—is you, Lord, my God! (cf Ps 46).

■

Our light and our salvation,
    God our Savior,
be our succor
    when distress threatens our hope.
Be our strength
    when our fidelity betrays its fragility.

37

Be our support
when we are overcome by lassitude.
Be our forgiveness
when the firmness of our faith grows heavy with slumber.

MONDAY OF THE 24TH WEEK

HUMILITY

1 Timothy 2:1–8: In Romans (8:26), Paul had pointed out that, on our own strength alone, we humans are incapable of properly orientating our prayer. But, he adds, the spirit comes to our aid. The First Letter to Timothy now proposes a model for this Spirit-inspired prayer. The most striking thing here is the universalism of the model. A prayer for all humanity merges with the petitions of the Our Father. The divine salvific will is concretized in Jesus Christ who, at the appointed time, became the servant of all, and delivered himself as a ransom for all.

Psalm 28 is of the genre of a complaint, and we have the characteristic alternation of intercession and thanksgiving (for the anticipated grace), along with the gesture of the hands uplifted toward God.

Luke 7:1–10: The sequence just concluded opened with the meeting of Simon and Jesus—the portentous encounter of Israel with its God, face to face in history. Now Simon gives place to the Roman centurion, and Luke invites us to consider an altogether different sort of meeting. Who is this centurion? Would he be the Cornelius of Acts? Like Cornelius, he is well-disposed toward the Jewish nation (cf. Acts 10:2).

In any case, he is a pagan, and Luke takes great pleasure in underscoring his marginal status. In contrast with Simon, and even with the centurion of Matthew, the officer is unwilling to approach Jesus directly. He sends lieutenants. Here is the prototype of all who will know Jesus by word of mouth alone. Thus he represents the "other" component of the Christian community. We have seen Simon, the Jewish Christian. Now we meet Cornelius, the pagan convert.

"I tell you, I have never found so much faith. . . ."! But what faith is meant? We see the faith that shows itself in this pagan's humility, of course. But especially (although it may be less evident), we discern the faith disclosed in his solicitude for a sick slave. On the part of a pagan, this concern is a complete surprise. The Good News, the burden of Luke's testimony, is addressed to all of those to whom the church, and even the sphere of religion itself, is a totally foreign thing. The evangelist's concern is not so much to attribute to these people an explicit faith, which indeed they do not have, as it is to reveal to them all of the "divine" that lies hidden in their everyday life. One day Peter will bear witness to his faith before Cornelius. And Cornelius will be astounded to see himself already alive in the Spirit.

■

"I am not worthy to have you enter my house"! Jesus is struck with amazement. In heaven, says Saint John of the Cross, "those of the elect who know God best are the very ones who best understand that there remains an infinitude to be understood" (*Canticle*, commentary on strophe 7).

For our own part, have we not wished to imprison God in dwellings made to order—our abstract concepts and our soulless doctrines? For our part, have we not thought to clothe God in patched garments? No wonder, then, if our images of the divine so readily unravel as soon as they are worn! Or else we have him wrapped in stuff so tightly knitted that it cannot "breathe"—rites without breath and spirit, habits without soul.

"I am not worthy to have you enter my house"! The basic attitude of faith, its first posture, is humility. Our words are incapable of uttering God. Silence alone, indwelt by the Word that utters him, can be the place of his revelation. Our definitions, our dogmas, will never be more than approximations. Only the Mystery unveiled in contemplation can provide us with anything like a picture of the true face of God. Our own images can only be sketches. Our behavior can only be faltering approaches. Only the Spirit can convert our heart. "I am not worthy to have you enter my house"!

But the believer's humility will find a response in the humility of God. After all, God will have no better words by which to utter himself than our clumsy ones. He will have nothing by which to reveal himself but a completely simple, simply human life, the life of a human being of Nazareth, together with the existence of such ordinary men and women as may have given themselves over to his word. To manifest himself today, God will have only the deeds of those who seek him. To sketch himself for us, he will have only their entreaties, tracing him out in awkward, babbling love. "Anyone who loves me will be true to my word," Jesus says, "and my Father will love him; and we will come to him and make our dwelling with him" (Jn 15:23).

God, infinite mystery,
we cannot know your Name
 unless you reveal it to us.
God most holy,
we cannot live according to your law
 unless you convert our hearts.
We are not worthy to receive you.
But speak one word
 and we shall know the joy of faith.
Only pour forth your Spirit
 and we shall be able to serve you.

TUESDAY OF THE 24TH WEEK

GOD IS HUMAN

1 Timothy 3:1–13: Like the other "pastoral epistles," the first letter to
Timothy pleads for a better church organization, focusing mainly on the case
of the bishops and deacons. The former are the same individuals as 1 Timothy
5 calls "elders." Their office is that of the ministry of the word. Their function
is like that of the father of a family: they preside over community life, and
represent their community to outsiders, as we see from verse 7. It will not be
suitable, then, to select neophytes for this office. Their pride will cause them to
"play into the devil's hands."

The deacons are Paul's co-workers. Like Paul and Timothy, they are to guard
the mystery of faith "with a clear conscience." Finally, bishops and deacons
must be "married only once." It will come as no surprise to our readers that
this last injunction has been the occasion of the spillage of a great deal of ink.
Depending on the commentator, the apostle is referring either to sexual
misconduct, or to remarriage after the death of a spouse, or even to the
repudiation of one's wife so as to be free to marry again. Or again, we may
understand the expressions "husband of one woman," and "wife of one
husband," which we find in Jewish and pagan epitaphs, as extolling a
particularly fervent conjugal love. Many commentators regard *Psalm 101* as a
royal psalm. E. Lipinski dates it from the era of post-Exilic Jerusalem.

Luke 7:11–17: Two processions wind their ways toward the city gates, as if in
hopes of converging. An only son is borne to his interment outside the city

---

40

wall. Jesus' disciples accompany him (accompany the Lord, in Luke's pointed language). The widow's son finds the Son of God.

At the head of the first cortege is a corpse. The second group swarms about the Living One. But who is dead and who is alive in this account? Must everyone play at hide-and-go-seek? At the city gate, the corpse and the One Who Lives will switch roles: the dead one will awaken to life, while the Living One will walk on toward the death foretold by old Simeon. And yet, in the youth restored to his mother's arms, the promise of the Risen One lives even now.

She would bury her son. Her only son. Now she would be alone, bereft of support and security in her declining years. No sunshine would ever brighten her daily task. Never again would she have a reason to live; after all, for whom would she be living? She would return to a house as silent as a tomb, and just as empty and cold. She was, in a way, as dead as her boy.

Jesus chances on the scene. He is seized with emotion. Before long, another funeral procession will wend its solemn way through the gates of another city. Jesus regards this woman in black, this mother in tears. She's aged ten years, go the whispers. So young, so beautiful, a matter of a few days ago! See her now, despondent and pitiable, this mother of sorrows! Now she is near. A hush falls on those about. There's the mother. The parents of one condemned always win a certain respect, do they not? Jesus is stricken at the sign. This young man, about to be laid to earth . . . is the living image of what he himself will be soon.

Jesus bids the pallbearers halt—compassionate Jesus. Oh, let there be no mistake—this is God's own compassion! Nor will there ever be the like!

■

When we ourselves are filled with pity, we have compassion. We "suffer with" the other, and when the vision of evil becomes insupportable, it is because it touches us, ourselves. And while we should, of course, wish to remedy the evil, this too is an expression of our need to palliate the sting we feel in our own souls. When Jesus has pity, it is out of mercy, *misericordia*. Jesus sees the misery of the other, as if it were his own.

And because Jesus is cut to the quick, fate undergoes a fantastic reversal. The young man rises, restored to life. God has pity on the human: he cannot abandon it to death. God's mercy is the other face of his creative power: God loves, and this love is life—rebirth, resurrection, salvation, grace, newness. God alone can love, can feel pity, at this point: Jesus will take the place of the widow's son. God's love, God's mercy, moves him to take the place of the being he loves, moves him to take that creature's place totally and without reserve, until God has become a human being himself. Jesus will stretch out on the bier and be laid to earth. "It is our infirmities he bore." But God will not let his beloved see corruption, as the psalm says.

It is because of mercy like this, God's own mercy, that we shall find it possible henceforth to believe that God hears us. Yes, now we can believe that human beings' sufferings, their rebellious outcries or their silent distress, have been anticipated. Love radiates from Jesus, and the beams of that love, shining on our hearts from the cross of Jesus Christ, tell us: God loves you. God created you, and he wants you alive. There was Easter in the air that morning at Naim.

■

God of life, blest be your name:
you will not abandon those who believe in you
to the dust of corruption.
Your Son sweeps us up in his Easter victory,
and your compassion is the wellspring of our life.
And so we confidently beg you:
have pity on such poor creatures as we,
and may our poor lives burgeon,
by your grace,
into life eternal.

WEDNESDAY OF THE 24TH WEEK

TO A TUNE ON THE PIPE

1 Timothy 3:14–16: Suddenly we hear a christological hymn, straight out of the community prayerbook! But while the independence of the hymn is beyond doubt, its choice has been dictated by instructions from Paul. The apostle has spoken of the various ministries. He now sets forth an excellent compendium of the nature and function of the church, in terms especially chosen for times of trouble. The nature of the church is to be the house of God. Its function is the tireless proclamation of the Christian message—a message that is not a theory, but a mystery.

In admirable detail, our hymn sets forth not only the various manifestations of this mystery, but their mutual enrichment as well, making use of a double chiasmus. The contraposition of "manifested in the flesh" and "preached among the Gentiles" is very suggestive for his purpose. It recalls the two fundamental stages of the economy of salvation: Jesus' historical position in the land of the Jews, and the "application" of this in pagan territory through the post-Easter mission. This mission has led to the reconciliation of Jews and pagans in one sole church, and this sign of oneness makes it possible for the angels to understand the mystery of the church (cf. Eph 3:10). "Believed in throughout the world," Christ is "taken up into glory."

While Jesus Christ is the summit and pinnacle of revelation, God has spoken to his people many times in the past. *Psalm 111* expresses this conviction. It is generally regarded as a hymn.

Luke 7:31–35: Luke knows how difficult it is for pagan Christians to embrace a strange tradition—here, the Jewish tradition. And so he gives us the parable of the children's game in the town square, to serve notice in no uncertain terms: non-Jews must make this quantum leap. Their refusal would associate them with the Pharisees and doctors of the law who have hated Jesus to the point of publicly insulting him ("Here is a glutton and a drunkard . . ."!), and who criticized John the Baptist with equal virulence and publicity ("He is mad!"). They would be like spoiled children, pouting instead of playing when invited to dance to a tune on the pipe. Only the children of wisdom will be capable of discerning the works of such a one as Jesus. For the pagans as for the Jews, Jesus is the last chance for salvation.

■

No man is a hero to his own valet. Nor has a prophet ever been listened to near home. Jesus appears, and the sign is vague and obscure. The sacrament of God remains ineffective. "We piped you a tune but you did not dance. . . ." To be touched by this sign, the heart to which it is addressed must be taken by surprise, astonished, seduced.

God is encountered. God is not forced on anyone. And the encounter is risk and chance. Jesus is the sacrament of God. A sacrament is like throwing a ball. If you only nudge the ball a little, you may have Chinese checkers, but you do not have sacrament. If you throw the ball, and someone catches it on the fly . . . ah, then you have the miracle of the game, the wonder of encounter. Something unexpected, something new happens. God could have handed us a theological treatise to transmit to posterity as one bequeaths an old vase. God prefers to throw a ball. And suddenly there is relation, and encounter.

God chooses to manifest the communion he proposes by taking the form of a human being. Only discover this human life, this too human life, and you shall discover a sign that will engender in you an astounding experience of nearness. God takes a human face, so that the human beings we are may be reborn to the life of God. God chooses to announce the Good News of his salvation in simple, everyday words. And we are astonished. These words become the route of access to the Reign. This life, these words, are the only opportunity God offers for the freedom of those he would have as partners in the covenant. These humble signs are the only signs God has available to touch the hearts of those he desires for his lovers.

A bouquet of flowers, a kiss, words of tenderness, gestures of affection, are nothing in comparison with the love to which they bear such humble witness. But what would love be without them? What would love be, had it not these lowly messengers at its disposal for its self-utterance— indeed, for its very existence? Without a kiss, without signs of communion, love would be empty air. To love will ever be to perform love's deeds.

A tune on a pipe in the market place? What could be less imposing? A few notes, a little rush of air. And yet, for those who allow themselves to be enticed . . . the piper's tune is all the wild gladness of the game, the joy of festival.

■

God of the dance,
you invite us to let ourselves be drawn
into the rhythm of the festival.
May your word of grace
open to us the mystery of tenderness.
May the bread of our tables
be the foretaste even now
of the feast to which you call us
for eternity.

DELIVERANCE

1 Timothy 4:12–16 opens a window on the primitive church. First we learn that Timothy's youth causes a lack of appreciation on the part of his elders. Saint Jerome thought he was at least thirty years old; but the stages of life were different in those days. For the ancients, one was not "grown up" until fifty.

According to C. Spicq, the intervention of the elders consisted in a consecratory prayer forming "one and the same sacramental action with the laying-on of hands." Timothy must hasten to develop the charism he has in virtue of his ordination. He must especially become an old hand at the public reading of the scriptures. His function is essentially that of instructor. After all, the community feeds on God's word. For the rest, it will be his whole life that must bear witness to the favor he enjoys in the sight of God.

Psalm 111: (See yesterday's commentary.)

Luke 7:36–50: A Pharisee and a public courtesan, in the same room! And two worlds collide. The woman acts her part. She is indeed a courtesan, and it is not difficult to understand Simon's irritation at Jesus' seemingly naive attitude of welcome. Of course, this prophet, this special guest, knows perfectly well that the presence of a "woman who was known in town to be a sinner" made the whole house unclean! And he proposes a parable by way of response to Simon's puzzlement. "Which of them was more grateful to him?" The Pharisee receives a polite hint that, far from being naive, Jesus has discerned a double meaning in the woman's actions, and found real love there too.

The two worlds actually have much to teach each other. I must have the experience of sin in order to taste the divine mercy. But I must have heart in order to discover, hiding beneath the opacity of a gesture, stuttering, nascent faith. "Go in peace." Jesus pronounces the word of grace that reveals to any lover of life the fullness of that life.

■

The gospel focuses our attention on an abandoned woman, a public sinner. In a woman of ill-repute, we are invited to share the mysteries of the Good News.

The experience of failure, of "missing the mark" (*hamartanein*, the word for "to sin" in the original Greek of the New Testament), of being in the wrong, of moral fault, has nothing specifically Christian about it. Nor indeed is the formality of sin as such entirely absent from the profane experience. I fail to do the good I should like to do. I have betrayed the friendship or the love of someone who has been loyal to me. In order to be able to call these lapses, these offenses, these breaches, by the name of sin, we must hear them so named by some Other, in whose eyes they are, precisely, sin. It is in being denominated that sin is unmasked and denounced as such. Sin *qua* sin appears only in the light of the word of the Other, for sin is sin only under the regard of that Other.

The weight of sin, then, will be the weight attached to it by the word and regard of the other. If another hands down a terrible, irrevocable judgment, sin will close me up in my failure, my fault, irrevocably. I shall have no recourse. But if the regard of that Other is tenderness itself—if the word of that Other unsnarls the knot that had seemed so inextricably, so irrevocably snarled—then the revelation of sin will also be deliverance.

Woman, your sins are forgiven! Our sin is healed by the very hand that lays it bare. Only Love itself has a forgiveness to bestow that will reveal our sin in the very act of forgiving. Why? Because only the light of mercy can show us the furthest depths of our ill. How often we fail to appreciate the extent of a danger until we have escaped it. We sinners are not sinners lamenting, sinners bemoaning shortcomings that we find to be such a terrible vexation; we are sinners forgiven, and sinners proclaiming our forgiveness.

Woman, your sins are forgiven because of your great love! The paradoxical experience of sin and forgiveness is precisely the locus of our experience of tenderness. Must we not have had at least some experience of the destructiveness of sin in order to discover the healing power of forgiveness? At the very heart of sin, there can be love—a love that heals, a love that redeems. Sinners are never really alone in their sin. They can have the experience of the presence of God there. Happy the sinner who can thus discover the irresistible passion of the One who loves us unto the forgiveness of sins!

■

God of mercy,
your word
    snatches the mask from our false pretenses.
Your light
    pierces every corner of our darkness.
We recognize and acknowledge that we are sinners.

Your word speaks to us again and again of your tenderness,
and your light is our rebirth.
Be blest, you for whom our sin
is not our last word.
May your forgiveness
be your last word to us
for everlasting.

FRIDAY OF THE 24TH WEEK

COMPANIONS

1 Timothy 6:2–12: One last time, Paul attacks false teachers. Like a physician looking for the cause of a painful symptom, he denounces the motivating force that drives them. These people are both prideful and dull-witted. On the one hand they refuse to accept the teaching of Christ as proposed by the church, and so they draw the community into quarrels and divisions. On the other hand, their inordinate attachment to money not only reduces them to the status of mere shopkeepers of religion, but threatens their souls, not to mention the souls of their followers. By way of contrast with this senseless attitude, the apostle proposes a doctrine of happiness founded on piety and disinterestedness.

Psalm 49 belongs to the sapiential genre. It endeavors to demonstrate the falsehood, indeed the stupidity, of a godless thesis. Riches are vain, it proclaims, and can do nothing whatever against death.

Luke 8:1–3: We are shown a picture of the Twelve, and a number of women seeing to their needs—a little community, then, a preliminary sketch of the post-Easter church, where the participation of women will break with the customs of a Palestinian world.

Indeed, there is organizational progress here across the board. After encountering Simon Peter, Jesus has indeed proclaimed the Beatitudes before all of his disciples. But for the discourse in parables, he surrounds himself with a more organized group, the disciples. Now we understand why the non-Jew can hear the Good News only through the intermediary of witnesses who live by it.

■

Jesus traverses the springtime countryside of Galilee for what has been styled, felicitously enough, the "great recruitment campaign." A little

group of men and women—"God's vagabonds"—have joined him for the great proclamation of the Reign. Here are my brothers, here are my own, Jesus will say, and he will mean those who hear, meditate, and make their own, his word. The whole gospel can be summed up in the one word, "accompanied."

"Accompanying" Jesus. . . . The New Testament writings have jealously reserved the use of this word to designate those who have given Jesus their whole existence. To accompany Jesus is to live with him, to pass one's time with him. It is in the intimacy of the common journey, of the shared table, of cares borne together, that familiarity is born. The disciple is a "companion," meaning, etymologically, one who shares the same bread. The disciples are Jesus' intimates. They anticipate his way of looking at things, his reactions. They know his tastes, and his favorite subjects. Familiarity is engendered in the everyday, in personal encounter.

To accompany Jesus is to awaken to a sameness of viewpoint with him. It means making his project one's own. A disciple is a follower, one who has opted for the program of the gospel. The disciple deciphers reality through a special lens. The Christian is not simply an honorable person. The Christian is "Christ's." And Saint Paul will cry, "For me, to live is Christ!"

To accompany Jesus is to keep him company. What would God be without these men and women who do his will? As Paul, once more, declares, we complete in our flesh what is missing from Christ's passion. There is a continuity between the disciples and Jesus, between the church and its Lord.

The disciple is Jesus' companion. That is, he or she does the same work, as in the Middle Ages brotherhoods of companions journeyed the highways and byways of a continent gracing it with the finest craftsmanship. A toiler for the Reign, the disciple actually constructs that Reign, causes it to appear. Without the disciples, what would become of the legacy bequeathed? Guardian of the traditions of the Reign, the disciple guarantees the future of the gospel.

"Father, I thank you: those whom you have given me have recognized that I have come from you. . . . Consecrate them in the truth." Such will be the last prayer of Christ (cf. Jn 17) for those who have been his companions. Such was his prayer for his church, for the number of those to whom we ourselves belong—"his own."

■

Father of Jesus Christ and our Father,
preserve the disciples of your Son in fidelity to his name.

He has made us the gift of his word—
  now consecrate us in the truth,
that he may reckon it to his glory
  to acknowledge us as "his own"
  in the eternity of the Reign.

■

  O God, who calls us to follow your Son,
send your Spirit upon us!
Grant that we may become the faithful companions
  of the shepherd of the flock.
May his Body, delivered up for our salvation,
  be the foundation of a communion in time
  called to be eternal.

FROM SATURDAY OF THE 24TH WEEK

TO THURSDAY OF THE 27TH WEEK

To Speak of God

The word of God is alive. It is found primarily in life, not in books. It rests in the precious reliquary of the Bible, to be sure. But it rises up before the eyes of all in everyday life. It is a word for each day, concealed in the humdrum of daily existence.

God teaches us life by having us live. Only someone who speaks knows what speech is. We submit to the apprenticeship of the word by exercising ourselves in that word. Only someone who performs the deeds of love knows what love is. This is the task and calling of the believer: to allow the word to appear in the world today by living the very Word, Jesus the Christ. The mission entrusted to the church is to reveal the hidden fact that the whole of reality is already the intimate universe of God. It is not a matter of a collage. We do not proclaim a paste-on word, ready to be affixed to the package of reality. The mission entrusted to the church is to tear away the veil and demonstrate that the word is at work even now—wherever men and women take the risk of living in some measure the values of the gospel.

Our task is to allow the word to sprout up by permitting ourselves to be initiated into the word. But this is a child's task. It will always be a child's task. Our vocation as God's daughters and sons is an initiation. Who could ever speak of God had they not opened their hearts to the wound of knowing God? Who will ever be able to speak of God without having taken the risk of sketching out a response to the questioning of faith: "Who do you say that I am?" And who will tell the weight of the word comprehended but those who are willing to allow that word bear its fruit in their hearts and to let the words of the heart, after their long, secret ripening, mount to their lips?

Yes, it takes a great deal of patience to learn a language. It takes a great deal of love to speak the language of the beloved. And it takes a great deal of boldness to dare to stutter words that will engage us in an encounter. But this is the grandeur of human kind: utterance. And this is our dignity as sons and daughters of God: the ability to utter God. Not to speak *of* God. But to utter God, as naturally as we speak our native tongue.

■

Lord our God,
*   behold your people assembled,*
*   your people gathered to hear you.*
Open our ears to your voice,
*   and our hearts to the Word that can transform them.*
Then shall we welcome as joyous news,
*   the message of your Son Jesus,*
*   your eternal Word, the sole Word of your mercy.*

SATURDAY OF THE 24TH WEEK

I CAST MY SEED UPON THE WINDS
1 Timothy 6:13-16: The apostle recommends a program of life for Timothy to follow. Authentic shepherds are just the opposite of false teachers. True pastors "first seek after integrity, piety, faith, love, steadfastness, and a gentle spirit" (v. 11). Thus they are faithful to their profession of faith and their baptism, for they are imitating Jesus Christ. The apostle concludes his exhortation on a solemn note: the doxology he selects glorifies the divine inaccessibility, thereby deliberately countering Gnostic pretensions to secret knowledge of God.

Psalm 100 prolongs the doxology, inviting the church of Jesus Christ to return thanks to its eternal shepherd.

Luke 8:4-15: The parable of the Seed—the mystery of a Word that wanders in quest of good soil and an abundant harvest! A little detail here betrays the special world of Luke. E. Delebecque (*L'évangile de Luc*, "*Les Belles Lettres*," Paris, 1976) has noted the finesse with which the evangelist speaks of only one portion of the seed at a time—including the seed that falls on good ground —when logically he should be telling us at this point about the "rest" of the seed as well. Delebecque suggests that "the good ground in question is not that of the field to be sown. It lies outside the field, where the good earth has shown itself exceptionally favorable." The hypothesis is eminently attractive. It allows us to interpret Luke as speaking, throughout the whole parable, not of the totality of the field to be sown—Israel—but only of the fringe. The evangelist seems to have "reread" the traditional parable, adapting it to the perspective of universal mission.

■

"Cast your seed upon the winds": a pretty maxim! It is also what today's gospel proclaims: the word of God is cast to the winds and bears fruit. For scripture says: "For just as from the heavens the rain and snow come down and do not return there till they have watered the earth . . . so shall my word be that goes forth from my mouth" (Is. 55:10-11).

The word of God is alive. It is found not primarily in books but in life. It reposes in the precious reliquary of the Bible, yes. But it springs up before the eyes of all of us in everyday life. It is a word for every day, concealed in the humdrum of daily existence.

"I cast my seed upon the winds," says God, and flings it into the air. Now the seed will belong only to itself, and its fertility will depend entirely on the soil where it falls. "I cast my seed upon the winds," says God, and henceforth his word, powerful in itself, belongs, as it were, no longer to God, but only to the liberty that will receive it. Finally, the Word reveals the depths of every one of us: by his sole presence Jesus obliges each of us to drop the mask and show what we really are.

"I cast my seeds to the winds," God says, and takes the risk of the broadcast. Need we be discouraged, then, at so much seed going for naught? No, the parable is deeply optimistic. Jesus is sure that, somewhere, the word will find the proper soil. Then there will be no withstanding its power.

■

We believe in God, our Father.
The earth, sprung from his creative word,
has bestowed its loveliest fruit:
Jesus, his Son, his eternal Word.

We believe in Jesus, seed of life,
the tiny grain sunken in the earth,
glorious ear of resurrection.

We believe in the Holy Spirit,
the power that fertilizes the Word
and upholds in the Church
the hope of the harvest.

■

Creator God,
grant that your seed may fecundate the earth.
As we have shared the bread of life,
may your word take flesh in the flesh of every day.
May our hope for the harvest
bear even now the sweet scent of tomorrow.

■

God our Father,
your word is accomplished in the coming of your Son.
Today it is offered to us in this eucharist.
Send us into the world
as bearers of the Good News that sets human beings free
from this moment forward, forever.

MONDAY OF THE 25TH WEEK

PORTICO OF THE REIGN

Ezra 1:1-6: Were the Jews actually authorized by the pagan king to repossess the land of their ancestors? Certain commentators have held the royal generosity in suspicion. Thus Cyrus' decree would be apocryphal. However, the document as it is reported actually contains nothing that would conflict with the general religious policy of the Persian princes. A year after the capture of Babylon in 538 B.C., Cyrus authorizes the exiles' return to Jerusalem, where they hope to reestablish the worship of Yahweh on Sion's hill. Actually many Jews who had settled in Babylon preferred to remain behind, while aiding those of their coreligionists who had chosen to return to their land. We cannot help noting the rather obvious parochialism of verse 5: for the author, the religious restoration was the all but exclusive deed of the tribe of Judah.

Does Jeremiah know what he is saying? He has proclaimed that the consequence of Israel's sins will be that the country will be "forever" transformed into a land of desolation. Now suddenly, in Jeremiah 25:11–14, the prophet restricts the period of chastisement to seventy years, the symbolic number representing a lifetime. But the prophecy was rooted in the curses of Leviticus 26 accompanying the legislation regarding the sabbatical years. "If the people refuse to respect the sabbatical years, the Lord will see to it that the soil itself will refuse to work, in order to recover the years of rest of which it has been deprived. This interpretation of the Exile as a time of desolation and forced sabbath (the soil transformed into wilderness) will be resumed in 2 Chronicles 36:20–22, which will in turn encourage the speculations of Deuteronomy 9 regarding the 'seventy weeks of years' in the time of the 'great desolation' under Antiochus IV." After this time of desolation, however, the great deliverance will be at hand.

Psalm 126, a "song of ascent," expresses the people's joy in the return of the prisoners. Even foreigners are dumbfounded at the omnipotence of Yahweh.

Luke 8:16–18: Word of warning, word of hope! First of all: the picture is optimistic, brilliant as a lamp on a stand. As the lamp lights up the entire room, so will God's word pierce the furthest recesses of the human heart. But who will measure the fecundity of the Word? Today Jesus is preaching within the boundaries of Israel. Tomorrow the hearers of his word will address the whole world. "There is nothing secret that will not appear on the great day."

But one must be careful how one listens. One must listen attentively—not negligently, simply untouched by its meaning taking care to put the word into practice, to see that it bears fruit. There's many a slip 'twixt the cup and the lip, and it is a far cry from the ear that hears to the heart that leaps to the deed.

■

We have only to leaf through the gospels to see that the parable is Jesus' special way of holding discourse.

The fact that the parables rest on a personal experience, and that they owe their power of persuasion to this experience, is not unrelated to their interpretation.

Most of Jesus' parables refer their hearers to their own life experience, and draw their effectiveness from this experience. Since this is the case, we can hope to assimilate their message ourselves only to the extent that we, too, recognize our own experience in them. The parables initiate us into the mystery of the Reign. And so it is not enough to ask ourselves what Jesus literally "meant" in the parables. We must also strive to read, through them, what Jesus has said of himself. The parables allow us to see reality as Jesus saw it in order to lead us to an encounter with Jesus himself.

"Take heed, therefore, how you hear . . ." A parable is a signpost along the road to mystery. Over and above the words, a story is being told. After all, only stories can describe what occurs in the Reign. As we teach children the meaning of life through stories, so we can acquire a mental grasp of God's project only by allowing ourselves to be carried along by the movement of a little story. The parables open to us the portico of the revelation of the Spirit.

■

Light engendered of Light,
Jesus, Word from all eternity,
    illumine our story,
    light up our history,
    be for us the word of initiation into the secrets of the Reign.

■

Be blessed, Father most good:
we have received the word of your Son
    and the communion of his body.
Grant us the desire to walk in his footsteps

    and to make our own the word to which he has given life.
May that word become our heritage,
    that we may know the joy of living as your sons and daughters.

"OUR" JESUS

Ezra 6:7-8, 12, 14-20: The generosity of the Persian kings redoubles. Darius, one of the successors of Cyrus, not only approves his ancestor's instructions, but orders his governors to finance the rebuilding of the temple by levying taxes on the province. The consecration of the altar in the spring of the year 515 B.C. is the occasion of great popular celebration and rejoicing.

Today's pericope identifies the theology of the author of the Book of Ezra, who is also the writer of the books of Nehemiah and Chronicles. All of his concerns center on Jerusalem and the temple. He dreams of a community, to be established in the holy city, that will be wholly sacred, entirely God's. It is from this perspective as well that he evaluates the age of the monarchy and the work of restoration performed by Ezra and his contemporaries. The reason for his obsession with the rebuilding of the walls of Jerusalem, then, is that he feels that the city should be walled off from the rest of the world. Similarly he proclaims the temple at Jerusalem to be the only legitimate one, in order to block the pretentions of the Samaritans. Finally we note his interest in the Levites: in Chronicles, too, the bearers of the Ark in days gone by are the principal ministers of worship.

Another song of ascent: *Psalm 122* is a song of pilgrimage, inviting its hearers to contemplate the wonders of the Lord.

Luke 8:19-21: The conclusion of Jesus' discourse in parables. In Jesus' eyes, ties of blood are of far less moment than the dispositions of the heart.

■

"My mother and my brothers are those who hear the word of God and act upon it." We are the family of Jesus. Hesitantly, yet trustfully, in the recollection of our heart, we make bold to call him . . . "our Jesus." To call him "our Jesus" is absolutely essential to our faith. Christ is no stranger. He is someone very near. To each of us he says, as he has said to his disciples, "You have not chosen me, it is I who have chosen you!" Christ is not our master but our friend. To each of us he says what he said to his disciples: "I no longer call you servants. I call you friends" (Jn 15:16).

The ties that lash us to Jesus are not the mere bonds of a mental grasp that seizes upon a word it knows to be the vehicle of truth. Nor are they the simple bonds of a will that has the docility to bow to a law. What binds us to Jesus are bonds of the heart—if by the heart we understand not the blaze of an affectivity equally prompt to flare up and to die away again, but a trusting communion, a communion in the choice of the same basic options, in the sharing of the same lot. What binds Christ and ourselves are those bonds of the heart that make for inseparability— despite the distance, the darkness, and the incomprehension that life or misfortune can erect between two lovers for a little while.

It is these bonds of the heart that found our faith, and it is surely for this reason that we can say, with love, "Our Jesus." Doubtless we have heard the curious expression sometimes used in family conversations. We designate a person by prefixing to his or her name "our." We say, "Our Katie," or "Our Bob." It is an expression that joins a tender affection to a special solidarity. "My mother. . . ."

■

God, Father of Jesus,
you alone can speak his name with tenderness,
    for he is your Son, your Beloved.
The Spirit has been poured forth in our hearts:
    and hence we make bold to pronounce the name
    that is above every name.
May our prayer be the sacrament
    of the family ties that bind us.
And may he acknowledge us as his sisters and brothers
    in eternity.

■

Be blessed, Father of Jesus Christ:
your Son reveals his face to us
    despite our little faith,
and gives us to share
    in his Body delivered to make us "his own."
May this eucharist manifest his power
    in our lives.
May it convert us:
    may it transform us into your family.

SENT

Ezra 9:5–9: The lectionary divides the Book of Ezra in such a way that we miss the reason for Ezra's prayer (see vv. 1–2). The prophet's concern remains ever the same—to assemble at Jerusalem a community that will be governed by Yahweh, and Yahweh alone. Naturally this community will need to be holy and unblemished. It is not for reasons of security alone, then, that the citizens of Jerusalem make such haste to raise its walls once more. They are equally zealous to preserve the city from all outside contamination.

The prohibition against mixed marriages has the same purpose. In Ezra's eyes these marriages have represented Israel's great sin in the time of the monarchy. He remembers the strange princesses who imported their gods along with their dowries, and so encouraged the idolatry so frequently denounced by the prophets.

Ezra's prayer is also the Bible's oldest "national confession," a literary genre developed at Jerusalem after the catastrophe of 587 B.C.

The canticle of *Tobit 13* is composed of two parts. First comes a psalm of praise (vv. 2–10) exalting Yahweh's sovereignty. The present selection is then complemented by a prophetic passage (vv. 10–18) that speaks of Jerusalem in universalistic tones.

Luke 9:1–6: Luke adds nothing to this missionary instruction, which has already been reported by Mark and Matthew. Let us notice, however, how quickly it comes after Jesus' identification of his real family as those who hear the word of God and act on it.

The missioners will fare no better than their Master. They will not find all doors open. It will even happen that, in contravention of the very laws of hospitality, they will be refused a welcome altogether. But they are always to come as harbingers of peace, the peace that is God's salvation. Their preaching is to proclaim the inauguration of the Reign, and their exorcisms will confirm the collapse of the rule of Satan. Luke tells more: these Twelve will prefigure the church. For in their person, the entire community of witnesses will rise up to bear testimony to Christ and his message.

■

"Jesus . . . sent them forth to proclaim the reign of God. . . ." From its very birth, the church is called to make proclamation. The church is missionary by nature.

Today we make a distinction between church and mission. Thereby we injure the church, its mission, and our conceptualization of both.

When we say "church" we conjure up a picture of a society established alongside the other societies in which people's lives unfold. The society of the church is then pictured as having its end in the exercise of so-called "religious activities." On the other hand the "missionary work" of the church is supposed to be the effort the church undertakes to absorb the greatest possible number of persons, thereupon to see to it that these persons accept a specific series of ideas, rites and behaviors.

This, in-barest outline, is our current idea of the church and its mission. Yet we ought to know that this mission, as God has effectuated it from the beginning by his creative Word, as it was embodied in the people of Israel, as it has been lived by Jesus—God become a human being—and as the church ought to be living it today, does not consist in transplanting human beings into a society where they will find salvation in the adoption of rites and an adherence to a system of thoughts. Mission is the revelation of the secret place where all reality already belongs to the intimate universe of God.

The believer and the church can only make this revelation if they plunge to the heart of all reality—all word, all thought, all love, all culture, all society, all civilization.

There is no believer anywhere else. There is no church without its roots there. The mission of the church is not to place Jesus where he has not been before, but to show and to say that Jesus is everywhere present, even now.

■

O God, who has held utterance since the beginning,
    steady our tottering faith.
May its rays pierce our life to the quick,
that we may become a living testimonial
    to the Good News that would seize and grasp
    the entire life of women and men
    forever.

■

Father of our Lord Jesus Christ,
God, Lord of your people,
    send your Spirit upon us!

May he descend upon those whom you call
   to undertake the building of your church.
May he be the breath that animates them,
   the thrust that sweeps them forward,
   the power that bears them up,
   and the bond that gathers them in.
Grant that we may be witnesses, immersed in this time,
   of a promise for all time to come.

THURSDAY OF THE 25TH WEEK

HOLY CURIOSITY

Haggai 1:1–8: Cyrus' edict occasioned the return of a first group of exiles, to the number of some 30,000, or a third of the deported population, to Jerusalem. There the order of the day was a massive effort of reconstruction. The returnees began their task by rebuilding the altar of sacrifice. Then they directed their efforts to the reconstruction of the temple itself. But the population who had not been deported created difficulties. They feared that the "newcomers" would seize their land, and the initial enthusiasm of the reconstruction project was quickly dampened. In 520 B.C. the temple was still a pile of stones.

But prophets now arose, and endeavored to shake the people from their apathy. Among them was Haggai, whose tirades fell on the ears of a grandson of King Jehoiakim, Zerubbabel—to whom the Persian administration had entrusted the civil government—and of the high priest Joshua. Haggai upbraided the pair, reproaching them for building a few luxurious dwellings in Jerusalem, and demanding that they cease to blind themselves to the signs of the times. Were not the drought, and nakedness of the people due to foot-dragging in the reconstruction of the temple?

In response to the prophet's exhortation, *Psalm 149* invites the people themselves to celebrate a liturgy in Yahweh's honor.

Luke 9:7–9: Curiously, Herod's question gets wedged in between the accounts of the sending of the Twelve and the multiplication of the loaves. "Who is this man about whom I hear all these reports?" wonders the King. One seditious movement after another has troubled this Galilee of his. But his question has a deeper meaning as well. It represents the sense of uneasiness we all experience in the face of the challenge of the person of Jesus and the testimony of the disciples. Who is this person who sends emissaries, and confuses people's minds?

59

■

People were talking about this person. They told a thousand-and-one stories about him. He was saddled with the most improbable claims and projects. His deeds were exaggerated by popular enthusiasm, by the heat of infatuation. Herod's curiosity had been piqued beyond enduring. Yes, this great puppet must behold with his own eyes the prodigies of which he had only heard tell. What an exotic subject roamed his too-provincial Galilee!

There is such a thing, we hear it said, as unhealthy curiosity. Unhealthy curiosity uses a person as a thing. It exploits scandal, thereby only adding fuel to the fire. It celebrates the incidental, promoting it to the status of the essential. Herod longed to see Jesus in order to display him to his court as a . . . curiosity. Ah, if perchance there might be a miracle! (See Lk 23:9.)

And yet curiosity can be the first stage of the encounter of faith! Astonishment, surprise, provocation, are the antechamber, the threshold of a discovery of the inner rooms of the house, an initiation into the mystery of the dwelling. Curiosity is synonymous with discovery. It is our straining toward an object glimpsed, surmised, and somehow desired, that leads us to the magnificent discovery. Woe to a love no longer curious! "A fire not fed might well be dead."

Am I curious about Jesus? We used to say that faith was strong if it was certain and sure. We reduced faith to the profession of soulless definitions and the "embracing" of cold, dry dogmas. No, faith is curiosity. Faith is astonishment, and then a willingness to risk the adventure. Faith is the glimpse of a possible encounter, and then this glimpse stirs desire. Faith is curiosity. Doubt is indispensable. Uncertainty and incomprehension are not the opposite of faith, as black is the opposite of white. They are the very domain of faith, as the empty stomach that craves satisfaction, the expectation that strains for encounter, the thirst slaked even now with the hope of the one thing that can satisfy it.

■

God of eternal youth,
quicken in us the thirst to know you
    and the desire to discover you.
Make us curious about your word:
may that word initiate us into the mystery of you

without ever exhausting the joy of an encounter
ever new and for everlasting.

■

O God, sought in the darkness of faith,
  no one has ever seen you.
But you have sent your Son among us.
Show us how to discover him ever anew.
May your Spirit initiate us
  into the knowledge of you:
we shall be astonished
  at what he would have us love
  throughout eternity.

READING AND UNDERSTANDING LUKE

The Reign of God Is at Hand (Luke 9:18–13:35)

This extremely complex sequence is an effort to respond to the question posed in the preceding section. Who is this Jesus to whom believers have given their faith? It is not enough to say that he is the Christ of God (9:20). We must go further: we must steep ourselves in the way in which he has understood his mission. It is not enough, in other words, to assert that Jesus is God's Son. We must go on to penetrate the manner in which he is revealed as this Son, for it is an eminently singular manner, and each of us is invited to imitate it. Luke gives his answer to the great question in three complementary moments. First there is Jesus' prayer. Then there is the proclamation of the passion and the ascent to Jerusalem: now Jesus has started down the road of fidelity that will show us how very committed his prayer has been. Finally we have the account of the transfiguration—a sort of contrast in light and shadow, in which Jesus both speaks of his exodus and appears in his glory (9:18–62).

Chapter 10 opens with a new mission, a new sending of the disciples. This time there are seventy-two (10:1–12), and their mission will be universal. Henceforth there will be, in all cities and villages, these joyous witnesses of things seen and heard, the reign of God come to every woman and man and recognized in Jesus Christ by the little, the small. After all, the Samaritan who draws so near the victim lying in the ditch on the road to Jericho (10:29–37) . . . is Jesus himself—just as it is Jesus himself who reconciles the different ideas of Martha and Mary about service. (10:38–42).

Chapter 11 returns to Jesus' prayer. That prayer must be one that leads to the gift of the Spirit. We have felt this from the moment Jesus began to indicate the manner in which he understood himself to be God's Son. Now, then, is the hour for decision, not for sterile discussions. Now is the moment when we must step forward and declare clearly for Jesus. Now is the time to listen to his solemn warning to the scribes and Pharisees who everlastingly distort the signs of the Reign, just as they denature the law and oppress the helpless with burdens too heavy for them. Who are they, for that matter, these scribes, to appoint themselves judges over others? Who are they to have power over life and death, when the Christ has been sent only to give life (12:13–15)? And there comes a new warning. But this time it is addressed to the disciples. The latter have received a grace, and a grace is not to be hoarded, but to be placed at the disposition of all. Then will the disciples be good stewards, and the Master himself will come to them and serve them (12:29–39).

Alas, life can be refused, as we see only too clearly in the opposition encountered by Jesus during his life. Israel has been unwilling, either to admit to its malady or to recognize Jesus as the one who can heal it, the one who would have been capable of bidding the chosen people to arise and walk once more (13:10–17). Revelation has run into a brick wall. And so God prepares to quit his "house," the temple, as the prophet Ezekiel had foretold—but only for a limited time, the time needed for conversion, the time of God's patience. God has taken up the defense of the sterile fig tree (13:6–9).

FRIDAY OF THE 25TH WEEK

THE WOUNDING
Haggai 1:15–2:9: "On the twenty-first day of the seventh month. . . ." Haggai has carefully selected the day of his preaching! The preceding oracle has been pronounced on the first day of a month. This one thunders its message on the last day of the Feast of Tabernacles, at a moment when pilgrims are pressing into the holy city in great numbers. And in addition, the liturgy of the feast invites the people to pray for the success of the coming harvest. The prophet takes advantage of this fact to set the people thinking about the spiritual future of the nation.

The times surely favored messianic speculations. The Persian empire had encountered serious difficulties. Despite its estrangement, then, the little Jerusalem community eagerly anticipated a change in the political situation.

Must not the upheavals all around them presage the Lord's decisive intervention in history? The prophet recalls the divine promises. Like the pillar of cloud of the Exodus, the Spirit rests upon the people. Haggai is arrestingly optimistic. Imagine speaking of the future splendor of the temple when that temple still lies almost entirely in ruins!

Psalm 43, a complaint, expresses both distress and hope. Must it not have been precisely such seemingly incompatible sentiments that tugged in two directions at the hearts of pilgrims who stood before a sanctuary that had scarcely begun to rise from its ruins?

Luke 9:18–22: Uneasy about the hubbub this individual has stirred up in his province, Herod asks a question. Who is this Jesus? Now, Herod is anything but a member of the church. But his question echoes in the hearts of the disciples. They, too, wonder: Who is this Jesus to whom they have given their faith?

Peter responds: "The Messiah of God." Ah, but he will not get off so easily! Faith is not restricted to an intellectual adherence. Faith arouses a personal commitment. Who is this Jesus to whom I commit myself? The gospel answers the question by announcing the passion. Jesus is the new human being, entirely submissive to the will of the Father. He must fulfill to the hilt the commitment he made in the synagogue of Nazareth. For Jesus, to be Son of the Father, to be his Father's child, is to obey, and obey unconditionally.

■

"But you—who do you say that I am?" You, not the crowd. You personally. No "canned answers." A delicate question. I should really like to know the answer. But . . . I hesitate. What will you do, lock me into facile definitions? Give me a name you scarcely comprehend? Whittle away at the mystery of my richness, a mystery whose depths I myself may not have plumbed? I know, you will answer me: Why, you are my child, the one in the manger . . . my friend . . . my "boss" . . . my love. . . . And so on. Yes, I am all of these things, surely. But I am something else, as well! How difficult it is to know another without wounding that one!

"But you—who do you say that I am?" Jesus asks us the question. He takes the risk. Answers abound. Books have been written. Jesus? Murdered prophet, Sacred Heart, "true God and true man," Superstar. Jesus imposes silence. How hard it is to know God without wounding him!

Jesus asks this question when he himself is at prayer. In the truth of his being and his existence, he can say that he knows God: "Father, Abba!" Here is a name I can pronounce without wounding God! For God allows himself to be wounded by that name. "Father, your will be done!" On

Calvary Jesus will show the lengths to which this answer will lead him. And in the hour of his passion he will truly be able to say: "Father . . . I have revealed your name. . . ."

To know God is passion, in both senses of the word. It is at once an immense love, and a profound suffering. To know God is a vocation, a call: "Whoever wishes to be my follower must deny his very self . . ." (Lk 9:23). One becomes a disciple by choice, and out of obedience.

Discipleship is a choice. I have been touched to the heart by a word that I fail fully to grasp. A vocation is a trial. The call burns like a brand, for it is radical as a judgment. To be a disciple is to open myself to a question—to allow myself to be "called into question." And discipleship entails no security, no assurance, but the grace to emerge victorious from the trial.

Discipleship is an act of obedience. I not only receive the gift, I "take it to heart." To all those who thirst for God, the God of life, Jesus grants his Spirit: for in baptism we have donned Christ, we belong to him. Our vocation is an initiation.

To know God will always be a new birth. Peter will genuinely be able to pronounce Jesus' name only after the denial and Easter: "Lord, you know all things, you know that I love you!" On that day, instead of imposing silence, Jesus will encourage Peter in his vocation of strengthening his sisters and brothers.

"Who am I?" What else, then, will tell us the name of God but the wound God himself has himself engraved on our hearts with the desire to know him?

■

What is your name, hidden God?
   Only the desire to know you can express our gratitude.
Your Son reveals to us your face:
   only the adoration of the face of the Crucified One
   can introduce us into your mystery.

"But you—who do you say that I am?"
This is your prayer, Lord Jesus,
and our response can only be prayer:
   May we glimpse your love.
   May we be granted your salvation.

THE SCANDAL OF FAITH

Zechariah 2:5-9, 14-15: Haggai bequeathed to the prophet Zechariah the role of providing Jerusalem's citizens with moral support. If we prescind from chapters 9-14, which are the work of another later prophet, we can say that Zechariah's work is essentially constituted of eight "visions," each followed by an oracle, and by a summary of his preaching which was written by his disciples.

Today's liturgy sets forth the third of these eight visions (2:5-9), together with a brief excerpt from the corresponding oracle (vv. 14-15). The vision is the rather classic one of the surveyor which Ezekiel, too, has reported (Ez 42-43) and which will reappear in Revelation 21:15-17. The most striking thing about it is surely the promise, the shining future, implied in the demand that the city remain open to the nations.

The oracle that follows is an invitation to joy, addressed to all who inhabit Jerusalem.

Jeremiah 31 is a collection of oracles originally addressed to northern Israel, and extended to Judah after 587 B.C. Here history is "reread" in the light of faith. The divine chastisement of the people is viewed as an instrument of rehabilitation.

Luke 9:43-45: The second proclamation of the passion omits any mention of the resurrection. For a good number of commentators this is a clue that Luke 9:44 actually goes back to the historical Jesus. It announces his death in terms borrowed from Jewish apocalyptic, notably from Deuteronomy 7:25: this innocent will be delivered over to human beings just as the "holy ones" of Israel before him were delivered into the hands of Antiochus Epiphanes. But if these commentators are correct, then Jesus' proclamation of his death will nevertheless imply his exaltation, since Deuteronomy 7:13-14 posits the ultimate meaning of the failure of suffering as the condition *sine qua non* and guarantee of resurrection at the last.

The disciples fail to understand. They have yet to become daughters and sons!

■

"But you—who do you say that I am?" Jesus has asked his disciples. Who will discover the mystery of the response except those who will share the depths of the scandal of a prophet sentenced for blasphemy, a preacher whose message has been rejected, a master ignored by his own? Who will recover the face of God but a woman impelled by the thrust of her heart and her compassion to defy men and wipe with her veil the face that, in the psalmist's words, is no longer so much as a human one? Who will be able to profess the true name of God but that individual, that despised foreigner of the army of occupation who, at the foot of the cross of this agitator and visionary will cry in astonishment, "The Son of God!"? Only those willing to walk the whole way to the cross will be able to comprehend, to seize, the victory of Easter.

Jesus must be delivered up. The expression is one of the refrains of the passion, as we know—verified in sinister images of Jesus passed from hand to hand, from Judas to the guards, from the Sanhedrin to Pilate, from Pilate to the executioners. But antecedently, the expression "delivered up," multiplied in its occurrences with the approach of the hour of destiny, is an excellent characterization of the disciple's path to the mystery of the God of Jesus. After all, that God is a God delivered over to human beings—a God faithful to his desire for a covenant, and yet respectful of the free response of a believer who must become a partner.

The sacrament of God's presence, this human Jesus, is a scandal and a trial for faith. Either it challenges faith and opens the way to the truth of the mystery, or it is a stumbling block for that faith.

■

God, who manifests yourself in your Son,
    grant us to draw near the knowledge of your mystery.
The cross speaks to us of your love,
    and your humility engages us in a covenant of tenderness.
Deliver to us your name,
    that we may deliver ourselves to your love.

■

Lord God,
    source of all wisdom,
you alone know the one you have sent us,
    Jesus, your son.
You alone could reveal him.
Grant us to discover in him
    the Messiah come to give his life for the multitude.
And instill in us the grace
    to profess his name before all humankind.
For he is risen, and he lives with you
    forever and ever.

Be blessed, most good Father.
Yes, the word of your Son disconcerts us.
   Yet we know that it is our life,
   the work of your Spirit in our heart.

Be blessed.
Yes, the Bread we share protests the paltriness of our love.
   Yet it creates our communion with you
   even today.

Permit us to embody your Word in time,
that we may become, day by day,
   the living Body of your Son,
the Sign, standing in this world,
   of the surprise of eternity.

MONDAY OF THE 26TH WEEK

IN THE MIDST OF THE CHURCH: THE CHILD

Zechariah 8:1-8: The last two chapters of Zechariah represent a compilation of disparate compositions, the work of disciples who have taken up their master's preaching. Chapter 7 portrays the arrival in Jerusalem of a delegation of Jews from Babylon asking the temple priests whether the fall of the temple of Jerusalem in 587 B.C. ought to continue to be commemorated by a fast. As it is Zechariah who answers, he was probably a priest.

The prophet gives his response in two parts. First he reflects on the meaning of a commemorative fast. In Zechariah's eyes, such a thing is useless. It looks to the past alone. But God is not a thing of the past. God "comes from the future" (P. Talec).

Chapter 8 follows without a transition. The scenery is altogether different, forming the backdrop for the new covenant that Yahweh longs to celebrate with his people. New names are given to Jerusalem, in token of reconciliation. The length of the life of its inhabitants is increased, and the country is totally liberated to a communion of faithfulness and justice.

Our liturgy selects from *Psalm 102* its promises of a brighter tomorrow. No sooner has the divine oracle been reported, than the psalmist intones his prayer of thanksgiving.

Luke 9:46–50: "Whoever wishes to be my follower must deny his very self, take up his cross each day, and follow in my steps" (Luke 9:23). Everything we have heard thus far in Luke 9 directs our attention to Jesus' passion, converging on how Jesus has been the Son, and hence on what the disciples must do to become daughters and sons in their turn. Surely this is the meaning of the Father's admonition in the transfiguration account: "Listen to him." There is a "greater than Moses" here: the Son, totally delivered up. This is how Jesus has been "the greatest," in the words of our gospel text.

Concretely, to be "the greatest" is to welcome not only our immediate neighbor, but outsiders as well. This emphasis on openness to the very poorest (to beggars and foreigners) is altogether typical of the Lucan style. As the outcast of all civil and religious society, these "little ones" have God alone as their defender. It is for their sake first and foremost that Jesus has been delivered into the hands of human beings.

■

Jesus is on the move, along the roads of a green, radiant Galilee. His step is resolute. His little group of pilgrims of the cross are a thousand miles from understanding what is occurring. Jesus advances alone, and lonely. His roadways are the ways of God. He pauses only to instruct his disciples. "The Son of Man must be delivered. . . ." The prophecy of the servant of Yahweh must be fulfilled. . . . But the disciples are too mired down in their own concerns really to listen. They are afraid to ask, and too busy to discuss the response in any case.

Jesus asks them what they have been discussing along the way. As he does, he lifts a little child into his arms and places him among the disciples. A child stands amidst the church. And Jesus kisses him—he, the Son of God who, all too soon, will be betrayed by a kiss, the kiss of one of the Twelve. But before delivering himself up to the fire of love, as a careless child might do, Jesus delivers to us words that signal an eternal revolution: "Whoever welcomes this little child on my account welcomes me. . . ." Yes, welcomes my Father and me. Did you not know that it takes only a kiss, only a little tenderness, to raise a child to life? Love is the only rule of behavior for those who enter the Reign of God.

Is there not born in our heart today, in the heart of a disciple, an overwhelming desire to run to the child within us? The life of that child has not yet been killed, despite all our adult desires, these desires for power. The child in us can teach us the path of grace, where the last become first.

■

We bless you,
     God whom neither earth nor heaven can contain.
For you have given us to know your name.
You manifested your face to us
     when the Child of Man, Jesus, your unique one, appeared.
Be blessed,
     God who overthrow the mighty
     and raise the humble.

When you will reveal your might,
you come to us as a child.
     For your might has the power of love.
Your Son takes on himself our weakness,
     he lifts up the poor ones that we are
     and makes us children, the heirs of your Reign.
Be blessed,
     you who fill the hungry with good things
     and sent the rich away with empty hands.

■

Yours is the power to bestow new youth
     on the gnarled face of our earth.
Father of the unique Son, our Father,
     come!
     By your Spirit restore to their youth
     these passions of ours, which grow faint
     in their search for other slaking than you.

When he comes in glory,
may your Son be able to cry out to us:
     "Come. You have my Father's blessing!
     Inherit the kingdom
     prepared for you from the creation of the world."

THE ROAD TO JOY

Zechariah 8:20–23: Is it the presence of the new temple, standing at last? Or the mighty walls that wrap the city once more? In any event the citizens of Jerusalem have set themselves to dreaming of the future—a grandiose future, in which all nations shall rise up and swarm toward the Jewish capital. On that day the promise God has made to Abraham will be accomplished: "I shall make of you a great people." And yet Jerusalem itself must one day lie in ruins again. For, while surely "salvation is from the Jews" (Jn 4:22), the hour is coming as well when the Father is to be worshiped neither at Jerusalem nor on Mount Gerazim.

Psalm 87 is to be ranged with the hymns chanted in honor of Sion. It sings the beauty of the city in which all peoples are to acknowledge one another— the heavenly Jerusalem, then, whose temple will be the Lord himself.

Luke 9:51–56: The die is cast! Jesus "sets his face" for Jerusalem. The journey will end only with the ascension, after the victory over suffering and death. It is Jesus' personal exodus. Along the way, day by day, Jesus will learn his Father's will, in his prayer.

He is sent to human beings, and he is delivered into their hands for judgment —his own judgment, first of all, which will bring him down to death, despite his innocence; and then that of his executioners which, Luke has already announced, will be a judgment of grace and forgiveness. It would have been easy enough to put the recalcitrant cities to the torch. But Jesus had not come for that.

■

To exiles scattered abroad, the prophet repeats the everlasting promise of God. We have heard it in yesterday's reading: "I have a burning passion for you. . . . Behold, I come to save my people!" In the dark times in which we live, we have but one hope to sustain us: God does not abandon us. For he is on fire with passion for us.

This faith that assures us, in the world, in the midst of the painful struggles and searchings of our times, that the human being is possible —this faith bears witness that life will have the last word. To believe in absolute Love is to believe that love, our human loves are, somewhere, guaranteed. To believe in supreme Life is to hope that our own deeds of life, fragile and helpless as they are, are being reaped somewhere, and that the harvest will be astounding. Yes, we are exiles still. Nothing of this has changed. And yet everything is different. The dark of our exile is lighted up by the promise of a return. The charm does not transmute our trial. Its only virtue is to conjure away despair.

Whence springs this hope, seemingly so unfounded? Only of a word, a mere promise? How fragile these would seem, were we not persuaded we perceive a spark of the promised brilliance on our very earth! For love has stooped to the very heart of misery, determined to sweep up our whole life. We have but one humble witness to proclaim: God has come to walk with us and make our trial his own. The end of our exile draws near. Once more we are on the road for the land of promise.

No wonder, then, that others join our caravan! They too are seduced by this incredible news. "Let us go with you, for we have heard that God is with you."

■

Faithful God,
> *you are on fire with passion for us.*
> *You long to rescue us!*
May our gladness be to the measure of your grace,
that our joy may serve as a witness to our sisters and brothers
> *that their hope cannot be in vain.*
We pray to you:
may they be able to share our thanksgiving.
For you are with them
> *as you are with us:*
> *for everlasting.*

■

God of the faithful promise,
> *who delivers us from anxiety and fear,*
your Spirit would spread your own gladness among us.
May our certitude grow into that joy:
> *for you save us, in Jesus, the Lord.*

■

Your Reign draws near, God our Father.
> *This communion is its sign.*
Make us witnesses of this hope.
To you we sing our praise
> *through your Son, who has walked on ahead of us*
> *to lead us to everlasting joy.*

71

THE STRIPPING

Nehemiah 2:1–8: The books of Ezra and Nehemiah are terribly contradictory. It is difficult to determine just when the respective prophets must have spoken their proclamations in Palestine. These two seem really to be "criss-crossing." It even seems that the prohibition of Ezra 4 against rebuilding the temple originally concerned only the walls of the city, and that the temple had already been rebuilt. On the other hand we do not know for certain which Artaxerxes is the one spoken of in Nehemiah. But problems of chronology need not detain us. What we should grasp and appreciate above all is the importance of Jerusalem in the eyes of the exiles. Here was the city of the temple, the place the Lord has chosen to establish his dwelling!

More than any other psalm, *Psalm 137* expresses the grief of Nehemiah and his exiled compatriots. "If I forget you, Jerusalem, may my right hand be forgotten!"—lost to me, useless.

Luke 9:57–62: To follow Jesus means a radical change in our lives. The missionary has neither home nor family. He or she must be prepared to pull up stakes on a moment's notice. Jesus shows himself even more demanding than the prophet Elijah, who at least granted his disciple time to bid farewell to his aged parents (1 Kgs 19). But Jesus is more than Elijah, and this time the disciple's mission is to announce the sudden, mighty coming of the Reign of God. Let the dead bury their dead. The order may appear harsh and abrupt. But this only underscores the urgency of the gospel mission, and the joy of the Reign. Indeed the real dead here are those who have failed to heed the Good News of salvation.

∎

One must advance, and resolutely broach the ascent. One must be unencumbered with any weight that would slow the march, then. Jesus has bravely taken the road for Jerusalem. The days of the great departure, the new Exodus, are upon him. "Whoever wishes to be my follower must deny his very self. . . ."! Ah, here is a candidate for discipleship, ready to follow the master wherever he goes. Does he have the slightest notion how rootless is the life he is embracing? And here is another, called by the Lord and not even given the time to bury his father! The urgency of the Reign brooks no delay. To follow Christ is a perpetual passage, an ascent, a Passover. Let us be plain. The time has come to leave, to be torn away, to be uprooted. The time of the stripping is at hand. Any who have heard the call must first be cleansed and refined, at great length. "Whoever wishes to be my follower must deny his very self. . . .!"

The words of vocation are hard, and hot. They can sear like a blazing fire. The gospel of Jesus is not a matter of words. Still less is it an "experiment." Either you are for or you are against. "Follow me!" And that means at once, right now, with no pussyfooting.

The time of vocation is the time of trial by fire. The call is desperate emergency, and radical judgment. Might we have missed something in reading the gospel? Might twenty centuries of habit have deprived us of a sense of the "end of days," a sense of urgency, of the headlong, passionate Reign of God among human kind? Today, in our own milieus at least, we are all politeness. But indifference can be more pernicious than a resistance that comes right out and calls a spade a spade. Might the lukewarmness of the disciples mean that the salt has lost its savor? The disciples will truly be Jesus' "followers" only when they have run the whole course, actually met with contradiction, and come to very Golgotha.

These followers must first be baptized by fire. They must first drink the cup. Then they can bear witness. The church will be born in the fire of Pentecost. To become the community of those called, the disciples will have to live the paradox of the Son who is willing to become servant, who is come not to rule but to serve. One day the community will bear witness to Jesus unto the very shedding of its blood. It will go the whole road—the road to martyrdom. But until that day dawns, it will have to learn from its Master and teacher the art of a total stripping, a complete self-divestment. A disciple of Jesus is one who has acknowledged the Lord, and made a total commitment to his exodus. Every step to the fore snatches the followers of Jesus from their securities, and thrusts them still further down the road.

■

God of the word and the prophets,
your call is like a burning fire,
*   the demand of your Law keen as any sword.*
Deliver us from our self-sufficiency,
*   yet calm our fears.*
Allow us to follow humbly in the path
*   of your Son, our Master and our savior.*

■

God of the living,
the communion of the Body of your Son
*   draws us into his footsteps.*

Preserve those who have put their hand to the plow
    from ever looking back,
and make of us, among men and women,
the laborers of your Reign.

THURSDAY OF THE 26TH WEEK

TO SAVE THE HARVEST

Nehemiah 8:1–4, 5–6, 8–12: Jerusalem has been rebuilt, and within its walls
the Lord's temple stands. But the main thing about a city is the people who
live there. Today's reading recalls for us the vocation of the community
assembled at Jerusalem. When Yahweh chose the temple to make his dwelling
there, he simultaneously entrusted his word to a people who would make it
their principal reason for living.

Behold these people—men, women and children old enough to have some
grasp of what is at stake—convoked, the first day of the year, by a holy
Word. Here is the Word that stirs hearts, and rouses them to joy! More than
ever, Israel, the old and the new, will be the people of the covenant, mighty
witness to God's love.

Psalm 19 sings the gratitude of a people who know that they are the dwelling
place of a divine promise.

Luke 10:1–12: Who is Jesus? Here he sends seventy-two disciples to all the
cities and villages where he himself is to come. They are ambassadors, like the
pair of disciples who will be sent to Jerusalem to prepare the Master's joyous
entry there.

These disciples have an altogether precise mission to carry out: to proclaim to
all the nations (the numeral 72 suggests universality) that the Reign of God
has drawn near indeed, in the person of Jesus—or rather in that of his
witnesses sent out into all the earth! The peace they bring with them is the
very peace of the Reign.

The missionary instructions have already been reported by the other
evangelists. The missioners are to greet no one on the way—the urgency of
mission is not compatible with passing the time of day. They are to take with
them neither knapsack nor money, as they will be living in people's homes.
They will wear no sandals. Easterners journey barefoot, and this journey is a

---

74

perpetual one. And they are to eat what they are offered. This last instruction has in view the disciples' coming sojourn in pagan territory: the missionaries must not scruple to eat food the Jews have considered impure.

■

Two by two they go, speaking with one another along the way of the beauty of God and the wonders of his mercy! Seventy-two they are, for they must go down every road! Urgently Jesus sends them, for the harvest is rich. Make haste for the golden fields of summer!

God is an optimist. At Jerusalem they prepare a cross, and God cries out, "The harvest is rich"! The urgency of the situation only provokes redoubled enthusiasm. Proclaim the word! Quickly. At any cost.

The harvest is rich. . . . Yet here we sit, bewailing the decline of religious practice and the loss of our old habits. Steeped in lamentation, we cry: Morality is no longer respected, tradition is forgotten! And we launch strategies that are more like rescue operations than the glad witness of a news that we cannot help shouting from the rooftops. We scarcely resemble an explorers' expedition! We are more like a headquarters losing a battle!

The harvest is rich. . . . Only the conviction of insatiable expectation, only the contemplation of the thirst for the infinite, for peace and happiness, still pervades our world, can fill the harvesters with enthusiasm. "The harvest is rich," says Jesus. Yes, and it is rich because he continues his ascent to Jerusalem. Soon the scythe will be sweeping through the stalks. Even now the axe is laid to the root of the tree. The harvest is rich because Jesus takes up, unceasingly, the deed of the cross and Easter.

The Reign of God is at hand. Strategies are all passé now. Any baggage will only be an encumbrance. Assurances, security . . . useless. And we watch the seventy-two spring to their feet and go, depart, without any other assurance than the knowledge that they are the bearers of peace and the witnesses to news of grace. The church of the gospel is an innocent church—so absorbed by the harvest that it is incapable of counting the cost, so charged with peace that it is astonished at its own daring. Our church is a church with but one word on its lips and one wish in its heart: *Shalom!* Peace to you! The harvest is rich because God's peace must be manifested. The reason why the church must live by the gospel? To save the harvest.

■

God, whose patience is everlasting,
you grant us to reap the harvest,
 and you rejoice when the fields are white with grain.

You find your happiness
      in causing your Reign to grow to greatness.
May the Church not fail the harvest:
may it be at the service of the Good News.

FRIDAY OF THE 26TH WEEK

CONFESSION

Baruch 1:15–22: Jeremiah's secretary, Baruch, is not the author of the book that bears his name. The latter actually dates from long after the Exile, and must have come into being in a community of the Diaspora at the time of the Maccabean revolt. This would place it at about the same time as the Book of Daniel. Indeed, Baruch's author has been struck by the similarities between the catastrophe of 587 B.C. and the persecution under the Seleucids, and has projected into the past the events he has watched unfold before his eyes. This was a frequent procedure in antiquity, and is known as pseudonymity, since, while writing of present events as if they were past, the author takes the occasion to place his work under the patronage of some great personage of national history.

In fact, the Book of Baruch is actually composed of four parts, none of them from the same pen or period. This admission alone will justify a post-Exilic dating, since it is after the fall of Jerusalem that there arose, in the plethora of collective lamentations, the literary genre of the "confession." The confessions usually served as part of the penitential liturgies, which were celebrated after the return from the Exile.

Psalm 79 is a good example of the national lamentation. We hear accusations against Israel's enemies, together with a description of the condition in which the people find themselves because of their enemies. God is reproached, then supplicated.

Luke 10:13–16: "If the people of any town you enter do not welcome you. . . ." The preaching of Christ's witnesses is humanity's last chance. But what is more striking, Jesus' lucidity in recognizing the failure of wonders as signs of the Reign—or his patience? The word pronounced on the refractory cities is neither invective nor curse. It is final appeal.

76

■

The Jewish communities of the Diaspora acknowledge their sin: "Each one of us went off after the devices of his own wicked heart, served other gods, and did evil in the sight of the Lord, our God."

We served other gods: our actions missed their mark. The Greek word for "sin" is derived from a translated Hebrew root that means "missing the mark," failing of one's proper objective. Like a careless shot, sin is an arrow that fails to reach its target. We need only allow the light of faith to shine upon our lives to see that our actions, whose more immediate purpose is to construct ourselves as we construct human communion, actually have a further, broader scope as well. We are grafts onto Christ—branches grafted on to the Spirit communicated to us by Jesus. And so our actions give rise not only to the human being as such, but to the very Son of God—the one who can say, with humble wonder, "Our Father."

But for this to come about, our actions must be fraught with love—propelled, shot like an arrow, by the force of our attention to others and our desire to see joy born in their hearts.

Let this power of love be lacking, and our actions fall short of their goal. Not only do human beings and their world dry up and harden, but the creative design of God, God's Reign, is blocked in its development. We have served other gods! We have "missed" God—fallen short of him. This is our sin—alas, our daily one, so poor are we in love!

But who will stem the rivulet in its plunge to the ocean? Who will stay the sap in its promise of a spring flower? Who will prevent God from loving? God *is* love. Inaccessible to disappointment, unable to condemn, tirelessly God offers us the riches of a love of which we deprive ourselves. God redirects our actions and our lives.

But let only the acknowledgment of our poverty, and a shy desire to love, open a tiny fissure in our hardened hearts—then the source, the wellspring, invades us, the sap of grace rises within us. Otherwise God can do nothing. Surely this is why the lot of Chorazin and Bethsaida is harder than that of Tyre and Sidon.

■

Lord our God,
in our frivolity we have failed to hear your voice,
and misfortune is our lot.

*We have wandered from your paths
   and lost our way.*

*Show us your love.
Guide us by your spirit.
May your loving-kindness be our help,
   and your forgiveness be our future.*

SATURDAY OF THE 26TH WEEK

THE RESCUE

Baruch 4:5-12, 27-29: To call on God implies a hope. In Baruch the response is generally formulated as an oracle. In the last part of the book an anonymous poet addresses the exiles, in terms recalling Second and Third Isaiah, to remind them that, even in a strange land, they remain the Lord's "chosen remnant." Let them not be discouraged! The chastisement merited by their failings does not mean their destruction.

Next it is Jerusalem's turn. She addresses her neighbor cities. For the moment, widowhood is her lot. But this is not her permanent state. God is the Eternal One, immovable in his being as in his designs. Consequently not even sin can shatter the covenant he has struck with humanity. Jerusalem has not been abandoned forever. When all is said and done, one name befits her: the "Espoused" (Is 62).

Psalm 69 belongs to the genre of individual lamentations. The liturgy retains only the conclusion, an invitation to praise God.

Luke 10:17-24: Hear the shouting in the Holy Spirit! Jesus has sent his disciples into the world, and behold they return filled with gladness at an amazing occurrence they have witnessed: the evil spirits themselves obey their commands! Instantly words of gratitude are on Jesus' lips. The mission—his and that of the seventy-two—show him that the end of days is at hand: "I watched Satan fall from the sky like lightning." The time of promise has yielded to that of the fulfillment. Truly the Reign of God has drawn near: it has arrived! Happy those who seize it and hold it fast!

But who can lay hold of it if not the very smallest? Once more Jesus can shout for joy. "The hungry he has given every good thing, while the rich he has sent empty away." The God whose witnesses are Jesus and the disciples is the God of the lowly, the poor, the "marginalized." The Reign of God is here!—in the victory of tenderness and love over pride and self-sufficiency.

78

■

"Fear not, my people!" You are God's remnant, and "he who has brought disaster upon you will, in saving you, bring you back enduring joy."

"Blest are the eyes that see what you see." The Good News has been proclaimed, and the Reign is reality when evil spirits find themselves subjected and the sick are well! Tokens of the divine mercy, pledge of salvation!

Mercy? That insipid obligingness? That sleepy indulgence? That make-believe oblivion of the past? No, mercy is hatred of evil in all its forms, for it is sprung from a love come face to face with the misery of another.

"Fear not, my people!" The church will always be distressed at the evil it must face. But it takes advantage precisely of the confusion of that evil to open the door to the invasion of a merciful love from on high. Now the way is clear for a mercy that is God's own passion for his creation, and Christ's very love for our misery. Poor hearts alone can understand compassion like that.

Blessed are you who behold the gift of God! We can surmise the measure of God's mercy only when we contemplate Jesus on the way to Jerusalem, Calvary and Easter. Only the victim, only the Son, sentenced to the gibbet of infamy, only the Master on his knees before his disciples washing their feet, only this human being willing to be deprived of a human face to show how deeply God is willing to bend in his concern for humankind—only the Son can truly speak of the Father.

Only the Son truly knows the heart of God, and only he can truly incarnate the Father's mercy. The Good News that gives Jesus so much joy is the radical manifestation of that mercy. He sees it in the radiant faces of his disciples as they tell of their own gladness. He observes, on the astonished faces of apostles thunderstruck at what the word will accomplish, if only it be preached. It is the power of a love at last made manifest.

"Fear not, my people!" The power of the church is only in the freedom that church can awaken in the heart of the poor. And the happiness of the church is in its realization that it knows the secret of the new world. "Blest are the eyes that see what you see"!

■

Be blessed, Father of mercy!
You reveal your name by showing us your compassion.
And the passion of your Son
   is the incarnation of your mercy.

Blest are we
to know such love!
Our faith is the foretaste
of the very gladness of eternity.

MONDAY OF THE 27TH WEEK

CHARITY

Jonah 1:1–2:11: A prophet rebels. Deeply religious sailors find fault with his attitude, but hesitate to jettison their dangerous cargo and save their lives. The Book of Jonah is an astonishing little work. It is the story of an historical personage, but its graphic style and didactic concerns place it in the genre of the wisdom literature. In fact it is a post-Exilic work, and its theme is the prophetic ministry. The hero's reluctance will recall the isolation and sense of abandonment of another prophet constrained to preach an unpleasant lesson to his contemporaries, Jeremiah.

The word of God, then, is the main "personage" in the book. It leaves the prophet no peace. But neither does it leave him in the lurch. The great fish, reminiscent of the Leviathan of the psalms, must give Jonah back. The word is life, and no force on earth can exhaust it. Matthew has understood this well, and he harks back to the symbolism of Jonah time after time. For just as the monster of the deep has been unable to hold on to Jonah, so neither can the tomb hold fast the Prince of Life, this Jesus who has commanded the sea and it has obeyed (Mt 9:23–27, 12:38–40).

Most judiciously, the liturgy now sings a number of verses from the psalm added to the book of Jonah (Jon. 2) by an inspired scribe. As in any lamentation, first we hear the psalmist's plight, then his act of thanksgiving for the favor he is confident of receiving.

Luke 10:25–37: "No one knows the Father but the Son, and the one to whom the Son would reveal him." Jesus is the true face of the Father. He shows us God's kindness and mercy, thereby permitting us to gaze into the very depths of God's heart.

But how does Jesus reveal this in everyday life? Here are only human beings in confrontation, looking into one another's faces, at times tearing one another to bits, and yes, at times seeking communion, for example in the Samaritan

---

80

who has approached the wounded Jew. The priest and the Levite will do nothing of the sort. Doubtless the scribe who is Jesus' interrogator would have done just as little. But the Samaritan has listened only to his heart, and in doing so has obeyed the only law of the Christian world, the law of the Spirit. He has allowed himself to be led by the Spirit, and the Spirit goes beyond the Law. But who is the true Samaritan? Christ, the true face of the Father.

■

The road descends sharply, through the rocky desert, from the holy capital where the temple priests celebrate, to Jericho the frontier town, city open to the world. "There was a man going down from Jerusalem to Jericho. . . ." If only one reads them well, the parables astonish, for their purpose is to stir the heart to conversion. Who is this helpless victim, robbed and thrown in the ditch?

He is the faceless one, anonymous, of no account, the victim of circumstances. After all, his story is like so many others. And yet it is by way of this "non-person" that Jesus is to reveal the astonishing novelty of the gospel.

A priest and a Levite appear on the scene. But they avoid the corpse— after all, might this not be a corpse?—and continue on their way. Oh, to be sure, they have their excuses. Their religion forbids them to soil themselves by contact with death, for they must be pure to ascend to the altar. Does religion thus stifle the impulses of the heart?

But a Samaritan, travelling the same way, is seized with pity for the poor victim, and hoists him atop his beast of burden, in the gesture of the good shepherd who lifts the lost sheep to his shoulders. This schismatic, this traitor, this creature legally impure for all religious persons, this excommunicate, "came on him and was moved to pity at the sight," as God is so often "moved to pity" in holy writ.

Jesus recounts this parable for the benefit of the doctor of the law he is addressing. His interlocutor is a high official whose function is to direct others in the performance of the duties of religion. For Jesus, the golden rule of morality is not the observance of a closely defined set of rules, but a norm welling up out of life experience and spelled out in the heart.

And yet one must go further still. The Samaritan "came on him and was moved to pity at the sight. He approached him. . . ." The Samaritan has exactly the attitude Jesus adopts toward the widow of Naim, the attitude the father of the Prodigal adopts toward his wayward child. This despised foreigner, this outcast, is the Christ, in whom God has drawn near every wounded creature. A human being was going down from

Jerusalem to Jericho. Jesus will soon be heading in the opposite direction. He will go up to Jerusalem, and there he will himself become a wounded human being, hanged by the roadside and left for dead. He will be ridiculed. He will be taunted as a Samaritan (Jn 8:48). His fellow human beings will all turn their faces away. And yet in him God will manifest his face of mercy and universal love. Brother, sister, go, do likewise! Salvation is on the side of the heart, the heart willing to feel compassion. Have a heart of mercy, for mercy is as the heart of God.

■

God of tenderness and pity,
bending low over our poverty,
and concerned for the sinners we are,
we know your mercy.

May we become by your grace
women and men of heart,
human beings consecrated to charity.
Charity alone will give us happiness today,
and charity alone abides
for everlasting.

TUESDAY OF THE 27TH WEEK

TO SERVE GOD

Jonah 3:1–10: No sooner had Jonah begun to preach than "the people of Nineveh believed God. . . ." The Book of Jonah is simply astounding. Its universalistic ideas outstrip those of, for example, Second Isaiah. The city of Nineveh was enormous. One thinks of Babel. It would have taken three days to traverse it on foot. But it takes Jonah only a single day to win its conversion. The force of the echoing word as it reaches the ears of the king only serves to demonstrate the power of the original divine word.

Psalm 130 prolongs the lamentation of Jonah 2. From the belly of the fish the prophet shouts his trust in the God of forgiveness.

Luke 10:38–42: First let us look at Mary. Not only is she seated at Jesus' feet, the position of the perfect disciple, but the context underscores her position as a daughter of Israel. She hears Jesus as the people have heard the word of

Yahweh. She has chosen the "better portion," the technical term for the role of a Levite consecrated to the service of the temple and of prayer.

At Mary's side we see Martha, "anxious and upset about many things. . . ." Martha is a dedicated one, like her soul mates the Samaritan and the Roman centurion. In fact the story is marred when Martha interferes to turn Mary from her chosen occupation of learning and worship. It is Martha's interference, not her devotion to duty, that provokes Jesus' reproach. Instead of seeking to pry Mary from Jesus' side, Martha ought simply to perform her service to the hilt. Then, like the Samaritan and the Roman officer, she too will find the "one thing required." Martha and Mary represent two ways of hearing the word. These two ways are complementary. Is not the "better portion" the worship of God, be it in the temple or in life?

■

Jesus takes the road once more. He stops, along his route, which will lead him to Jerusalem and the end of his mission, with old friends at Bethany. On his way to the Reign, Jesus stops at the house of friends. And the church, in the person of the two sisters, welcomes him.

As homemakers will when overanxious about details to be attended to in receiving a guest, Martha forgets the one essential thing: the guest. She runs to the kitchen, from the stove to the parlor, from the parlor to the pantry. She really ought to be concerning herself with her guest, anticipating his wishes. It is he whom she ought to be serving. When everything is perfectly prepared, nothing new, nothing unexpected can occur. The church can apply itself to the task of imitating Martha. It can forge a chain in which each link is carefully programmed, letter-perfect. The menu will be precisely *comme il faut*. Like the well-mannered hostess, with more delicacy than spontaneity, it can be careful to avoid any unpleasant confrontations. Everything will go swimmingly. But once the candles are out . . . the celebration is at an end. The church can, if it wishes, rely on its wisdom and prudence, its organization and *savoir-faire*, and be a church of influence, pressure, and missionary strategies. But then it will hear: "You are anxious and upset about many things. . . ."!

"Mary has chosen the better portion"—as does a church receptive to its Master's word, a church for whom nothing matters but his presence. Oh, the meal is a bit improvised? What of it? The church has chosen the better portion when it has the candor of children who forget everything when they are listening to a thrilling story that snatches them from reality to a land far away, a land where life is different. The church has chosen the better portion when it is wide-eyed, seduced by a traveller who has stopped at its house. The church has chosen the better portion when it is a church of genuine contemplation, contemplation that goes straight to the heart of the matter—when it is a free church, preferring the bitter winds of the road to the familiar, bland flavors of closed-up kitchens—when it prefers the rigors of the nomad's tent to the security of a solid house that so soon becomes a burden and a prison. The church has chosen the better portion when it is a church of passion and heart, like Mary racing to the tomb while human reason laughs at a hope like that. For Mary has contemplated Jesus. Mary savors his words, and the words engraved on the tablets of her heart will be the source of a thrilling, joyful, sure discovery: beyond all the evidence, beyond death itself, she will discover the surprise of Easter.

The church has chosen the better portion when it is a church of contemplation, when it looks beyond hard human reality to discover the wild, impossible novelty of Easter, and the other face of things—when it is a church astonished. Then you have chosen the better portion. You shall not have it taken away! For your hope is rooted in the very promise of God.

■

God who makes your dwelling among us,
do not permit us to become accustomed to your presence.
Grant us to savor your word,
        this word ever new.
May we be astonished at so much love.

■

God our Father,
who grants us the Word of life and the Bread of the Reign,
        this is the better portion for us.
Grant us the gift
        of bearing this gift to our sisters and brothers.
May they see us as witnesses of your generous bounty.

And permit not that vain cares
        prevent us from seeking the one thing required:
        Jesus Christ, the Word who utters your grace
        and the Bread that nourishes our faith.

ALLOWING GOD TO RESCUE US

Jonah 4:1-11: Which is the more to be admired, the perspicacity of the sacred writer or the irony of God? We can learn a valuable lesson from the Book of Jonah. It is a lesson valid for all times and climes. For there will always be Jonahs, more concerned with their gourds than with the salvation of Ninevites. The prophet is scandalized, then, when he learns that his God is actually a "gracious and merciful God, slow to anger, rich in clemency. . . ." What did he think—that God was petty and sulky? How correct of Voltaire to observe that, if God has created us in his image, we have certainly repaid him in kind!

Let us admire the poetry of these passages, and let us dwell on the concluding expression—"persons who cannot distinguish their right hand from their left," which will doubtless remind us of the theme of the two roads leading to life or death. Finally we note that the use of the number "a hundred and twenty thousand" connotes universal salvation.

Psalm 85 is, once more, a lamentation, presenting by way of consolation a catalog of reasons why the psalmist ought to have trust in God.

Luke 11:1-4: For Luke prayer is a life commitment, a way of being. Jesus' prayer, then, is unconditional acceptance of his Father's will. This is why the "Our Father"—the prayer of sons and daughters—is so crucial to our faith.

With J. Radermakers let us observe that the last three petitions of the Lord's prayer—illustrations, as it were, of the first three, which bear on the Reign—will become more explicit in the succeeding chapters of Luke's gospel. The petition for the bread of life, in its acknowledgment of God as that life's only source, is the antithesis of the first of Jesus' three temptations in the wilderness (Lk 4:4), and will find its prolongation in his promise to serve his disciples (12:35-40). The forgiveness of debts, which is an invitation to imitate the divine gratuity, will be illustrated by the parable of the Prodigal Son (see Lk 15, 16), and is opposed to the temptation to power (4:6-7). The third petition, finally, will be illustrated by the refusal to accept God's salvation (Lk 17ff.), and counterbalances the temptation to force God into one's own service (4:9-10).

■

"Teach us to pray"! The humble appeal, "Our Father," will ever stand as the model for Christian prayer. With these two words we enter into the heart of the simplest, most authentic prayer. I say, "Our," and all women and men are with me. In this one word, I assemble the vast totality of creation. Then I say, "Father," and in the presence of this tremendous assortment of humanity I call on God to engender us to his own life.

When, in a spirit of recollection and with a serious heart, then, I say, "Our Father . . ." I provoke the vivifying encounter of all humanity with a God who seeks to be its Father, Father to perfection, Father in every possible way. In my own attitude and act of prayer, the whole human race opens to the recreative action of God, this Father who tirelessly revives, in all its hidden foundations, the creative act that he has begun. His love knows no term, for he must have his fatherhood ever present, deliberate, intentional. His is a fundamental fatherhood, a parenting always in act. At each and every instant God creates and molds us in accordance with his design. Though the lacerations and distortions of our sin turn us from God's dynamic deed, from his fatherly will to sweep us away and hide us in the secret recesses of his love, this deed and this love prevail.

And there are times when humanity finds itself struck dumb, as it were, smothered . . . and perchance turned around the other way. But by the prayer that asserts our belonging to God as his child, and the choice of our engagement and commitment, we break a trail, we throw open a road. Casting ourselves into our Father's arms, we allow him to possess us once more, take us back, take us by the hand and lead us again into the house we ought never to have deserted. Through us God receives and accepts our own humanity—the vessel of our prayer—and all humanity. And he breathes into it his love.

It is at this basic point of our being that we find prayer. We find it in the place where God re-creates and remodels us, the place where he gives us a rediscovery of the authentic locus of our existence. In calling him by the name of Father, we acknowledge not only his ongoing, incessant activity, but we consent to that activity. In calling God our Father we are asking him, on behalf of ourselves and of everyone on earth, for the gift of becoming his sons and daughters, his children animated by the love of his Son. Then at last we understand that the gift of prayer, prayer learned and acquired in the prayer of the Our Father, is not a matter of formulas, phrases, or words. Simply, we surrender ourselves to grace. We fall into the hands of God. And he re-creates us. And this is what it means to pray.

■

O God whom no name can name,
God whom no image can describe,
alone the words of your only Son
    can reveal to us who you are.
Be blessed for the words he speaks to us
    and the face he gives to you.

Be blessed for his prayer,
    which becomes ours.
With him and through him
we can repeat, indefatigably,
    the words of our tenderness:
    Be praised, our Father.

THURSDAY OF THE 27TH WEEK

"WE DARE!"

Malachi 3:13–20: The presence of the temple has failed to maintain the religious fervor of Jerusalem's inhabitants for very long. The prophet addresses a totally disintegrated community. Of course! Once more the people have fallen into their past mistakes. Not only is worship neglected, but social justice is trodden underfoot. Above all, Malachi denounces mixed marriages, by means of which the returning exiles climb the social ladder, to the detriment of their souls.

The literary genre of our text is that of controversy. The prophet endeavors to make a response to a question that well shows the skepticism of the Jews. Why do the wicked prosper? Why this injustice on God's part? Malachi's answer opens with a theodicy sprung from reflection on recent events, and constitutes an advance over the Book of Job. Today God tests his people's patience. Tomorrow he will deliver his judgment. Then shall the faithful discover that they have never ceased to be Yahweh's "chosen remnant."

Psalm 1 returns to the theme of the two ways. With Jonah we have learned that only the road to the right leads to happiness.

Luke 11:5–13: "If you, with all your sins, know how to give your children what is good, how much more will your heavenly Father give good things to anyone who asks him!" we read in Matthew (Mt 7:11). Luke replaces the "good things" with the Holy Spirit, who for him is the gift par excellence. Only the Spirit can teach us true prayer, prayer that commits the whole person to activity calculated to hasten the coming of the Reign of God.

The promise of the gift of the Spirit to those who persevere in prayer is illustrated by a parable fairly charged with symbolism. We hear of bread, a closed door, and a harassed friend who finally gets out of bed. The presence of verbs of resurrection (*anastàs . . . eqertheis . . .*), together with the mention of a door closed like a tomb, can scarcely fail to evoke the image of the first Easter morn. For those who persevere the door will open, and the Risen One will enter to bestow the bread of life.

How often in our lives have we had the feeling of running into a brick wall? It is then that one must persevere, especially in prayer. Blest shall we be when the door opens and the light floods in!

■

Prayer is a source of God's recreation in us. Prayer attests within us the bond that links our birth with the coming of the convenant. To pray is to allow God to come to tell us his name, and it is to hear our own: God is our Father, and we are God's daughters and sons. In prayer the world of God becomes visible to us. Prayer evangelizes us, then. It teaches us that God is to be discovered not in the conclusion of a syllogism, but in the astonishment of a heart that finds itself loved.

Prayer attests our profound identity. Surely it is on this account that it is heard. God's promise is no longer of the order of the merely possible, the "chancy," the "long shot." In Jesus the only and true Son, promise has become reality. Our prayer is petition, yes. But it is not as if we were asking anyone to buy anything! It is not as if we were trying to "get something out of" someone! Our petition is a simple appeal to an acknowledged reality and (dare we say?) right: "Remember, O God, what you have accomplished by your beloved Son!" Here is the deeper reason for our daring, and our familiarity. We dare to "lay siege" to God because we know that we are only confronting him with his (dare we say, once more?) responsibilities. God is caught in a trap. After all, he started the whole thing. It is because he himself has tied the knot of familiarity that we dare risk asking.

The words of the eucharistic celebration invite us to dare, to have the boldness, to pray the Our Father. But our audacity is not the sauciness of ill-bred children. It is the perquisite of daughters and sons, who "have the run of the house" because they are "of the household." Our prayer can be importunate because God himself grants us the assurance of a heart renewed by the Spirit.

■

God our Father, be blessed:
   hallowed be thy name!
The very Spirit
   comes to the aid of our weakness,
   and bestows on us faith's daring.
We stand before you
and pray to you with confidence:
   give us of your very best.
And may we know even here
   the happiness with which you mean to overwhelm us
   in eternity.

■

God our Father,
   you have given us the Bread of which we have such need.
May our communion in the Body of Christ
make us partakers as well in the Breath of his life,
   the Holy Spirit who alone can draw from our hearts
   a prayer you will hear.
To you we shout our thanksgiving,
   now and forever.

FROM FRIDAY OF THE 27TH WEEK

TO SATURDAY OF THE 28TH WEEK

The Economy of Faith

"Tame me!" says the fox to Saint-Exupéry's Little Prince. Faith is like that. Faith is humble supplication. We are "God-sick." The lover feels the beloved's absence. Love is always request, supplication, beseeching: "I need you! Without you I am unbearably deprived." Faith is not first and foremost an adherence to a code of truths to be believed, or the voluntary choice of a rule of life. It is first of all this prayer of love: "Tame me. Tell me your name. I cannot live without you." We ask God to grant us an understanding of the hidden mystery of Jesus' words and deeds because God has only these words and deeds with which to speak to us. "Tame me!" is both the prayer of desire and the richness of encounter. This humble request contains within itself the whole power of the covenant. In order for a communion to be inaugurated between God and ourselves, it is enough that we ask God to tame us. After all, God, from all eternity, is infinitely poor and a beggar, for he is infinitely love. From the first morn of the universe, God is in supplication. It is God who first begs of us, "Tame me!" And we reply, "Tame me!" as our desire reaches out and touches the outstretched will of God. Standing before him as suppliants, we become, by this our supplication, sons and daughters—loved, and hence able to love.

"Tame me, so that the wheat that has meant nothing to me may remind me of your golden hair!" added the fox. "Tame me!" Our very request transfigures reality, which suddenly finds a tongue and speaks to us of God's loving-kindness. Our "today" is transfigured, in the fire of God's glance. Because we are "tamed," the banality of our everyday reality suddenly has the value of eternity. Now we live a life of God's sons and daughters. For the believer life is altogether different, just as it is with lovers. The words are the same words, and yet they are suddenly words capable of truly uttering God. The deeds are those of every day, and yet behold, they summon up eternity. The events of history are "ordinary," and yet they suddenly become the trail of another history—the same—a history that "leads somewhere." Because it is suppliant regard—"Tame me!"—faith lends life another color. It transforms it.

"Tame me . . ."! We become . . . domesticated. Now we belong to another world. Suddenly, we are God's. Now we live where God lives. We can no longer live according to the norms of the world. Now we must live by the norms of God, the rules of the Reign. "Tame me!" Our very request is a commitment. We want to switch sovereigns. No longer do we wish to belong to ourselves, to be our own. Here again is the dispensation, the "economy," of faith. Faith has persuaded us to "change worlds." Now we are attached to God. "Tame me!" is a supplication, and a responsibility, for we become responsible for being tamed, and we are bound to the one who has tamed us.

"Tame me!" says faith—because it loves.

■

God beyond knowing, blessed be your name!
No one has ever seen you.
But you have sent us your Son
        to give you a name.
He has proclaimed words of ours, our human words,
        and behold, in faith we know
        the Word pronounced from all eternity.
He has lived our human life,

and behold, in faith we discover
the deeds of your covenant.
He has taken on himself our poor life and death,
and behold, in faith we stand in wonder
at what your Spirit accomplishes:
in your beloved Child we become your sons and daughters.

May the Spirit now animate our prayer,
and may the deeds we do in faith
become as well, by your grace,
the sacrament of what we receive from your mercy.

Your Breath gives body to your promise:
in faith, we become sharers already
of the mystery manifest in your only Son.
For, as we remember his death
and celebrate his rising,
already we pass to the new world,
to the heritage of believers,
to the promise made to your daughters and sons
and kept, to their everlasting gladness.

May the teaching of your Son
transform our thoughts,
and may his life, offered in sacrifice,
nourish our existence.
Renew for us today
the word he proclaims.
Reanimate our will to follow him.
And may your church, under the guidance of those who have its charge,
reveal your tireless fidelity,
and your will to make all things new.

At one with all who, throughout the ages,
have given their faith to your promises,
we bless you and thank you,
in your Son, our Lord and our Savior.

FRIDAY OF THE 27TH WEEK

WHO IS THIS PERSON?
Joel 1:13-15, 2:1-2: The personage and book of Joel are the subject of still more debate. Then let us simply sketch the message of this prophet who, as so

many authors have noted, is very like the prophets of the end of the seventh and the beginning of the sixth century. Joel's great preoccupation is with the "day of the Lord." The theme had originated in the victory bulletins of the conquest of the Land of Promise. The day of Gibeon's victory, especially, was still alive in the memories of all (Josh. 10:12–14). And in times of distress the memory of those swaggering hours quite naturally sustained the morale of the population. Now this people consoled itself with the expectation of a divine intervention that would restore Jerusalem to its radiance of yesteryear.

But the prophet Amos had already denounced the naiveté of this expectation. How could his hearers fail to perceive that the catastrophes that crushed their nation were but the consequence of their infidelity? For this prophet "the day of the Lord will not be a day of light, but a day of judgment and chastisement."

In Joel's descriptions the day of the Lord is all but personified. It appears as a "frightful monster, rather like the condensation of an incommensurable force, a radically incomparable, foreign energy, an energy that can only be described in inadequate language borrowed from natural catastrophes or a murderous war, an energy that by comparison with earthly life is but darkness, whose assault annihilates life and blows out the stars, whose manifestation implies the condemnation of everything that would dare rise up against the Master of the universe." Joel calls for penitential rites, then, the outward expression of a conversion as radical as its terrible occasion.

Psalm 9 is extremely heterogeneous in content. The verses appearing here are basically optimistic. The day of the Lord is a day of mercy, as well.

Luke 11:15–26: "As Jesus was casting out a devil. . . ." The devil was mute, and this is not without its importance for the rest of the chapter. The verses to come bear on the word of testimonial to be delivered by the disciples. In Luke's eyes, the missionary word, like the sufferer from whom the demon of dumbness has now been expelled, is a sign to its hearers of the Spirit, at work in the world.

But a sign is ever ambiguous. It respects the liberty of the one receiving and interpreting it. Even so with the miracles of Jesus: so many have seen only the devil's work there.

A sign calls for a decision, an option. If a demon is cast out, it is because one "stronger than he" has come on the scene, proclaiming the Reign. The fate of the chosen people is here compared to that of a person suddenly relieved of every manner of impure spirit. If they fail to welcome the Reign for which they have been prepared, their condition will be worse than before their deliverance. And today, the chosen people are the church.

■

"Blest are the eyes that see what you see"! A few days ago Jesus was blessing believers. Today he reproaches those who fail to decipher the signs granted to those who believe.

Who is this person? That is the question. The peasants of Nazareth, the fishers of Tiberias, the merchants of Jericho and the Pharisees of Jerusalem have had thirty years in which to discover the secret of the one they called Jesus. They have failed. Who is he, then, this carpenter's son who heals lepers and strives to remodel the human heart by delivering it from its sin? Who is he, this spellbinder, this inflated ego? "You have heard it said. . . . But I say to you. . . ." Why does he take his meals with persons leading loose lives? Who is he indeed. It will take us a lifetime to discover his secret.

"If it is by the finger of God that I cast out devils, then the reign of God is upon you"! God has only a human life—the life of this Jesus—to teach who he is. He has one entire human life to lift the veil of his mystery. We have only this same human life, the life of Jesus, to discover who God is, for we have no other place to know him than the life of this Human Being!

Who is this individual? One day he will go down to the secret dark of the tomb. Who is he who permits himself to be annihilated like a grain of wheat buried in the earth? Yes, here is the human being who tramples the death that could not quite hold him in its chains. From him we shall learn our destiny, for God has raised him from the dead, and now his life can become for us the sacrament of what God wills for us.

Who is this person? We only understand someone we know. But to know someone we must live with that person. We must share his or her existence. We shall have no other opportunity to speak Jesus' true name than that of a life lived in familiarity with him. The entire history of the church will not be too long for the church to learn to recognize the One by whom it lives.

■

Father, how could we utter your name
unless your Spirit enlightened our intelligence
and your mercy warmed our heart?
Be blessed for the grace of our faith:
it allows us to recognize your ambassador,

the perfect Image of your Glory,
Jesus our Savior.
And we pray to you:
grant that we may ever sound the depths of so great a mystery,
until the day of perfect knowledge.

SATURDAY OF THE 27TH WEEK

WORD AND LIFE

Joel 4:12–21: The prophets, then, have warned the Jews that the day of the Lord could turn against them unless they abandoned the error of their ways. These same prophets frequently regard the pagan nations as the instrument of the divine punishment. They are simply projecting into the future the situations they observe around them. But they warn the pagans, as well: they will be judged in their turn, by the protector of the small and the poor. Their excesses will not go unpunished.

And yet no prophet has reduced the day of the Lord to a day of vengeance. Their message, however unsettling, has always left room for hope. When they threaten the people it is to lead them to conversion. To be sure, Jerusalem will be chastised. But if she turns from her evil ways the Lord will show mercy, and restore her to a splendor greater than any she has ever known.

Psalm 97 is well-suited to a celebration of the day of Yahweh—a song of enthronement, proclaiming God's triumph over the enemies of his people.

Luke 11:27–28: It is the word that is crucial. Jesus is clear and forthright. The Reign is not of those who boast of their privileges, but of those who receive the witnesses of the word that proclaims freedom, and God's gratuity.

■

Have we truly taken the measure of the mystery of the word?

Before all else the word is the victory of human beings over things. In its profession of reality, that reality finds its name. It would be too easy a victory, however, were it to be this and no more. It would lack the quality of an invitation to response. The "other" must enter the picture, if the word is to find an echo that will be a message in its own turn. The word becomes a human word only in the presence of this echo, this exchange. The word is a call awaiting a response, which it arouses, to

which it gives birth. A child learns to speak by watching the lips of those who love it sufficiently to address it and then to let it take its own turn in speaking. The word I address to another is fully and genuinely a word only when it returns to me, only when I receive it as something "other." The word is, we might say, everlastingly conjugated: two voices in quest of one another, two voices in alternation and mutual appeal.

"Blest are they who hear the word of God and keep it"! Until the word flung to the winds by God returns in a profession of faith, it remains somehow without signification, objectless, empty, hollow. God's word is exchange, dialogue, covenant.

"Blest are they who hear. . . ." The word instills silence. Chattering murders dialogue. A game of familiar words, lightly swapped, without a struggle, without a surprise, is not dialogue. Dialogue lives by silence. After all, only in silence can we measure another's word. "Blessed are they who hear the word. . . ." If Mary is to be called the Mother of all believers, it is surely because, as the evangelist notes, she "treasured all these things and reflected on them in her heart."

■

Lord our God,
your Son, your Ambassador, is in our midst.
Word from all eternity, he speaks with authority.
May his Spirit repeat to us
  your wish for his disciples,

and may his Word reveal to us
  your tireless fidelity.

■

Deliver us, God our Father,
  from sounds without savor, words too familiar,
  words too easily exchanged, the covenant aborted,
  murderous silences, words stillborn.
May your eternal Word, contemplated in silence,
well forth in a word of life,
  in the Spirit's stutter,
  in our heart's conversion.
Then shall your word be a birthgiving,
  engendering the joy of encounter
  for everlasting ages.

■

May the teaching of your Son, Lord our God,
  transform our thoughts,
and may his life offered in sacrifice, received in this communion,
  nourish our existence.

MONDAY OF THE 28TH WEEK

A HUMAN BEING WHO . . . UTTERS GOD

Romans 1:1–7: The Letter to the Romans dates from the spring of the year 57 or 58. Paul has now passed three months at Corinth, upon completion of his third missionary voyage, and is on the point of embarking for Jerusalem with the collection taken up in behalf of the mother church. But Jerusalem would be merely a stop along the way. Now that he had concluded his task in the eastern part of the Empire Paul dreamed of sailing for Rome, or Spain. Commentators frequently remark the circumspection with which the apostle addresses the church of Rome, which he had not founded, but which, like others, was divided into Jewish and pagan-convert factions.

The apostolic mission consists in proclaiming to the world "the Good News that God had promised of old by his prophets in the holy scriptures"—the sending of a Son to inaugurate the Reign. Here Paul inserts a profession of faith in the form of a christological formula shared by all the churches and hence known to the Romans. He proclaims a "Son, who was descended from David according to the flesh, but was made Son of God in power, according to the spirit of holiness, by his resurrection from the dead. . . ." This profession of faith emphasizes not only the continuity of the messianic function, but the difference in Jesus' condition in the two phases of his earthly and heavenly life, as well. During the former phase, his status as Son of God has been "marked by the weakness and lowliness of the flesh"; in the latter phase "it is marked by entry into possession of the fullness of the divine prerogatives," customarily translated, "lordship." Paul's ministry has been "to bring to obedient faith all the Gentiles"—that is, to lead them to the acceptance of the divine revelation.

"Sing joyfully to the Lord, all you lands. . . ." *Psalm 98* invites all nations of the earth to sing the glory of the God who has wrought salvation in his Son, Jesus Christ.

Luke 11:29–32: In Luke 11:16 Jesus' audience has asked him for a sign, when he has just exorcised a demoniac. With this skepticism Jesus contrasts the

---

attitude of the Ninevites, who were instantly converted at the word of Jonah. And yet one greater than Jonah is here, one greater than the Queen of Sheba.

But like Matthew, Luke has "reread" the parable in the light of the resurrection, and in verse 30 he speaks of a sign to come: ". . . So will the Son of man be a sign for the present age." The resurrection becomes the sign par excellence of Jesus' messianic status—a sign for pagan and Jew alike, but a sign which so many will fail to perceive. Indeed the Lucan (or the Matthean) rereading of Jesus' declaration in the light of Easter implies that God's word has been embodied in the testimony of the disciples—in a missionary word regarded simultaneously as proclamation of an accomplished event, and as original wisdom.

■

There will be no sign but this human being! Await no sign but the person of this artisan from a little village in the Galilean hills, this itinerant preacher, this head of a troublesome school, this walking sign, this story one day to be dramatically, and yes, tragically, climaxed with a sentence and a pitiable execution, as the misunderstood are always pitiable.

There will be no sign but this human being! For us Jesus is more than a figurehead of the adventure of freedom. And more than a magnetic personality. Jesus is also the one who gives God a human form. He dares name the Ineffable, whom he expresses in his word and in his being. In this sense too he is the Word of God: in the age-old stammering of human beings and their religions, Jesus, too, is an inventor of God.

There will be no sign but this human being! Jesus rises out of the compost of humanity and takes his turn at living and uttering God, with every fiber of his being, to the jolts of death itself. Jesus is, we daresay, God's "creator." To "come up with" God, Jesus took as his vocabulary his own person, his body, his hands, his face, his speech. His word is his life and his death. Jesus can be God's creator because his humanity is totally impregnated with God, in a transfiguration such that one rightly refers to him as "God totally given to a human being," or "a human being who has totally received God."

There is no other sign than he. For he utters the whole of the human being and the whole of God. Indissolubly. He pronounces the human being and he pronounces God.

■

God, who reveals your name and unveils your face,
    enlighten our understanding.

Discover to us the hidden sense of our human words,
   that, transformed by your Spirit,
   they may utter to us the Ineffable.
Warm our hearts:
may they be our love's secret strength,
   that, transformed by your Spirit,
   that love may sing the covenant to which it leads us.

There will be no sign for us
   but our stammerings and our strivings.
May they open us to the joy
   of the communion that is everlasting.

TUESDAY OF THE 28TH WEEK

BY FAITH

Romans 1:16–25: Having spoken to the Romans of his deep longing to visit them, Paul promptly comes to the main point of his letter: justification by faith. He opens his considerations with a declaration of his pride at being in the service of the gospel, which is the "power of God for the salvation of anyone who believes." Thus he forestalls the objections on the part of Jewish Christians claiming the right to subject the salvation of the pagans to the observance of Jewish practices. Surely the power of God was first manifested for the salvation of the Jewish people, especially in the Exodus. But its real scope was broader. It envisaged the salvation of all, Jew or Greek, who would give their faith to God. Salvation, then, while only for believers, is for all believers, as the Old Testament had itself proclaimed (Hab. 2:4).

Then the apostle invites his readers to contemplate the spectacle offered by the pagan world. He sees a fallen, idolatrous world, where men and women pursue only the surfeit of their momentary passions. In the style of the prophets, who saw in the misfortunes of the people the just chastisement of their sins, Paul regards the situation of the pagans as the consequence of their behavior. Our sins dog our footsteps! He further observes that, at all periods in history, God gave women and men the opportunity to know him, but that many refused to live in conformity with that knowledge, and then attracted others to their own corrupted ways. Indeed the apostle is conscious of the fact that this danger threatens as well those who have received the gospel. There are, after all, those among them who fail to live by that gospel. Would he have in mind those who questioned the teaching of justification by faith? Finally we note that, as for the "wrath of God," Paul emphasizes that it comes down not on humanity as such, but on the "irreligious and perverse spirit of men who, in this perversity of theirs, hinder the truth."

Psalm 19 confirms the word of the apostle. "The heavens declare the glory of God. . . ." And yet his "handiwork" is not limited to the first creation!

Luke 11:37–41: Before we examine Jesus' virulent attacks on the Pharisees and jurists it will be helpful to recall two things. First we recall the beatitude pronounced on all who hear the word of God, the word that comes to women and men through the testimony of the disciples. Next we remember the promise of the gift of the Spirit, a promise made to those who beseech the Son with perseverance. This double reminder will enable us to grasp the Lucan intent here, which goes beyond the simple fact of Jesus at loggerheads with the Pharisees and scribes. Jesus denounces, primarily in the Pharisees, a conceptualization of life that tarnishes the word, and prevents it from reaching all persons. Indeed, Pharisaic practices like an over-solicitousness for legal purity had ultimately imperiled the entire missionary effort, as it had divided humanity into "clean" and "unclean," into Jews and non-Jews. These practices had rendered the Samaritan's deed impossible, then, thus distorting the actual face of God. Does Christian practice consist in "giving alms from your possessions" (Tob. 4:7; etc.)? But which of our possessions is more precious than the assurance of salvation freely bestowed in Jesus Christ? This is the "possession" we should be sharing. Could anything be more clear?

■

How ever could we understand what Paul has to tell us of faith without meditating on his own personal experience? What Paul will all his life consider his "grace"—his friendship with God, a friendship altogether unmerited on his part—is founded on this living experience of the Crucified One who has manifested himself to him as the one who lives, the true Lord. With no ifs, ands, or buts, Paul will henceforth defend the utterly basic importance of faith in Christ received by pure grace. He will defend it against any attempt to superimpose other factors. "The just man shall live by faith."

"By faith. . . ." Our encounter with God is textured of purest trust. To have faith in someone is to give myself, abandon myself to that person, place myself wholly in that person's hands. To have faith in someone is to believe so much in that person's word that it becomes my own word: I have nothing to say but what you say of life. I give myself to you. Faith is a clinging.

"By faith. . . ." Faith is inextricably bound up with this basic *abandon*, this abandonment to another. Faith is a combat, a conversion. I give you my faith: I unite my lot with yours. Your norms will rule my life. Your teachers will henceforth be mine. Faith is a communion. It models and fashions us. Once more faith is a clinging.

"By faith. . . ." The sole foundation, the sole criterion, is firm attachment to God through Jesus Christ in a trustful faith—an attachment which no failure of mine can cheapen nor any of my good works elevate, but from which proceed, naturally, the works of love.

"The just man shall live by faith"! Only by clinging to God in Christ shall we make the most of our freedom, our wisdom, or the love and hope that sustain us in the vicissitudes of life. We cannot forget that the gospel is Good News!

■

O God, who saves us by your grace,
blessed be your mercy!
You initiate us to freedom
      and rear us to your wisdom.
You enlighten us by the knowledge of your name
      and sustain us by the gift of your Spirit.
As you make us to live,
permit us to bestow ourselves upon your goodness,
      that our faith may be the wellspring of rebirth everlasting.

WEDNESDAY OF THE 28TH WEEK

DRIVEN TO CONVERSION

Romans 2:1–11: "Every one of you who judges another. . . ." Naturally we suppose Paul to be writing to Jews. And indeed tradition has it that the Letter to the Romans is addressed first to the pagans, then to the Jews. Actually Paul's addressees are not explicitly identified as Jews until verse 17, although phrases like "kindness and forbearance" are consecrated expressions of Yahweh's behavior toward his rebellious people. Let us simply say that Paul is still speaking to those "who, in this perversity of theirs, hinder the truth" (Rom. 1:18), whether by confusing the freedom of the gospel with libertinism, or (as some Jewish Christians) by continuing to expect the divine promises to work their automatic salvation on the last day.

"With God there is no favoritism." There are no infallible privileges, then. Or, better: privilege always entails responsibility, and Paul indicates this with his formula, ". . . the Jew first, then the Greek," whether he is speaking of judgment or of salvation.

Psalm 62 proclaims the psalmist's unshakable trust.

Luke 11:42–46: Here is a jurist who would have done better to hold his tongue! Jesus wishes to show his solidarity with the Pharisees and at the same time distinguish himself from them. Here he accentuates the differences, and discloses the specific danger represented by the lawyers. What he reproaches them is not narrow-mindedness—the Pharisees' prerogative—but their lack of discernment. All their great knowledge has not enabled them to recognize the Messiah in the person of Jesus! Besides, this knowledge has invested them with a terrible prestige and power, that of burdening consciences. Thus they can prevent their listeners from hearing the Spirit, who speaks in a person's deepest heart.

■

Anyone even casually interested in the person of Jesus feels challenged by that person. To cling to Jesus—which is what faith is, as we were saying yesterday—is to make of him the norm of my life.

God seems to drive people to conversion. Will Jesus become the norm of my life? The question is an altogether personal one. The decision is mine alone. No church, no dogma, no pious declaration, no profession of faith, no testimony by another can force me to make a response or make a decision. This is a decision ultimately to be made in all freedom. This decision is an interchange between Jesus and myself, without intermediaries.

God drives us to conversion. The response is up to us. And response is commitment—commitment for, or commitment against. Why, when all is said and done, do we give Jesus our faith, if not because we trust him beyond all testimony, beyond all the examples of the lives of those trustworthy persons who have already given him their faith? We do not make our decision blindly. But neither are we overwhelmed by evidence. We make our decision . . . reasonably, merely—and yet in unreserved trust and absolute certitude. Ultimately our faith is like love. And indeed it is transformed into love.

■

God, who judges our hearts:
*   fill us with your wisdom,*
*   overwhelm us with your Spirit.*
Drive us to conversion,

and may our faith be our joy
now and forever.

■

That your Church be the fire
that consumes every dried branch
and renews everyone who sits in ashes,
Lord, hear our prayer.

That the baptized may not be oblivious of the Spirit
in which they have been new-created,
Lord, hear our prayer.

For a peace that fears not truth,
amends,
and reconciliation,
Lord, hear our prayer.

That conflicts occasioned by faith be but the beginning
of rich Christian discoveries,
Lord, hear our prayer.

Lord, when we pray,
place your spirit within us:
that Spirit alone can create in us
a new heart,
and an endless harvest of life.

THURSDAY OF THE 28TH WEEK

JUSTIFICATION

Romans 3:21–30: "What is the advantage, then, of being a Jew?" (Rom. 3:1). To be sure, a Jew is a member of the people of the covenant, the trustee of the divine promises (3:2). But Paul is far too aware of the false certitudes which that membership has generated in his former coreligionists to neglect to point out the equality of pagans and Jews in the matter of salvation—after first pointing to their equality in the matter of sin and the divine wrath. Verse 28 is a perfect summary of his thinking: ". . . We hold that a man is justified by faith apart from observance of the law." Not that the law is useless. On the contrary, in the past it has been the vehicle whereby the Jews have become aware of the reality of sin. By way of its reports of the divine intervention, the law has borne testimony to God's salvific desire, a testimony that it shared, for that matter, with the prophets. But "today" a new age has dawned, for "the justice of God has been manifested . . . for all who believe." And this has happened "apart from the law."

Salvation, then, is for anyone who believes, Jew or pagan. After having depicted the distress of both, the apostle will now describe the justification effected by Christ. After all, salvation does not rest on the works of the law. It rests on faith in Jesus, whom God has raised aloft on the cross that he may be "the means of expiation for all who believe." The word "expiation" is a reference to the old "propitiatory"—the golden plaque hanging over the ark of the covenant, which the high priest sprinkled with blood in the ancient rite of the Day of the Great Atonement. The Letter to the Hebrews regards this yearly ritual as the image and prototype of the Christ's own sacrifice. By the blood of Christ, which is immeasurably superior to that of animals, Jesus becomes, once and for all, absolute perfection for all believers; that which the "propitiatory" was incomplete, and for Jews alone. The latter, then, have no reason to be puffed up. Is God not one? Then he is the God of pagans and Jews alike, and his oneness demands that both Jew and pagan look upon him as their only savior. In Christ, the deed is done.

Continuing to emphasize the expiatory nature of the deed of Christ, *Psalm 130* implores God to deliver, to rescue, believers.

Luke 11:47–54: Ah, these lawyers, these tomb-builders! Over the course of time the Jews had come to regard the prophets, whom their forebears had persecuted and murdered, as martyrs. Beginning in the reign of Herod the Great they had even begun to build tombs for them as monuments to their memory.

Jesus has discerned the murderous intentions of his compatriots. He seizes the occasion to remind them that the only prophets they can abide are the dead ones. These, at least, can do no more talking. In saying this, Jesus himself joins the long list of God's envoys. And now their lot will be his. But be on guard, Israel! The measure of your sins may have reached its limit!

■

God wished to manifest that it is his justice that saves! Salvation and justice are synonymous in scripture. Of course "justice" is not to be understood in the juridical sense of the word. The sinner's justification does not mean acquittal. It does not even mean pardon. When criminals are pardoned, they have to "make it on their own" after that—start a new life as best they can. When God justifies, he communicates his justice—his own holiness, which is Love. God's justification is recreation, renewal, reconversion.

The world justified, the world sanctified, the world rectified! A world in which every failed human being on the face of the earth can live in the rectitude of the Spirit! God makes us a gift of his newness of life. Such is salvation, such is our justification. We become just, we become "the way we ought to be." It is not that we *are* free. But we *can* be freed—freed by the one who is absolute freedom, our Savior.

We need not plead mitigating circumstances. We need draw up no brief for the defense. We are made just. Faith consists in submitting to this decree of grace, to this Good News. After all, this is how faith saves us.

■

God of tenderness and mercy,
it is your will that the multitude of human beings be saved.
Open our eyes to the obedience of Christ,
prevent us from setting up obstacles to your will.
Make us living proof
of your all-powerful love,
God of mercy.

■

God of love,
you have created us for a future of joy and glory.
Open our hearts to the gift of wonder:
give us to recognize in Jesus
the one who has come to deliver us from failure and death.
For, in the might of the Spirit,
he lives with you, Father, forever.

■

God of all grace, be praised!
You shower us with your grace,
your mercy is our justice
and your love renews our hearts.
For we are sanctified, rendered holy,
by your loving-kindness.

Therefore we beseech you: may your grace be our gladness,
that, overwhelmed with so grand a gift,
we may bless you for all eternity.

OUR FATHER ABRAHAM

Romans 4:1-8: The Jews based their certitude of their salvation on their carnal descent from Abraham. And so the apostle rereads what scripture says of the justification of their great ancestor. This rereading only confirms the thesis of justification by faith. It was not in virtue of his works, but by his faith, that Abraham was declared just.

We recall that the term "just" must be defined as "an attitude that bases and maintains, between two persons, a covenant of communion" (Xavier Léon-Dufour). It was Abraham's trusting attitude toward God that placed him in a position to benefit from the covenant. He was as yet uncircumcised.

Resuming *Psalm 32,* the liturgy celebrates the happiness of those who owe their salvation to God alone.

Luke 12:1-7: A crowd of thousands gathers. The number obviously suggests the eschatological assembly so often proclaimed by the prophets. And indeed God comes on the scene in our text as the great judge of the last days, the one "who has the power to cast into Gehenna. . . ."

Jesus asks his disciples to mistrust the yeast of the Pharisees—in Luke, their hypocrisy. (In Matthew their leaven is their teaching.) The endless laments of the Pharisees betray this hypocrisy. As we see, they and their lawyers have reduced religion to their own dimensions. They have become relentless propagandists of the law only in order to seize control of the law. They perform their judicial function in such a manner as to place themselves in direct competition with God.

"A crowd of thousands had gathered. . . ." It had gathered while Jesus spoke —that is, according to J. Radermakers, when word had spread of the great revelation that Jesus had enunciated (Lk 9:18). That revelation had focused on the Father, knowledge of whom is precisely the goal of the apostolic mission, and on the Spirit, whose signs can be perceived only by receptive, open hearts. Chapter 12 will now depict the life of the disciples in light of this double revelation—in light of what they are to shout from the housetops. And the revelation they are to proclaim is: the very heart of the One for whom a human being is worth more than all of the birds in the world.

■

Because Abraham had faith in the Lord, God pronounced him just. Abraham, the "father" of believers! The reason the Bible uses such an expression is obviously to make it clear that Abraham is the beginning point of all that multitude of women and men who call themselves believers. But the Bible is also eager to present Abraham as the believer par excellence, the prototype of the believer—and present his attitude, his behavior, as the wellspring of the attitude and behavior of all those who call themselves believers.

With Abraham, believing consisted in constantly living and acting in such a way as to plunge into the life and action proposed by God's word, and by this path to reach God's presence and life. At the critical moments of his existence, the moments that demanded he adopt a new orientation, cross a threshold—as with his departure from his native land, the announcement of his son's birth, so long despaired of, or the sacrifice of that only son—Abraham embraced the challenge and responded to it. Yes, for Abraham, believing, faith, in these mighty moments, consisted in always behaving as one who takes his life in charge, in conformity with what he believed he was discovering.

This sense of faith—Abraham's manner of believing—is indeed wondrous. It involves him in an existence that, on the level of his actual reflection and experience, offers him no promise, affords him no certitude, and even seems destined to lead him up a blind alley to his death. But Abraham believed, against all the evidence, that this journey would lead somewhere—that it would carry him to success and not sterility. "Abraham believed," and his faith was purely and simply his full commitment to his life, whatever might be its failures, its fears, its despair and disillusionment.

Existence is joy and happiness for me, of course, and this is a fine thing. But I know that this joy and happiness will never fill me to the brim. Why? Because it does not save those who suffer and who, at least obscurely, wish to be rescued from their suffering. And yet I know, I believe, that this life to which I commit myself each morning sparks the genesis of the Reign of God. And for me to join the Reign of God means to become a child of Abraham, father of all believers.

∎

God of Abraham, our Father,
your call impels us to leave our familiar lands.
Yes, your word rouses our obedience.
By your grace
*   we risk our lives for your promise.*
Then grant us to know the peace of faith:
*   may our trust be the foretaste*

*of the life we shall have
for everlasting ages.*

SATURDAY OF THE 28TH WEEK

THE LIFE OF FAITH

Romans 4:13, 16–18: It is in virtue of their faith, writes Paul, and not on account of any deed of theirs, that Abraham and his descendants have been designated the heirs of the "world." In the Old Testament that promise had only been of a land to be possessed. But the preaching of the prophets, once the Land of Promise had been possessed, had afforded a glimpse of the birth of a whole new world. Nor had the prophets ever flagged in their insistence that the promise would remain in force until it was fully realized. In order to benefit from the promise, Paul explains, it was enough to be found in the same dispositions as those of its first beneficiary, Abraham. Verse 18 places the faith of the mighty ancestor in perspective. When Yahweh promised Abraham a child, Abraham believed. His age, and Sarah's sterility, would be no obstacle. And lo, the way was clear for God to exercise his creative power.

Psalm 105 is a hymn, recalling the divine promises and counseling trust in God and his omnipotence.

Luke 12:8–12: "Whoever acknowledges me before men—the Son of man will acknowledge him before the angels of God." The testimony borne by the disciples will be the object of the eschatological judgment. Indeed, that judgment is carried out in this very life, Luke knows—whenever Christians must bear testimony before the authorities. It is a judgment to be pronounced by the Father, as we see by the repeated use of the passive voice. The Son and the Spirit assume, respectively, the roles of witness (for the defense) and defense attorney.

What are we to say of the apparent opposition between the Son of man and the Spirit? Probably Luke is contrasting the time of Jesus' earthly mission with that of the apostolic mission, which is conducted by the Spirit and which constitutes humanity's last chance for salvation. It will be helpful to compare the present passage with Mark 3:22–30, where Jesus' apostrophe follows his accusation as a worker of miracles in the name of Beelzebul: "It is possible that one may not recognize the mystery of the Son, but there is no excuse for misinterpreting the sign constituted by the exorcism performed by Jesus in the Spirit." When all is said and done, the culprit is bad faith—a hardened heart.

Hebrews tells us that "Abraham believed and so became the father of many nations. . . ." The Genesis account had already proclaimed God's promise: "I shall make your posterity as numerous as the dust of the earth." Again, the Letter to the Hebrews asserts: "By the faith of one man—who was already as good as dead—was born a multitude like that of the stars of the sky, numberless as the sands of the seashore."

We must admit that we are not accustomed to making this sort of link between faith and fecundity. The terms that spontaneously cluster around the word "faith" in our language are "light," "truth" and "certitude," as opposed to "ignorance" or "darkness." The example of Abraham stands as a reminder that it is not in confrontation with ignorance and error that we assert our faith but, far more basically, in a face-to-face meeting with death—death in its daily guise, where the grim reaper steps forward in the form of sterility of action, or as the uselessness of life that would have us formulate the despairing admission: "It's no use! Nothing can be done!"

It was this crucial experience, in its most elementary form, that confronted Abraham. He had no child. And his old body was "as good as dead" in the sense that it no longer contained the germ of new life. And yet, relying on God's word, and despite so much experience to the contrary, Abraham believed that the deeds of life, infected though they be with the power of death, would become life-giving. And Isaac came into the world. Isaac is a symbol—and his father, in his old age, becomes for us the sacrament, the outward sign—of our faith, when, in spite of all our experience to the contrary, we believe in life, and on God's word risk actually taking that life in hand.

God of our faith,
enable us to risk our very being,
on the basis of the assurance of your promise.
Fecundate by your grace
the deeds that texture our lives,
that those lives may expand, in all directions,
for everlasting ages to come.

In this bread broken for us,
God our Father, we recognize

the One who gives life to the world,
Jesus, your Passover for our earth.
As he is our savior,
may he continue to be our strength each day,
and keep us in oneness with you
now and forever.

FROM MONDAY TO SATURDAY

OF THE 29TH WEEK

New Life

Before knowing God's law, we can have the impression of being alive. But that life is only a death. From the moment of our first contact with the law of God, we awaken to the truth. We awaken to ourselves: our existence has meaning for God!

Confronted with God's own desire for us, we awaken to our helplessness to respond to this desire perfectly. And we are devastated. Luther described the Christian as "simultaneously sinful and justified" by God in Christ—*simul peccator et justus.* And to be sure, the Christian is not impeccable. Far from it. But the fact remains that, though we are sinners, we are no longer under the domination of sin. And this is Paul's message. Thanks to Christ, we have passed to an entirely different mode of existence before God. Our bitter struggle with evil has been transformed into trust.

And at the same time, God appears entirely different to us. God had been the God of the law, in the good sense of the word—the God who means to rehabilitate humanity. But their moral and religious calling confronted "carnal" human beings with the impossible demand of fidelity. Then, joined to Christ's own attitude of surrender, Christians received Christ's Spirit.

Doubtless we Christians remain, in some sort, carnal beings—fallible, struggling to live according to the commandments of Christ, never entirely faithful. Surely. But this fact may not be allowed to function as a pretext for regarding ourselves as "simultaneously sinful and justified." After all, while we are unfaithful at times, sin no longer dominates us. A superior strength has filled us, and that power sets us free.

■

How can we thank you, God our Father?
You have delivered us from the power of death,
    you have set us free from the slavery of our sin.
In your Son, the new Adam,
        we are consecrated to a new life,
        woven of grace and of mercy.
Following his law,
    we reap life.
Watchful in faith,
    we burn with a fire that warms our hope.
With all who share this heritage,
    God, our Life, we praise you.

■

The peace you give
    is not as the world's peace.
    For your fire will not mix with our tepidities.
Lord, plunge us in the ardor of your passion,
    that our life, seared with the breath of the Spirit,
    may expand into life everlasting.

MONDAY OF THE 29TH WEEK

THE STRENGTH OF FAITH

Romans 4:20–25: Far from weakening his faith, Abraham's trials actually strengthened it. Now the apostle turns to his fellow Christians. The promises attaching to Christ's resurrection, he tells them, place them in the same situation as their great ancestor. Be they Jew or Greek, their justification will be commensurate with their assimilation of Abraham's attitude of belief. Paul concludes with a formula frequently found in the early Christian professions of faith. The first part of the formula draws its inspiration from the Songs of the Servant of Yahweh: "delivered for our sins and raised for our justification."

With the help of a number of verses from the Benedictus, the liturgy situates Christ's resurrection in the overall context of God's salvation deed.

Luke 12:13–21: Jesus is asked to arbitrate a dispute over an inheritance. Taken in itself, the episode is banal enough. Rabbis were frequently besought to perform this kind of service. But Jesus' response gives us a feeling that something far more profound is transpiring. "Who has set me up as your judge or arbiter?" And once more we sense the theme of judgment.

Luke addresses the task of clarifying what this judgment will be. We hear the answer in Jesus' attitude. Jesus refuses to become involved in questions of money. Life, in his view, does not consist in having. And we discern the first faint light of a theme that will soon dawn in all its brightness: the judgment of which Jesus speaks is a judgment of salvation, a wellspring of life.

■

Abraham is our father. He had faith in God, and this was credited to him as justice. And so he became the father of a great multitude. He found his strength in faith, Saint Paul observes. Faith is not a pious sentiment. Faith is active. It is more than a mere attachment to dogmas or truths. It is a clinging of the heart, a concentration of all our faculties upon a single goal: to live according to God's call, which is beyond all rule and measure. Faith is to-believe: faith is a verb, a movement, an acting.

"He was strengthened in faith"—that is, it was in faith that Abraham found his strength. For Christians, to believe in God is inseparable from believing in the human being. Faith adds no new capability to our becoming. Faith is not the spare tire on my pickup. Faith steeps our whole becoming. There is no separation of worlds here—the world of our human expansion from the world of our holiness. There are correspondences, and there are passages, from the one order to the other. Our strength is our faith. Because we are believers, we must have faith in life, and cling, bind ourselves, to its simplest, most immediate realizations. We must have faith in life so that it may enter upon, venture upon, its consummation—arrive at its supernatural dimension.

Our strength is our faith. Unless I believe in myself as the artisan and creator of my today, how shall I be able to commit my freedom to the supernatural, creative space of the invisible universe? There is no access to God but by the humble everyday, and there is no means of engendering holiness but through fidelity to the movement that makes us exist: living. The faith of my mind, and the clinging of my heart and my freedom, to a call that comes from God himself, is inoperative unless I feel at one with the creative strength of my person. Unless you hope, you do not find the unexpected.

Our strength is our faith. I know that God's love is not imaginary—that it is positive, and creative, and that in loving me God enables me to love. For he would not love me had he placed nothing lovable within me. In the act of believing, then, I deliver myself to this strength. And then I try, I do my best, simply to live.

Creative God, source of all life,
blessed be your name!
Your promise is fulfilled for our happiness,
    and in the Passover of your Son
    we discover our future.
May our faith be our strength,
    and our hope the joy of our living.

TUESDAY OF THE 29TH WEEK

ATTIRED IN LIVERY

Romans 5:12, 15, 17–19, 20–21: This particularly difficult passage calls for a systematic approach. First let us recall something we have said before: everyone is equal before God, who has not based salvation on privileges but on faith. The apostle has already described the state of a sinful humanity condemned by God but capable of being justified by faith in Christ.

Now the dominant theme is the victory of Christ. Now Paul will demonstrate the superiority of the deed of Jesus to that of Adam. The deed of the first human being was an act of death. That of Jesus is a deed of life. And the consequences for the humanity of which both Adam and Jesus are an inseparable part? The Pauline theology of the consequences of Adam's deed has posed a tremendous challenge of interpretation. In verse 12 the apostle embarks on a comparison, and then omits the conclusion: "Just as through one man sin entered the world and with sin death, [and] so death came to all men inasmuch as all sinned. . . ." The last clause poses a problem. It appeals to a personal transgression, and thus seems precisely to contradict the thesis that human death is the result of delinquency on the part of a single individual at the dawn of history.

The explanation comes after verse 12, in verses 13–14. In these verses, which are not included in the reading, Paul insists that personal transgressions could only be imputed to the persons committing them once the Law had been introduced. Of course, this also implies that from Adam to Moses sin must already have concealed a maleficent force entailing death. Accordingly, certain interpreters judge that Paul is considering Adam as the representative of a collectivity rather than as an historical individual. The power of death would thus be identical with the force of alienation to be described in chapter 7.

Whatever the merit of this interpretation, the comparison initiated in verse 12 gives place, beginning in verse 15, to a demonstration of the superiority of Christ's deed to that of Adam. "But the gift is not like the offense," writes Paul, introducing a series of comparisons to show the difference in status between sin and grace. In verse 19 he expounds the causes of this difference, which are to be sought in the respective attitudes of Christ and Adam to God: the obedience of Christ versus the disobedience of Adam. And the apostle concludes with a brilliant formula (and incidentally an intentional slur on a Law that cannot save): "Despite the increase of sin, grace has far surpassed it. . . ."—where sin abounded, there grace abounded the more.

Paul's appeal to Christ's obedience inspires us to sing certain verses of thanksgiving from *Psalm 40,* which is often cited in this connection.

Luke 12:35–38: "Let your belts be fastened around your waists and your lamps be burning ready." The atmosphere is that of Passover. A belt, while belonging to the attire of a livery, was also part of the traveller's garb worn by Jews when they celebrated Passover. This is how Jews awaited the Messiah— with their lamps lighted, in loving watchfulness, as suggested, for example, in the parable of the ten maidens in Matthew 25.

What will the master do when he finds his servants keeping watch? He will don his own livery, seat his servants at table, and personally serve them. And this is literally what Jesus will do on the eve of his death—gird himself with an apron and wash the feet of his friends and followers. It is the new Passover, then, that is suggested here—that of Jesus' total gift of himself, the Passover of the wedding feast of the Lamb. And so, just as yesterday's reading spoke of the salvific nature of judgment, today's explains the content of that salvation. It will consist of an unheard-of gift: the Lord himself will serve his disciples. After all, is it not this that is meant by: "The Son of Man is come not to be served but to serve"? To die as a ransom for the multitudes—behold, Jesus' service.

■

In the name of those who take the risk of bringing children into the
    world . . .
In the name of youth who do not do as everyone does . . .
In the name of those marginalized for their nonconformist venture . . .
In the name of all those committed to the rejected . . .
In the name of all men and women experiencing the night of faith . . .
In the name of the Lord who became Servant
    and the Master who donned the livery of a slave
    to wash his disciples' feet . . .

I adjure you to keep your lamps lighted: faith is active when it watches in darkness to hasten the first light of dawn.

We have toiled, now, and we have watched—in livery, investing our treasure at interest. It is not really very much to have accomplished. But endlessly we have rekindled our flickering flames, thereby serving notice on the night that all its ruses stink of death, and that it will not succeed. Yes, let us endure to the end. Let us remain on our feet, though we stagger with sleep, to catch that first faint glimmer, in our own times, of the dim rays that herald tomorrow: lives more or less surrendered to love, communions of persons laboriously launched and precariously afoot, solidarity struck by a promise, a fairly sincere quest for justice. Yes let us endure, and for one reason alone—what would tomorrow be, were it not to dawn in faith?

Listen to your heart, and not to all those excellent reasons you have for taking your rest, falling asleep, or even dying. Remember—Jesus, too, kept vigil, that your heart might watch with his. It was in the bright light of dawn that he, too, having struggled in the darkness, appeared, the firstborn citizen of a new world, the new Adam of a world raised to life again, to don the apron of service and set the table—to break bread for us.

■

Surely we may tell you of our impatience,
    God who promises to come!
Have we not relied on you for everything?
Be our assurance
    when doubt displaces our trust.
Be our courage
    when the temptation comes to drowse.

WEDNESDAY OF THE 29TH WEEK

KEEPING WATCH
Romans 6:12–18: In the first part of his letter Paul has stigmatized the attitude of Jews who think the divine election shields them from judgment. But this attitude is not the monopoly of Jews. Christians share it, especially those Christians who look on baptism as a talisman automatically assuring

114

them of salvation, independent of real life. Vigorously the apostle explains that baptism is the pledge of life only if it entails a real death to sin.

Beginning with verse 12, doctrinal presentation yields to exhortation. Christians ought to live according to the logic of their baptism. Since they are dead to sin in order to live a new life with Christ, they should repel any temptation to return to the slavery to which sin might still subject them. Their bodies, "the locus of their presence to the world" should choose justice— should choose the covenant struck between God and human beings in baptism. The thing is possible, ever since grace replaced a law helpless to save from sin.

Redacted in the style of individual thanksgiving, *Psalm 124* is nevertheless intended for community prayer. It recalls the slavery of sin, from which Yahweh alone can deliver.

Luke 12:39–48: Peter's question focuses Jesus' discourse on the group of the disciples themselves. They have received much; much will be asked of them.

The passage resumes all of the themes broached since Jesus was asked to arbitrate a dispute over an inheritance. The disciples are compared to stewards. They are to parcel out to their fellow servants each one's respective share of the harvest. But there are two kinds of stewards. There are the "farsighted," who perform their task in conformity with the instructions given them. And then there are those who are like the "fool" in the parable (v. 20) who pulled down his grain bins and built larger ones to accommodate his harvest. We recall the reproach Jesus has addressed to lawyers who have confiscated the key to knowledge (Lk 11:52). Christian leaders must avoid the same sin. They are trustees of the divine grace, not its proprietors. They hold it not for their own profit, but for that of the communities. Were they to forget this, they would be nothing more than so many impediments to the implementation of God's salvation plan.

■

Be on guard! The syllables ring like a call to our faith, and a call of hope.

Be on guard! The slow numbness that paralyzes the reflexes of our attention, shrivelling our reasons for living and camouflaging the urgency of existence, threatens our vigil. Countless times, an insidious wind has swept in from the open sea to extinguish our lamps. "Be on guard"! Tirelessly we have rekindled the lamp that thrusts away the night. We have watched, we have toiled, we have done our best. It is when the night goes on forever—when night stands stock still—that the day is sure to come. The lamp incessantly rekindled serves notice on the night that, with all its ruses, it cannot win. Be on guard, church.

Rise early. Go meet the dawn. Toil till morning, when God will manifest his deed: you have received the inheritance of hope. Be the lighted lamp that guides us. And thus reveal to those of us who have let ourselves be overcome with drowsiness, how good a thing it is to stride toward the stars.

"Be on guard"! Denounce the merchants of illusion, unmask all who would cast a sleep or a spell on you. Be servants expecting their Master's return. May he find you awake and at work, impassioned by his word. "Not the one who cries, "Lord, Lord," will enter the Reign, but the one who does the will of the Father."

"Be on guard"! Do not let fear get the better of you! How many watchful vigils have collapsed in defense reflexes! We feel we must leave no margin for error, no room for the unexpected. And on the day of the longed-for visit we forget about our friend who has come and think only of all we have to do! We brook the approach of no messenger to our well-guarded walls unless we know the message! No, leave your security instructions at home, and venture out the gate. Live in the open air!

The Master of the house is away. Watch and pray! Let not night gnaw away at your hope. The One who comes will take you by surprise, come upon you in the midst of your task. There will be so many things left to do, yet there he will be. Happy those who will be found watchful then, for they will recognize, in the Reign of God when it comes, something of what they have patiently carried in their heart. The Master is on his way. But understand well—you have nothing to fear from his return. He himself will reawaken us in the land of his Reign, the land of a new day, for he is the night sentry who has kept watch through all the hours of darkness, to be born again in the morning—he, the Easter Conqueror.

■

Happy shall we be if you find us on guard!
Lord, stir up our faith once more
    for the day of your coming.
Do you not come
    each time hope stirs our hearts?
What would become of us
    if sleep overpowered us?
Lord, arouse us yet again, even now.
    Wait not for eternity.

SOW FIRE, REAP LIFE

Romans 6:19-23: Apologizing for the inadequacy of his language—doubtless for his use of a vocabulary of slavery to characterize the new life inaugurated by Christ—the apostle exhorts the Romans one last time to place themselves entirely at the service of this life. Thus they will accomplish the concrete realization of the vocation implied in their membership in the people of God. When they were at the service of injustice, they reaped only death. Now, if they persevere along the path opened by their baptism, they will reap life everlasting. This life springs from God's free mercy, while death was but the wages, the normal outcome, of sin.

In a meditation on conversion, on changing one's life, *Psalm 1* extends our Pauline reflection on the two paths offered to the baptized.

Luke 12:49-53: The earth is on fire, with a fire that destroys the wicked and purifies the good, as fire refines gold in a crucible! God has come to render judgment, and verses 49-50 express the prophet's haste to reach the term of his mission. And suddenly we learn that this judgment is to be carried out in the passion of the Son of man, in language conjuring up the image of a "baptism." Not only will the coming judgment be unforeseen—as intimated in the image of the thief in the night (v. 39)—but it will divide families: "three against two and two against three . . ." suggesting the number of fingers on the hand. It goes without saying that families should be joined, as are the fingers of the hand. But with Jesus, nothing is any longer the way it "should" be.

Is the judgment always one of salvation? True, Jesus' discourse has suddenly turned harsh. Besides, verses 49-53 introduce chapter 13, which will focus on the inescapable death of the Just One. But we must not forget that, when Luke was actually composing his redaction, the old symbols had been enriched with new meanings. Baptism, for example, which Jesus mentions, suggested the Christian baptism for the forgiveness of sins, while the symbol of fire was reminiscent of the baptism of the Spirit and the fire of Pentecost. Jesus is surely come for a judgment of salvation, then. The only question is whether there will be "faithful, farsighted" women and men to receive him!

■

Our Jesus, an arsonist? The gospel certainly has no fear of contrasting images. Meek and humble of heart Jesus surely was, but in how passionate a heart that meekness rested! Oh, the violence of the peaceful! Jesus struggled to the death, and the fire of Pentecost is in his resurrection!

Fire warms. Fire is life. But life is risk, and the brasier purifies. When Jesus kindles the fire of the Spirit, he kindles a conversion. "When you were slaves of sin, you had freedom from justice." When Jesus fans the fire, we shall have to accept risks.

And behold, the fire of the gospel attacks our very homes. The sweet peace of the family circle changes to strife. "My peace I leave you," Jesus says, "but not as the world gives peace!" We thought we were going to live in peace. We had trimmed the word of God to our dimensions. But it is enough that one among us take seriously this Jesus who strides toward his passion, and lo, we are divided. "Who is not with me is against me!" You have "become slaves of God."

The gospel is fire. The church is not a gang of pals, and it is not a social club. The kiss of peace we exchange is not a piece of urbanity. Baptism is not a sinecure. We have become slaves of God! And "the gift of God is eternal life." Only those whose houses have been purged by fire and rebuilt by the burning call of Easter have the promise of eternal life.

"The gift of God is eternal life"! Any who take Jesus' yoke upon them know that it is light, for Jesus was the first to be cast into the fire of the Spirit. Because he has known the baptism of blood, he—and he alone—has the right to demand it of others. You have won life by becoming God's slaves. After all, the baptism of blood swells into resurrection. It flares into a refiner's fire that none can extinguish.

We shall hear: Do not be so demanding! Quench not the smoldering flax! No, of course not, that is just the point: the smoldering flax must be rekindled—fanned into a blaze again! It must feel the flame once more, and take the risk of a new conflagration.

■

Jesus Christ, plunged in death
  to renew all things,
  have mercy on us.
Lord, delivered into the hands of sinners
  to stir up new peace,
  have mercy on us.
Son of God, transfigured in the fire of the Spirit
  to give life to the world,
  have mercy on us.

God who loves rectitude,
convert our hearts by your Word of fire.
Keep us from facile compromises,
    dishonest silences,
    and the indifference we call peace.
So shall we love the truth that was in Jesus.
    For it he died.
    In it, he lives at your right hand.

FRIDAY OF THE 29TH WEEK

AND YET. . . !

Romans 7:18–25: Isolated from its context, this passage could read like a psychological analysis. Actually Paul is still addressing the same problem. He is still obsessed with trying to show the possibility of a new life—a possibility that is Christ's deed, and not that of a Law helpless to save us though it show us our sin. At the same time I must not saddle the Law with my own guilt and responsibility. The sole culprit is the "me" who, subject to sin, cannot break loose from its clutches and subject itself to the Law.

Paul speaks in terms of alienation, then. For him, sin holds people captive. We "intend well, but evil is here—indeed, within us—and it strives to make [us] submit to it" (A. Viard). Prisoners of sin, we are "caught in a destiny that contradicts [our] profound aspirations." Human beings are deeply divided within themselves.

But if the Law cannot deliver us from this slavery, then who can? "Who can free me from this body under the power of death?" The answer has been given in chapter 6. Jesus Christ is the only savior. He delivers us by transforming us in his Spirit.

God answers the prayer of those the Law cannot save. How? By sending Jesus Christ (*Ps 119*).

Luke 12:54–59: The dominant theme of these transitional verses to chapter 13 is "warning." A discernment of the signs of the times, and reconciliation with one's adversaries, are urgent tasks, incumbent on anyone seeking to enter the Reign of God.

119

Verses 57–59 also prepare us for chapter 16, which will emphasize the importance of forgiving our sisters and brothers, the urgency of cancelling their debts. When all is said and done, we are being "farsighted" disciples when we make peace. In doing so, we are not scrambling to get all the grace we can while there is still time—that would be selfish—we are only opening ourselves to the salvation freely bestowed by God upon all women and men.

■

"What a wretched man am I! Who can free me from this body under the power of death?" The world seems destined for disintegration. The human race seems doomed to annihilation. We learned in our catechism that "man" is "fallen," and that all creation bears in some sort the mark of this trauma. And indeed every woman and man of us discovers, in the furthest depths of us, the rending of the sin of Adam, whose guilt we bear.

We should like to preserve our optimism intact. And yet, do we not, from time to time, feel the clutch of terror? We see worlds born and disintegrating. Behold the great cosmic law, which we find governing the life of societies as it controls the biological order. And this law pursues us right down to the conflicts and sufferings of our own lives. Death steeps all things, and nothing can exorcise the specter of evil, of wars, of terrible injustices, of famines. Nor can anything ever heal me of the anguish of the death inscribed on the heart of all life.

We live as on a great seismographic fault, stretching from the cosmos into our lives all the way to our own responsibility. "I do . . . the evil I do not intend." I know only too well how to shut myself off from the call to believe and to love, to be genuine and to act. We dupe ourselves by pride and fear. There are days when we play out a gigantic comedy. We sally forth to do battle with one alienation, while eagerly permitting ourselves to be taken captive by another. My cowardice and my stubbornness are frequently stronger than I, and yet I am not only the victim, but the very perpetrator of this cowardly, stubborn life of mine! As an old rabbi said long ago: we are each our own Adam. Indeed, is not the original sin that scars us more than likely this network of evil in which each of us must frame our lives? The forces of destruction are at work, and who among us never permits them to take the field unhindered?

"All praise to God, through Jesus Christ our Lord"! For I see my existence inscribed in a twofold solidarity: that of evil and death, to be sure—but also that of love and life. After all, both the universe and our lives are attracted by the magnetism of Christ. The prospect of solidarity with him seizes us more radically and more profoundly than does the milieu of sin. Every life must weigh in the balance this solidarity of love, of the love of Jesus, against the lethal solidarity of the old Adam. We find this twofold solidarity carved into our hearts as a call and an appeal. In a world in a state of sin, we are called upon to toil for the transfiguration of that world into a land of justice. In a world of disintegration, we must tirelessly see to the regrouping of the forces of communion. In a world of hatred, we must mend the rents. In a world of war and ruin, we must ceaselessly reopen the construction site of peace. In a world of despair, we must allow the seed of joy to sprout. "Praise to God . . ."! For our condition as sundered beings is but a challenge we must take up in the footsteps of Jesus of Nazareth. Ultimately we know only the cry of Easter: "O death, where is your victory?" (1 Cor. 15:55).

■

Be blessed, God of life,
for the hollow pit our hunger delves,
and for the face of the darkness that cries for your light.
Death and decay cannot have the last word:
speak to us once more the words that lift us up again,
raise what our sin has destroyed.
By your grace may our life be the struggle
that never fails to engender our everlasting happiness.

SATURDAY OF THE 29TH WEEK

THE SPIRIT GROANS WITHIN US

Romans 8:1-11: "Who can free me from this body under the power of death?" Faith's answer strikes like a thunderbolt. But the lightning is charged with promises: "There is no condemnation now for those who are in Christ Jesus." What? How is this possible? Paul explains by way of a reflection on the two covenants. On the one side there was the old covenant, founded on the law of Moses. This law has demonstrated its impotence to free the Jews from the dominion of sin. On the other side there is the new covenant, based on the promise. Where the Law had failed, God has succeeded. By sending his Son to share the human condition, God has succeeded in "condemning sin in the flesh," and thereby putting an end to its dominion.

Here the apostle inserts a parenthetical observation on the manner of Christ's activity. He borrows a technical expression from the sacrificial vocabulary of the Old Testament: "sin offering." A sin offering is a sacrifice offered for the purpose of overcoming and defeating sin. In this kind of sacrifice, we recall, the death of the victim manifested the divine condemnation. Christ's death has permitted this condemnation to have its effect. This "act of obedience and love" has permitted the realization of the promises contained in the oracles of Jeremiah 31 and Ezekial 36: the old Law has yielded to the Law of the Spirit. The law had been external to us, and hence constraining. Now it resides deep within our existential being. No longer living in the clutches of the flesh, in revolt against God, we have become capable of carrying out the demands of the Law. Our body may remain pledged to death, on sin's account. But we have become the daughters and sons of life.

The responses sung by the Old Testament faithful at the moment of the entrance liturgies (*Ps. 24*) furnish a contrast with the statements of Paul. Only one saved by the activity of Christ can "ascend the mountain of the Lord."

Luke 13:1-9: Two tragedies are on everyone's lips: a killing ordered by Pilate, and the collapse of a tower, leaving eighteen dead. People were ascribing these incidents to the divine wrath. The victims must have been sinners. But Jesus hastens to disillusion them: they are sinners themselves, every last man and woman of them. So they ought all to have perished. On the other hand, the tragic, seemingly unfair deaths due to these twin catastrophes do presage the final judgment, which has already begun.

But the question returns with a vengeance. If all are sinners, why are some spared? This again is a sign to be interpreted, and a parable can help. Here is a tree that bears no fruit. Its owner is angry. For three years now, he has had it carefully tended, and for what? Yet his gardener is opposed to cutting it down. One must be patient—as Jesus must be patient. For three years he has carried out his ministry, and for what? But God gives Israel one last chance.

∎

Each of us is guided by our own desires. We are virtuous for ten years, twenty years . . . we toe the mark for a while . . . and then comes the day when we can no longer hide our true colors. "I want it all!" we say. Actually, perhaps we should not complain. After all, nothing happens without passion!

If each of us is led by our own desires, why should the Spirit of God not have his desires, within us?

"Those who live according to the flesh are intent on the things of the flesh, those who live according to the spirit, on those of the spirit." If God's Spirit in us is to be nothing but a law, a morality—in other words a beautiful ideal or program—the Spirit himself carries no weight in our lives. The gospel as a law, as a program, will last five years, perhaps ten, then fall apart. Except we have a taste for God, except we find our pleasure in him, except our truest being be found in him, we are not genuinely freed by the gospel, and the gospel fails to be Good News as far as we are concerned.

"You are in the spirit, since the Spirit of God dwells in you." There is a desire in us that lives in terror, that convulses, that lusts, that raves. We have been "under the law" of death (Rom. 6:15). We were prey to all manner of strange, irrational fears when we were delivered to ourselves. But likewise implanted in us, by the Spirit, are the very desires of God. These strengthen, these give peace and tenderness. These are the desires that give life.

■

No longer do we belong to the world.
Nor are we still in the clutches
of our fears, our doubts and our lusts.
God our Liberator,
fill us with the Holy Spirit.
May that Spirit be the breath that opens us to the future,
the breathing that keeps us alive
and the desire that bears us
toward everlasting ages.

FROM MONDAY TO THURSDAY

OF THE 30TH WEEK

Hoping . . .
Where is life headed? In our daily existence, through all our working hours, swallowed up in the nameless crowd, faced with so many dramas that find us helpless, we are pierced to the quick with the question: Is life headed only for death? Is life only life?

Where is life headed? The question calls for, not an answer, primarily, but an extension of the question. For, we notice, the first answer is not of the order of ideas at all. Each of us knows: you cannot keep someone from despairing. No argumention, no promise, no light, no love will prevent someone from despairing, if he or she is in despair. But each of us must also acknowledge that no disappointment, no horror, no suffering, no darkness can prevent someone from hoping if that person hopes. These are two facts of life. And we make bold to say: it is hope, and not its alternative, that is objectively justified.

Not that Christians possess some secret weapon with which they justify their hope. We have but one piece of news to proclaim: hope is right, for we dare to hope! It is from within the very fact of hoping that I cry: Anguish does not have the last word! And I have no other way of saying it. We can tell the world that hope is right only by the very fact of our hoping against hope.

It is in the desert of our mangled humanity, in the solitude of battles that break out in the dark, in dry loves that barely register, that the Good News begins to make itself heard. Let the earth be desolate—we testify that no winter despairs of spring, no night is too long to harbor a hope of dawn.

Yes, we dare to hope! Whence springs this outsized, disproportionate hope of ours? From a word, a promise? But how fragile these would be, had we not caught, on our very earth, a glimmer of the blinding flash they proclaim! We dare to believe in life because God has believed in it first. Our hope is not a mere plunge into the hopes that spring from the human heart out of human need. Our hope does not spring up from below, like an exploratory rocket that we might launch into the infinite. Our hope springs from this assurance of ours that, in Jesus Christ, God has taken sides with life. God has opened our eyes, which had been unable to see—and suddenly we behold our future. God has raised up the crippled, paralyzed creatures that we are, and suddenly we are on our feet again, we can "get going"—delivered from the fears that had rooted us to the spot. God has unswathed the shrouds of the dead, and deeds that had been fruitless suddenly engender peace, communion, justice.

We dare to hope! But we hope not only, and not mainly, because we need to hope. No, our hope does not depend on our dispositions. We do not create our hope. We receive it, we live it!

MONDAY OF THE 30TH WEEK

THE ENERGY OF HOPE

Romans 8:12-17: Now the apostle draws the appropriate conclusions from the fact of Christ's salvific deed. His first observation: Saved by Christ, Christians have contracted a debt. But let us not mistake the creditor. No debt to the flesh has been contracted.

We should notice that the word "flesh" here denotes the human "race." As Paul is addressing Jewish converts, we may conclude that he is insisting primarily on the new status that is theirs: having become Christians, they are no longer in the clutches of the "flesh." They have no more obligation to the Law. The slaves have become sons and daughters. Joined to Christ, they can call on God as he does, crying, "Abba, Daddy." Being sons and daughters, they are also heirs. For this, one condition is required: union with Christ who died and was raised again.

Psalm 68 is a collection of poems on the subject of the divine might. But God's fairest victory is to have made of us his daughters and sons.

Luke 13:10-17: Jesus has not set foot in a synagogue since the cure of the person with the paralyzed hand (Lk 6:6ff.). Now he does so for the last time in his life. One reason for Luke's omission of such visits is the evangelist's preoccupation with the openness of the gospel to pagans. But he is also inviting us to pay a great deal of attention to this last visit. We are deep in the heart of the land of the Jews. The synagogue is a veritable tract of the Holy Land. The woman's sin, for its part, recalls the sin that holds Israel captive.

Jesus frees the victim and lifts her to her feet. His deed is typically messianic, and surely there is no better day than the sabbath on which to perform it, since the sabbath is the Lord's day par excellence. The woman's cure is the vehicle of a twofold sign, then: it points to Israel's hidden iniquity, and it discloses Jesus' mission. And now is the moment to interpret these signs. But who will be the interpreters? Certainly not the false hearts who look at Pilate's massacre and the incident of the tower in Siloam and take refuge in their smug, impregnable consciences. It is time—high time—those consciences were converted!

■

The Spirit makes you daughters and sons! We say it, we repeat it, but can we ever really grasp the import of a like statement? The Spirit has us say, "Abba." Were we ever to venture upon the Our Father "for real," were we ever really to stake our lives on it—those lives would be upset, turned upside down, for good and all. We might never again dare utter those formulas of fire!

Do we call God "Abba, Father"? Do we realize to what lengths we go? To call God . . . to speak to him and say to him . . . "Our Father. . . ." casually, perfectly simply, with the assurance of Jesus alone! To saunter into the house of God, completely at home, and call, "Dad!" The Spirit has us say "Father." The "Our Father" is a prayer of such breadth, such space, because it discerns, proclaims, awaits, seeks, another shore. It protests because it attests. It knows that the response to its demands, to those improbable demands it makes, is there for the asking.

Humanity is on a quest that leaves it everlastingly unsatisfied. Our taste for the future fills us, and spurs us ever onward. Stubbornly we invent the possible. Relentlessly we march toward the promise that shines like a beacon in the night: you are children of a Father who tells you his name. And when, in the poverty of our prayer, we dare to take the risk of uttering the words we have received as our inheritance, at that moment we breathe, even here, the air of the Land of Promise: joy, peace, love, forgiveness, deliverance and . . . expectancy.

Who will take the measure of what is given to us to know? The Our Father will always revitalize the men and women of the future, for it is the refrain of the Exodus and the song of Easter.

The Spirit has us say, "Abba," and that is our inheritance. In other words, it is given us as a program, since an inheritance is bequeathed to be invested, to engender, to bear fruit. When we pray the Our Father we protest, we are impatient, we are stimulated, we build. They alone can claim this inheritance who are willing to live the passion whose floodgates this mighty invocation opens—those willing to choose and to realize the possible, those willing to make the possible swell to reality. This prayer that the Spirit stirs to life in our hearts is the raw energy of hope.

■

The Spirit comes to the aid of our frailty.
The Spirit utters words
    we should never dare to pronounce ourselves,
The Spirit reveals to us your name and our own.
And so we dare to say:
    "Our Father," be blessed.
May the inheritance we have already received
    be token and pledge of all that you promise.

TUESDAY OF THE 30TH WEEK

ETERNITY ALONE HEALS
Romans 8:18–25: Paul has just explained that we are "heirs of God, heirs with Christ, if only we suffer with him so as to be glorified with him" (v. 17).

In the Old Testament, "glory" denotes the splendor of God precisely as manifested. And where is that splendor manifested? In the divine prodigies of which the resurrection of Christ is the culmination. As Xavier Léon-Dufour writes, meditating on the saying of Irenaeus of Lyon: "The glory of God is God manifested, is Jesus Christ, is the human being alive."

How can human beings who cry out in their suffering ever be apprised of their salvation? Languishing under the dominion of sin, the "old man" was deprived of God's glory (Rom. 3:23). Now men and women are clad in it to whatever extent they allow themselves to be transformed by the Spirit. This transformation does not reach its perfection here below. It is limited by whatever refusals human beings oppose to the divine action. And so Paul characterizes the gift of the Spirit as the "first fruits" of that Spirit—a partial gift, bestowed in token of the whole. But while these firstfruits must await the final adoption that will transform them to the image of Christ, Christians are aware that this legacy, this adoption, is already in their hands. Henceforward the sufferings that weigh upon humanity are but the pangs of birth.

But no man is an island. The human being is an element of the cosmos, a piece of creation on its way to completion and screaming in its suffering. The creative act consisted in the subjugation of the cosmic forces. Then the human being's sin introduced disunion and disorder in the world, in such a way that relationships among God, human beings and creation were modified (cf. Gen. 3). But now the world's sufferings conceal a promise, a future. As the prophets never tire of reminding us: There will be a new earth and new skies, and no more sorrow or sighing!

Old world, new world: "They that sow in tears shall reap rejoicing" (*Ps. 126*).

Luke 13:18–21: The planter cast (*ebalen*) his seed into the garden. (Mark and Matthew say *espeiren, spare*—he "sowed" it, it was "sown.") The yeast is kneaded into three measures of dough. And thus shall it be with Jesus' persecuted body: it will be cast into the tomb.

But after three days he will rise again. For, from death, life wells up. Both of our parables teach us that failure is part and parcel of the growth of the Reign of God. These parables were a great comfort to the young church. In them Christians could read that persecutions would not carry the day against the Christian mission.

■

Anchored in our being, in our deepest being, is a need for expansion, a basic tendency toward a destination which is the plenitude of happiness. That desire mobilizes all our volitional powers, all our thrust, all our daring, all our stubbornness. At stake is a conquest.

An endless conquest. Creation cries out in the pangs of a birth not yet ended. And the desire is insatiable, for we are structured for more than the temporary satisfactions of our quest launched ever and again. "We are disappointed," writes Simone Weil, "by the pleasure we have expected and received. The reason we are disappointed is that what we expected was future. Once we had it, it was present. What we need is the future, present—and still future. Only eternity can heal this absurdity." Creation cries out in the pangs of a birth that is not yet finished. . . . We need to be cured of our thirst.

Do you remember the "habit of sanctifying grace" in the catechism? The *Letter to the Hebrews* asserts that the hope we cherish in our souls is like a strong, sure anchor. In order to heal our disappointments, or our too narrow realism, in order to bear up under the tragic element of our existence, we receive the virtue of hope, our anchor in the storm. We shall survive.

Hope is the child of eternity. It is like a transfusion of blood—the blood of the Redeemer—into our world. Hope is entirely different from a "hope" kept up "for whatever it's worth." Hope is a virtue. That is, it is revealed by, and we must receive it from, Someone Else. Only the spoken word we hear, only the blood transfusion we receive, can be our certitude, and only the Spirit can speak this word or impart this transfusion. And the content of our certitude is this: the redemption is accomplishing its task. It was Julien Green who wrote: "We are all poor Christians. The poorest, perhaps, that the earth has seen. But in a world collapsing about our ears, the certitude of the redemption is without a doubt what keeps us from dying like mad dogs."

"All creation groans and is in agony even until now." And yet: "In hope we were saved." Evil suffocates us. You may be undergoing torture at this very moment. But do not condemn without due process what God found to be good in the springtime of his creation. Whatever we have on our hearts can, with the help of hope, prepare—roughly, doubtless, and poorly, perhaps, but with passion, and reality—the world to come, by making the present world a new one.

Only eternity heals. But even now, in our very today, the gladness of hope springs up laughing—the sprout that will grow to be an enormous tree. The yeast is already raising the dough.

■

God, our future,
what can heal us of our thirst but your promise?
How shall the history of the world be able to spread out and grow
*   unless you raise our crushed hope from the earth?*

We beseech you: may this, too, pass,
 swept up by the might of your word,
 until the coming of the everlasting ages.

WEDNESDAY OF THE 30TH WEEK

A RESCUED HOPE

Romans 8:26–30: A world in the midst of its becoming, crying out its suffering, the baptized in possession of the deposit of the Spirit—both, the cosmos and the baptized, share one certainty: that of their salvation. For the Spirit intercedes for them, and the intercession of the Spirit is effective. Human beings are incapable of discerning what is for their good, or what corresponds to God's designs. But the Spirit comes to the rescue of their weakness. He knows what God wants, and transmits to the Father our prayer in such a way as to engage it in God's creative act. Thus does our faithful God conduct to a successful outcome the work he has begun: what he wishes is the glory of the human being, who has been chosen for this purpose. He has called that human being. He has justified that human being. Even now he glorifies that human being.

"All my hope, O Lord, is in your loving kindness" (*Ps. 13*). The psalms of complaint often end with a vow: to celebrate, in praise or sacrifice, the petition heard and granted. This promise obviously implies the certitude of being heard by Yahweh.

Luke 13:22–30: The road to Jerusalem! Luke does not forget the goal of Jesus' journey. It is his death on the cross that bestows on him the status of obedient Son. And the "narrow door" that so many Jews cannot stoop to enter, despite their membership in Abraham's race? Would it not be the tomb of Jesus? This would make the connection with the preceding parables.

Chapter 12 has spoken of life offered in abundance. The healing of the crippled woman, the images of the seed and the yeast, all lay in this direction. Now Luke warns that life itself can be refused. Some of the first will be last! Nonetheless salvation is on the way: some of the last will be first, to find themselves reclining at table with the patriarchs and prophets. The seed is buried only for a time. It will remain hidden only until all the dough has risen.

■

Jesus advances toward Jerusalem. Somehow he knows that, in Jerusalem, the last act of the drama will be played out. The road that

---

129

stretches before him is barred by two wooden beams. Luke's gospel has a grave, sometimes tragic, echo.

"Lord, are they few in number who are to be saved?" How many will have access to the Reign? The subject was hotly debated in rabbinical circles. Who will be saved? The whole of humanity? Israel, to the exclusion of other nations? Only the just in Israel? Jesus refuses to answer. What good would it do to know the number of the elect? More important is to know what to do to belong to that number! "Try to come in through the narrow door." Try to follow Jesus, then. This is the first lesson of Jesus' reply.

A second lesson is grafted upon the first: the urgency of the decision. The feast is ready. All men and women are invited, from north and south, from east and west. But the door to the banquet hall is narrow, and the vestibule a cluttered one. And the hour is the last. Even now the axe swings for the root. The moment has come to decide for the Reign. It is time to invade the banquet hall, for the Master of the house is about to rise and shut the door. Then it will be too late for those who have not taken care to profit by the time of salvation! "It is not those who say, 'Lord, Lord!' who will enter the Kingdom of Heaven, but those who do the will of my Father." Some will appeal to their familiarity with the Master of the house. Their appeal will be in vain. They will claim their "rights." But they will be greeted only by a sign over the door: "Do Not Enter." By contrast, the joy of the patriarchs and prophets will be shared by the multitude of the poor come from the four corners of the earth.

Our hope is not intended as a means of glossing over our capitulations. Hope is not only revelation, but vocation. Our hope is not easy. It is provocation, and engagement in a dynamism that originates with the road to Jerusalem.

"Try to come in through the narrow door"! The name on the door is "Jesus." Oh, you prefer a road where there will be no ambushes? Very well. But then do not cry, "Injustice!" on the last day if you discover you have been running up a blind alley. "Try to come in through the narrow door." That door is the gate of Jerusalem, through which Jesus now will pass—the door of the passion. But what an escape into the infinite for the one who has chosen it and entered there! For it is the door to Easter.

"Try to come in through the narrow door"! How unhappy our hope would be, aroused as it is by such a call, were we to be abandoned to our own devices when it came to making a response! How insecure our hope would be, given over as it is to the hazards of a conversion, were that conversion to be the sole fruit of our own gyrations! But, thanks be to God, the Spirit comes to the rescue of our weakness: he knows that, in intervening on behalf of the faithful, he wills what God wills. Our hope will be ever a hope rescued.

■

Lord, give us to know your ways:
may we not die enmired in the clayey ruts
of our attachment to ourselves.
Open to us the door of life,
and may our hope, nourished by the Spirit,
bring us to eternity.

■

We have dined in your presence.
You have given us the body and blood of your Son.
Lord, set us on the road again:
let the passion of our Master
steep us to the quick,
to lead us to resurrection and new life
now and forevermore.

THURSDAY OF THE 30TH WEEK

COME WHAT MAY AND AGAINST ALL ODDS

Romans 8:31–39: Side by side with his absolute assurance of our salvation, Paul's other obsession is the precarious character of existence. Is not the creation to which we belong caught up in a perpetual process of change?

Our adoption as Christians by God is signed and sealed. But what we are to be as adopted daughters and sons has not yet been revealed. Since this is the case, have we no reason to fear lest, on the day of judgment, powers hostile to humanity may carry the day? These reflections lead the apostle to display before his readers' the long parade of pledges the Spirit has made to believers. Adopting an ancient literary technique, the forensic analogy, Paul engages in a kind of cross-examination. For the apostle, that God is on our side is altogether evident. Has he not delivered up his own Son for us? Furthermore, salvation is assured, since even the ambushes we encounter along our way represent the birth pangs of the new world. No power, then, can prevail over the divine love. God wills the salvation of those he has justified. As for the question of possible condemnation, Paul observes that, on the cross, it was sin, and sin alone, that was condemned. Nothing, then, can separate the human being from the Love made manifest in Christ Jesus.

Sure of God's love, the believer can call on him in moments of distress. *Psalm 109* is a complaint.

Luke 13:31–35: Herod has drafted a plan to do away with Jesus altogether. And his machinations leave Jesus supremely unconcerned. Jesus' death, freely accepted, will take place in Jerusalem, the city that murders prophets. His mission has consisted in gathering to himself the children of Jerusalem, but the majority of them have turned a deaf ear. They have not heard the appeal for conversion issued by the last of the prophets. It must be made clear to them that God will react to this rejection by forsaking his temple (cf. Ezek. 11:23).

Is it all over, then? Is this the last act? Does the curtain fall on an utter tragedy? Has the Word of grace been reduced to silence for good and all? One hope remains, actually. The temple has been forsaken, but only for a time . . . until the day when Jesus' hearers, whose cowardly silence today is fairly deafening, will be heard to sing: "Blessed is he who comes in the name of the Lord!" Although the death of us all (cf. vv. 1–9) shows us our sin and calls us to conversion, sin is no obstacle to the infinite patience of the One whose word is from everlasting to everlasting.

■

"I must proceed on course. . . ." There is a kind of necessity in the gospel, as if something more were at play here than Jesus' simple decision. There is more afoot here than an individual's loyalty to a project ever more patently doomed to failure. But neither is it a case of addle-pated, suicidal obstinacy. "I must. . . ." It is the very logic of the covenant: Jesus takes the road to Jerusalem, the city that murders prophets, because he is impelled to do so by the Spirit. "I have come to do your will"! After all, "The works of God must be made manifest." Here is the hidden mechanism of this journey to Jerusalem.

"I must proceed on course. . . ." This is the disciple's program. And as disciples we continue the journey, come what may and against all odds. For we are not on the road alone. How fragile a thing our hope would be, were it to be our personal possession. But this treasure is the property of an entire multitude. We participate in eternal life, even in this world, as members of a society that we might call—and our hearts beat high as we think of it—the Community of Hope of all centuries and all climes.

With our companions on the road—our companions in misery, frequently —we share the certitude of a happiness begun. Indeed is it for any other purpose that we are a people? "Who shall bring a charge against God's chosen ones? God, who justifies?" Each one of us can fail. The hope of the church cannot. Ordinarily, outward events upstage everything else in the human drama. But for the church, real history is the sacred history of the Body of Christ raised to life on the third day, that history of ours in which the last word belongs to Love. "Who will separate us from the love of Christ?" That love is the source of the disciple's assurance. We the people of God are patient because we have God's faithfulness as our pledge and warranty. The promise "must" be kept, God says.

Not that we are never impatient! The community of hope is both patient and impatient. Its patience convinces it that the glory of God will burst forth one day. But it is impatient precisely to hasten that day. Together with so many of our sisters and brothers who do not share our creed, we condemn human beings' injustices, their exploitation of one another, their murderous assaults on life—at home or thousands of miles away—because all of this constitutes evil, and we are impatient with evil. But we are particularly impatient with evil because, in our Christian eyes, it belongs to a world of the past, a world dead and gone, a world that has rotated on its axis and now bathes in a new dawn. It is the negation of the universe recreated by Good Friday and Easter. It is not only our human conscience that rebels. It is our resentment at the attempts of the old world to reclaim us. In evil we see the choking residue of a world that Jesus came to abolish in his blood.

"I must proceed on course. . . ." The "must" that sounds in our ears rings with the necessity of the Reign of God already come. In love received, we are the great conquerors. But this "must" is also the call of our project, our task, and that project has bogged down. Redemption is delayed. And this is precisely why we *must* keep marching to the fore, come what may and against all odds.

■

God, our hope,
what will separate us from your love?
    Not our sin, not our hesitations,
    not even our delays in following the trail your Son has blazed.
Nothing can withdraw us from you.
As this is our assurance,
grant us to live in the peace
    that comes with your grace:
for we must resume the journey
    that leads to eternity.

Mercy

The gospel is a proclamation. And it is Good News. Jesus speaks of God in story and parable. Only in tales, in comparisons, can we catch a glimpse of the incomprehensible behavior of God. When Jesus speaks of God he performs deeds. He receives at his table the outcast and "worthless." Only in deeds can we glimpse the life of God. "God so loved the world . . ." Saint John will say in his old age.

God so loved the world! This is the only profession of faith we are required to make in order to be faithful to the inheritance bestowed on us. God loves the world, and loves it with an incomprehensible, disproportionate love. The God revealed by Jesus is not a God in the image and likeness of ourselves! God is neither the guarantor of the world order, nor a super-power, nor a super-engineer surveying the scenario and blueprint of the world, nor the guardian of the social or moral order. God loves. Never again can a concept of God be without this attribute, this qualifier, which touches the human heart so profoundly, plunging to the very marrow of our being: God is love. Only Jesus —and only the Jesus whose word and deeds lead to the cross, only Jesus crucified—could have given us a glimpse of this: that God is a God in love. The God of the philosophers would tell us, "Whatever will be will be. All is chance and necessity. Strive to understand." The God of the sages would tell us, "Wait and see. You shall find Truth." The God of the moralists would tell us, "You have to. You must. It is your duty." The God of the ideologues would tell us, "What have you built? What struggle claims your engagement?" The God of Jesus Christ, because he is in love, asks only, "Will you?"

What a disarming, what a disarmed, "Will you?" Disarmed, because God is infinitely poor. Mercy is first of all God's own supplication: "Let me love you." And disarming, because God's call is infinitely challenging. Mercy is the most radical challenge that our being could ever be given.

Disarming and disarmed: behold, God. The gospels offer us only some stories and some deeds to impart to us some notion of an appeal that reaches down to our deepest being—to let us hear, faintly, what God wants to tell us: "I love you. And you . . . ?"

Servants of Grace (Luke 14:1–17:10)

Chapter 14 represents a studied contrast with chapter 13. The healing of the dropsy victim, precisely on a sabbath (14:1–6), is an exact replica of the healing of the crippled woman (13:10–17), with the sole exception that here we have no synagogue. The urgency of renunciation on the part of the disciples (14:25–35) corresponds to the necessity that Jesus die (13:31–33). But we find the dominant element of this section in the parable of the prospective guests at a great banquet (14:15–24). Chapter 13, as we have seen, concludes on a note of failure. Jesus has come right out and announced his death at Jerusalem and the forsaking of the temple. And yet the parable of the sterile fig tree, like those of the yeast and the mustard seed, presupposes a judgment that will be one of grace. This "death of God" will be only a temporary one. It will continue only long enough for the conversion of humanity.

Once more Jesus seizes the initiative. Once more he calls women and men to his banquet, addressing his invitation to all: the crippled, the blind and the lame, on all the highways of the world. He offers us a glimpse of God's infinite patience, a patience unwearied by human infidelities.

And suddenly the Pharisees are back, and with their eternal question. By what right does Jesus act in this manner? By the right God has to be God! In the parable of the prodigal son, as in those of the lost drachma and lost sheep, Jesus lays bare his Father's heart—a heart ready to rejoice because a child who had died has come back to life.

Not only this, but the Father invites the elder son to rejoice as well. The Father's joy is not complete as long as the reconciliation is less than total. Paradoxically, the elder son is invited to imitate the cunning of the devious manager (16:1–8). This parable is worthy of the greatest attention. "Managers" or stewards play an important role in Luke's gospel. They symbolize Jesus' disciples, since disciples must be concerned to distribute a proper share of bread to every hungering person. Jesus readily contrasts them with the Pharisees, then, whom he accuses of monopolizing the Law for their own advantage. The manager to Jesus' liking is the one who condones his Master's debts—the steward who has comprehended that he will never extricate himself from this plight of his own making without imitating the generosity of God himself. Here are the real disciples: "useless" servants, yes, but remember, servants of grace, and very aware of having been "graced" by God.

■

Be blessed, God our Father,
      for Jesus, your eternal Word, your Word of Light.
In him we know the secret of our life:
      you love us without reserve,
      and your mercy is beyond all measure.
Grant us to bear witness to this grace,
      and to be the artisans
      of a world renewed by your love.

GOD OF OUR FOREBEARS

Romans 9:1–5: The solemnity with which Paul opens this new chapter, and his appeal to two witnesses (the number required to establish incontrovertible evidence), Christ and the Spirit, indicate its importance in his eyes. His point is: Yes, he has become a Christian. But by no manner of means does he deny his roots. He is a son of Israel, and it is not in the merriment of his heart that he has ignored the opposition of so many of his compatriots to the message of the Christ. His reaction is even stronger than Moses' had been: Moses had offered merely to share the lot of his sisters and brothers (Exod. 32:32). Paul would choose annihilation, could that serve the salvation of his compatriots.

But make no mistake! As in the rest of his letter, the apostle's word is charged with hope. "Not that God's word has failed . . ."! Just as he has repeated his conviction of the salvation of humankind, now Paul proclaims the validity of that conviction for the particular case of Israel. Jacob's sons and daughters have a shining future in store! Of this Paul is altogether sure.

Psalm 147, crafted as a hymn, is yet another recital of the uninterrupted list of gifts received by Jacob-Israel.

Luke 14:1–6: Jesus heals another sufferer. But this time he forestalls the objections of one of the leading Pharisees. Yes, he knows very well that he is doing work on the sabbath. But precisely, it is one's view of the sabbath that should be changed. Jewish jurists regarded any healing activity as a medical procedure, and hence work, occupation. And this was forbidden on the sabbath day. But for Jesus the sabbath is, above all, the Lord's day. What better day could there be for doing good and proclaiming salvation?

Chapter 13 ends with Israel's apprisal of its sin and the abandonment of the temple. But God will seize the initiative once more. He means to dispatch his servants with an invitation for humanity. There will be a new banquet.

■

"Theirs were the adoption, the glory, the covenants, the lawgiving, the worship, and the promises; theirs were the patriarchs, and from them came the Messiah . . ."! How can the Church, in certain centuries, have read the scriptures, and then forgotten its origins and renounced the stock onto which it had been grafted? How can we have forgotten that, in our soul and our flesh, we are Semites?

How often must we hear that the Bible does not reveal God himself, but his image, refracted in the turbulence of a recalcitrant people? Chosen? This people? Yes, but in what sense? Surely because, in their resistance to the divine activity, they serve as both an example and a witness of a revelation that has no intention of resting on reason alone, but will appeal to the whole human being.

We recall the wonderful words of Peguy: "Lord, who molded them from this earth, are you surprised to find them earthy?" No, God is not surprised. Far from it. Their earthiness is precisely the occasion of God's love for them. God is determined to save the universe. So he must take human beings in their root, in their most nocturnal zone. Then he will see them burst into light in the dawning that is Christ. Could ever a people have been more privileged than Israel? Surely not. But what about Israel's failure to adapt to God's extraordinary call? Like the flight of the prodigal, it is their flight from God that is the very occasion of their election! O infinite tenderness of God, embracing this earth that cannot respond in kind, that his breath may descend there and stir it to life!

God chooses a people even in its unwillingness, its premeditated distance? Yes. God is ever present to this people, throughout its history, as the day is present just beyond the closed shutters and ready to stream in through the narrowest chink. It is God's impatience, accumulated, that constitutes his indefatigable patience.

O people chosen for our grace! Behold the earthy people whose God will ever be the Lord. Behold the people chosen, for our grace, in their very thickness and torpor. To rescue us from temptation, what else but a stronger temptation? And what temptation could be stronger than gift?

God of Abraham, Isaac, and Jacob,
God of Moses and God of the prophets,
God of the Word and God of the Book,
    God of the Land of Promise,
    of the Election and the Awaiting,
praised be your name forever!

O unfathomable mystery of your love:
    you remain forever the God of the children of Israel!
We, the new graft
    on the trunk of this revelation,
    beseech you:
Grant us to inherit their marvellous history!
And may it expand into communion
    through ages without end.

SATURDAY OF THE 30TH WEEK

IN AN APRON
Romans 11:1-2, 11-12, 25-29: Paul's reflections on the history of Israel tell him why he should believe in the ultimate salvation of the Jewish nation. When all is said and done, he argues, the current situation of the chosen people is no different from what it has been in the past. A few concrete examples, such as the rivalry between Jacob and Esau, show that the divine election has always been a free gift. It has always descended on a mere fraction of the carnal descendancy of Abraham. Indeed, what prophet has transmitted the promise to any but the chosen remnant? Today, this remnant —Israel according to the spirit—is composed of those who have clung to Christ.

But the divine election of some does not prevent others from playing a role in God's salvation plan. Thus Israel's refusal has made it possible to save the "nations." After all, that refusal induced the apostles to abandon the synagogues and go out to the pagans. A. Viard goes further: a mass-conversion of the Jews "would have entailed the maintenance of their particularism," while their rejection of the Christian message was the occasion of an explosion of the church and its openness to the pagans. But if the hardening of one part of Israel has made possible the conversion of non-Jews, what may one not expect from the plenary realization of God's design? All is grace!

Psalm 94 is a complaint, interspersed with a poem in the wisdom genre composed in the style of a refutation. The liturgy has concentrated on the verses expressing trust in God.

Luke 14:1, 7–11: "Do not sit in the place of honor. . . ." A lesson in humility? A counsel for those who would attain life? There will be Christians who will use Christ's words as a pretext to slip into the back pews in church! No, "none of the above." Jesus is speaking of the Reign of God. We need only observe that he is talking about a wedding feast. In biblical language a wedding feast always stands for God's covenant with humanity.

What is required for admittance to the divine wedding feast? The answer is very simple: a behavior just contrary to that of the Pharisees. The latter are altogether too self-assured. They set more store by their virtues and merits than by divine grace itself. They claim the first places in the Reign as well. Are they not called the "pure," the "separated"? The very name "Pharisee" is from *parûsh,* "separated," "set apart." They must learn that their attitude is the wrong one where the Reign of God is concerned. If they are indeed to have the first places one day, it will be because God will have freely bestowed these places on them. For God is about to take the initiative of a new call.

■

Then he rose from table, took an apron, and began to wash his disciples' feet. And he said to them, "What I do, I your Lord and Master, you also must do." God in an apron!—lovely scandal, summing up, simply of itself, the immense failure of Christianity when it attempts to replace the gospel with the good manners of the world. When God celebrates his Son's wedding he goes out looking for the poor, the sinful, the good-for-nothing, the crippled—and he washes their feet. God is the God of mercy, and therefore very different from the God of the Pharisees: the God of ceremonies for show, with reserved seating lest the high and mighty have to rub elbows with miserable common folk! God is the God of mercy, and his only law is humility.

Humility. A misunderstood virtue. Humility is the virtue that smacks of the soil, of humus, of truth patiently worked out, of grace received that becomes grace lived, of gift become interior law. The humble one is the poor one, who awaits all grace and judgment from God alone. Have you ever noticed the humility of genuine scholars? They are women and men of patience. Far from censuring everything, they are just the opposite of persons of doctrine, religious or political, who must always have the last word on everything.

God is humble. His Son stoops to the very soil of the tomb and the table of the sinful, without passing judgment. Because God is almighty, he invents forgiveness and love. Birds of a feather! When God brings us together at the wedding banquet of his Son, he alone knows our deep, internal appearance: we all bear on our interior countenances the look of his Son. And thanks to this resemblance, God can place us all in the same row.

■

God of the poor and the little,
you engage your omnipotence
in the manifestation of your mercy.
Create in us a heart of humility,
to receive your benevolence
and live by your grace.

■

Lord God,
you disconcert us ever:
at the table of your Reign,
the places of honor are for the poor.
Thanks be to you
for the tenderness you reveal to us in Jesus Christ.
Through him we hope to sit at table
at your eternal banquet.

MONDAY OF THE 31ST WEEK

FREELY AND GENEROUSLY

Romans 11:29–36: Aghast at the scandal of Israel's incredulity, Paul does all he can to integrate this attitude into the divine economy of salvation. In this fashion he demonstrates his fidelity to the thinking of the ancients, for whom nothing, not even the human being's refusal, escapes the divine omnipotence. This is the burden of verse 32, especially when it concludes, from the slavery in which disobedience has walled up the human being: "God has imprisoned all in disobedience that he might have mercy on all."

Once again the dominant idea is that of the remnant—the remnant of which God has systematically made use to save his people as a whole. What the Jews ultimately lack, says Paul, is an appreciation of the fact that salvation is

---

the fruit not of their specious privileges, but of grace. True, the disobedience of the sons and daughters of Israel has furnished occasion for the explosion of a church gone in search of the pagans. But the conversion of the Jews will become possible only when their present jealousy yields to gratitude for what God has done for them.

Gratitude, acknowledgment. . . . Paul expresses his admiration and wonder in a hymn that includes two Old Testament citations. The first, from Isaiah 40, observes that God has used the Exile to purify his people. The second repeats, with Job, that all is from God.

Psalm 69 is a complaint, concluding with a promise to celebrate Yahweh. Let the poor make festival—for God is on their side!

Luke 14:12–14: Despite the refusal encountered by his messenger, God is set to launch a new initiative. He is determined that the eschatological banquet will take place. Once more this initiative will be gratuitous. Its addresses will be the poor, the crippled, the blind, the lame, and all those to whom human beings assign the lowest places. In God's eyes they are precious, for they have nothing to turn to account, and so can have nothing to give in return.

■

"Then who has set the table where the bread awaits us? It is you, Jesus, who have led us to this repast" (From a popular French hymn). It is he who leads us to the table we set, and it is he, we know, who dons the apron of the slave to wash his disciples' feet. Our Lord and Master is the Servant. Jesus is "in our midst as one who serves," (Lk 22:27) then, one who presents himself in the frailty of a word so feebly transmitted, one who offers himself to us in the seeming insignificance of the banal everyday.

The words of today's gospel are not those of human wisdom or facile calculation. They unveil the depths of the heart of God, in order to convince our own hearts. For we are invited to a wedding—Jesus' wedding. God is marrying the world. "When you're invited to a wedding you don't take your friends along," says the world. But the etiquette of the Reign and the wisdom of the world are poles apart. In a world where everything is all calculation and measure, where profit is the norm and success the highest value, in a dog-eat-dog world where my neighbors count for nothing unless they serve my interests, and satisfy my needs and desires, in this world where the first are those who know how to take care of themselves, we receive this word as a call to conversion. Suddenly our scale of values is reversed, upset. Now the great one is the one who serves. The living are those who have died to themselves. The wealthy are those who free themselves from wealth to be filled to overflowing with pure gift. Behold the gospel revolution. God has freely called us, and our life must become a parable of this gratuity.

Give without counting the cost. Keep no books on your virtues. They are God's grace. Do not trim your universe to the confines of your expediency: is not God's love—your destiny—universal? You are called to glory, and that glory bursts forth in the supreme gift of Golgotha. If you hear God's invitation, you are blessed, for the one who receives you at his table is already saying to you: My friend, come up higher—in you my grace has not been in vain.

■

Lord God,
will your surprises ever have an end?
Your Son must take the last place
to enter into his glory.
May your Spirit overturn our evidences
and initiate us into the new world
that you inaugurate through Jesus
now and forever.

■

We bless you, God our Father,
Parent of all women and men.
You call yourself Love,
and your tenderness awakens our love.
Your omnipotence becomes our self-despoilment,
and you promote us to royal rank.
Your wealth is grace,
and your Spirit makes us the heirs
of your well-beloved Son.
Be blessed,
you who cause us to ascend to the table of mercy.
Be blessed for the immense multitude of humanity
who hunger for feasting and love,
for renewal and resurrection.
With them, poor in their poverty
and rich with your presence,
O God, we bless you.

BELONGING

Romans 12:5-16: As Paul begins to bring his letter to a close, chapter 12 invites the reader to recall the various themes that letter has developed. They are themes springing from a meditation on salvation history, and they can be summarized as follows: God calls all men and women without exception; his salvation, based on faith rather than on privilege, is offered to Jews and pagans alike. Whatever be their origin, then, Christians ought to demonstrate this fundamental oneness of human nature.

How are they to accomplish this? Essentially, in daily life. "Renouncing all self-seeking, Christians will seek the good of others, and do all that is in them to avoid what might threaten their solidarity among themselves or with any of their neighbors." Christians form one people, as there is but one mystery: the reconciliation of human beings with one another, with creation and God (cf. Eph. 3:6). To manifest this oneness in a life surrendered to God, as Christ has surrendered his life to God—this is spiritual worship.

Concretely, the apostle lists a series of charisms, services inspired by the Spirit. He adopts the celebrated comparison of the body and its members, which he has used before, in 1 Corinthians 12. In Corinthians, however, his concern was to show the unity of the body identified with Christ. Here he emphasizes that the actions of the various members of the body are to be wholly and entirely at the service of that body.

In keeping with Paul's own exhortations, *Psalm 131* invites us to humility.

Luke 14:15-24: "Lord, are they few in number who are to be saved?" (Lk 13:23). The question supposes very strict conditions for admittance to the banquet. Actually it is the wrong question. Despite the refusal of the first to be invited—and invited long in advance, in accordance with eastern custom—the master of the house prepares to dispatch his servants with fresh invitations. The couriers will begin in the squares and streets of Jerusalem. Then they will take to the highways and byways of the world: they will go out to the pagans.

But the parable reveals all its richness only in contrast with chapter 13 as a whole. That section of our readings ended with rejection on the part of the Jews and the divine threat to abandon the temple. The parable reveals God's response: God proceeds with his dialogue with humanity. What response will be forthcoming on the part of the latter? Will human beings continue to refuse these ever more pressing invitations? Or like the blind and the lame, who have nothing to lose, will they take advantage of this opportunity and surrender to God?

■

Call the people from the public squares to the banquet hall! It must be full! The parable shows us something out of the ordinary, something we have never seen before. And it is a scandal and a provocation.

Our parable speaks of God. Through Jesus, God tells his story. God is like a king who has gone to a great deal of trouble to prepare a wedding banquet for his son, all through the bustling, anxious days that precede such a celebration. And he has sent word: "Come along, everything is ready." But the aroma from the kitchen can be enticing, the table beautifully set, the lamps lighted and the festal board strewn with flowers—and the dinner can still be without the one essential: What if no one comes? Imagine the magnificent royal table—without diners! The expected guests—old acquaintances, friends, relatives—have turned a deaf ear to the royal invitation. And God is left alone with his meal. Will he extinguish the lamps? No, he sends for the poor, the crippled, the blind and the lame. No one—but no one—will be shut out of the great feast! From this moment forward, the table in God's house is set for all.

God sends invitations to his Son's wedding. To whom? To a dream humanity, holy and pure? When the bride is a profligate who has squandered and soiled her innocence in the back alleys of history? When she bears the stigma of such immense promiscuity? Here is a King's Son who will scarcely "marry well"! "She's not good enough for him," think the invited guests, and send regrets. But the poor, the kind of persons who "get left out," rejoice. God has not shuddered and turned away, sickened at the sight of sin. God has no illusions about humanity. His tenderness takes on, by turns, accents of betrayed love, jealousy, threat and insane passion. But he keeps his incredible promise, and no person or thing can make him do otherwise. "I will espouse you to me forever" (Hos. 2:21). You will be reclining at table with Zacchaeuses, Matthews, Mary Magdalenes, the blind one of Siloam and the paralytic of Capernaum, the Samaritan leper and the forgiven adulteress. God is going on a spree. His Son is marrying the human race!

God is racing through the town squares today. Can it be true? Are we invited to God's royal dinner, to the wedding of the King's Son, to the paschal table? Out of the question. Better think up a convenient excuse and send regrets. Ah, if humanity but suspected God's designs on her! It is precisely lame, crippled, blind humanity whom God invites to the wedding—and not the citizens of some dreamland! Do not expect the artificial hilarity, the momentary exuberance, of a soulless business lunch. Our gladness will be in proportion to our surprise at finding ourselves there—right there in the banquet hall, despite our handicaps and our sufferings.

■

God, whose love is beyond anything we can measure,
    blessed be your name!
You open wide the doors of your house
    and we poor human beings enter,
    to sit at the banquet
    where your Son will give himself as food.
Grant that we may sing your goodness and kindness
    all the days of our lives,
    till the day you clothe us in the wedding garment
    of eternity.

WEDNESDAY OF THE 31ST WEEK

FOLLOWERS

Romans 13:8–10: Having reminded Roman Christians of their obligation to submit to legitimate authority and, in verse 7, of their duty to pay taxes, Paul draws their attention to the only debt that they can never totally repay: that of mutual love. But as he is also addressing Jewish Christians, so concerned to comply with the prescriptions of the Law, he also insists that this charity attains the goal set by the Law. Jesus, too, had declared that there is no greater commandment than that of love of God and neighbor.

"Happy the man who is merciful and lends to those in need." *Psalm 112* welcomed pilgrims to the temple and congratulated them on their fidelity to the divine law.

Luke 14:25–33: The divine invitations wax in their urgency. Human beings must take on their responsibilities. The perspective of judgment is not absent from chapter 14, if we understand judgment, like death, as what makes life a serious matter. God's patience is not weakness. Jesus knows that his call is the last we shall receive.

And yet we must also understand what we commit ourselves to in following Jesus. This is what the two parables recall. The authentic disciple is the one who places Jesus Christ above all else, and is ready to share his lot. Verse 33, obviously appended, shifts the sense of the text and speaks of the renunciation of earthly goods, a favorite theme of Luke.

■

What does Jesus want, then? If we look at the gospel the answer is clear. Jesus has come to defend God's cause and take sides with humanity. God's will be done!—the message of the coming of the Reign. "Thy will be done." This is how it will be with Jesus from now on—to his very passion. The will of God is his sole rule, and it must be the same for his disciples. "Whoever wishes to be my follower must deny his very self, take up his cross. . . ." (Lk 9:23).

To follow means to hear a word that is grace. The reason why the path followed requires a determinate behavior is that it is forged by *someone*. Gospel "morality" is primarily an attachment to a living person. Liberality, gift and grace precede norm, ethics, demand and precept. Each of us is called, each is offered salvation, and no other demand is made on us but that we hear and follow. The very exhortations we hear are but the ineluctable conclusions of the proclamation of God's Reign.

"Follow" also suggests a dynamism. The road is journey and promise. Reflect before you build your tower. But never forget that "unless the Lord build the house, they labor in vain who build it" (Ps. 127:1)!

"Follow" also means to strive for a goal. God demands more than a particular external comportment. God requires your heart. He absolutely does not want only good fruit. He wants a good tree, too.

Jesus leaves for Jerusalem. There is no time for hesitation. The axe is swinging for the root of the tree. From the viewpoint of the ultimate, the definitive—the Reign of God—we can only choose the rough ascent of Calvary, the ascent of a life surrendered, and destined to burst forth in resurrection.

■

While we still have today
*   to struggle along our path,*
God our Father, we pray to you:
You entrust your Reign to those alone
*   who have sold all they have*
*   to go out to meet your Christ.*

May the Spirit rekindle our ardor
    when the temptation comes to turn back.
We offer you our little faith.
Do not measure your grace.
May it enable us to reach the end of the journey.

■

Who could follow your Son, Lord our God,
    unless you came to set us free
    by the gift of your Spirit?
Strip us of our false security.
    May the cross of Jesus
    be the foundation of our hope.
We build our lives, then,
    on the sole assurance of your love,
    a love that abides forever.

■

Be blessed, God of love.
You give us bread for our journey,
    and, in this bread,
    the daring to wish to be disciples of your Son.
Renew in us the freedom
    to renounce ourselves
    and follow him to the end—
    the Christ: the Way, the Truth, the Life.

THURSDAY OF THE 31ST WEEK

EXTRAVAGANCE

Romans 14:7–12: In a discourse to the Romans on charity, Paul will surely have to deal with the friction arising in such a heterogeneous community. In Rome as elsewhere, there were the "strong" and the "weak"—Christians profoundly liberated by the proclamation of the good news, and the more timorous, especially those who still felt bound by the prescriptions of Jewish law. The apostle advises both groups to act in conformity with their respective consciences. All, whoever they are, are persons of good faith, and what they do they do for the Lord, who is their only head. The Lord alone can judge their intentions.

Psalm 27 fuses a complaint (vv. 7–14) with a royal psalm of trust (vv. 1–6). Today's liturgy places its emphasis on the trust of those who know in whom they have placed their hope.

Luke 15:1–10: The context of chapter 14 raises a question. By what right does Jesus promise sinners they will be saved? Chapter 15 answers the question, above all in the parable of the prodigal. And the answer is most remarkable in its simplicity. Jesus claims no right. He simply imitates his Father's attitude.

The parable of the prodigal has been read on Saturday of the second week of Lent. It is preceded in the text by those of the lost sheep and lost coin, which express God's zeal to bring back the sinner and the joy that reigns when someone lost is found again. These two parables are not of a piece, however. The parable of the lost sheep is recounted against a Jewish background, while that of the Greek drachma envisages the pagan world. Incidentally, we shall do well to recall that Matthew 18 uses the parable of the lost sheep to underscore the responsibility of the heads of the church.

■

We may as well come right out and say it. Jesus' parables do not have very likely endings. In everyday life the shepherd will, of course, prefer to save the ninety-nine sheep than go running after the hundredth. A woman who loses a coin will shrug her shoulders and try to forget her loss. After all, as popular wisdom has it: "A bird in the hand is worth two in the bush."

True enough. But Jesus is speaking of God and the ways of the Reign! To reveal the Father to us, Jesus can only tell a story. After all, God is totally different from what we think. God is extravagant. Jesus alone can speak of God in this way, because he speaks from experience.

Jesus' experience! He has watched sinners listen to his voice: Matthew and Zacchaeus have shared his table, publicans have received the proclamation of the Reign, and so many rejected and marginal persons have flocked to his side. The lost sheep that was found again? Jesus has been there. The feverish quest of the wielder of that broom? Jesus has seen her—in the leap of his own heart toward all the lost sons and daughters of Israel. Jesus has lived his parables. In narrating them, he invites his hearers to acknowledge the action of God in his own dumbfounding deeds.

Extravagant God! God does not act like God! God is not reasonable. God abandons everything to look for one sheep that he may or may not find. He scrapes his feet and he goes on looking. Crowned with thorns, Jesus will yet proclaim his Father's love. They tell us love is blind. Lovers do unexpected, imprudent things. Shall we ever be able to speak of the God of Jesus and fail to mention that love makes him behave foolishly? "Come on, let's celebrate!" God says. "I've found what I'd lost!"

■

God of great patience,
    you go in search of us.
    Ever you welcome us in your grace.
Grant us to find the way that leads to you,
and your tenderness will fill our joy to the full.

■

In gladness we give you thanks,
    God our Father,
    through Jesus, your living Word.
Jesus is the shepherd who surrenders his life
    that a new people may be born.
His mercy bars sinners' roads,
    his arms reach out to receive the wandering,
    he holds all men and women in one love.
Tenderness is mightier than sin, then,
    and love has conquered death.
Therefore with all who hear his voice,
    and all who are borne up by his presence,
    God our Savior, we sing your love.

FROM FRIDAY OF THE 31ST WEEK

TO SATURDAY OF THE 33RD WEEK

Faith Saves Us

The gospel is a provocation to resurrection. It sets before our eyes two scales of values, and two paths of life before our feet. There is the path of slavery and death. And then there is the path of liberation and communion. Faith is a choice and a risk, a logic and a commitment.

But while the gospel is a challenge, a demand to be lived, and while this makes it a new Law, its provocative call is not satisfied with just any response. The provocation of the gospel is a call to actualize in the present the gift already bestowed, a challenge to give thanks for a grace already made manifest. Our response will be, "Increase our faith" (Lk 17:5). Somewhere within us we have already experienced the violence of the gospel, and tasted the newness of mercy. True, so often we have heard the cry of the gospel and resisted with a stubbornness that rivals the malicious strength of our sins themselves. But has our deepest heart not already been swept toward the Reign of Love? That Reign is here in our midst. It is here in our hesitating acceptance of a Word come from somewhere afar.

It is here in our little, self-seeking charity. It is here in a stuttering prayer. Yes, our hearts already flicker with enough of the light of the paschal victory that we venture to say that the gospel has "taken" in our lives—somewhat as we say that faith has already saved us.

The victory of the gospel is no longer a mere possibility, or a temporary alternative. The victory of the gospel is sure and definitive. And this is doubtless why we can look at everything—our lives, even our infidelities— with new eyes. The call has already received a response in our lives. The Spirit of the Son has been given to us. And this is doubtless why we still dare risk a response to the challenge of grace, and reach out to the mighty hands that welcome us even now. For good and all, we are daughters and sons.

■

Lord, eternal Father, blessed be your name!
You manifest your mercy
*   and raise us up to joy.*
How could we ever be separated from your love?
Who could ever question
*   what we are by your grace?*

You are for us,
*   who can be against us?*
God, our help, be blessed eternally.
May our Savior, your Son Jesus,
*   bring you our hymn of thanksgiving!*

DECIDING

Romans 15:14–21: In his peroration as in his exordium, Paul seeks to justify the project of his letter. Some will judge his efforts to have been somehow "out of line." For one thing, why has he written to a community that he has not founded? For another, are his addresses not world-renowned for their faith and knowledge? The apostle's justification is the mission entrusted to him by God, which he recalls in terms calculated to underscore both its sacred character and its specificity. Paul has been sent to proclaim the Good News to the pagans, and to make those pagans an offering acceptable to God (Rom 12:1). His pride is the assurance he has in knowing that he has acted in communion with Christ Jesus, as the spiritual power accompanying his ministry will attest. As long as he lives, the apostle will have but one desire— to carry the Good News ever further, and one rule of conduct, not to go where others have preached before him.

"Sing joyfully to the Lord, all you lands. . . ." (Ps 98). The toil of laborers like Paul have shown the world the justice of God!

Luke 16:1–8: the parable of the prodigal. It is interesting to compare the father's expressions with those of his elder son in their dialogue. "This son of *yours,*" says the brother, contemptuously. "This *brother of yours,*" the father retorts—reminding the elder son of his responsibilities. After all, the joy of the parents of a family is complete only when reconciliation is complete. And the Father's forgiveness comes by way of the church's forgiveness.

The parable of the manager pursues the same idea. Is Jesus referring to an actual incident? A manager, a steward, was in deep difficulties in his employment. He is reported to have extricated himself from a delicate situation, and even made friends, by means of a stratagem as daring as it was devious. How surprised Jesus' hearers must have been to hear the Master compliment the dishonest servant!

But as a matter of fact, what is the basis of the Master's compliment? To see the answer, we must situate the parable in a much broader context. In so doing we shall see it as a summary of the whole gospel of Luke. In chapter 12 we have already heard of a "faithful, farsighted steward" charged by his master with dispensing to all their ration of bread. In Luke 6, we learned that this ration is to be abundant: "Be compassionate, as your Father is compassionate" (Lk 6:36)—that is, in a measure "pressed down, shaken together, running over. . . ." (Lk 6:36–38). We may well imagine that Luke recalled these words as he contemplated the scene of the manager receiving his master's debtors and writing off what they owed. And suddenly he saw that scene as an image of the revelation of divine grace, which now opened a new age for humanity. "Farsighted stewards" are Christians who imitate with their own sisters and brothers the very forgiveness of the Father.

■

Now, here is a capable individual if ever there was one. He knows how to make decisions! Blessed is such a one! God willing, this beatitude will describe Jesus' disciple as well.

For it is not those who cry "Lord, Lord!" who will be saved, but those who do the will of God (Mt 7:21). Our faith would be ludicrous indeed were it not a decision to change the course of things. Faith is not a matter of "Live and let live." Faith is a choice we make for a time of crisis.

God has been gracious with us. He has "graced" us without calculating and without reneging. Now is the time of crisis. It demands a decision in keeping with the urgency of the situation. We are not saved because we recommend ourselves to God by our merits. We are saved because God wishes it so. We run a risk, then. For we must rely more on God than on our good works.

"God has 'graced' you and loves you. Return him his grace!" A decision in keeping with the urgency of the situation? To believe is not only to hear the word. It is also to be attentive to the path traced out by that word. Love begets love. Our wonder at the Word of grace opens an unsuspected space for us, and an unsuspected future.

Instead of bobbing in the backwaters of death, begotten by values helpless to bestow life, we can now respond to a word borne on the breath of a recreation.

The wily manager has been obliged by circumstances to take the necessary decisions and invent a new life for himself. In ourselves, the gospel is a challenge to resurrection.

■

Lord our God, you call us
to enter your Reign.
The end of the ages has come.
It is the hour of faith.

We pray to you, then:
by your Spirit, set our hearts free.
Intensify our decision.

The time has come
to follow in the footsteps of your Son.

■

Lord our God,
in giving us, in this Eucharist, the life of your son,
you commit us to live by his own love.
Grant that we may faithfully manage
the part of the Reign you entrust to us,
that one day we may enter into possession
of the inheritance you promise us.

SATURDAY OF THE 31ST WEEK

THE GOODS OF THE EARTH

Romans 16:3-9, 16, 22-27: Paul's letter has consisted of a series of lengthy disquisitions, and we are gratified to discover a warm, affectionate close. Here is language in which we can feel the intimacy prevailing between the apostle and the church of Rome. Here is a list of names of pioneer Roman Christians and their families! Paul is no stranger after all, in this church not of his founding.

The letter closes with a doxology that has analogies with the themes Paul will develop in a later day, in the so-called "letters from captivity." We are struck by its beauty and majesty. The church, after its long contemplation of its past, is "glad to be alive in the age when the name of Jesus Christ revealed becomes the key to universal history and the destiny of every human being for all time to come."

Jesus Christ manifested! Let all God's creation give thanks to its creator. (Ps 145).

Luke 16:9-15: "I have it! Here is a way to make sure that people will take me into their homes when I am let go" (Lk 16:4). Expanding on the theme of the manager's reflections, Luke now favors us with a series of verses that interpret the parable in the sense of a lesson on the right use of money. These verses are based on a series of puns in the Semitic style, an interplay between the words *mamón* ("money") and *aman* (the "worthy," the "genuine"). What is to be done with Money the Deceiver, Money the false God, a power capable of enslaving the world? Imitate the manager. Like him, make friends to receive you—in heaven.

153

At stake is the difference in behavior that will distinguish the authentic disciple from a Pharisee (v. 14). To illustrate that difference, at the beginning of the chapter Luke contrasts the genuine manager, who is concerned to distribute a fair share of bread to each of his fellow servants, from the Pharisee, who is not only the friend of money and honors, but above all the proprietor of the Law. Thus chapter 16 once more presents the theme of greed, previously developed in chapter 12. To the Pharisees, who have not understood the meaning of the invitation addressed to the poor and sinful, Jesus retorts that there is but one admissible attitude on the part of one who has received the revelation of the divine gratuity: the imitation of that gratuity. Woe to the one who hoards this grace to selfish advantage, like the Pharisee, or like the rich farmer piling up his grain in his barns! (See Luke 12:16ff.). Such an attitude can only breed death. The true, the genuine disciple is the one who "manages" this grace to the profit of all humanity, and thus behaves as a trustworthy steward. The hoarder serves Mammon. The true disciple serves God. And these two services (these two religions, really) are incompatible.

■

"The children of darkness are more astute than the children of light!" Jesus has taken sides in the story that has the whole countryside talking. He is astounded at the faithless steward's ingenuity. And once again we are constrained, under the impact of the gospel, to transcend our spontaneous outlook on things and come to Jesus' viewpoint. Then Jesus continues: "No servant can serve two masters." In setting this wily steward before our eyes as an example, Jesus means to lead us to a discovery of the finitude, the meaning, of what we may call the "goods of the earth."

As if it went without saying, we are told: money is made to be shared, tables to be sat at, words to communicate with, culture for an understanding of others, and warmth of heart for consoling the lonely—for snatching from their loneliness anyone isolated by misfortune or grief. Money, intelligence, culture, art, love, are all forces tending, in their profound dynamism, to gather, to assemble, to unite. And we call all these forces "goods of the earth" precisely because, of themselves, their thrust is toward the creation of relations. They "reconnect." They engender communion. And that is the "good" of these "goods."

The goods of the earth are "goods" because they are intended for sharing. But, to our misfortune, we so often pervert them. As if we did not know that to live is to love, to create bonds, we utilize these goods to assert ourselves against others, to crush, to dominate, to escape having to strike or maintain any solidarity with others in our lives.

When our pride or our hearts pervert these forces, we change their meaning. Thus we change their name as well. The gospel calls the goods of the earth by the monstrous name of "riches"! The Reign of God is built in acceptance, in forgiveness, in sharing, in mutual responsibility, and in a community of sisters and brothers. Money, on the other hand, locks us greedily up in our treasures. You cannot serve God and Money. They are exact opposites.

Here, then, is the call and challenge of the Word of God, which once more places two scales of values before our eyes, and two pathways before our feet, along which to lead our lives: a way of death and a way of communion. Clearly, we have already answered the call, the challenge, in part—here and now. Behold our goods: the bread and wine of our open tables, a gesture of peace that becomes a promise to live in communion. God accepts our simple gifts. His Spirit steeps them, transmutes them—and behold, our poor goods of earth become the goods of the Reign of God.

■

God of generosity,
in Jesus Christ you have given us all things.
We pray to you:
>   *may he be the treasure of our lives,*
>   *and give us knowledge of the Reign*
>   *where all is grace.*

MONDAY OF THE 32ND WEEK

THE PRAYER OF FAITH

Wisdom 1:1–7: Surely the author of the Book of Wisdom, the last book of the Old Testament to be written (mid-first century B.C.), hoped to win a hearing with pagan readers. But mainly he was addressing his coreligionists. To these Jews, shocked and disturbed as they were at the prestige of the Greek culture they encountered in Alexandria, he proposes, like his predecessors, a quest for the authentic wisdom—the wisdom that comes from God and that can only be obtained by the virtue of an exemplary life. He recommends above all a great simplicity of heart, for God is pleased with neither deceitful thoughts nor hypocritical hearts.

As for defining this wisdom, the author of the Book of Wisdom does not seem to have gone beyond his predecessors. And yet he "has taken a decisive step in the direction of a mythical, speculative divinization" (G. von Rad). For he makes an effort to "fine-tune" his definition of wisdom by taking advantage of the wealth of the Greek vocabulary. He calls wisdom "spirit." In chapter 7 he will speak of the "breath" of the divine omnipotence, and will characterize the radiance of the Almighty's glory as "resplendent."

Psalm 139, the prayer of an innocent, contains a lengthy reflection on the divine omniscience, thereby echoing the exhortation from the Book of Wisdom.

Luke 17:1-6: The discourse ends with directives to the disciples bearing on the whole of community life: occasions of scandal, forgiveness, faith and the like. Let us recall once more that "scandal" in the Bible does not mean a bad example. A scandal is a trap laid along someone's path, something to cause a person to stumble. Thus Jesus has been the occasion of a fall for the Jews whenever, to their great astonishment, he invites sinners to his table.

But Luke focuses on the astonishment aroused by the revelation of the divine grace. Like God, the disciple ought to give in abundance—and hence forgive as often as necessary. This is how the Christian communities, animated by the Spirit, ought to live. "Increase our faith," the disciples beg (Lk 17:5). Jesus will respond to their petition at his last meal, as he strengthens the faith of Peter.

■

Lord, increase our faith! Jesus has warned us in advance. And so, in response, the church walks its path repeating this humble prayer: Enable us to discover faith, and the newness of the Reign! Increase our faith, for we are of this world and we cling to it. Shall we ever reach that other shore with Jesus, shall we ever climb that bank and find God? Increase our faith! See how we keep on praying, over the years. We pray and we pray, but we see no results. Increase our faith, for we do not see the will of God being realized. We do not see temptations subsiding, evil disappearing. We do not see the Reign of God becoming reality.

"Increase our faith!" In response to Jesus' forewarnings, we have only this humble prayer to offer. Ah, really only this? No. . . . For if this invocation rises to our lips, must it not be that, somewhere in the depths of us, we have already tasted this new reality, already experienced the violence of faith? Must not that grace have already borne the deepest part of our being to the farther shore? If we refuse to resign ourselves to the fragility of our successes in changing the face of the earth—if we "get back to work," despite so many defeats, which are our grief, and so much half-heartedness, which is our shame—if, confronted with such

flimsy results, we are nevertheless "darned stubborn," and stay on our guard—must it not be that the strength of faith has already swept the deepest part of our heart into the kingdom of love?

"Increase our faith!" It is the call that comes to us from elsewhere, surely, the call from the realm of our desire, that endlessly rekindles within us, despite our failures and our cowardice, the irrepressible desire to love.

By faith, then, which is a vigil, a new order is inaugurated, at once a quest and a promise—which, once fulfilled will endure forever: the Reign of God.

■

God, Lord of the unexpected,
    in you are our lives,
    with you rests our future.
Let not the vicissitudes of this world
    lead us to despair to the depths of our soul,
nor let the challenge of the impossible
    drag us to earth utterly.
Each morning revive in us our faith
    in a world re-created by your love.
Crown the deed you have begun:
    may our faith be a match for your promise,
    and our vigilance to the measure of your will—
    your will to hold us in your embrace
    for all eternity.

TUESDAY OF THE 32ND WEEK

BY GRACE
Wisdom 2:23–3:9: The wisdom literature had always been interested in the destiny of the individual. The Book of Wisdom is no exception to this rule, and in the first chapters the author is manifestly concerned with the lot of the just who have died before receiving their reward. His response is interesting, as it benefits both from the development of the idea of the resurrection of the dead, and from Platonic philosophy, especially the doctrine of the immortality of the

soul. At once the question arises: Is the Book of Wisdom applying the notion of survival to the soul alone? Or does it understand it of the body as well? The question is a disputed one. Many authors admit that the glorification of the just (3:7) and their eschatological participation in the government of the nations (3:8), of which we read in this passage, imply some manner of bodily survival. But the most characteristic thing about the doctrine with which we are confronted is that the notion of immortality seems, as it were, included in the present life. For the author, true death is not of a physical, but of a spiritual order. Already present in the life of the impious, this death will become manifest in the beyond. By contrast, the life of the just will be eternally prolonged in God.

The end of *Psalm 34*, in the alphabetical genre, also transmits a wisdom teaching concerning the respective lot of the just and the impious.

Luke 17:7–10: Verses 7 through 10 complete this section of the gospel of Luke, which opened with chapter 14 and was entirely devoted to the theme of gratuity. The familiar personage of the servant is with us once more, together with the scene of the heavenly banquet. Once more the passage underscores the gratuity of service: the disciples' sole title to glory is that they are the servants of grace. We note, too, that community service is illustrated by the images of the laborer and the shepherd.

■

"If you had faith the size of a mustard seed . . . !" Jesus had told them. A grain of mustard? Now, that's really small! A negligible quantity. But what a taste!

If you had a little faith! But faith is not what you think it is. The fidelity of the believer is not that of the beast of burden, stomping straight ahead, with nary a falter, and nary a new idea. Faith is a regard, an outlook, a light, a way of seeing the world as God sees it, an out-of-the-ordinary way of living. Believers are eccentrics, who let God do anything he wishes with them. With God they are like a fish in water. Whatever they do, they know that the doing of it is a gift from God. They are, shall we say, in complicity with God. Shall we simply sit down and wait, seeing that we are useless servants? "When you have done all you have been commanded to do, say, 'We are useless servants.' " When you have done all. . . . Can love be discovered anywhere else but where it has been patiently engendered? Love is at once a gift and a quest, a grace and a birthgiving. The word is at once received and returned, learned and invented. Prayer is at once revelation and invocation, enlightenment and combat. When you have done all. . . . What would love be without the deeds that enflesh it, what would the word be without the syllables that search it out, prayer without the desire of the heart—faith without life?

When you have dared invent charity, dared babble the prayer whose words leave you so unsatisfied, when you have permitted your desire to find God to grow, and the breath of the Spirit to rise up within you—then, in wonderment and as a sort of by-product, you discover love right in your lap. Word is ever-astonishing encounter, prayer seduction, and faith a revelation. You have done all, and all has been given to you. By grace.

■

God of the unexpected,
blessed be your name.
Your grace is our aid,
your promise our assurance.
and our very faith but another gift of your goodness.
Therefore we beseech you:
fill us beyond all hope,
that our fidelity may gasp in astonishment
at your gift to us
through everlasting ages.

■

Father of heaven,
you call us to cooperate in your work:
blessed be your name.
You have given us to share the bread
that is the strength of our faith.
Grant increase to what you have preserved,
that our fidelity may respond to the gift you bestow on us
in Jesus, your Son,
whom we bless forevermore.

Face to Face with the Coming Reign (Luke 17:11–19:28)

"On his journey to Jerusalem. . . ." The die is cast. The road ends in Jerusalem.

What will be the consequences for human beings? Will they be willing to link their destiny to that of the "Son of Man"? To do so they will have to acknowledge Jesus as their only source of salvation. This is what the Samaritan does. Healed along with his companions, he alone retraces his steps and prostrates himself before the source of life.

When will the Reign of God come? The rabbinical schools had striven to determine the signs of this coming, never thinking to seek them in the ordinary things of every day—in the very things in which the Reign will be manifested. Then let them reread the story of Noah, or of Lot! People ate, drank, married. . . . "When the Son of man comes, will he find any faith on the earth?"

Pray! Pray so as not to enter into temptation, so as not to be lacking in faith, so as not to doubt the Reign! One must pray without ceasing, for the Reign is a thing received. In the parable of the Pharisee and the tax-collector (Lk 18:9–14), Jesus contrasts the attitude of the Pharisee, so glued to himself, with that of the tax-collector, who is so open to the unexpected. Riches, of whatever kind, can befog the way to the Reign (18:18–30). That road is negotiable only by those who have a heart to receive (18:15–17).

For it is the road to Jerusalem. We are no longer far from the city that murders prophets. Already we are in Jericho, the gateway to the Land of Promise. Two persons await Jesus here. The first will show him the way. He is blind. The second will offer him hospitality. He is a tax-collector. Each of them, in his own fashion, will welcome his salvation.

■

You have left us in charge of your house,
*   God our Father.*
Will we be bold, trustworthy managers?

Your word is life.
*   What will we do with the Good News?*
Your love is passion.
*   Will we live to the limit the exigencies of the Law?*

Give us faith's daring,
and the fidelity of those who know
*   that their treasure is in the future,*
*   promised by you for everlasting.*

SUMMONED TO SALVATION

Wisdom 6:1-11: Chapters 6-11 place an encomium of wisdom on the lips of Solomon himself, the wise ruler par excellence. Solomon is represented as addressing his royal peers, especially the rulers of pagan lands. His exhortation, reminiscent of Psalm 2:10, emphasizes the responsibilities inherent in the exercise of authority, which has its origin in God.

Psalm 81 is a psalm of judgment. It contains a prophetic oracle, probably directed against the kings of Israel, whom it reminds of their sacred duties of justice and the protection of the weak. Verses 6 and 7 thunder with the language of a death sentence.

Luke 17:11-19: "I must proceed on course today, tomorrow, and the day after, since no prophet can be allowed to die anywhere except in Jerusalem" (Lk 13:31). Jesus is on the way to his fate, and the question arises for those who, from the outset, have heard the Word of grace: Will they follow Jesus to the end? Will they go with him to Jerusalem? To be sure, the invitation to enter God's salvation is gratuitous. But it calls for a commitment of the whole person. The temptation to hesitate—in other words, to refuse—is very great, and it is not without reason that Luke urges Christians to reflect very carefully (cf. 14:28-32). The church is a people of individuals with minds of their own!

And we have the story of the ten lepers, nine Jews and one Samaritan. All ten had been healed. All ten had obeyed Jesus' order to "show themselves to the priests." But only one returned to Jesus to thank him. Only one understood that henceforth it was neither at Jerusalem nor on Mount Gerizim that one will celebrate worship agreeable to God, but in the person of Christ. It is he one must follow now, in life as in death.

■

This passage could easily have been no more than the account of a healing. A leper comes to Jesus. In conformity with the dispositions of Jewish law, he stands at a distance. But he cries, "Jesus, Master, have pity on me!" Jesus sees him and calls, "Go show yourself to the priests!" And on the way to see the priests the leper is healed. A very simple story. But the genius of Luke has been to seize this text and make it a hymn to faith.

"Keep in mind Jesus Christ: with him we shall live!" The profession of Christian faith begins when we fall at Jesus' feet to give glory to God. There is no other name by which we may be saved! The passage could so easily have been no more than the account of a healing. God saves, God delivers, God heals. But Luke's genius makes it a revelation account. The word that saves is the word of this individual from Nazareth who incarnates the creative might of God. And the church learns its identity —we are the people who worship God in Jesus Christ: "through him, with him, in him."

The passage could so easily have constituted a simple exhortation to gratitude. The Samaritan is the only one to return to Jesus. He prostrates himself before him and gives thanks to God. His behavior contrasts starkly with that of his companions. But the contrast is not in the thanking. The other lepers may very well have gone to the temple to give thanks. The scandal of this gospel passage is: Jesus praises a Samaritan, someone excluded from membership in God's holy people. For it is to him that the Samaritan has come to pay worship to God. "Believe me. . . ." Jesus has said to the woman of Samaria, "an hour is coming when you will worship the Father neither on this mountain nor in Jerusalem" (Jn 4:21). The true locus of the encounter between God and human beings, the name by which one is saved, is Jesus.

A stranger is called to salvation and enters the Reign, while everything about him—his leprosy, his sin, his origin—fairly screams the contrary. The excommunicate par excellence! Really, now! A leper, and a Samaritan besides? And he becomes the model believer. His faith has not only healed him, it has saved him. In relating this story, and applying it to an unexpected problem, Luke surely has in mind the Christian communities in Samaria, cut off from any program of evangelization. And out beyond these communities, he surely recalls, are all the "foreigners" to whom Jesus opened the doors of the Reign of God. Yes—even to us!

■

God, Friend of humanity, Father of the poor,
    God whom no one has ever seen or contemplated,
be blessed for Jesus Christ—
    for the fascinating glance that heals our leprosy,
    and the breath with which he gives body to our flesh.
He has walked the pathways of humanity,
    his hands lifting the legions of the paralyzed
    that they might walk on to the land of freedom.
Be blessed for the words of grace you have uttered,
    the echo of your mercy,
    the secret revealed, the good news proclaimed.
Be blessed for the One who has become your face,

your compassion for us,
  and, for you, our face and our suffering.
By him you inaugurate a festive celebration without end,
  you who consecrate us in him:
upon us you place his mark,
  you who make his Spirit to dwell in our hearts.

THURSDAY OF THE 32ND WEEK

NIGHT

Wisdom 7:22–8:1: "In Wisdom is a spirit intelligent. . . ." The sacred writer's character as representative of a specific earlier biblical tradition has not prevented him from integrating into his composition notions foreign to the Bible. Thus as he observes the scant emphasis his predecessors have placed on the presence of Wisdom in the world, he utilizes the Stoic concept of *pneuma* to underscore that presence. We learn that Wisdom had come to Solomon himself in the form of a "spirit," and that it is owing to this *pneuma* that Wisdom "knows the universe through and through, rules it with power and certitude, ceaselessly renews all things, and enters the pure of heart" (C. Larcher).

The author lists twenty-one attributes in his encomium of Wisdom (chaps. 6–11), grouping them by twos and threes, and presenting them as quasi-physical qualities. We are struck by how many of these properties, while calling attention to the presence of Wisdom in the world, nevertheless insist on the nonidentity of Wisdom with that world. The *pneuma* is distinct from all created being, transcending even the subtlest of spirits.

After having depicted the presence of Wisdom in the cosmos, the author attempts in verses 25–26 to identify the relation of Wisdom with God. His vocabulary betrays his concern to posit a close dependence indeed. The word "mirror," for example, is very suggestive. In presenting the activity of Wisdom as the faithful reflection of the divine activity, the author is inviting us to contemplate the action of God in that of Wisdom. Well has it been said that the mission of Wisdom to men and women, and its governance of the universe, is the prelude to the doctrine of grace in the New Testament.

The verses selected from *Psalm 119* sing of the divine activity in the world.

Luke 17:20–25: "When will the Kingdom of God come?" The question was hotly debated in Jesus' time. In the apocalypses as in synagogical reflection, an effort was being made to identify reliable signs by which the actual date of the event could be set. For Jesus, however, the real problem lay elsewhere. The important thing was: Are you going to be left out when the Reign of God does come? But it had already come! In Jesus' own person. The Reign of God is already here.

If we read on to verse 37, we appreciate the intent of Luke's apocalyptic style. He is attempting to communicate, in dramatic form, the high stakes of the present moment. He shows us a Jesus come to the end of his mission and aware that any who reject his message reject the Reign. And he shows us the Pharisees—rejection personified—still asking when it will be midday at two o'clock in the afternoon. But Jesus' word applies not only to them. It is addressed to all persons of all times, and urges them to stand honestly before the Jesus event—an event that ever strikes where least expected, unforeseeable as a thunderbolt.

■

Today we no longer say, "He is here!" or, "Over there!" But our religious nature is just as quick to get the better of us, and we have often thought that we could draw up a blueprint for God's coming—sharply define his place in our lives, present him with an itinerary that we could understand.

For believers of bygone times, the universe rustled with divine voices. At any moment, in any place, the Word, the Presence could strike. Visions and dreams cast their spell, but of course one did not speak of them. The events of nature, of collective life and daily existence were just so many immediate expressions of the divine Will. Everywhere the inexplicable attested its presence. Today we have curiously shrivelled the field of the unknown, and it has become intolerable to us to connect God with the incomprehensible.

Then cannot God be discovered in the ascent of history? Could he not be there as the hidden, inevitable figure whose dabs of pigment, when once we have managed to see them together on our canvas, gradually fill in the picture? Do not the happenings of history appear, to an attentive faith, as a slow interlacing of elements that, once they have achieved their critical mass, will snap together into the dénouement of tomorrow's fulfillment? "They will say to you, 'Here he is!' Or, 'He is there!' But do not go." The Bible had long since been warning believers that only God's back, and not his face, is visible to human beings. We cannot discover his presence until it has transformed itself into absence. Moses only saw God's back, we must remember. Elijah found him only in the faintest of breezes. And the disciples of Emmaus saw him disappear once he was recognized in the breaking of the bread.

Or perhaps God has died, as the frontiers of the unknown have receded. Perhaps he has abandoned us in the maelstrom of history. We would never actually say that, of course. We could never speak of the death of the Living One, of our abandonment by the Faithful One. But our hope has only the present to cling to: "The reign of God is already in your midst" (Lk 17:21). The word of grace is available in the scars with which it has marked the Book. We can experience the power of Love in the communion of sharing, whose earliest crystallization has only just begun. We can taste the ineffable Name revealed in the silence of our own lips when the heart abandons itself to contemplation. "The reign of God is already in your midst"! It is in your midst in your hesitant acceptance of a strange piece of news from far away. It is in your midst in a charity barely practiced, but surely willed. It is in your midst in the babbling prayer whose own words surprise it. Night is all around. But the first faint glimmer of daybreak already quivers in the East.

■

God, our future,
blessed be your name!
> *Your word is born in our silence,*
> *your love is revealed in our humble fidelities,*
> *your promise is confirmed in our fragile faith.*
Strengthened and comforted by the signs of your presence,
> *we can advance toward the Day that will be yours.*
And it is this that we ask of you in trust:
> *hasten the day of eternity.*

FRIDAY OF THE 32ND WEEK

THE DAY OF GOD IS HERE!

Wisdom 13:1–9: The last part of the Book of Wisdom is more concrete, concerned as it is with giving a description of the activity of the divine Wisdom in the actual history of Israel. The method used by the sacred writer is a consideration of the contrast between the respective lot of the Israelites and the Egyptians. His intent is polemical, as we may gather from the long digression on idolatry (chaps. 13–14), introduced by a series of allusions to animal worship. We find the theme, classic in Greek thought, of the artisan who is recognized in his handiwork, together with the doctrine of the perfection of the cosmos, so dear to the Stoics. Actually our author is denouncing the foolishness of the pagans. Their regard for creatures has led them to celebrate the beauty of the universe, this is true. But instead of ascribing the basic unity of that universe to its factual author, they attempt to explain it in terms of the primacy of one or another element. With this sole exception, the Book of Wisdom is strikingly tolerant of other ideologies. It criticizes the pagans, but does not blame them. It seems to say: We may reproach unbelievers about their confusion of appearance with reality; but at least they have sought God.

Psalm 19 repeats the doctrine that the creature is a reflection of the Creator.

Luke 17:26–37 follows immediately upon yesterday's reading. Luke is merely borrowing an apocalyptic theme familiar throughout Judaism, indeed one used by the other evangelists. In the same spirit, in verses 31–32 we have the theme of flight, which is found in so many of the prophets. The reference to the indifference prevailing in the days of Noah and Lot is intended as a warning not to misunderstand the Reign as an exceptional event. No, the Reign happens every day!

And yet its irruption demands, on the part of human beings, a prompt, personal decision. Board the ark or tumble into the deluge. Leave Sodom; and not in the manner of Lot's wife. The gospel passage is very concrete. But Noah and Lot are also salvation figures. Yes, for Luke the judgment is always a judgment of grace.

■

Jesus breaks the anguished vicious circle of the prophets of woe, with their sense of impending doom that inspires such fear in their hearers and all but hauls them bodily to conversion. "You know not the day or the hour!" Jesus insists.

"The reign of God is already in your midst"! The Reign pounces upon us, wherever we happen to be in life. We eat, we drink, we marry, we work. And it is in our most ordinary experiences that the coming of God is accomplished. Concerned as we are with all of this exteriority, we forget to take the true measure of things: Christ is alive. We can speak of him in the past tense: "He came. . . ." We can speak of him in the future tense: "He will come again. . . ." But we must always speak of him in the present tense: "He comes!"

He comes, and a new world has begun. Fear may seize us, personally or in society, but he proposes we board the ark of the new world dawning, he would have us plunge into our interiority, and then dwell in a heart that loves. He comes, to open a world that had been closed, walled up and walled in. He pierces the wall of indifference and fear. He vaults the barricades of tribulation and death.

He comes, and the humdrum of the daily round is suddenly the chrysalis of tomorrow, a sign of what is to be. They were eating, they were drinking. . . . Noah's fellow-citizens had not grasped the dimensions of their "today." They had failed to appreciate their capacity to lay hands on banality and make it be novelty. Our everyday is ever "tomorrow." Our tedious "today" is the eternity of love victorious, even today.

■

Abandon us not to our threadbare ideas,
     God of eternal youth!
Place within us a new heart.
By your Spirit, convert us:
     turn our regard toward that future
     that you prepare for us for ages to come.

■

God, ever faithful to your promises,
     who deliver us from uneasiness and fear,
     the Spirit is the source of our hope.
May this, our conviction,
     mount in a hymn of praise.
And then accomplish what you have decreed:
     our happiness for ages without end.

■

God of everlasting tenderness,
     in these apprehensive times of ours
     the Eucharist gives us hope.
May it preserve us from evil and fear,
     and keep us watchful in your service.
Thus shall we share with all men and women
     the happiness of your Reign.

THE LABOR OF PRAYER

Wisdom 18:14–16, 19:6–9: A meditation on the events of the Exodus enables the author of the Book of Wisdom to serve notice on any who might be contemplating an assault on Israel. They shall have to reckon with the protection with which Yahweh has always surrounded his people. With a series of comparisons, the sacred writer shows that each of the instruments serving for the chastisement of the Egyptians was transformed into a boon to Israel. For example, the meat that disgusted Egypt (the frogs) nourished Israel in the desert (the quail). The author progressively comes to a consideration of the mightiest of those punishments: the death of the firstborn of Egypt and the miracle of the sea. On the one side, behold a decree of death upon the daughters and sons of the Hebrews; on the other, the death of all the firstborn of Egypt, including the Prince Royal. Finally, in a style not without grandeur, the author describes the night of Passover, when the word of God brought death to Egypt. This word, identical with the judgment it executes, is powerful, and the cosmos obeys it. And once more we observe that the sea, which at first rendered the position of the Hebrews so precarious, was finally their salvation. And the author interprets this miracle as a new act of creation. Earth and sky have been, we might say, "remodeled."

In its own meditation on the events of the Exodus, *Psalm 105* invites us to give praise to the One who has been mindful of his promises.

Luke 18:1–8: The parable of the judge must be understood in the light of the Jesus event. In itself it proclaims the certainty of final salvation, since the judge finally succumbs to the widow's insistence.

Luke's interpretation of the parable links it with the classic theme of God's apparent inaction. In proclaiming the imminence of judgment, the evangelist is doubtless still thinking of the unexpected nature of the irruption of the Reign. This is confirmed by the concern of verse 8 with human beings' response to the Reign. What will they do? Will they accept it? Yes or no?

■

Mark my words: God will one day show that she was right to be so insistent! Prayer is that powerful! We present the world to God, and that world, thus positioned under the regard of the Father, is taken up and accepted by him. I tell you, God will do it justice! A footbridge between the world and God! Our toilsome today lashed to the unexpected accomplishments of God! Such is the grandeur of prayer.

The prayer of Christians—which is that of Christ, since his Spirit prays in us as we cannot—appears as the great, heaving respiration that lifts the world to its promised destiny: God's justification of the efforts of human beings.

Too often we regard prayer as a kind of esthetic gesture or gratuitous activity. And we know the impatience with which people criticize contemplative nuns: "Of course they pray! That's all they have to do!"—as if prayer were a pastime, something you do when there is nothing else to do. (Or when there is nothing else to be done!) No, prayer is a mighty shout: "Give us our rights!" Prayer is not some vague sentimentality. Prayer is a function we have to perform. Christians have a vocation to pray. They have a job to do. Ours is the task to give life to the world by praying to God.

And this demands that we "stick to the world." If by indifference, contempt or cowardice we withdrew from the world and stood somewhere along the parade route to watch it go by, how ever should we be able to consecrate human effort, and how ever would God finally give human beings their rights? The toil of prayer restores us to our rightful position as the artisans of a new creation.

■

In saving us, you manifest your glory,
    God our Father.
Hear our burning prayer.
We come before you
    our hands lifted in offering.

Reach down and take what they hold:
    a world that cries out
    in birthpangs that have not abated.
By your Spirit,
    grant that we may believe in the impossible
    every day.

■

Just and holy God,
    you will never disappoint those who cry to you.
By this communion
    you grant us to share in the Spirit of Christ.
Once more, then, we beseech you:
Keep us strong in faith
    against the day of the coming
    of your Son Jesus, our Lord.

HEART AND EYES

1 Maccabees 1:10-15, 41-43, 54-57, 62-64: When Alexander the Great died, his generals divided his empire. The lion's share went to the Lagides (Egypt) and the Seleucids (the Middle East, with Antioch, in Syria, as its capital). In 175 B.C. Antiochus IV, surnamed Epiphanes, a Syrian, ascended the throne of the Seleucids and launched a policy to unify the royal domains. Even in occupied Israel there were those with whom his project found favor. A number of Jews there, conscious of the isolation in which the law of Moses had confined their nation, now petitioned Antiochus to abolish their privileges. Not surprisingly, the King welcomed the invitation, and undertook to bestow on the Jewish provinces all the benefits of Hellenistic civilization. A gymnasium was built in Jerusalem, and athletic games were held. The celebration of the beauty of the human body served as a pretext for the rejection of circumcision as the outward sign of attachment to the Covenant of Sinai. The scrolls of the Torah were burned, and in 167 (the year 145 of the Seleucid era) Antiochus pillaged the temple and erected in Jerusalem what the Book of Daniel calls the "horrible abomination"—an altar to Zeus of Olympus, identified with the Baal Shamem, of whom the King claimed to be the reincarnation. This was the last straw. And Israel erupted in revolt.

Psalm 119 sings the love of the Law.

Luke 18:35-43: Ever since the time of the conquest (Josh 6), Jericho had stood as a figure of the gate of entry to the Land of Promise. The evangelists had adapted the notion, letting the city represent the gateway to the Reign of God. But the disciples had begun to realize that access to that Reign is possible only through the activity of God himself (18:27). Jesus comes as "the way, the truth, and the life . . ." (Jn 14:6). He is the salvation we must seize and hold fast.

Once more Luke gives us two mutually enriching accounts. The flavor of the first is unmistakably Jewish—the episode of the blind person. The second is intended for pagan readers (19:1-10). But both reassert the doctrine that the Reign of God is for the little, for those out on the margins of a society that has thrust them there for a life of shame and misery. Among the "Jewish" traits of the first account is its explicit petition to the son of David, its emphasis on a salvific faith, and the reaction of the beneficiary of the miracle of healing— the blind person, who suddenly sees and who, in the best rabbinical tradition, now sets out to "follow" Jesus.

He is always there, in the same spot, part of the street scene, disturbing no one. Then one day his closed universe is penetrated by a presence. Who comes? Jesus of Nazareth? Suddenly the blind one is on his feet: "Have pity on me! . . . I want to see"!

God who is Light, invented the eyes of Jesus that the world might suddenly be perceived as it never had before. Now that world would find itself pierced with a gaze whose intensity and truth would be as merciless with a lie as it would be merciful to human frailty. "Have pity on me!" And because Jesus is the Light of the world, he invented eyes for this blind mendicant: "Receive your sight. Your faith has healed you"!

An Arab proverb says: "Bring me your heart, and I shall give you my eyes." Bring me your heart, Jesus says to us. "Have pity on me!" we say with the blind beggar. Our part is to bring Jesus our heart—our courage to see, and see everything, our courage not to flinch, not to blink when reality whips into our faces at full speed, whether it is our own reality or that of the world. We must dare to see our darkness. Faith is first and foremost a trial and a cry: "Have pity on me!" For example, in the following graphic description of *acedia*, written by a great playwright, do we not discover our own personal reality? "I opened my eyes in the morning with, yes, a real pleasure at beholding the light of day. I rose; and after a few minutes, lassitude bore down upon my shoulders like a mantle of lead. . . . It was like gazing upon the night in broad daylight —night mingled with day, the black sun of melancholy" (F. Ionesco, *Journal in Crumbs*). "Bring me your heart. . . ." There is but one cry that can mount to our lips before all that we behold. "Have pity on me!"

"I shall give you my eyes." Only the eyes of the Risen One can rescue us from despair, and give us a new outlook on the world. Only a blinding light can invest the whole of reality with radiance. "Receive your sight"! The view to which Jesus opens our eyes is no ordinary one. Surely we only dare look reality in the face because it is revealed to us as reality rescued and saved.

■

Light of light,
Jesus, Son of the living God,
    have pity on us!
Snatch us from our darkness,
    and show us your salvation!

Blind us with your mercy,
and teach us to see our world
as you see it
for ages to come.

TUESDAY OF THE 33RD WEEK

"I SHALL STOP BY TODAY"

2 Maccabees 6:18–31: "But many in Israel were determined and resolved in their hearts not to eat anything unclean. . . ." (1 Mc 1:62). In the martyrdom of Eleazar and the seven brothers, Second Maccabees gives us examples of the stubborn resistance mounted by certain Jews to Antiochus' unifying measures. Contrary to appearances, however, Second Maccabees is not the sequel to the first book. Both works cover almost the identical period; but while First Maccabees, written by a Palestinian Jew, is of undeniable historical worth, the scope of Second Maccabees—a résumé of a more extensive work—is religious. Its intent is to move the reader emotionally: its literary genre, exceedingly popular in the Hellenistic world, is that of "pathetic history" (W. Harrington).

The death of Eleazar is presented as an example to be followed. Here is an eminent doctor of the Law constrained to sit at a sacrificial meal. He is told he must eat pork, a favorite dish of the Greeks, but forbidden by the Mosaic law. His apostate companions, who know the value attached to the prestigious old man's example, go so far as to propose that he make a pretense of eating the pork and thereby preserve his life. But Eleazar refuses, with the noble observation there are things worth more than life.

Psalm 3 is an individual complaint by the martyr about the machinations of persecutors and false friends. But it expresses an invincible confidence in God.

Luke 19:1–10: The theme is the same as in the previous narrative. But the Zacchaeus account is crisply distinguished from the one that has gone before. This time Luke elects to describe the encounter in terms of characteristics that will appeal to pagans. Thus we observe that Zacchaeus asks nothing of Jesus. On the contrary, it is Jesus who calls to the tax collector—granted, in response to the latter's quest. Jesus no longer insists on the prerequisite of faith. Now he lays the emphasis on his own gratuitous initiative in taking the risk of lodging with an individual legally stigmatized with uncleanness. And finally, Zacchaeus does not embrace Jesus' discipleship. He offers hospitality and shares his goods. Just as he has done in chapters 5 and 7, the evangelist

172

accentuates the differences in the steps taken by two beneficiaries of Jesus' miracles—here, by the blind person and Zacchaeus.

In this last reading, joy is everywhere—Messianic joy. The Lord has kept his commitments to Israel. The time of the promise has yielded to that of realization, and this has happened *today*. While everyone else regards Zacchaeus as an outcast, Jesus tells him that he is a son of Abraham. And to boot, in the reconciliation of this lonely excommunicate we have a preview of the universal reconciliation proclaimed by the prophets. In the words of Ambrose of Milan: "Zacchaeus in the sycamore is the new fruit of the new season."

■

He was someone wanting to see Jesus. Little did he suspect that he would be the one "seen"! It would not be the last time that someone was "caught" trying to spy on another! "Zacchaeus, hurry down, I mean to stay at your house today!"

Contrary to what we imagine, it is not we who search for God. God first searches for us. We have not been made primarily to love God— although this, too, is the purpose of our creation. Primarily we have been made that God may love us—that he may invite us to enter into this free exchange of shared love. Someone has sought us out. There is the secret of our faith and our happiness! "Zacchaeus, hurry down, I mean to stay at your house today!"

The gospel goes beyond the revelation of the parenthood of God. If the mystery of God were revealed to us merely in an infinitude of dependency—in an impenetrable transcendence, however open the latter might be to a communion with the inferior partner—this would be nothing startlingly new. But Jesus is not an incarnation of God: he is the incarnation of God's heart.

"Zacchaeus, hurry down!" God is demanding. Why? Because God is love. Jesus is the incarnation of this "formless" God, a God poor as the love that is prayer and as wounding. It is this, really, that will be the scandal. No one misses the point. When Jesus visits public sinners in their homes, he not only provokes reprobation on grounds of loose morals, he calls religious representations into question. God is not an infinitude. God is not even an infinite Father who oppresses because he must. God is a beggar. A wounded infinity, then. "God, too, has his hell—his love for us," wrote Nietzsche. Saint Paul went further: "God became tender . . ." (Rom. 9:16).

Zacchaeus "wanted to see." And what was revealed to him was a wounded God. He had asked nothing. And suddenly it is God who begs him: I want to stay with you. . . .

■

God of the little, God of sinners,
your mercy reveals your might:
your love can do all things!
Look on us:
may your tenderness be manifested to us.
Become our guest.
Then we shall know, from this day forward,
a communion destined to last forever.

WEDNESDAY OF THE 33RD WEEK

TAKING THE RISK

2 Maccabees 7:1, 20–31: "Having shown us the example of an elderly man who was also a scholar of the law, the author now presents a woman of the people and her seven youthful sons, that every class and age of life may have a model to imitate in time of persecution" (F.-M. Abel). The liturgy has actually retained only the mother's exhortation, and the dying declaration of the youngest son. In so doing it has omitted the author's insistence on the cruelty of the torments which, like the mention of the presence of the king, is typical of the hagiographic style. Along with the mother's greatness of soul, what strikes us are the allusions to a resurrection of the flesh, along the lines of Daniel 12, in a context of the divine omnipotence manifested on the day of creation.

The martyrdom account has a historical basis. Two traditions vie for the location: the first would place it in Judea, the second at Antioch. In the fourth century of the Christian era, Saint John Chrysostom situated it at a short distance from the latter city where there was a basilica with the relics of the martyrs. The veneration of these Old Testament martyrs passed to the West at this same time.

Psalm 17 is another complaint, protesting the innocence of one tormented. The latter, expecting nothing more from human beings, has placed all his trust in the divine justice.

Luke 19:11–28: Has the splendor with which God's "today" is manifested in the reconciliation of Zacchaeus been the occasion of any false complacency in Jesus' disciples? Jesus is always concerned lest his hearers not be too naive in their eschatological expectations. In its own way, the parable of the various sums of money once more insists on God's "today."

Luke has taken his inspiration for his portrait of the king who went abroad to be crowned from the actual coronation voyage of Archilaus, one of the sons of Herod, who had to journey to Rome after his father's death to be confirmed in the paternal legacy. Arrived in Rome, Archilaus actually did encounter the obstacle of a Jewish delegation that had come to petition for the abolition of the monarchy. The parable ends on a note of royal wrath. But Luke uses this historical recollection to call attention both to Jewish opposition to Jesus' messianic claims and to the consequences of this blindness. At bottom, the parable of the various sums of money serves as an antithesis to the account of the Zacchaeus incident. Not salvation, but judgment, is contemplated here.

We shall be judged by the concrete element of our lives. The amounts of money entrusted to the servants turn the spotlight on the activity in which the disciples are expected to engage while they await their Master's return. When all is said and done, happy are those who, instead of spending their time calculating the date of the coming of the Reign, apply their intelligence to the question of how not to miss out on it when it does come! The amount of the sums to be invested, as gathered from the Greek text (by contrast with the huge amounts of the Matthean parable), is calculated to indicate the disproportionately great reward such prudent disciples can expect to receive from the responsible execution of a relatively modest task.

■

So he had hidden his little gold coin for safekeeping. He was anxious about the future. Therefore he would risk nothing. However, the money was not his. He would have done better to be more prudent with it!

It is altogether off the mark to reduce this parable to an invitation to "make the most of our talents"—our intelligence, strength, courage, spirit of enterprise, and so on. No, this parable is still speaking of God and his Reign!

So the Master has gone on a journey, then. The community of the first Christians finds itself orphaned. Christ has departed, and has left the fate of the Reign in the hands of his disciples. Now it is we who are responsible for the Reign of God!

Then what have we done with the Word? The scribes and the teachers knew very well that they had been entrusted with a precious deposit. Jesus reproaches them with having merely preserved this Word, when it had been intended to germinate and produce fruits of life. What have you done with the Word? This is what Jesus is asking the scribes; but his question strikes into our own hearts as well, where this gospel echoes: How about you? What are you doing? There are a thousand ways to put the Word to death and still preserve it. Money that makes no money quickly becomes worthless. Bury love and grace and what will become of them? Bury Jesus, and how will he still be the living Christ?

Transmit it, yes. Hand it on, yes. But this is worlds apart from merely "preserving" it! Our "capability," as the gospel calls it, our fidelity, is not to be enclosed in the careful preservation of a legacy. Our fidelity is not reducible to holding wakes for the dead and conducting tours of their souvenirs. Our loyalty to our Christ is altogether different from the well-oiled mechanism of memory. Our fidelity is a risk. It is a fidelity on its feet!

What are you doing with the Word? The church is "incapable," unfaithful, when it disguises that Word with the heavy mask of custom, of habit, when it succumbs to an exaggerated regard for minutiae, or to a parching, desiccating addiction to control. The church is unfaithful when the Word is no longer a cry, a desire that engenders life; when questioning is strangled on the pretext that it is impertinent or unbelieving; when scholarship is shackled because it is provisional; when we freeze with fear instead of seeking new paths for the gospel; when justice and love, truth, reconciliation and peace remain soulless words—while, of course, we faithfully repeat that they are principles of our lives.

We must take risks. After all, the Reign is all in seedlings, and seedlings relish risk and adventure. Shoots have a taste for life. The church has received only one "unit." Its name is Jesus, and Jesus is alive. "Living," henceforth and for eternity, is a present participle. And faith is always conjugated in the active voice.

■

Grant us faith's daring,
and the faithfulness of those who know
that their treasure is in the future
promised by you for everlasting.

The Coming of the Son of Man (Luke 19:29–21:38)

Jesus is on the heights of Bethany now, (Lk 19:29), about to descend the Mount of Olives to enter the temple by the Eastern gate. To grasp the whole significance of the procession now under way in this crowd, this crush—the procession we celebrate each year on Palm Sunday—we must reread the prophet Ezekiel (11:22–24, 43:1–4). His oracles enable one to discover, in this individual who advances through the crowd mounted on an ass, God himself coming to judge the city that will momentarily be murdering the last of the prophets.

The scene in which the eschatological discourse is couched only brings it into sharper relief. However, we must read that discourse aright. When Luke cites Jesus' proclamation of the destruction of the city and the ruin of the temple, he knows that these events have already taken place. His purpose, then, is not to turn his readers' minds from the vicissitudes of this world and project them into an indefinite future. On the contrary, the evangelist would have them return to these concrete events and reread them in the light of faith.

For that matter, it is intentional on the Synoptics' part that they place their account of Jesus' death and resurrection immediately following the eschatological discourse. This, after all, is the moment of the definitive shift in the center of gravity of the history of the world. With the eschatological discourse Luke poses the following question: What becomes of human history now that the visible temple has disappeared? And he answers his own question. In fact, he gives two answers, both drawn from scripture as well as from the facts he has witnessed with his own eyes. On the one hand he registers the destruction of Jerusalem (Lk 21:20–24) and, after the fashion of the prophets, sees in this devastation the logical consequence of the sins of the holy city. On the other hand, while he is acutely aware of the bitter persecution that the disciples of Jesus have known by now (Lk 21:12–19), he is equally conscious that the Good News has spread through the empire as far as Rome itself. Thus he can end the discourse on a note of optimism: Jerusalem's ruin is not God's last word. Indeed, among Jesus' warnings to his opponents, has he not told them that the Son of man will come only when men and women cry, "Blessed is he who comes in the name of the Lord" (Lk 13:35)? Consistent to the last, the evangelist concludes the discourse with content that embodies the notion of salvation.

■

God, Lord of the impossible,
*   to whom might we go?*
You have the words of eternal life.

Guide us by your Spirit.
Stripped of our false wealth,
  may we enter a new world—
  our own world, turned back to the Sun for good and all,
  that night may be forever day.

THURSDAY OF THE 33RD WEEK

ATTACHMENT

1 Maccabees 2:15-19: On one side stand the envoys of King Antiochus, charged with the task of spreading the cult of the deified king. Their antagonists are Mattathias and his family, determined to defend the faith of their ancestors, come what may. On the one side, evil waxes with all determination. On the other, saints are ready to resist, and with equal determination. We are in the little town of Modein, some twenty miles north of Jerusalem. The royal commissioners are aware of the repercussions that an apostasy on the part of the Maccabees would have on the people. The situation was the same as it had been with Eleazar. And their discourse is persuasive indeed. Mattathias and his sons will be showered with gifts and admitted to the royal entourage. They need only abandon the faith of their forebears. Really, why does Israel isolate itself so stubbornly from other nations?

But the priest of Modein refuses, and exhorts his sons to do battle to the death. In his zeal for the Law he kills an apostate comrade and an emissary of the king. He flees into hiding. Other Jews withdraw to the desert.

Psalm 50 emphasizes the importance of the Modein incident. It is phrased in the form of an indictment pronounced by Yahweh personally before all the earth.

Luke 19:41-44: "As he approached Bethphage and Bethany on the mount called Olivet, he sent two of his disciples with these instructions . . ." (Lk 19:29-30). With these words Luke embarks upon his account of Jesus' messianic entry into Jerusalem. After the parable of the units of money, then, we suddenly find Jesus on Mount Olivet. The place is important. It recalls the oracle of the prophet Ezekiel proclaiming the return of the glory of Yahweh to the temple "by way of the gate which faces the east" (Ezek 43:4). In the person of Jesus, then, the evangelist is sketching the eschatological visitation of the holy city by God himself. And yet we see that Jesus enters Jerusalem as

---

a messenger of peace. This is how he is welcomed by his disciples, whose acclamations are reminiscent of the song of the angels at Bethlehem (cf. Lk 19:38).

But Jerusalem will reject this peace. Then the peaceable king will turn prophet and judge. Thrice Luke will thunder the judgment of God on the city that has derided its Lord. Here he does so in terms reminiscent of the siege of Jerusalem by the Roman legions (A.D. 70). Thereby the evangelist indicates that he, like his Christian contemporaries, regards this event as the execution of a divine sentence.

■

Offer sacrifice, and you shall be rich! Strange . . . the world we live in is peopled with idols. Some idolize the objects of their desire. Misjudging these creatures, they forget that the objects of human desire have only a symbolic bond with the happiness whose quest is the motive force of our entire existence. The journey becomes the goal, and the stages along the way become ends in themselves. Others, their gaze fixed on a single value, which they isolate from the rest and make absolute—truth, knowledge, art, and so on—subject themselves and others to a tyranny that transforms them into fanatical propagandists, inquisitors, yes, terrorists. Still others, of more modest pretentions, perform their furtive genuflections, in the semi-secrecy of every day, before their custom-made idols of money, prestige, pleasure and enjoyment. Offer sacrifice, and you shall be rich! How many are our gods—in the image and likeness of our fears, our aspirations, our fatalism itself!

"God forbid that we should forsake the law and the commandments"! Henceforth this prayer will become part and parcel of our lives—both as an actual experience, and as a demand never to be fulfilled. At the heart of this world sown from end to end with the foolish fetishes of our own fashioning, our faith has a task for us—that of leveling an accusing finger at each fetish in turn and saying, "You are not a god." Yes, we have a vocation to atheism! The first Christians did not create an edifying impression. Far from being regarded as virtuous persons, they were looked upon as immoral. They refused to offer sacrifice to the Emperor. Then they were atheists! Our faith is iconoclastic: its vocation is to denounce false absolutes, to relativize fanaticisms, to criticize the alienating compromises of daily life.

Offer sacrifice, and you shall be rich! Our faith denounces illusions. We find our happiness in contemplation and silence, and in a relentless struggle to be free. The idol that fascinates, that rivets the attention, must die, in order that the name of the true God may live. When the idol tumbles, the mirage of a "substitute absolute" vanishes. Then appears the Divine Word, the image of the Invisible One, sole access to the Father. And our desire fuses with God's: "Ah, how I should wish to gather my children!" (cf. Lk 13:34).

■

God, the one and the true,
    you call to your children.
Strip the mask from our deceitful attachments.
    Denounce to us our illusions.
Gather us by your word:
may we find it sweet
    to attach ourselves to you
    forever and ever.

FRIDAY OF THE 33RD WEEK

LET US GO UP TO PURIFY THE SANCTUARY

1 Maccabees 4:36–37, 52–59: First Maccabees can be considered as a trilogy. It recounts the shining deeds of the three sons of the priest Mattathias, especially the six-year struggle of Judas Maccabaeus with the representative of King Antiochus. After his first victories, Judas Maccabaeus resolved to restore the legitimate worship, and to this effect ordained the purification of the temple, built a new altar and, in mid-December, 164 B.C. (the 148th year of the Seleucid era), on the third anniversary of the sacrifice offered to Zeus, offered a sacrifice in conformity with the Law.

Thus the Jewish calendar was enriched with a new religious feast: *Channukah,* or the Dedication. The eight-day celebration included a sacrificial rite, with the singing of psalms (the *Hallel*) and processions with palms and green branches. But lamps were also lighted in the windows of homes—one more each day as the celebration progressed—and this gained for it the name of Festival of Lights, endowing it with an enormous popularity. Second Maccabees itself underscores *Channukah's* similarities to the Feast of Tabernacles—a happy correspondence, as *Sukkoth* recalled the dedication of the first temple.

Instead of a psalm the liturgy sings parts of a hymn of praise placed by the Chronicler on the lips of King David (*1 Chron 29*). This prayer is part of a royal testament, and stresses the monarchy's concern for the temple.

Luke 19:45–48: The Old Testament always hesitates to ascribe extensive priestly prerogatives to the Jewish kings. But since "the king was the founder or benefactor of the sanctuary, since there were times when he took charge of the construction or maintenance of the buildings, and since he still played a special role in the actual liturgy celebrated in this sanctuary," he was regarded as enjoying "a genuine right of patronage" (L. Monloubou). Even the prophet Ezekiel, who had so radically modified the status of the king, left him certain privileges, notably that of presiding at sacrifice on a raised dais at the Eastern Gate, through which, unlike the rest of the populace, he could actually enter the temple building itself.

"Jesus entered the temple." What has Jesus come to do? He has come to manifest the meaning of his kingship by restoring a worship worthy of his Father. Jesus has not entered the temple purely and simply to restore the Jewish worship. He has come to proclaim a new worship, one "in Spirit and truth" (4:23, 24)—the worship he will actually inaugurate in the guest hall of the Last Supper and on Golgotha. From the outset, the sanctuary at Jerusalem had been under a cloud of ambiguity. Had it not been erected in contravention of the express prohibition of the prophet Nathan? From the outset, then, the temple had been the fruit of an act of disobedience, and succeeding generations had crowned the work of their refractory forebears by making it into a "den of thieves." When Jesus, coming to be acclaimed as a king, entered the temple by its Eastern Gate, he implemented a very specific project: the inauguration of a "living sacrifice, holy and acceptable to God" (Rom 12:1)—a sacrifice in his own blood.

■

"My house is meant for a house of prayer." Jesus is speaking of the temple, to denounce what human beings have made of it: a house built to human specifications.

Our house is where we are at home. Our house is where we lodge, the place where we "find ourselves," where we can drop our mask and just be ourselves. Our house is our life. And we have furnished it to our own taste—to suit ourselves.

"My house is meant for a house of prayer"! This is the Christian's decision. Our life is no longer our own property. Our home is no longer our castle! Our house, the place where we are at home, has become the dwelling place of God. "My house is meant for a house of prayer," and prayer is creation.

My life will be a long apprenticeship in freedom, at the very heart of my burdens. No longer is my life a refuge where I cower amidst my securities. Now my life—in my personal faith decision—opens out upon the unexpected. I am like a potter who, after the long apprenticeship of his hands, and after the slow maturation within him of the thing struggling to be born—raises an unexpected new form and shape out of the mass of his clay.

My house is meant for a house of prayer, and prayer is trust. Prayer is surrender to a word of grace. When the acrobat's body has flown the trapeze and abandoned itself to space—trajectory lovely, perilous!—a partner stretches out a pair of strong hands, and now the human projectile can gracefully, fearlessly sweep up toward those hands and the sky of the big tent. Let my life, far from being confined in the narrow walls of a dwelling bereft of space or scope, take the risk of shooting for the sky, and for the hands reaching to receive me.

"My house is meant for a house of prayer." Instead of being built to our own measurements, now our life will open out to the power of the Father: "Unless the Lord build the house, in vain do the builders toil." Now instead of being merely a human life, our life becomes a consecrated one, a holy temple. "You must know that your body is a temple of the Holy Spirit . . ." (1 Cor 6:19).

■

You make your dwelling in our house,
*   a house built on your word, cemented by your grace.*
God, our rock, our salvation,
consecrate us by the power of the Spirit,
*   that we may be the temple*
*   raised to the glory of your name*
*   in this present time and forever more.*

SATURDAY OF THE 33RD WEEK

NEW LIFE

1 Maccabees 6:1–13: King Antiochus is thrown back. He fails where the great Alexander had triumphed. Elymais is the mountainous region of Elam, east of the Tigris. Here stood the treasure-crammed sanctuary of the goddess Artemis, which the natives had successfully defended against the greedy designs of the Seleucids. Bitter and vengeful, Antiochus had retreated, only to learn of the restoration of Jewish worship. What is interesting here are the reflections placed by the sacred writer on the lips of the king. Now on his deathbed, Antiochus attributes his misfortunes to his profanation of the temple at Jerusalem. The historian Polybus attributes them to the profanation of a temple, as well—but of that of Artemis. Actually Antiochus died before the completion of the work of restoration that had been undertaken in the Jewish capital. What fascination a religious edifice held for antiquity!

Psalm 9 is a collection of snippets of many genres. The verses selected for today's liturgy express satisfaction at the defeat of one's enemies.

Luke 20:27–40: Now in the interior of the temple, Jesus faces his judges alone. The high priests, the scribes and the elders are all present. The prophet from Galilee is at odds with the most influential party of the Sanhedrin on a number of counts. The question of the resurrection of the dead still divides the Jews after two centuries. The Pharisees share the popular belief in a resurrection of the body, envisaged in very materialistic, very naive images, while the Sadducees, who reject the prophetical books, refuse to embrace this new teaching. And so they pose Jesus a scholastic conundrum obviously calculated to hold him up to ridicule.

Jesus' response is twofold. He asserts his faith in the resurrection. Not wishing to appeal to the prophet Daniel, however, he calls to witness the Book of Exodus, which the Sadducees of course recognize. There God has revealed himself to Moses as "the God of Abraham, the God of Isaac, the God of Jacob," a powerful expression of the divine protection and favor. The question, then, is whether this protection is abrogated at death. From the time of the Maccabaean martyrs, the answer has been more and more in the negative. God had claimed to be "the God of the living," and his promises accompanied his creature across the threshold of death. Jesus shares this popular belief. At the same time, however, he warns against too naive a representation of the condition of the risen. "They become like angels," he says. They are heirs and sharers of a new world.

■

Aha! Seven brothers and their hapless sister-in-law. Now this Jesus will be put to the test. But Jesus pronounces all the current criteria irrelevant, without application. You cannot speak of the Reign of God in old images. New wine? New bottles.

How would we have anything at all to say of this new order unless we already experienced, deep in our heart, our passage to the farther shore with the Risen Christ? In him we are the vanquishers of the powers of death, though these imprison us still. The old being is gone for good! Through our Easter experience, the world learns what it would otherwise never have dared imagine. Now it knows that death is counter-nature.

In the humility of our faith, in the fragility of our hope, we make a mighty claim: we belong to a new world. Now we can call by the name of sister and brother even those who are strangers to us by culture, birth, or opinion. Now we can say that we are one body, despite so much still dividing us. Now we can say that we are saints, despite our personal and collective sin. We still see death at work everywhere; but we never pause in our cry: "He is risen!"

The question posed to Jesus by his adversaries centers entirely on death. Death makes the decisions, Death makes the rules. But because we believe in Jesus' resurrection, henceforth everything is polarized by one great reversal: now life, not death, is the motivating force in our lives! Yes, we are impassioned with life. We are alive, we are "full of life"! Why this belief in life? Because in Jesus' resurrection we experience the luminous secret of the world: Our God is the God of Abraham, Isaac, and Jacob—the God of the living. This is why we are so in love with life.

■

We thank you,
*   God of Abraham, God of Isaac, God of Jacob.*
You have struck a covenant with our ancestors,
*   and they live forever in your sight.*

We thank you,
*   God of Jesus Christ.*
You have struck a covenant with him,
*   and he, if not we, remains faithful.*
You called him to life Easter morning.
*   He lives forever in your sight.*

We thank you,
*   God of all the living.*
You renew your covenant with human kind
*   that we may all live with your life.*
Even beyond death
*   you call us by our names.*
Therefore we can join our voices
*   to those of all the living who throng around you*
*   to sing the victory of the life you bestow on us.*

The Virtue of Hope

Each day we must rebuild. We must rebuild the world, we must rebuild hope. Our times, like all times, are times of resurrection to the work of the age. Some will show you an isle of dreams where everything is "better than you have it here." But the gospel tells us: Live where you are! The Good News comes into our daily lives, and nowhere else. The gospel is written in the present tense. Yes, God is the God of every day!

It is by your patient endurance that you will have life. Hope is a grace offered. Hope is something to be received. The theological virtue of hope lives by the blossoming of our little hopes, and by the resumption of those hopes every time they are dashed. Hope teaches us that the church is falsely spiritual when it is no longer interested in human beings. Hope bears testimony that the Reign of God is granted to us only in our attachment to the beauty and grandeur of this world. Hope is woven into the tissue of today.

Now is the hour. Now is the everyday hour when men and women give themselves to life and to death. Our hope will ever be molded of the joys and sorrows of the world, of the world's sufferings and longings. Our hope will be like a hidden, secret tapestry that gives meaning to a far broader tissue: hope leads history to its term. And if Christians are no longer "of the world," it is only because, even in this time, it is given to them to view the term of history and its finality: "Where I am, there shall my servants be, as well" (cf. Jn 17:24). Such is Jesus' promise on the eve of his dying. And that promise has the force of a testament.

■

Father most holy,
it is your Son who prays to you
*   for those whom you have given him.*

Sear us in a new fire,
*   that we may know the glory that is within us.*
Deliver us to love without division,
*   that we may know perfect joy.*
Plunge us in the death of your Son,
*   that we may rise again to Life*
*   in his resurrection.*

The Universe of the Apocalypses

Meditating on the events of their age, the prophets proclaimed a general, unspecified confidence that a turning point in history was in the offing. But the time came when the prophet no longer discerned any possibility of renewal and rebirth. Then hope disappeared in its turn. At the time of the Book of Daniel, even the prophets were gone. History was mute, and God himself seemed to have fallen silent. What had happened?

Let us recall the circumstances surrounding the redaction of the Book of Daniel. In 164 B.C. Palestine belonged to the Seleucids of Syria who, along with the Lagides of Egypt, were the successors of Alexander the Great. Antiochus IV Epiphanes dreamt of unifying his vast empire by imposing on all of his provinces the same language, the same customs and the same religion. In Palestine, however, he collided with lively opposition, culminating in revolt and a declaration of independence. How does the author of Daniel react?

Actually he reacts as the prophets reacted. He continues to scrutinize history and tell its meaning. But Daniel's horizon is considerably broadened. Contemporary events still form the visible face of the combat between good and evil; but now this combat has assumed cosmic dimensions. Hence it comes that, in the apocalypses, this combat, while continuing to be rooted in the history of human beings, so often unfolds between heaven and earth—as if their authors were seeking to give token of their determination to gaze upon events from above. It is as if these writers were no longer interested in events in themselves, and wished to behold only their more profound meaning.

Just so, we see the apocalyptic writers broaden their vision of time. Starting as they do with the notion that the events they are witnessing constitute an episode in the struggle between good and evil, they are tempted to compare their own times with other periods of history. Thus to the author of Daniel, the Jews' revolt against Antiochus recalls the combats they once waged against Babylon. In the one instance as in the other, the author of Daniel registers the will to rescue, if not national independence, at least the national identity.

When all is said and done, the role the apocalypticians take on is that of a sentinel—which, after all, was the role of the prophets. Persuaded that they stood at a turning point in history, they contemplate the past and the future in an attempt to decipher the present. They are interested in antecedents, and strive to unsnarl the tangles that have led to the contemporary crisis. They wonder about the "end" of history, "that *eschaton* toward which history, as the accomplishment of the secret designs of God, is ever moving" (P. Grelot). They labor to discover, in the segment of history that they have selected, "the vector leading in the direction of the goal willed and foreseen by God" (Grelot). Thus the apocalpyses come on the scene of history as a "revelation," an "unveiling."

■

The determination of the apocalypticians to take their distance from the course of events has two consequences. First, they are no longer artists of the word, but visionaries. Their language is no longer discourse but image. The struggle between Good and Evil is symbolized. The eschatological future is depicted graphically, and in vivid color. The authors have frequent recourse to myth, notably to the traditions of the Book of Genesis. Secondly, as they lengthen the time period with which they are concerned, they can now antedate their visions, and even place their entire composition under the pseudonymous patronage of some Old Testament hero. The adventures of the people of the Book of Daniel, for instance, are situated not in the time of the Seleucids but in that of the Babylonian Exile. This procedure, like symbolism itself, has the added advantage of safeguarding the confidential, underground character of the book.

Finally, what lesson do the apocalypticians draw from their meditation on history? Once more, these writers cannot be separated from the prophets. The prophets stressed that human history was a sacred history, polarized by the fulfillment of a divine promise, which at the same time could be blocked off by sin. History was shot through with divine judgments—always accompanied by the glimmer of a promise of salvation. The authors of the apocalypses generalized the experience of the prophets. For them the combat between Good and Evil culminated in a last Judgment, the prelude to a definitive Salvation. Thus they replace a world in which God has not yet achieved his goal with a world in which he has achieved it. They are messengers of hope.

■

God of the future,
could we ever doubt your promise?
Your Son is risen from the dead,
to lead us from death to life.
Firstborn of the living,
he walks on before us.
As we struggle under the terrible weight of our times,
we know he leads us,
even now, toward the light of your day.
And we pray to you:
As we believe in his word,
may he abide with us
each and every day,
to the end of time.

BLESSED ARE THE POOR!

Daniel 1:1–6, 8:20: Chapter 1 serves as a general introduction to the entire Book of Daniel. It presents, in a fictitious-historical framework (the customs recorded are those of the Persian court rather than the Babylonian), four noble youths exiled to Babylon with the King of Judah and destined for the service of the new suzerain. They are educated in schools presided over by the scribes, where they are taught the use of cuneiform writing, and are maintained by the King of Babylon, an important mark of distinction.

Nevertheless they refuse the King's viands, lest they transgress the dietary prohibitions of the Mosaic law. Two lessons emerge from the chapter: first, the young people's asceticism; second, their respect for the Torah. All of this secures them a wisdom superior to that of the magicians and diviners of the kingdom. This wisdom must be understood in a context of the occult sciences, and Daniel 2 and 5 proclaim the vanity of this knowledge as contrasted with the wisdom bestowed by God. And so the first chapter of the Book of Daniel betrays its literary genre. Here as elsewhere in the first six chapters of the book, what we have is an edifying account, calculated to establish that the observance of the Law is possible, even in a pagan milieu. Daniel and his companions constitute the paragon of the faithful Jew who, in the age of Antiochus, resisted—to the death, if need be—the Hellenization of their homeland.

Daniel 3:52–90 are older than the rest of the Book of Daniel, and constitute a canticle of benediction. At the moment when King Antiochus was raising the statue of Olympian Zeus in the temple at Jerusalem, this song recalled to those who could read between the lines that God alone has the right to the worship of all creatures.

Luke 21:1–4: Now the people must choose. In the guest hall Jesus will soon be giving his all, his very body and blood, like this poor widow who has emptied into the treasury "every penny she had to live on." Jesus' adversaries, the scribes who seek the first places and devour the substance of widows, lay hands on everything, religion included. At the moment when, in a final discourse, Jesus undertakes to announce the collapse of the temple of stones, whom do we choose? The mighty ones of the old regime, or the One who says he can raise the temple in three days? The temptation is great to give in before the last. We must remember that Jesus is in Jerusalem, and that he will be drinking to the dregs the cup of his destiny.

■

Blessed are the poor! There is no escaping the fact: the gospel is on the side of despoilment.

The widow in the temple with her two cents is held up before the disciples as an example. She has given all, and without counting the cost. She has given all, and for what? What are two cents in the temple treasury? She has given everything, and without expecting any return.

Obviously Jesus presents the example of this woman because the faith of the disciple ought to be modeled on her attitude. We must give all—not just the assent of our mind to truths believed, not just the consent of our heart to certain values, not just the attachment of our will to a project that seduces by its loftiness. We must give our *all*—detach ourselves, pry ourselves away, from our very selves. Then we can make a gift of ourselves to someone else. Blessed are the poor, when they deliver themselves into the hands of another!

Jesus proclaims this woman blessed because, having given all, she can receive all. Poverty is the other word for liberation. Poverty is to be poor in definitions and dogmas, to be free to receive a living word. Poverty is to be poor in religious feeling, to be free to contemplate a face and a mystery. Poverty is to be poor in behavior and morality, to be free to invent a response in keeping with the call.

She had given all, without counting the cost, and without asking for anything in return. And what she received was beyond all measure: Blessed are the poor, for theirs is the Kingdom of Heaven!

■

Your love is beyond reckoning,
God our Father,
and your grace is profusion.
Create in us a heart that is free—
poor in assurance,
to be able to recognize your Word,
poor in certitude,
to be able to discover your face,
poor in a good conscience,
to be able to live by your mercy.

IS IT ALL OVER?

Daniel 2:31–45: The ancients attached a great deal of importance to the premonitions they received in dreams. Even the Bible ascribes a certain value to dreams of premonition, while regarding them as inferior to the prophetic word. But in giving a first example of the wisdom received by Daniel as a reward for his fidelity to the Law, the second chapter of the Book of Daniel criticizes pagan divination. None of the Babylonian sages had managed to interpret the King's dream. True, the King has set them a particularly difficult task: not only to explain the dream, but to recount it without having heard it.

In his dream, the King had seen a statue made of various materials, some noble and some ignoble. The dream is an allegory of the history of earthly realms, from the Babylonian Empire (represented by gold), to the whole territory inherited by Alexander (iron) only to be partitioned between the Lagides (iron) and the Seleucids (tile). The mixed composition of the feet of the great idol reflects the rivalry that set the Lagides and the Seleucids at mutual enmity. At the same time it indicates the frailty of the Seleucid Kingdom that sought to impose its law on Israel. One small stone could bring it down to dust.

That stone, we hear, has hewn itself from a mountain "without a hand being put to it." The point being made is the unimportance of human intervention. The collapse of earthly empires is the deed of God, who "will set up a kingdom that shall never be destroyed. . . ." The Book of Daniel is a radical criticism of all totalitarian regimes. Only the Reign of God, a reign of justice and peace, will have eternity as its inheritance.

Luke 21:5–11: When Luke places on Jesus' lips the proclamation of the destruction of the temple, the temple is already a heap of ruins. Titus' legions had put it to the torch August 29, A.D. 70. The evangelist is less interested in the proclamation of the event, then, than in its meaning. God's covenant with humanity is sundered. The locus of his presence has vanished.

There is a remarkable difference between the respective apocalypses of chapters 17 and 21. The former seeks to deduce the consequences of the coming of the Son of man where individual human beings are concerned. The latter considers this coming in terms of the history of peoples, even citing the repercussions of the event on the cosmic framework in which the destiny of societies unfolds (cf. Lk 21:10–11). Ultimately the question is what is to become of human history once the temple is no more. To put it another way: Henceforward, how will God allow himself to be "read" by human beings? The comprehensive answer to this question can be given only in the light of Jesus' death and resurrection. In the meantime, however, this postponement does not prevent Luke from drawing certain conclusions from the eschatological discourse.

We note first of all the care with which the evangelist has adapted this discourse to the mentality of his readers. In verse 9 he writes, apropos of wars and uprisings, "These things are bound to happen *first*, but the end does not follow immediately." The word "end," however, did not have the same meaning for Jewish and Greek readers. A Jew would understand "end" in the sense of fulfillment. A pagan, too little sensitized to the eschatological value of the event, will understand it as the conclusion of an ever-recurring cycle. In carefully distinguishing the "end" from what precedes that end, Luke is deliberately placing the end of the ages in the present moment. Today becomes the "qualified time" par excellence (Xavier Léon-Dufour), the special, crucial moment of history, the time of salvation. Henceforward all happenings must be situated in the context of the breach in history opened by the Incarnation.

■

"Nation will rise against nation. . . . There will be great earthquakes. . . ." But "the end does not follow immediately"! The end of the world. . . . There will be those who will seek to take advantage of the description Luke places in Jesus' mouth to stimulate confusion or fear, to reduce people's hopes to a shambles. These are impostors! What genuinely counts is to hold up your head and live.

Naturally we should like to be able to program the future. We should prefer days of security and repose to a struggle in which no light can be seen at the end of the tunnel. But be on guard against dreamers. They are refusing to live!

We Christians in a capsized world—what testimony do we render? Of what are we witnesses, when peace never comes and the earth trembles beneath our steps? Wars and conflicts ceaselessly rend our world. We acknowledge that humanity's heart is sick. But we want that humanity to be happy, and our testimony moves us to protest, in season and out, the creeping death we see all around us. And we continue in our flesh Jesus' passion for life.

"There was darkness over the whole land until midafternoon," the hour of the death of God's Son. And "the earth quaked. . . ." (Mt 27:45, 52). Was it the end of the world? The disciples had thought so. It was all over. There was nothing left but to despair. Yet over Golgotha itself flashed the first faint glimmers of Easter.

Every day we must rebuild—rebuild the world and rebuild hope. Our times, like all times, are times of resurrection to the work of the current age. There may be those who will show you an isle of dreams where everything will be better than it is here. But our sun of Justice, Jesus, has risen from the dead. And he tells us: Wherever you are, live! I am with you all days! "By patient endurance you will save your lives."

■

God of the future,
your promise is for everlasting.
May it be the assurance of our faith
*   and the source of our hope.*
And may it be our joy in eternity.

WEDNESDAY OF THE 34TH WEEK

PERSEVERANCE

Daniel 5:1–6, 13–14, 16–17, 23–28: Chapter 5 opens with another portrayal of Daniel's clairvoyance. To the great fright of King Belshazzar (Bel-shar-ousour, son not of Nebuchadnezzar, but of the last Babylonian king, Nabonides), the official diviners have pronounced themselves unable either to read or to decipher the mysterious writing on the wall of the banquet hall. Daniel arrives, and does so without the slightest difficulty. His interpretation: For having profaned the sacred vessels of the temple of Jerusalem, Belshazzar will be assassinated, and his realm will be divided between the Persians and the Medes.

But Belshazzar is obviously only a pseudonym for the real villain of the Book of Daniel—Antiochus Epiphanes, the impious Seleucid who had pillaged the temple at Jerusalem in 169 B.C., then profaned it in December 167 by erecting an idolatrous altar. We likewise note that Belshazzar's banquet ends in a drinking bout, which could be an allusion to the bacchanalian orgies introduced by Antiochus at Jerusalem. The fifth chapter of Daniel, then, with its veiled attack on King Antiochus IV Epiphanes, is a fine example of historical fiction.

Luke 21:12–19: Old Simeon's oracle had foretold it. Jesus has become a sign of contradiction. Like a beacon, his coming lights up history, in its very

---

192

unfolding. It is in the light of this coming that Luke rereads the destiny of the church and of Jerusalem.

Luke reflects on the destiny of the church. The still young community is suffering persecution at the hands of Jews who, after the fall of Jerusalem, have acquired a more vivid awareness of their identity, and hence of the danger represented by the Christians. Luke's picture is a miniature of the one he paints in the Book of Acts. And so we should regard it in the light of the hope springing in the Christian heart with the spread of the Good News to the imperial capital itself. Luke's exhortation ends with an appeal for perseverance. The greatest trial of all, in the evangelist's eyes, and one that must be withstood, is the temptation not to trust God's salvation.

■

"By patient endurance you will save your lives." How could we not hope? Hope is the elastic force of life. Once it is no longer provoked and challenged, it goes soft and collapses.

But where may we obtain it? In the free life of which we say with such admiration, "Now, that's living"? We seek it unflaggingly, and unflaggingly it eludes us, whether in the oppressive personal or social conditions of our life, or in the bottomless gulley of a desire that yawns ever wider until one day we must admit the difficulty—the impossibility?—of filling it!

How can we justify this hope? We dream of a life no longer merely endured but created, no longer imposed but invented, no longer coveted but shared, no longer feared but loved. And we continue to experience a life that is limited and conditioned. Our hands, called to open, stay closed. Our hearts remain frozen with fear. No, our road leads not to the penetrating sweep of the light of day, but to choking, stifling night.

The danger of this moment is that we may see the mirage of hope—a false hope—rise up before our eyes. We may seem to discern, beyond time, the wonderful thing we are denied today. And suddenly we feel we should only wait in resignation for some Other to bestow on us, in a dream universe, what we are no longer willing to strive for today, in this reality of ours that has become so harsh.

This is the moment of witness. Jesus tells us, "I come"—in a present tense that lasts an eternity—and we know the grace of being discovered by hope. Ours is the great hope that, far from taking the place of our little hopes and strivings, revives them, grafting them onto itself, and conferring on them an unexpected fulfillment. Great hope, the theological virtue, lives by the revival of our little hopes, not by dashing them. Great hope teaches us that the church is falsely spiritual when it is no longer interested in human beings. Great hope, the theological virtue, testifies to us that the Reign of God is given us only in our attachment to the beauty and grandeur of this world.

"By patient endurance you will save your lives." You have received hope. It will lead you to testify, in this time, that tomorrow is already at work in the present age.

■

God of yesterday, today and tomorrow,
your Spirit traverses our history
    attesting the faithfulness of your promise.

May that Spirit be the breath of our witness.
May our labor in this age
    be only the birthpangs of tomorrow.
And may our endurance rescue our lives
    to everlasting ages.

THURSDAY OF THE 34TH WEEK

PREGNANT
Daniel 6:12–28: The Book of Daniel makes Darius a Mede, while history knows only Darius the Persian, successor of Cyrus and Cambyses. It makes little difference, as the present recital is an edifying narrative, not history. The courtiers, jealous of Daniel's meteoric rise (reminiscent of that of Joseph in Egypt), have set a trap for him. They have persuaded the inconstant Darius to forbid the worship of any god but himself for the space of one month.

Royal deification would have been an anachronism in the time of Darius. But it was certainly up-to-date for the age of Antiochus. The latter had indeed obliged all of his subjects, including the Jews, to offer worship to the god Baal, identified with Zeus. The Seleucid sovereign regarded himself as the epiphany of that Greek God (hence the surname, "Epiphanes"—"God manifested"—on the coinage of the realm). The royal pretentions aroused resistance in certain Jewish circles, and Antiochus determined to eliminate the recalcitrants through persecution. Chapter 6 of Daniel, then, is both a political pamphlet and an exhortation to martyrdom rather than apostasy.

Luke 21:20–28: Luke has witnessed the success of the Christian mission. He is concerned with transmitting an optimistic vision of the future of the church. Here he turns his attention to Jerusalem. What will be the future of the faithless city? At the time of Luke's writing, Jerusalem already lies waste. Roman troops have already dealt with the resistance there. What the evangelist is doing, then, is not foretelling the event, but subjecting it to an in-depth reading. To this end he has recourse to a mosaic of Old Testament texts, all speaking of the "devastation" to which Judah and Jerusalem will be delivered by reason of their chronic infidelity to the covenant. What has happened to the city is a consequence of its sins.

Is all hope lost? Nebuchadnezzar of Babylon had destroyed Jerusalem, but Jeremiah 25 had set a limit to his repression. It would not exceed seventy years. In this same spirit, Luke writes: ". . . until the times of the Gentiles are fulfilled." Jerusalem will be chastised, yes. But only for a set time. For that matter, it is possible that by "the times of the Gentiles" Luke means the time necessary for their evangelization. Luke would then be sharing the Pauline hope of a universal conversion.

What will occur after this set time? "There will be signs in the sun, the moon and the stars. On the earth, nations will be in anguish. . . ." Now we are privy to the fate of the "nations" delegated by God to chastise the rebels. Now it is their turn to know the terror and anguish of being enemies of God. The situation of the peoples will be reversed, as foretold in the prophetic oracles, especially in Isaiah 13, which was pronounced upon Babylon. Because the nations have transgressed the prescribed limits of their intervention, God will rise up against them. Thus Luke rereads the events of his time in a perspective, and with a vocabulary, that are altogether traditional.

"After that, men will see the Son of man coming on a cloud with great power and glory." The Son of man comes, with all the attributes of a judge, to pronounce final sentence on the history of humankind. But on that day humanity will be prepared to say: "In the name of the Lord, blessed be the one who comes" (cf. Lk 13:35). The judgment of the Son of man is ever a word of grace.

■

The French language uses the same word to designate a woman carrying a child in her womb and the wall of a fortified city: *enceinte,* "girt about." Thus we use the same expression for the most fragile as for the mightiest, for the humblest as for the most prideful, of creatures! A pregnant woman is a vessel of hope. A city's fortifications represent human beings' desperate attempt to ward off misfortunes and generate a sense of security. Fortifications would fain guarantee life. But the fissures in the walls admit the terror of the instruments of death. Precious little chance a city will have to "withdraw and regroup"— injustice besieges it from all sides, selfishness overwhelms it, intolerance divides it. And if, from time to time, justice, respect, goodness, peace and reconciliation seem to have the upper hand—how often are these victories anything more than respites? Then must we say that pregnant women, these vessels of our hope, our life and our future, are themselves condemned to despair?

To the prophets of doom, to the fatalists who insist they are only transmitting the lessons of history, to the discouraged, the crushed, the disappointed, the failed—behold, an incredible invitation. "Stand up straight and raise your heads, for your ransom is near at hand"! The church sounds a stupendous call down through the centuries, through all the hazards of history!

Yes, the church, the spouse of the beloved Son, is with child. No fortified wall protects her. She has only her hope, founded on God's promise, to bring the human adventure to term. "Stand up straight and raise your heads . . ."! The church has no antidote for human adversity and despair but the News it carries under its heart. But that News is the germ of life. In the face of defeat, it has nothing to cling to but this humble, fragile embryo that it will surely carry to term. "Lift up your heads"!

There will be signs, in heaven and on earth! It is the defeatists and the prideful who must lower their heads. A sign will be given: a babe in a manger, a criminal on a gibbet—but angels in heaven, too, singing the glory of God, and an empty tomb proclaiming the irruption of a new life. Justice and peace will have the last word, because some of the poor will patiently endure to the end, to the coming of the promise fulfilled.

Our strongholds are crumbling. The uncertainties of our time are bringing them down. But we shall not be "like those who have no hope" (1 Thes 4:13). For, together with our mother, the church great with child, we believe that the new City is a-building even now, through our watchfulness. It will be the city of peace for women and men, and the glory of God our Redeemer.

■

May your Word, O God, Guide of our history,
*   be the light of our lives.*
May fear never get the better of our hope.
Hold us in trust,

and grant that we may lift up our heads
to see the coming of endless ages.

■

Be blessed, our Father, our Redeemer.
When we share the bread of our human tables,
    you consecrate it by your Spirit
    and it becomes the firstfruits of the new age.
As it nourishes our hope,
may it give us the foretaste
    of all you prepare for us in eternity.

■

Lord Jesus,
    taking leave of your disciples,
    you committed yourself not to leave them orphans.
Look on the faith of your church,
    and grant us peace once again—
    peace in our days.
For now are the days
    of our hope in your glorious coming.

■

Ruler of time and history,
    blessed be your Name.
Father of life, God of longsuffering,
teach us the secret of time
    and the wisdom of gestation.
Let our hope not falter:
    for even now your Reign is near,
    to grow, to swell, through ages without end.

■

May we never attempt to mend
    an old garment with a new patch!
Lord, despoil us of our narrowness,
    strip us of our shabbiness.
Make our hearts young again,

that we may enter into the feast
of the Spouse who comes in search of us
because he is moved by love.

FRIDAY OF THE 34TH WEEK

CONVERSION
Daniel 7:2-14: With chapter 7, the second part of the Book of Daniel, the visions, has begun. The sacred writer is explicit: these are the night visions of his mind, purely symbolic dreams, first recounted by Daniel (vv. 2-14), then interpreted by an angel.

First of all, Daniel sees four winds that stir the great sea. The winds are doubtless those of the Babylonian cosmogony. As for the sea, the whole of the biblical literature regards the sea as the lair of powers hostile to God. The sea is the disquieting "abyss" of the Book of Genesis, the Tiamat of the Babylonian creation poem. From this sea emerge four monstrous beasts, identifiable with the earthly empires, the last representing that of Alexander the Great. This fourth beast, whose appearance translates the terror inspired by the Macedonian power, is crowned with eleven horns. These represent a succession of eleven kings, the last being Antiochus.

Daniel's dream is purely and simply an allegory—very closely akin, all things considered, to the edifying story of the statue of Nebuchadnezzar in Daniel 2. The terrifying aspect of the sea monsters is an expression of the violence of the struggle being waged between the Reign of God and the terrestrial empires. And in its frantic references to blasphemous reforms and the persecution of Jews loyal to the faith of their ancestors, the recital gives us to understand that that struggle has reached its paroxysm with Antiochus.

But it is also evil's last assault. Yes, the Ancient One—God—has seated himself on his fiery throne. The books are opened, the judgment has commenced. Now shall sentence be pronounced upon the rebellious nations. The last beast is slain, the others reduced to servitude. Then a new character enters the scene, his aspect in striking contrast with the appearance of the monsters. He is "one like a son of man," a child of humanity. Enthroned beside the Ancient One, he receives the everlasting empire.

Luke 21:29-33: "Notice the fig tree, or any other tree." Read the signs! But which signs? The evangelist has just commented upon those he and his community knew: on the one hand the fall of Jerusalem; on the other, the success of the Christian mission. The Reign must be at hand.

198

Thus does history reveal to human beings the presence of God. Jerusalem and the temple have been moments in this history. But they are gone now. After all, "in times past, God spoke in fragmentary and varied ways to our fathers through the prophets; in this, the final age, he has spoken to us through his Son, whom he has made heir of all things and through whom he first created the universe" (Heb 1:1–2). For, with the incarnation, the last stage of history is under way, and the commotion of the cosmos testifies, in its way, to the breach opened by Jesus Christ. Creation is literally undone, to return to the original chaos and permit the genesis of a new world. With the coming of Jesus, time dissolves, and henceforth has no density but in him, to the point that everything is defined in terms of "before" and "after" him.

■

How wide of the mark are those who claim that our faith is the opium of the people! And how equally mistaken are those who would have us turn our faces to the sky and snatch us from an earth become a "vale of tears"!

Our faith challenges us to be accepting of the slow, patient travail of childbirth. After all, there is no other place for the Good News to come than to this deep void in our human earth.

I recall the very dry little cellar in my parents' house where fruits were preserved for the winter. It smelled good—it smelled of pears and plums. These had had to be harvested at just the right time if they were to be just ripe enough when the time came to make them into savory winter desserts!

Our earth must be able to recognize the right time—the season of harvest—if it is to grow and swell into a new earth. Only time's slow maturation will give birth to eternity. But even now, in the charity that contradicts the powers dividing and separating human beings, in the hope that clings to life despite all of the disappointments and failures of our personal and collective history, in the faith that beholds the invisible, real as real can be but at a distance, beyond our uncertainties and our questionings—in all of this we contemplate, even now, the fresh shoots of tomorrow. When the sap swells the fig tree's buds, spring is just around the corner.

"The reign of God is at hand"! Far from plucking us out of our human condition, our faith returns us there. For it is there that, as the espoused, we shall discover the seedlings of the new world. There is no other means for us to reach Jesus than to plunge into our human lives. There is no other place for us to find God than our faithfully espoused existences, with their peaks and their valleys, their hopes and their successes. After all, God, for all eternity, has espoused our history. God is Emmanuel, a God with us and for us.

"Notice the fig tree. . . ." Secretly the sap works in the seemingly dead, lifeless tree. Slowly it mounts to the branches, whose future had seemed all sterility and death. And—marvel of life—the branches begin to green again, and their promise of new birth is fulfilled. Our faith and our hope fairly shove history toward its accomplishment. They convert our times. That is, they bestow upon our age its full dimension, its true measure, its real density. "The reign of God is near"!—and there is no other place for it to come but into our poor, human lives. Here is the true grandeur of our history: that it alone can become history-with-God—sacred history. Then notice the fig tree indeed. It will teach you that our age, too, must be able to recognize harvest time if it would become the age of God.

∎

Ruler of time and history,
   Father of life, and God of longsuffering,
teach us the secret of the season.

SATURDAY OF THE 34TH WEEK

BE ON THE WATCH!
Daniel 7:15–27: The Seleucid persecution, then, represents the finale of the struggle mounted against God by hostile cosmic forces. Solemnly the author of the Book of Daniel maintains that the victory will be God's.

Who was this "Son of man"? His identification had evolved over the centuries. Daniel is a compilation, and the definitive redaction, of earlier traditions. In a first acceptation, the Son of man had been the symbol of the divine lordship at the end of time. Everlasting dominion would be entrusted to him when the terrestrial empires had lost their power. The angelic interpreter identifies him with the "holy ones of the Most High"—that is, with the Jews who will have remained faithful to Yahweh. Thus the Son of man becomes the representative of the authentic Israel, which Daniel asserts will replace the fallen empires.

But history does not stop with the Book of Daniel. The figure of the Son of man gradually came to be individualized. Finally it merged with that of the Messiah. The evangelists would have us understand that Jesus used the title of himself. Indeed, we hear, Jesus announced his passion in the very terms of Daniel: like the "holy ones of the Most High," this "Son of man must be delivered into the hands of men" (Lk 9:44) before he can be exalted to the right hand of God.

Luke 21:34–36: If the "end of the world" is a matter of today—that is, if the Son of man pronounces his judgment in history—the exhortation to watchfulness only takes on more weight. "Be on the watch. Pray constantly for the strength to escape whatever is in prospect. . . ." In the context of this final discourse, placed just before the accounts of the passion and resurrection, the formula clearly designates the passion of the Son of man, in which, like it or not, the disciples will be involved. Thus the exhortation is calculated to encourage them against the moment of their brutal confrontation with the mystery of the cross.

But Luke is thinking of his readers of today and tomorrow, as well. Confronted with the mysteries of existence, will they not be tempted to abandon all? It is then that they must remember that the times of the Reign are already fulfilled—"that our histories are testimony and sign of a coming all glowing within them, and that what to our as yet unopened eyes seems but grim autumn and decay, for the believer, rooted in prayer, with eyes wide open, is springtime, full to the brim with the coming of the Son of man" (P. Bossuyt).

■

"Be on the watch"! And with this injunction, the liturgical year comes to an end. The new year will take up the same invitation: the theme of Advent will be "Watch!" Arrived at journey's end, we find ourselves once more on the frontier of the land of hope.

Have we been traveling in a circle, then? Are we forever condemned to retrace the selfsame course?

Or will our course be . . . "the same but different" every time?

"Be on the watch"! Yes, we have been refreshed along the way, but with a water that leaves us thirsting. Yes, we have been fed by the roadside, and have regained our strength, but the bread we have eaten has only sharpened our hunger in its very allaying. "Be on the watch"! To be sure, our memory pricks us to watchfulness. But the injunction launches us once more toward tomorrow, sets us "on the road again," and prevents us from confusing the destination in the distance with the still more distant horizon. Still more importantly it prevents us from identifying that horizon with the authentic term of our hope. "Be on the watch"! That is, advance courageously. Our trek has not been mapped out for us in advance. We must prepare the passage ourselves, and in myriad ways, but we must also allow the way to open where we do not expect it. "Be on the watch"! Lest we nod, lest we give way to dreaming, let us seek to prepare the passage actively.

Without stint. But neither with fear. After all, *En garde!* is neither a warning nor a threat, but a battle cry—the call to the combat between life and death.

En garde! How could the liturgical year have ended with any other cry? For only this challenge can launch a new year. All by itself it summarizes, it condenses, our faith experience. The issue of the struggle will not be of our making. Perhaps when the Bridegroom comes knocking we shall yet be awake. Or perhaps he will find us like a child who has drifted off at last, dropping some toy as one lays down one's weapons. Then he will whisper to us, with a smile and infinite tenderness, "Be on the watch!"—and take us up in his arms to rouse us in the land of Day.

■

God of infinite patience,
tireless is your quest for us.
Tirelessly you strive
to lead us to your covenant.
Grant that we may stay watchful in faith
and persevere in hope.
Thus will you fulfill our desire
and hear our prayer:
to belong to you in a world without end.

■

Be praised, God our Father.
In the bread that sustains our journey
we receive the life of Christ.
Keep us watchful in hope,
that the coming of the Lord Jesus
may not find us in slumber—
and yet, do catch us ever by surprise
with your infinite love,
God blessed now and forever.

EVEN YEARS
ORDINARY TIME
WEEKS 22-34

Gospel According to Saint Luke
First Letter to the Corinthians
Proverbs
Ecclesiastes
Job
Letter to the Galatians
Letter to the Ephesians
Letter to the Philippians
Letter to Titus
Letter to Philemon
Letters of Saint John
Revelation

Church and Gospel

As we know, Luke wrote a two-volume work: the Acts of the Apostles, and the Gospel according to Luke. They are like the two leaves of a single diptych. They ring with the same intuitions. The third gospel is called the gospel of the Spirit: for only the God's Breath, who traverses human history, gives the church a soul. There is no vacant interval between the time of Jesus and that of those who believe in him. The church is both the product of the gospel, and its vehicle. It used to be said that the Good News is somehow opposed to sacred tradition. This is a false antagonism. The church occurs both in, and for, a community of believers. The mission of the church is to live and spread a proclamation. And it is born of this very proclamation.

The word of God proclaimed by Jesus Christ is the word of the apostles. They testify to what they have seen and heard. There is nowhere that the word of God can make itself heard but in the clumsy words of believers attempting to utter the unutterable, as they bear witness to what they have contemplated. The word of God is molded in the human word; henceforth and forever, then, the divine word will flow in the clumsy, but indispensable word of the church. According to Acts, the word of God is a word of salvation, (13:26), a word of life (14:3, 20:32). One encounters the Good News in virtue of the provoking, challenging preaching of the church. The gospel recounts the salvific power and force of Jesus' word; thus it becomes the prehistory and foundation of the action of the word in the missionary preaching of the Acts of the Apostles.

The bond between sacred tradition and gospel is at the very roots of our faith. The God of the Christians ties his revelation to the testimony of believers. Have we genuinely grasped what it means for this God to call himself the "God of Abraham, the God of Isaac, and the God of Jacob," and henceforth to call himself the "God of Jesus"? God bears the name of those who believe in him, for he has never shown anything of himself but the face of those who believe in him. Even when he was transfigured on the hill, manifesting his status as the Image of the invisible God, Jesus showed as yet only the dazzling countenance of a human being transfigured by total faith and obedience. The foundational relationship between God and his church is a bond intrinsic to the revelation of an incarnate God, and a bond at the basis of our faith and the originality of the God of the Christians: God binds himself to a people of believers. This is the glory of the church, and its responsibility: God will be what Christians make of him.

The bond between tradition and gospel, then, is foundational for our faith. And so we shall do well to ponder the testimony of the first communities, together with the gospel that brings this foundational bond into such striking relief. Like all histories, this will be a story woven of babblings, hesitations, questioning, search and even error. The church is inventing itself, the church is seeking itself, the church is alive. And it is in these slow adjustments that the word of God takes shape and form. The word of God is always, inextricably, a mixture: a *mélange* of human words and the transcendent word of God. And the reason why we are still interested today in the very particular problems of the young communities of Galatia, Ephesus or Philippi, the reason why we attach any importance to Titus and Philemon, the reason why we listen to what the communities at the close of the first century are saying—is not that we are overcome with nostalgia, or loyally enslaved to the past. It is only that we have no other way of reaching the living word of God! The respiration of the Spirit is in the life of the church.

FROM MONDAY TO WEDNESDAY

OF THE 22ND WEEK

Converted

"These have been recorded to help you believe that Jesus is the Messiah, the Son of God" (Jn 20:31). What else is the object of the gospel? The gospel is this initiation, and this passage. It leads us to posit the act of faith. A human creature has appeared in human history. He has dwelt among us, as life, light, salt and leaven in the human mass. With him, human taste has changed. For we have seen his body heaving on a gallows, we have witnessed the victory of his life over death, we have received his words of grace. And we human beings have been moved to cry: Today the promise is fulfilled! And this everlasting marvel is the church of all times. For the church has discovered with what great love God has loved his human creatures, and is unable to keep this good news to itself.

And if this news can seem a bit threadbare after so many centuries, if perhaps we must acknowledge that we have neutralized its explosive force—we must also repeat and testify today that it can turn a life upside down. The Spirit can come in a squall, and simply sweep away our personal and collective pettiness. Despite our failures, which are our afflictions, and our desertions, which are our shame—we dare to say and proclaim: the gospel has converted us.

■

Can your Word be locked up
within the confines of a book?
Lord Jesus, make your Church
the book, open till the end of time,
in which we read the startling story
of your infinite love—
Good News and tireless hope
forever and ever.

■

Lord Jesus,
may your voice not die out in our hearts.
May your love
not dim in our memories.

Stay with us,
O Word welling up from our silences.
O Charity who satisfy our desires,
may your Reign and glory come!

TODAY

1 Corinthians 2:1–5: The church of Corinth has fallen victim to division. A pagan influence on all sides, a series of sterile discussions, an immoderate love of the philosophy of raw speculation, have all conspired to create a very stormy atmosphere. And yet the Christians of Corinth have recruited the little and the lowly. Paul does not overlook the paradox of the divine choice: "God . . . singled out the weak of this world to shame the strong" (1 Cor 1:27).

At the same time, as he is wont to do, the apostle cites the other side of a coin whose face is scratched and marred. Paul knows the taste of the Greeks for the art of oratory and philosophical discussions, and has not wished to rely on the prestige of the Word, or on wisdom, to win the adherence of his hearers. He has preferred the path of the Spirit, who speaks to the heart and leaves its owner at liberty. In speaking of the "power of the Spirit," Paul is alluding not to miracles that would have guaranteed the truth of his preaching, but to the "fruits" that had ripened in every community animated by the Holy Spirit: fervor, the charity of sisters and brothers, joy. Indeed, in a world as cynical and sophisticated as the Greco-Roman empire, such manifestations must have come as a surprise. And in their own way, they have testified to Jesus Christ crucified.

"I have more understanding than all my teachers," sings the writer of *Psalm 119,* referring to the benefits of the law. The Christian knows another law: that of an exchange of love.

Luke 4:16–30: (See p. 7.)

■

Today! Everything in Jesus' programmatic discourse turns on this word. Here is Good News for today, says Luke to his church. At the moment he writes, Christians are awaiting the Lord's second coming. They expect this coming presently. After all, the Lord had said that their generation would not pass away without seeing him again. And many among them, fixing their gaze on the time to come, are utterly unconcerned with the world in which they live. Luke undertakes to proclaim to them "the currency of God." Do not be inactive! Do not turn your backs on the world. That word is being fulfilled today. Today has salvation begun. "Today this scripture is fulfilled in your hearing"!

Christianity is a faith in reality. Christianity is the living of "God's today."

We nurse no nostalgia for a past that cannot return. "Why do you stand here looking up at the skies? This Jesus . . . has been taken up from you. . . ." (Acts 1:11), said the angels of the Ascension. Our faith is not the cherished memory of a time whose end we must lament. The church is not a community of the past. But neither are we utopian souls, homesick for tomorrow. Yes, we have been instructed to stay on the watch. But to Christians awaiting the Parousia from second to second, Paul is saying: "Does someone not work? Then let that one not eat!" We do not say, "Well, I don't know what good it is to hope, but I do hope for a time when everything will be lovely at last and a paradise will tumble down from heaven." Our faith is not that kind of hope.

We are creatures of the present—God's eternal present. If the word of God changed no one, if it had no effect on the world—starting right now —that word would be bland and tasteless. In fact it would be ridiculous. But God's word is life. God's word is the welfare of humanity. The Good News is really good only if it is the germ of a human life. We turn to our past only for the sake of today—only to decipher the hope that is our heritage in the present moment. Despite all appearances to the contrary, life has the last word, because one morning someone rose from his tomb. And we turn to the future only because we desire to see more clearly what, for now, we only see in the chiaroscuro of faith.

The mystery of God does not depend on our demonstrations. The mystery of God is a new life, a life led according to the Spirit. And it is in the only too familiar hazards of everyday living that this re-creation is effected. It is here, in the banality and insignificance of every day, that the Christian meets God. Yes, we happen to speak of eternity. But we do so not in order to belittle time, we do so in an attempt to utter the infinity of God, the inexhaustible source of life, the depth of mystery that will never run dry. "Today," Jesus says. To speak the name of God, must we not live each day as God's "today," a day ever new—and rediscover the Word that gives us rebirth, day by day, in God's sight and in God's care?

■

God, who is Good News in the hearts of the poor,
     Lord, have mercy.
O eternal burst of freedom in the depths of our imprisonment,
     Christ, have mercy.
Word ever fertile,
     Lord, have mercy.

■

Today is your Word fulfilled, Lord our God:
  your consecrating Spirit is upon us.
May our life proclaim your peace,
  our joy:
  the good news we receive from your lips.
And may we enjoy what you promise
  throughout all eternity.

TUESDAY OF THE 22ND WEEK

SPIRITUAL PERSONS

1 Corinthians 2:10–16: Divine wisdom is a gift of the Spirit. After all, only the Spirit penetrates the secrets of God. And it can be communicated only by those who have received this Spirit, for it is thus that they are enabled to understand. Being placed in a position of false rivalry with Apollos, and finding himself at odds with persons who rely on purely human eloquence— the mere philosophers of truth—Paul claims to speak the language of the very Spirit of truth.

The terms he uses are important. On the one side there is the "natural" person, "who has only his human forces" to rely on, as well as the person of mere "soul," who is nevertheless dubbed "perfect" by the mystery religions. These individuals have participated in the rites of initiation, and thus have been informed of the knowledge to which their particular sect is privy. This raw learning is characterized by the mystery of mere enigma. On the other side, however, as Paul asserts (v 7), a "mysterious . . . hidden" wisdom reveals the secret of God's design realized in Jesus Christ. Would the Corinthians have mystery? Here is mystery. Then Paul launches a polemic against the gnosis and the mystery religions, those so very questionable efforts of the human mind. His letter, we see, reflects the world well—both the mysteries that world has concocted, and the true mystery that lies at its secret core.

Here again is a hymn in the alphabetical style so dear to the wisdom schools. *Psalm 145* restates the truth of the divine message, while exalting the mission of the faithful, who are to shout to the world this message of a God of tenderness and pity.

Luke 4:31–37: (See p. 10.)

■

Who has known the mind of God? Who will be his counselor? Be that as it may, we have the mind of Christ! This is the Christian claim. Pretentiousness? No, simply the difference between Christians and others.

What is special about us is not our morality. Surely not everything true, good, beautiful and human, is specifically Christian. Nor is it our sincere quest for truth. For not everyone animated by a genuine conviction, a true faith, an upright will, is a Christian. Nor is what differentiates us from others our profound search for the meaning of life and history. After all, the Christian Church is not present in every meditation group, every cell of activists and every community of the committed. Christianity is not always present where a combat is being waged against inhumanity.

No, the originality of our faith resides in this, that we have recognized the face of God, and our own face, in the human being who is the eternal Word of God. Christianity is the activation of "a dangerous, liberating memory" (Johannes B. Metz). The difference between us and the rest of the world is a person with a name: Jesus professed as the Christ. What is specific in Christianity, what is absolutely original there, is that Christianity regards Jesus as an absolutely critical, crucial personage— as the determining factor, the norm, of all dimensions of human existence. Christianity is the profession of a unique name.

"No one knows what lies at the depths of God but the Spirit of God." Need we be surprised that, once they had recognized in Jesus the depositary par excellence of the Spirit ("He has anointed me . . . to bring glad tidings. . . ."), the first Christian communities regarded Joel's prophetic outcry as having been accomplished by way of their very existence? The Spirit, who had been "extinguished" with the last of the prophets, would now be poured out on the entire people, for the last days are upon us. "God's Spirit, helping us to recognize. . . ." This, and this alone, is our originality. The Christian is a "spiritual" person, a person filled with a Spirit, and their Spirit is none other than God, who is so very near to us and our world, a power and a force seizing but unseizable, prodigal in gift but unavailable to manipulation, creator of life, and its judge.

Do we appreciate the extraordinary liberating power of this statement: "The spiritual man . . . can appraise everything"? Invested with the Spirit, we are freed—set free from the judgment of God, set free from our neighbors' judgments, set free from our own judgment. In this freedom, a great multitude of anonymous persons, extending from the apostolic age to our own day, have never failed to find courage, support, strength and consolation in their decisions, their anguish, their dangers, their aspirations and their hopes. Possessed by the Spirit, ever and again we rise up and turn toward life.

■

It is good, Lord, to thank you
    for the gift of your Spirit—
    Jesus' Promise, kept!
May this Spirit whisper to us the human words
    that will worthily praise your name.

May this Spirit of all joy
    be the wellspring of our faith
    and the pledge of our freedom.

May this Spirit of truth
    confirm your presence
    by awakening our hope.

WEDNESDAY OF THE 22ND WEEK

TO BE CHURCH

1 Corinthians 3:1–9: Divisions in the church are a scandal. They show only too clearly that those who foster them, or even tolerate them, are bereft of the maturity of persons animated by the Spirit of God. Paul asserts the importance of a catechesis suited to the hearers' capacity to understand.

"We are God's co-workers. . . ." Paul and Apollos both toil at the building up of the Body of Christ, each in the measure of the talent with which God has entrusted him. Paul plants, Apollos waters, but God alone gives growth. The growth of the church, like the knowledge of God's secrets, is a gift of the Spirit.

"Happy the nation whose God is the Lord . . ." (Ps 33)! Paraphrasing the scriptures, let us cry: Happy the church that is animated by the Spirit!

Luke 4:38–44: (See p. 12.)

■

The church is Spirit-sprung. The church is the community of those who believe in Christ—of those who have committed themselves to the cause of Jesus Christ and who testify that their church is hope for all. The task of the church is to serve that cause, to defend it in the spirit of Jesus, and to bend every effort that it may succeed.

We could never hope to live, and to live together, as church, without this common origin of ours. We are all born of the Spirit. Whatever our age, our mentality or our culture, our birth is registered in the one book of life. And this registration is much more than a record of identity. It is a matter of our very blood, our life's breath. We have all been engendered by one and the same Word, and by a grace that none can imprison. The unity of the church is not some scholarly, balanced, bland compromise. The unity of the church has its origin in a shared gift: the gospel alone is our rule, and we are all at its service.

To belong to the church, then, is to make room within us for the gift of the Spirit to grow, make room for this grace to display its power. Membership in the church will never be limited to adherence to such and such a teaching, or defined by such and such a lifestyle. To belong to the church is to let ourselves be attached to the person of Jesus Christ—to permit the tying of a bond of love and faith that will both establish us in communion with one another, and root this living communion in Jesus himself.

"You are his cultivation. . . ." The Word becomes seed. By the gift of his Spirit, God cradles our hearts in the rhythmic tide of his love. Thus he draws us into a life in accordance with his design—just as a soft melody soothes the soul, then gradually gathers power until it sweeps our very body into the dance.

My sisters and brothers, you belong to no human being. You are born of God, and to God you belong, wholly and entirely. To belong to the church is to become church—to walk in the footsteps of Jesus, to be molded by the Spirit, to be "God's cultivation."

■

Your Spirit, God our Father, molds us:
your grace arouses our faith,
your love calls forth our own.

As we belong to your Christ,
may his word bear fruit in us,
that you may take pride
in what that fruit will accomplish for eternity.

Blessed be your name, O God,
for your Word made flesh
and for his body become our bread!

For the life of your Son us,
and for his blood given for love,
    be blessed!

May the Spirit he has poured forth in our hearts
    consecrate our human lives.
Sanctify our present time,
    as you sanctify—even now—
    the everlasting ages.

FROM THURSDAY OF THE 22ND WEEK

TO FRIDAY OF THE 23RD WEEK

Novelty of the Spirit

Why liturgy? Why do we celebrate? We shall grasp the originality of worship in this "time of the church," wherein our existences flow, this time of Luke's great concern, only if we grasp the importance of the reversal, the complete turnaround, inaugurated by the coming of the Word and the rush of Pentecost. "Our worship is the result of a liberation. It becomes possible in virtue of an event that transcends humanity. That event is the gift of the Spirit. The Spirit bestows tokens or pledges of the world to come. That is, in and through the Spirit the Reign of God, the future age, bursts upon our world and establishes something like a colony, a bridgehead to the world where, as the Book of Revelation says, there will be no more weeping, or sorrow, or suffering, but everlasting life. The Holy Spirit evokes by his presence an eschatological situation, and this situation calls for and is expressed in worship. We are worshiping beings not only because, in the power and exaltation of these pledges of the future, we cannot refrain from returning thanks, but also, and perhaps especially, because it is in worship that we find our true role, the one for which we have been created—a liturgical role. Worship has an essentially eschatological scope, and Guardini is certainly not wrong to call it somewhere, 'eschatological athletics' " (von Allmen, *Prophétisme sacramentel*, p. 289).

Why liturgy? So that the revelation of our election and sanctification may reach us. So that a word may be pronounced today that sets the world on its ear. So that, today, our vocation may be placed before our eyes. Why liturgy? Because the gospel becomes our Bread.

■

We thank you,
Father of tenderness, God the source of all love,
by Jesus Christ your beloved Son.
In him you have chosen us to celebrate your name
and the novelty of the Word.
By him you have consecrated all things,
pouring forth your Spirit
to inspire, to enliven, our lives.

You the Most Holy, the Most High,
you upset our evidences
and you become God-close-at-hand—
God-among us.

Astounded at such mercy,
as we await the return of your Christ,
O God, we bless you.

THURSDAY OF THE 22ND WEEK

CAUGHT OR CAPTIVATED?

1 Corinthians 3:18–23: This paragraph functions as a conclusion to what has now been said, and it is an interesting example of Paul's "chiasmic structure." First he has denounced the pair of disorders peculiar to the church of Corinth —divisions (A:1:10–16) and human wisdom (B:1:17–25). Next he has posited the principle in virtue of which he condemns these deviations: Christian existence is an existence in Christ who has become "our wisdom and also our justice, our sanctification, and our redemption" (C:1:30). On the basis of this principle, the apostle can draw up a list of the characteristics of true wisdom (B':2:6–16) and deplore the scandal of division (A':3:1–16).

There is another chiasmus at the end of the paragraph. It resumes both of the above cited themes (divisions and false wisdom) and reverses them. First, wisdom: the one who is wise after the fashion of the world must be converted to divine ways, which will make that person a fool in human eyes. As for divisions, it is to Christians' own advantage to cause these to disappear, for they make us the slaves of a particular party, while Christ has come to deliver all humanity, and the true preachers of the gospel have no other ambition but to be the servants of the community.

Psalm 24 is taken from an entrance liturgy. It is used here for the sake of its first two verses: the earth belongs to God as the Corinthians belong to Christ.

Luke 5:1-11: (See p. 15.)

■

Jesus' friends have been fishing all night, but have returned without a catch. To their astonishment, Jesus instantly challenges them to sail once more for the deep, and again cast their nets. They comply, and their catch is beyond their wildest dreams. The nets begin to snap, and all succeeding centuries will hear of the miraculous catch of fish.

It all could have ended there. Then of course we should have had a different story to tell. But it did not end there. Jesus went on: "From now on you will be catching men." The image is a startling one, and it transforms the wonderful event into a parable. On this morning, Jesus has unveiled the mission of the church.

Catching men! But see the competition along the docks! All manner of sects, gurus and ideologies vie with one another to bait the men and women swept hither and yon in the treacherous currents of their meaningless lives. Is the church nothing but one fishing company among many?

"From now on you will be catching men"! But one can be caught as fugitives are caught, or as lovers are caught! "From now on you will be catching men"! The church can only cast its nets as its Lord did. He caught them by calling them, not tricking them. He enlightened them with his truth rather than manipulating them. He strengthened them with his Spirit, but without doing them violence. Yes, Jesus catches us, but for our joy—he sets us free. Jesus captures us by captivating us.

From this moment on, the church will have the mission of casting the word to the four winds, and men and women will be seduced by a countenance that awakens them to life and freedom. "From now on . . ." means not only: "From this time forward," but: "Because of the experience you have just had." Though seduced, the church will not turn seducer. Pressure, stories, slogans and blackmail are altogether foreign to authentic mission. The church has not received the vocation to catch anyone in nets. It has not received the task of "having," of possessing, a human being. Only those are touched to the quick who have felt a freedom awaken within them, who have seen their liberty aroused, resuscitated, raised from death. And out of the freedom of a converted heart comes the cry, "You know that I love you" (Jn 21:17). Only lovers are caught in the nets that plunge them into the freedom of life.

■

God our Father,
your Son has seduced us:
　　possessed by your Spirit,
　　we are captivated with his word.
And so we ask you:
　　at his invitation, may we take the risk
　　of going where you call?

■

God our Father,
we have toiled to build a world of peace,
　　and our toil has borne no lasting fruit.
Now, at your Son's word,
　　we cast our nets again.
Fulfill our hope,
sustain our courage:
　　may your promise be our life.

FRIDAY OF THE 22ND WEEK

A WEDDING FAST?

1 Corinthians 4:1–5: "Who in your opinion is that faithful, farsighted steward whom the master will set over his servants to dispense their ration of grain in season? That servant is fortunate whom his master finds busy when he returns" (Lk 12:42–43). Jesus is placing his disciples before their responsibilities. They are the first servants of the Christian people. Just so, Paul submits his cause to the Lord: God alone can pass a serene judgment on Paul's apostolic activity.

Psalm 37 is constructed alphabetically, and this is because of its scope. Like the wisdom writings, it lists "from *a* to *z*" the prescriptions to be observed by the righteous if they would obtain salvation, which can come from God alone.

Luke 5:33–39: (See p. 18.)

■

Why ever would one want to go on a fast when the Groom has arrived? The habits we have acquired in our quest for God, all our old criteria, are reversed, upset. Can you ask guests to fast at a wedding? The moment he enters our history, Jesus confers on that history an utterly radical newness. Since the Incarnation, since the Passion, since the Resurrection, nothing in our relationships with God, with one another or within our own life and death can be "the way it was." A new wine is seething, and Jesus tells us we had better have our new wineskins ready! When Jesus is "called to order"—to the law and order of an austere piety—he responds with a discourse on love and weddings!

You poor, poor folk, exuding the ennui of your deadly religions, the insipidity of your flat, colorless virtues—will you ever understand that when God comes it is to bring us something new, and to speak of love and feasting? Jesus is here! He invites us to enter into the rhythm of his word, and his word is a proclamation of renewal. He invites us to share his passion—to receive from his hands this new wine, the blood that he will give that his beloved bride may live. The cup of our covenant overflows! For it is to our own wedding that Jesus invites us. It is time to drink new wine and not look back. It is time to forget all the infidelities of the past. For this is the feast of love. And yet . . . at this very moment we are encouraged to fast, and to fast to the very depths of our souls! For suddenly the Groom is gone, and we are left with a house to tend, and a prayer: *Marana tha!!* On and on goes the wedding banquet, and our longing for the endless banquet waxes apace. And we stand astonished that mere servants can have received such responsibility: a world to give life to, a piece of News to reinvent. Stewards of the Reign of God, we are charged with the task of drawing the new from the old— the task of incarnating, along our hesitant path, the blunders, the errors that are the price of any quest. We are assigned the mission of bestowing flesh on God's own wedding celebration with our poor humanity.

CONSECRATION

1 Corinthians 4:9–15: "I am writing you in this way not to shame you but to admonish you as my beloved children." Wake up, Corinthians! You rely much too heavily on the assurance of your bare intelligence. You wish to seem sensible, strong, respectable. No, see that you look like fools! See that you are weak and despised. Imitate Christ, whom I, Paul, have shown to you as the sole source of salvation.

Alphabetical in its structure, *Psalm 145* sings the qualities of Yahweh, and is addressed to all who place their trust in him.

Luke 6:1–5: (See p. 20.)

■

"The Son of Man is Lord even of the sabbath." The Groom is here! It is time for the wedding, and the old commonplaces no longer hold. On the evening of the sixth day, God had taken his rest, to consecrate his creation, and human beings had consecrated the sabbath to the praise of God and his wondrous works. The sabbath is a day for sanctifying time. But Jesus is here! Henceforward every human life is declared holy. Every human life is now human time and God's time. Henceforth nothing human is foreign to God.

O scandal of our faith: the sacred is profane and the profane sacred! The first Christians were caught dead to rights: yes, they were atheists! For the gospel is no ordinary religion. Nor, surely, is it a religion of sentiment and feeling. A religion that flows from feeling monopolizes God. A religion of feeling reverences, posits, invokes, desires a God who is elsewhere, far from human events. Like the prophets before him, Jesus overturns this image. Religion proceeds from faith, from the hearing of a word. In order to enter into contact with God, we are no longer required to forsake our human condition. No, God has entered history now, and become a human word, human littleness. Faith effects a turnaround that is well-nigh incredible. Instead of erecting a barrier between the world of earth and that of God, it sanctifies our worldly condition! How ever can we have made of God our enemy, our competitor? How can we have been so poor and petty in drawing back the veil of the secret meaning of the enormous toil of the women and

217

men who devote themselves to making the world livable and humane? For it is precisely there, in this patient birthgiving, that we find the coming of the Word and the surge of the Spirit.

"The Son of Man is Lord even of the sabbath." Through the deed recorded in today's gospel, Jesus has made of the Incarnation something more than a theologian's theory. God speaks in human life alone.

MONDAY OF THE 23RD WEEK

LEAVEN OF THE SPIRIT
1 Corinthians 5:1–8: So much for the scandal of division. Now for the ethical problems. Not without a touch of irony, Paul addresses the case of a Christian living with his stepmother. How can such wise folk as the Corinthians tolerate a like situation? They ought to have excluded the sinner from their community.

This situation is an instance of the problems raised by the spread of Christianity in a pagan milieu. Corinth was a port city. Its pleasure-dome atmosphere was conducive either to extreme moral laxity, or to the contempt for the flesh preached by certain philosophies. Faced with these questions, Paul makes an effort to promote a balanced approach to them, one inspired by his Christian vision of the human being. "Everything is lawful for me," he cries—but that does not mean that everything is good for me" (1 Cor 6:12)! True, Christians have been liberated by Christ's death, and need no longer take cognizance of any morality of permissions and prohibitions. But they must still make an effort to lead a life in conformity with what the Spirit of love inspires in them. In other words, the life of the Christian should concretize an identification with the immolated Christ, just as the life of the church should reflect the holiness bestowed on that church by Christ on the cross. Consequently, when sin threatens the community it must be torn up by the roots. The immolation of Christ, the true paschal lamb, has dissolved the old yeast of sin once and for all, making it possible to lead a genuine paschal life of purity, as symbolized by the unleavened bread.

Psalm 5 is a complaint. The psalmist protests his innocence, reasserting the incompatibility between God and evil.

Luke 6:6–11: (See p. 22.)

■

Jesus heals the hand! Once more a sabbath cure testifies to his messianic authority. Through the prophetic deed of his messenger, God the Master of time and history consecrates our entire life. God saves. This is his very name, and he will brook no obstacle to the Good News. The gospel is salvation and wholeness: the cure of the withered hand testifies to that.

As a consecrated life, a life made holy, our life is "religious" through and through. There is no "profane" in life any longer. The locus of the coming of the Word of salvation, the place of his incarnation, is everyday life. True, Christians have been liberated by Christ's death. They need no longer take any cognizance of a morality of the permitted and the forbidden. But they must still lead a life in conformity with what the Spirit asks of them. "Get rid of the old yeast to make of yourselves fresh dough, unleavened loaves, as it were; Christ our Passover has been sacrificed." Life according to the Spirit will not be primarily the observance of rules or norms. Primarily it will be a breathing, a respiration. We have been set free by the passover of the Lord—free from guilt, the law, death. The Spirit we have received is the freedom and courage to act, to love, to live in peace, justice, joy, hope and thanksgiving. And despite all the lapses and failures of the church from the apostolic age to our own day, countless believers have found strength and consolation in their decisions, their anguish, their dangers, their aspirations and their hopes. The Spirit is leaven, and nothing in our lives is beyond the Spirit's reach. The Christian life is primarily an existence conducted under the name of Jesus, not a number of observances that leave everything else unconsecrated. Either all of the dough rises, or it all remains heavy and tasteless. You are a new yeast. Then live in the truth of the Gospel.

■

You are as Passover bread.
 "Get rid of the old yeast"!
Do not profane love!
 Lord, have mercy.

You are as Passover bread.
 "Get rid of the old yeast"!
Stop coddling sadness!
 Christ, have mercy.

You are as Passover bread.
 "Get rid of the old yeast"!
Why are you mired down in mediocrity?
 Lord, have mercy.

■

God our Father,
your Son is the firstborn of a new world,
        a seed cast to earth for our salvation,
        and he has sprung up for an abundant harvest.
His resurrection is the leaven that lifts our earth
        and thrusts it toward the day of fulfillment.
Pour forth your Spirit upon us:
        may he be the germ of the birthgiving that must be,
        and the breath to guide our history.

TUESDAY OF THE 23RD WEEK

CHOSEN

1 Corinthians 6:1–11: "The community of believers were of one heart and one mind," we read of the first Christians (Acts 4:32). But we can scarcely say this of the Corinthian community! Division among Christians had reached such a pitch that they were hailing one another before the courts! Paul reproaches such very wise ladies and gentlemen with their inability to settle their own differences, so that they had to go running to the civil tribunals. Not that Paul is without regard for these tribunals. Does he not urge Christians, in Romans 13, to submit to legitimate authority? The point is only that unity, peace and the charity of sisters and brothers must come first in the community. These are its foundation and character.

Psalm 149 is a hymn, and a most festive one. It expresses the Lord's love for his people, a people at one despite their divisions.

Luke 6:12–19: (See p. 24.)

■

Jesus selects twelve followers—and twelve that know the winds over the lake, the art of hoisting sail! Was the night rebellious? But they had learned at an early age to cling to hope till morn. And it was they he called. Without any other apprenticeship, Jesus entrusts them with the word. In their hands the Word becomes flesh and history—a Word with a name and a face, a Word that is health and wholeness for the human beings that we are because he has a name: Jesus, Emmanuel, God-with-us. "The whole crowd was trying to touch him because power went out from him which cured all."

On the strength of their faith in this call, the Twelve set out, leaving father and fortune behind. They will decipher the word and its mystery. Along their way, the blind will cry out for the light of day for their eyes, and slaves will beg to be delivered from their chains. And the Word will open those eyes and break those chains. The Good News is abroad in our land!

"He called his disciples. . . ." This little phrase contains the whole of the faith and life of the church. Ours not to ask whether we "have it in us" to respond to this call, ours not to examine whether we are worthy of it. Ours not to worry about the frailty of our freedom or our capacity to commit an entire lifetime. The church springs from a calling, a vocation. After all, there is not the remotest similarity between a decision that rests on our own freedom, and a decision based on the freedom of Christ. It is God who calls, and so it is God's to know whom he calls and how. When God takes this risk, ours is but to accept the risk he asks of us. God is only too familiar with the risk of incomprehension: "Will you also go away?" God has known the betrayal of Judas and the denials of Peter. The wager of faith is first and foremost God's wager. "He called his disciples. . . ." Sisters and brothers, if you doubt God, do not risk this adventure. If the mainstays of your faith are only yours, woe to you indeed.

"He called his disciples. . . ." And they go! They take the risk. Surely the adventure of faith is a leap in the dark, a departure without travellers' insurance. Only *in via*, on the road, do the Twelve begin to grasp in depth how well-advised their undertaking has been. From century to century and age to age, we shall be the vessels of the Word to the extent that we are the receptacles of our fellow human beings' agonizing questions. From Galilee to the Parousia, from creation to the resurrection of the dead, men and women will testify that the Word of God vanquishes death. Christians are as frail as any of their sisters and brothers. They are devastated by the same sufferings. They live the same hopes. The hope that distinguishes them is their knowledge that, from the first morning of the universe, God has called his human creatures. And this too is grace.

■

O God, who call us to adventure,
grant us to recognize your invitation,
*   and set out on the road to your Reign*

in freedom and gladness,
in the footsteps of Jesus, the Christ, our Lord.

■

It is good to sing of your tenderness,
    O God who never ceases to shed your grace!
It is good to bless your faithfulness!
Daily you raise up apostles
    to bear witness to the Gospel.

Today your church is still the light
    in which every man and woman can find hope
    and the strength to advance along the pathways of life.

Be blessed for your messenger Jesus,
    in whom the world has seen the dawn
    of the day of promise.
Filled with the power of these glad tidings,
    O God of apostles and prophets,
    we celebrate your name!

WEDNESDAY OF THE 23RD WEEK

THE OTHER WAY AROUND

1 Corinthians 7:25–31: In chapter seven, Paul treats successively of married couples, virgins, and widows. If we are not to miss the thrust of the apostle's thinking, there are a number of things we must note. First of all we shall do well to reflect that Paul has never undertaken to compose an exhaustive treatise on marriage and celibacy. He only responds to certain precise questions that he has been asked. Next, we must call attention to the fact that, except in the matter of divorce (vv 10–11), he repeatedly states that his opinions apply to himself alone. Would it be honest to absolutize what the apostle himself was at such pains to relativize?

Further: we must note the climate that surrounds Paul's thinking. In the midst of his directives, he enunciates a general principle: Let his hearers remain in the state in which God's call has found each of them (vv 17–24). Is he alluding to the discussions that divided the Church of Corinth? Doubtless we must keep in mind the philosophical currents that despised the body and erected celibacy

222

into an absolute ideal. At all events, Paul insists that marriage, like celibacy, is God's gift (v. 7).

Christians should make no change in the state in which they had been living before their conversion, then. Christ's return is in the very air, altogether relativizing mere everyday considerations. And yet Paul is not counseling indifference. On the contrary, he appeals for watchfulness. We are instructed to discover the essential values in order to range the others in their proper order.

Psalm 45 is a poem composed for a royal wedding. Verses 11–13 are addressed to the bride, a foreign princess, to encourage her to enter into the marriage bond without hesitation, while verses 14–16 describe her cortege. Verses 17–18 are to the king, and promise him sons.

Luke 6:20–26: (See p. 29.)

■

"Blest. . . . Woe . . ."! Let us not be misled by the ringing antitheses of Luke's Beatitudes. When God addresses us, and sets before us both blessing and curse, he does so only for our happiness. God's promise is always a word of grace. A crowd gathers. They are to hear the one who speaks in the name of God! And the whole country of Judea, with its capital, Jerusalem—even the neighboring regions of Tyre and Sidon, foreign lands—swarm to the spot. Luke is thinking of the teeming church of the early communities, the church of Jerusalem and the church of the Greek world. The church hears its Lord, and attends to the path he is about to reveal.

"Blest are you poor . . ."! Poverty! We are dismayed that Jesus could place happiness in poverty. Not to mention the tears and persecution of the poor! "Blest," happy! Here the human response is: Impossible. If there is happiness there, it must be a false happiness. If this is the price of happiness, we cannot afford it. Be on your way.

Happy! We believe that Jesus was the Poor one, the Abandoned, the Condemned. Yes, he has trodden the royal road. The path to happiness is the one he walked to Calvary. Insanity! (To human beings.) Scandal! (To the "wise.") And yet—this is the path to Easter.

The poor, the starving, the weeping, the persecuted . . . are all the same persons! It is ever the same folk who have nothing, and at the same time are the object of ridicule on the part of wise, realistic persons. It is to these that Jesus addresses his word of consolation. "For the Lord comforts his people and shows mercy to his afflicted" (Is 49:13). In God's name, Jesus opens up the way of salvation, and cries to the poor: This is for you!

We think we can build our happiness by playing our cards in just the right way. Then along comes God and reshuffles the deck. The Reign of God is a grace, a grand reward! What was called "death" becomes life. Sin is transfigured into pardon and grace. The world of humanity has collapsed, and God's antipodes has sprung up in its place. Surely there is no happiness in being poor. The weeping have never been told to keep on weeping! All the evidence is against us. But blessed are those who choose the way of the Risen one. They forge ahead only on the strength of their belief in the Word that overthrows the world. Like acrobats, they swoop down into space, and the Word, fragile as a thread—in human eyes—catches them up to their destination.

Blest are you poor. . . ! Poverty will never liquidate our riches as long as we remain rich. We can only sketch its outlines within us, like children's drawings. God alone bestows it (M. Debrel). Happiness and salvation are grace.

■

Blest be humanity!
Such is the promise
of a God who wills life.
I believe in One
who accomplishes what he promises.

Blest be humanity!
Blest be Jesus Christ,
the new Adam!
Here is the human creature of whom God has always dreamed,
a poor one overflowing with grace,
glorified because he has traversed the path of love
from end to end.

Blest be humanity!
I believe in the Spirit who regenerates us.
For by the Spirit we reach the wellsprings of life.

INSANE LOVE

1 Corinthians 8:1-7, 10-13: In antiquity, meat for human consumption came from temples. What had not been used in sacrificial worship was sold in the market place. The question arose whether, by eating this meat, a Christian was compromising with idolatry. In his answer, Paul makes a careful distinction between theory and practice. In theory, it is obviously impossible to serve false gods, since they do not exist. And so, just as Jesus had already declared that what enters us from the outside cannot soil us, Paul responds that the Christian is free: " 'All things are lawful for me'. . . ."

". . . But that does not mean that everything is good for me" (1 Cor 6:12), the apostle hastens to add. After all, there are scrupulous Christians who are convinced that it is idolatrous to eat meat that has been offered to idols. If they hear that one may eat this meat, they might leap to the conclusion that idolatry is not so terrible a thing after all! And so we must keep such people in mind. Finally, charity must come first, and for the sake of good community relations, one must sometimes keep silent about one's own legitimate rights.

Psalm 139 is a lengthy individual complaint. The psalmist acknowledges God's omniscience, and implies his own innocence, of which, therefore, God cannot be ignorant.

Luke 6:27-38: (See p. 32.)

■

God's world is certainly a topsy-turvy one. The one Sent dies on a gibbet of infamy, and behold, death collapses at his feet. When sin seems to carry the day, it is then that salvation is accomplished and grace manifested. ("O happy fault!" we sing at the Easter Vigil.) And when Luke looks at the communities that have sprung up in pagan regions, he sees precious little to gladden his heart. People living in misery and destitution, without any outstanding virtues, the dregs of society. (Ah, the milieu in which the faith has flourished!) The gospel is sheer unreason: "Do good to those who hate you. . . . When a man takes what is yours, do not demand it back." The gospel is modeled not on the human beings we are, but on God. Jesus can ask us to love insanely because he alone has followed this road to the very end.

Henceforth we can take love's measure by contemplating the love of the Father as revealed in Jesus. Jesus forgives his murderers, he takes a traitor into his confidence, he entrusts his flock to the most cowardly of his shepherds. Struck, he is silent. Falsely accused, he refuses to defend himself. So has God loved the world! Passionately. Insanely.

The Christian is no hero, no prodigy of virtue. The Christian is a convert. The Christian is one who has been seared in the fire of the Spirit. Blessed are the gentle? Of course! Not the milksops, not the ones without character. Nor the unconditionally resigned—those who will put up with absolutely anything. But the patient, the dogged. Those who foil the hellish circle of violence by daring to believe that they can have the strength to love. Blessed, not those who are afraid of conflict, but those who are at its very heart without harboring hatred or resentment. Blessed are the merciful! Not those who "forget" without forgiving, but those who forgive while still remembering. Blessed are God's "fools." Blessed are those who will dare to weigh the anchors of reason and loose the hawsers of the good reasons that hold them to their little terra firma. Blessed are those who will trust the Word of life and place all their hope in the Ocean that can bear them up. No one who refuses to risk the high seas will ever know the intoxication of the billow and the fog, or the seduction of the sky that kisses the earth. "The measure of love is to love without measure" (Saint Bernard). The landlubber will never lose the taste for the solid earth—the earth of "reasonable people," so sure of themselves, so wise, so reflective. They think they have built something, and what they have built is a heap of ruins. Love is like one's dreams: anything can happen! Know this before you risk the unreason of the gospel!

■

God our Father, can we do good to those who strike us,
    forgive those who have offended us,
    or love without limit?

And you—what are your doing, letting your sun shine
    on the evil as on the good,
    forgiving seventy times seven times,
    and going back after the lost sheep or the prodigal child?

Make us like you,
    that we may become the reflection
    of your matchless love.

226

■

God our Father,
    we cannot claim your love.
And yet you have invited us
    to the table of mercy.
We have communicated in the passion of your Son.
Then make us artisans of peace,
    that your Reign of Love may begin.

FRIDAY OF THE 23RD WEEK

A HEART IN GOD'S IMAGE

1 Corinthians 9:16–19, 22–27: Paul's expressions are powerful, and they could make us forget the context of the discussion on meat that has been offered to idols. The apostle is attempting to make us understand that, out of charity toward the weak, the strong must at times renounce their most legitimate rights, as indeed he has himself done for the sake of the gospel—or for that matter, like the athletes of sports-hungry Corinth, who so readily embrace their difficult sacrifices in order to win championships.

Paul has consecrated his entire life to the cause of the gospel. He is the steward, the manager, of the gospel with which he has been entrusted. He asks no salary, for he is steeped through and through in the grace he proclaims, and so he offers it freely.

Luke 6:39–42: (See p. 34.)

■

"Preaching the gospel is not the subject of a boast . . ." (2 Cor 9:16). We are sent as witnesses of mercy, and this grace, which does not come from us, is the source of our humility. A spokesperson for the gospel lives a life of gratitude.

Witnesses of mercy. . . . Mercy? Oh, surely one is always "for" something as nice as mercy. At least we are always willing to be its beneficiary. But to be "for" mercy because it suits us, because it fits in with our plans, because we profit from it, is to lose it utterly. In order to receive its fruits, we must have an altogether different attitude from this. We shall adopt, love, mercy as one loves a face—as one loves the greatest, sublimest face of all, the face of God.

"The well-formed one will be as his master." How do we know that we have entered into the life of God, the new life, the Easter existence? We have entered into that life if we accept the task of conniving with God's gratuity. How ever could we be witnesses of mercy unless the manner of God's activity became our spontaneous reaction, the reflex action of our own lives? How shall we ever be vessels of the gospel of liberation if we behave the way humans behave, imprisoning others in their inadequacies or their faults, injecting our partisan evaluations into decisions from which there is no appeal, establishing ourselves as sovereign judges of good and evil? Blessed are the merciful!—those who forge a heart to the image of God. If your self-styled justice blinds you, if your merits give you the illusion of having rights, when the grace of which you are the beneficiaries bestows on you only duties, if forgiveness justifies your pride—then you are still in the dark, and your pretentiousness is leading you to your ruin.

"The well-formed one will be as his master"! Happy the disciple who is an artisan of peace! Happy the one who sees only signs of hope and renewal! Happy the one who dares to believe in the best part of everyone! Happy the church whose standard of conduct is the good of the poorest in virtue, that goes out of its way, departs from its path, to find those whom the world rejects! The gospel is the pride of such as these, and the liberation that they proclaim—become reality in their manner of life—is their gladness. The crown of the saved will be their only title of excellence.

■

God, Father of Jesus and our Father,
*   lead us to the light of your grace.*
Enroll us in the school of your Son,
*   that his word may become our gospel,*
*   his mercy our rule of life.*

May your Spirit draw us ever farther along the road
*   of fidelity to your call,*
that, when the race has been run,
*   you may bestow on us the crown of glory,*
*   the reward of the saved.*

■

Be blessed, Father of mercies!
For you regard not the hypocrisy of our hearts,
*   but measure us by your Word.*

May the table you set for those who follow the call of your Son
be the source of our charity.
And may the Spirit bring to fruition in us
a harvest of truth,
as Jesus Christ has promised.

FROM SATURDAY OF THE 23RD WEEK

TO WEDNESDAY OF THE 24TH WEEK

Charity

The church is born of the Passover of the Lord. It is from Jesus' pierced side that the church is sprung. Then let it ever cling to the Passover of its Spouse. The church must "pass over" into God. This two-way street between the election and task of the church is symbolized by its Eucharist: "The church confects the Eucharist and the Eucharist confects the church," said the Christian fathers of old. The church lives, and receives, the Lord's Passover—to become, in this Passover, the Body of Christ.

"It is your own mystery that is placed on the Lord's table; and it is your own mystery that you receive. The 'Amen!' you cry is your response to the declaration of what you are, and your answer is as your signature. For you are told, 'You are the Body of Christ!' Then let your 'Amen' be true!" (Saint Augustine to the newly baptized). The mystery of the church runs this deep: its oneness is not comparable to that of a social body, for this oneness originates in the Eucharist. And the ancient Bishop of Hippo tells more: "Why is this mystery accomplished in bread? Let us say nothing of our own invention. Let us hear the apostle himself, as he tells us, speaking of this sacrament, 'We, many though we are, are one Body, for we all partake of the one loaf' (1 Cor 10:17). Understand, Christian, and rejoice! Unity, piety, charity—one Loaf! And what is this single Loaf? One body made of many. Think how the bread is not made of a single grain of wheat, but of many. In the exorcisms, you were as crushed by the millstone. At the moment of baptism, you were made a paste, with water. Then the Holy Spirit came upon you like the fire that bakes dough. Be what you see and receive what you are!" This patristic text takes us to the heart of the Eucharistic dynamism of the church. Why do we receive the Body of Christ? To become his Body—to be able to love. Charity, the foundation of the unity of the church, is not the product of sage compromises or arbitrary decisions. Charity is life, received in communion. Charity is a theological virtue: it is a gift of God, and it inserts us into God's own life.

■

God our Father,
consecrate us by your Spirit.
May we become your church in our times!
May we each devote all our strength
to the upbuilding of the body of your Son,
for the holiness of our world!

SATURDAY OF THE 23RD WEEK

COMMUNION

1 Corinthians 10:14–22: To Paul, it makes no difference whether you eat meat offered to idols in your own or others' homes. The only requirement is charity.

With verse 14, the apostle moves from this question of the private meal to problems posed by a participation in the sacred meals of pagans. But such participation is obviously forbidden to Christians, as it engages the whole of their humanity. After all, what is the meaning of sacrifice? In Israel as in pagan religions, sacrifice implies a desire for communion with the divinity, as indicated by the gesture of placing one's hands on the head of the victim. The entire ritual is calculated to convey the image of a gift of oneself to God, through the intermediary of the victim.

Paul is dealing with a question of faith itself. Participation in a sacrifice implies faith in the divinity concerned, and in the efficacy of the sacrifice. This holds for the Christian sacrifice, as well, as it is communion in the body and blood of Christ. In other words, participation in the Christian sacrificial worship presupposes faith in the salvific value of the cross. But then I surely cannot proclaim my faith in Christ and in pagan idols at one and the same time. Taking another line, the apostle observes that our communion in Christ is so profound that it symbolizes the union of Christians, especially in the gesture of the breaking of the bread.

Psalm 116 is part of a long psalm of thanksgiving that actually begins with Psalm 115. The psalmist expresses his desire to offer the sacrifice he has promised, as he is sure that his prayer will be heard.

Luke 6:43–49: (See p. 36.)

■

Sacrifice is part of humanity's "religious soul." To offer a sacrifice is to express the desire to be one with the one to whom it is offered. To eat of a sacrificial victim is the very realization, in symbol, of this union, and thus at the same time an act of unification with those who have offered the same victim and taken it as their nourishment as well. The discussion on meat offered to idols, then, is no small matter for Paul. Where are your communions? Such is the question, essential for the life of Christians, with which the apostle challenges the young communities sprung up in a pagan world.

Where are your communions? All Christian discourse, all Christian declarations, all the programs aiming at a "new person," a "new creation," will remain without effect—and will even serve for the pure and simple reproduction of inhumane social relations—unless Christians today make this "new human being" and this "new creation" visible to the eyes of the world by means of a struggle with injustice in all its forms. The church leaves no doubts as to the locus of Jesus' solidarities. The Christ was only to be found where men and women were despised and diminished, where the honor of the human being was to be rescued.

After all, our dignity is God's glory, as old Irenaeus knew. "Why do you call me 'Lord, Lord,' and not put into practice what I teach you?" (Lk 6:46). Christianity is not mainly a theory or pious discourse. First of all Christianity is life. The tree will be judged by its fruits! Where are we in our personal and collective life, where are we with the authentic image of the church, where are we in our identification with the weak, the sick and suffering, the poor, the lowly, the oppressed and, yes, the lost sheep? What has become of the Pauline dismantling of barriers between foreigners and compatriots, good and evil, in a love that includes even adversaries and enemies? Is the God of our lives a God in the image of the gospel—a God who enters into solidarity with human distress and hope, who does not demand but bestows, who does not crush but raises up, who does not condemn but delivers, who unstintingly places grace on the erstwhile throne of law?

Where are our communions? You cannot drink of the Lord's cup and at the same time imbibe the potion of the evil spirits. You cannot drink of the chalice of a life consecrated to love to the point of passion, you cannot drink to the testament of the Master on his knees at his disciple's feet, to the act of the Servant bestowing the legacy and testimonial of bread shared, and at the same time maintain communion with the spirit of the world that crushes the weak, abandons the hopeless, enslaves the hesitant, and slaughters lost sheep. Sisters and

231

brothers, dig deep: build on the love that will "go the whole road." Then your house will stand in a storm. Your life will expand into an eternal communion with God.

■

You will have no sacrifices, Lord,
*   or pious discourses.*
It is in a heart surrendered to love
*   that your covenant is established.*

When we break bread,
*   make us faithful to the testament of our Savior.*
May his life, delivered up for our happiness,
*   be the rock on which we build our own lives.*

■

Lord our God,
*   without love, faith and hope are unavailing.*
May this communion give us strength
*   to share the longings of our brothers and sisters,*
that we may testify
*   that you are the source of love*
*   forever and ever.*

MONDAY OF THE 24TH WEEK

THE BREAKING OF THE BREAD
1 Corinthians 11:17–26: Paul's discourse on pagan sacrifices leads him to speak of the Corinthians' deportment in the liturgical gatherings. The apostle begins by denouncing the hypocrisy of the Eucharistic meal as it is lived by the Christians of Corinth. For Paul, this repast ought to "proclaim the death of the Lord until he comes!" In other words, as chapter ten has shown, the Corinthians' participation in the Eucharist ought to be an actualizing of their communion in the body and blood of Christ, and thus a contribution to the upbuilding of the church. Indeed this meal has no meaning unless it expresses the unity lived by those who share it.

Instead, what do we see? First, the Corinthians are split into various cliques and coteries. Paul has spoken of this at length in the beginning of his letter. Now social divisions appear, and are manifested in the liturgical gatherings. At the meal preceding the Eucharist, the Corinthians gather by kinship and class. Obviously this attitude is inconsistent with the meaning of the rite.

And what is the meaning of the rite? After Paul's diatribe, a consideration of the significance of Jesus' death will be in order. To this purpose the liturgy employs the great verse from *Psalm 40:* "Holocausts or sin-offerings you sought not; then said I, 'Behold I come.' "

Luke 7:1–10: (See p. 37.)

■

They had transformed the Lord's Supper into unseemly feasting. They had converted a communion of sisters and brothers into a series of exclusive social clubs. What was left of the Eucharist? "When you assemble it is not to eat the Lord's supper. . . ."

The fathers of the church said: The church makes the Eucharist, and the Eucharist makes the church. The church creates the Eucharist! But what will be the state of the Christian community if its meal, the symbol of its communion, becomes a hotbed of divisions? We have forgotten the truth of signs: there is a threshold beyond which signs become counter-witness! Might we not perhaps occasionally do better to abstain from the Eucharist when there are quarrels among us? The Eucharist is a table of sisters and brothers, and it is laden with the life of the church. Placing upon this common board their desire, their hunger, their hopes, and their clumsy efforts to enflesh love, these sisters and brothers daily build the community of those who live by the same heritage. The Eucharist is the place where this communion, this family, grows and spreads out. The Eucharist is the sign in which this communion finds its meaning, its origin and its destiny. The church builds the Eucharist! Brothers and sisters, let us not force the sacrament to lie. Let us not despise the church!

The church makes the Eucharist, the Eucharist makes the church! We do not gather at this common table, in one family, on the strength of our mutual forgiveness, our reciprocal compromises, our patiently forged solidarities. This sacrament is not only the expression of what we live, it actually establishes what it shows forth, it reveals the life it bestows. "Every time, then, you eat this bread and drink this cup, you proclaim the death of the Lord. . . !" At the table of the broken bread, we proclaim that the true name of life is patient love—love that begins again, that starts over, that forgives, love that welcomes, that invents. The bread we eat is our communion in the surrendered life of the Lord. The bread that we receive is the bread bestowed on us by Jesus in the moment of his consecration of his life—a consecration to the hilt, to the very end. For he said, "The bread I will give is my flesh, for the life of the world" (Jn 6:51). The new world is, at one and the same time, grace received, and the fruit of a life signed by the toil of the Spirit.

They had transformed the Lord's supper into a revel, and the communion of brothers and sisters into coteries and cliques. They had scorned the church, and rejected the Lord's legacy. Bread is only for breaking and sharing. The church lives only in communion received, for it is founded on grace received and lived. From the moment of the Last Supper, church and Eucharist are indissociable. Destroy the one, and you make the other a lie.

■

Lord our God,
    your Spirit gathers us around this family table,
    the place where your church is refreshed, restored, revived.
Renew this communion,
that our sharing of this food and this cup
    may be the signs of a covenant
    that is your gift to us.

■

Each time we eat the flesh of your Son,
    you come, Lord, to renew your promise.
Each time we drink of the cup of redemption,
    you give us to taste of the joys of your Reign.

Permit not that our lives
    should give your word the lie!
As we communicate in your love,
    may we move into a new world.

THE BODY

1 Corinthians 12:12-14, 27-31: "One person goes hungry while another gets drunk" (1 Cor 11:21), writes Paul—of the Eucharistic meal! This little sentence speaks volumes on the atmosphere prevailing at Corinth. It also says a great deal about the milieu into which Christianity was penetrating. We must not forget that, before their conversion, certain Christians of Corinth had known the euphoric exaltation of the mystery religions. It is not improbable that something of this unhealthy ambiance had infiltrated the Christian assemblies, which would explain the presence in the letter of Paul's strong exhortations concerning the proper use of spiritual goods.

The verses retained by the liturgy transmit only the great guiding principle Paul proposes to the Corinthians: There is no such thing as a private charism. All charisms are ordained to the good of the whole community. Paul illustrates this assertion by citing the solidarity that binds the members of a single body.

Psalm 100 calls us to praise. Dying on the cross, Jesus Christ willed to gather together all men and women, and make of them a single people.

Luke 7:11-17: (See p. 40.)

■

One body, of many members. A comparison between the human body and the body social is an ancient commonplace. Will the unity of the church, then, be simply a species of the oneness that binds human beings together? Will our union be based on a sage consensus, an orthodoxy acknowledged or imposed, a comportment embraced or obligatory? Will we be cemented by fine organization, or patiently constructed compromises? Will the oneness of the Christian community be one and the same as a judicious division of labor?

"You, then, are the body of Christ"! Saint Paul emerges from the sociological analogy to turn to the christological facet of the church. We are of a body that belongs to Christ, a body that is "of Christ." (Cf. Rom 12:5: "We, though many, are one body in Christ and individually members of one another.") The unity that Paul exhorts the Corinthians to pursue as a goal, this oneness in Christ, is a unity to be contemplated, and received. Our union is a Person—a common breathing, a word exchanged, a life shared because it is one. Our unity is a matter of blood, and our life's breath. The unity of the body we constitute is far more than a mere wholesome cooperation among many members of a social unit. For Jesus is the whole body, and each of his members lives only by the Spirit. It is the Spirit that allows us to be disciples–imitators, witnesses of the one Son of God.

The oneness of the church comes from on high. At the same time it implies the conversion of each one of us. We must never, therefore, either force it by constraint, or renounce it in a liberalism sprung from some universal axiom of free enterprise and free thought. Our union is realized in the formation of a "we," in which no "I" is dissolved, but rather asserted, opening up, dilating into the "I" of the church, becoming ecclesial. Each of us finds his or her true dimensions in living for the single body of the Lord.

If truth be told, this mystery can be revealed in the church, all modestly, only because it is first revealed between Christ and the church. The church is Christ's Body because it is the Spouse he has loved, and loves, as his own body, his other self. And if by this life of ours, a life of sisters and brothers, we can become the church built on love, it is only because the roots of our charity reach this deep. The variety of gifts of the Spirit is not only ordained to the common good, it is also the diversified manifestation of a single grace.

■

God our Father, consecrate us by your Spirit.
As that Spirit has come upon the bread and wine
*   placed by you in our hands,*
so may he descend upon us.

May he become the breath that gives life
*   to the visible Body of your Son.*
May he be strength, prudence and courage
*   in those who have the charge of your church:*
*   the pope who presides at this feast of charity,*
*   and our bishop.*
May that Spirit be the wisdom of faith
*   for those who bear witness to your word,*
charity for those who give flesh to their love
*   in deeds of your own solicitude,*
wonder in those who guide the prayer of your people,
and the germ of unity
*   in those who have charge of this communion.*

Send your Spirit upon us:
may we become your church!

LOVE

1 Corinthians 12:31–13:13: Still in a context of the good order that must prevail in the liturgical gatherings, Paul enunciates a concise critique of the charisms. All are subordinate to that other gift of the Spirit, the charity of sisters and brothers. His argumentation follows the outline we have seen in his treatment of the divisions in the Church of Corinth:

A. The most eminent charisms are useless unless they are rooted in love (vv 1–3).
B. Verses 4–7 describe the works produced by love. The accumulation of verbs, indicating the manifold activity aroused by charity, permit the apostle to escape the pitfall of too abstract a definition.
A'. Verses 8–13 return to the theme of the superiority of love, enriching it with a consideration of love's everlastingness. Love alone will endure. All else is doomed to dissolution.

In response to Paul's hymn to charity, *Psalm 33* exalts the source of all love, God himself.

Luke 7:31–35: (See p. 42.)

■

The mystery of the communion established among Christians can only be revealed, and modestly at that, because it is first revealed between Christ and his church, as we have said yesterday. The church is Christ's Body because it is the Spouse he has loved as his own body, his other self. No wonder, then, that Paul proposes a higher life for the construction of the church. Love alone builds the body of the Lord in this world. Charity is God's child. "Contemplate the mystery of charity: then you shall see the heart of the Father, which his only Son has given us to know" (Saint Clement of Alexandria). The only charism indispensable to the life of the church is love—a love born of God and returning to God. The church is born from the pierced side of the dying Christ. In less

---

237

graphic terms, the foundation of the fecundity of the church is the death of the Lord, his radical love-to-the-limit, his gift of himself.

At such depths does love—the Christian's vocation—have its origin! Charity is a theological virtue. It comes from God alone, and shares in God's very being. Jesus has allowed himself to be "opened," emptied of himself, and in the water and blood that flow from his pierced side we find the source of our charity. Charity is God's child. The church is drawn from the Savior's side, the new Eve from the side of Adam. In our search to imitate the love that was Jesus' reason for being, we are as "married" to the Word. One who loves is already born of God.

FROM THURSDAY TO SATURDAY

OF THE 24TH WEEK

Yeast of Life

What a deep desire we feel within ourselves to live! How we wish to be free of our alienations—both those we find within ourselves, and those that come to us from without! What a longing we experience to be ourselves in the transparency of our being, expansively, free of all the limitations imposed on us by suffering and evil!

And we discover that all of this is endlessly doomed to failure by our own limitations—by the limitations of our body, by our sin, and yes, by our death.

The first Christians lived in a perpetual state of astonishment at the certainty that a particular individual, this Jesus, who like themselves had lived all of these hopes and contradictions, was now the Living one: God had brought him to life for good and all. It is not just any death that has issued in resurrection. It is this particular human being, who died on a cross, who has entered into life, and it is his death, the death of his obedient love, that has become the death of death itself.

This Jesus is a sign for us. In the Risen one we already glimpse the end of the journey. It is the entire sense of our human existence personal and collective, that is revealed to us in this Jesus. In him we contemplate a totally successful life—a life after God's own heart, a life such as the creator dreamed for us on the morning of Genesis. Indeed, Jesus' resurrection is more than a sign for us. It is in some sense our own accomplishment and fulfillment. In the risen Jesus,

God has filled the entire universe with the "sacrament," the efficacious sign, of our passage. All human and cosmic realities are transfigured. The whole world has become the body of Christ, textured of our flesh, of our most concrete existence, of all the flesh of the earth.

■

We sing your glory,
  God our Father,
  Father of Jesus Christ, our Lord.
You have raised him from the dead
  and you make us to live again in him.

You instill the heart of your church
  with the strength of hope,
that, through all the trials of our times,
  we may tremble with joy
  at the promise of our incorruptible heritage.
renewed by the power of your Spirit,
  God, our life,
  we bless your name!

THURSDAY OF THE 24TH WEEK

GOSPEL OF THE RESURRECTION

1 Corinthians 15:1-11: The final question to be taken up by Paul is that of the resurrection of the dead. Tomorrow's reading will afford a better glimpse of the origin of the Corinthians' uneasiness about this Christian dogma. For today, let us merely note the solemnity of the apostle's response. We observe it particularly in the rabbinical expressions Paul employs to introduce the traditional enunciation of faith. "I handed on to you first of all what I myself received. . . ." Paul has no intention, then, of making an unheard-of proclamation. He simply recalls to the Corinthians the content of the faith common to himself and them. The stereotyped formula delivers a datum of faith, older than Paul's considerations and itself testifying both to a rereading of the Easter event in the light of the scriptures, and an appreciation of the redemptive value of the cross.

By way of an act of thanksgiving, we sing a few verses of *Psalm 118*, frequently applied by the infant church to Christ's resurrection and exaltation.

Luke 7:36–50: (See p. 44.)

■

"He is risen! This is our faith!" cried the first Christians, all enthusiastically, and this has been the profession of faith of all those who, down through the centuries, have accepted the gospel. The church is the community of those who believe that the human Jesus has entered into the divine communion, that he is God and Lord, that he can open to those who believe in him the route of access to the divine life, that he is at the head of the line of all those who, like him, wish to enter into communion with God. The church is the church of the resurrection. It is borne through history by this profession. And it is still the church of the resurrection, for it lives by this proclamation alone: I hand on to you what I have received. This is the whole of church *traditio*—everything the church has to "hand on": He is risen!

I hand on to you what I have first received. The meaning of life is there for the taking. For Christians, who have their eyes fixed on Jesus—this unique sufferer, raised to life—resurrection is not behind them, but ahead of them. With their regard fixed on Jesus, whom their forebears in the faith proclaim to be alive, believers attest that God stays near his creatures, to the point of the absurdity, the inanity, the dereliction, the solitude, and the "nothing" of a life condemned to death. To profess the resurrection is to testify that, in Jesus' life and activity, in his passion and death, God has taken sides with us without reservation. To profess the resurrection, beyond all hope and come what may, is to manifest that God is a God of compassion: He is with us and for us, and he raises us up again.

And suddenly, to transmit what we have heard becomes something very different from the repetition of soulless words. Resurrection is life before it is a dogma. Tradition is a vocation. I hand on what I have received. The church will have nothing else to repeat or live. Either its witness is a word that raises up—either its life is a liberating deed—or the church is simply being disloyal to its birth certificate, resurrection. The gospel is Good News, and the proclamation of the resurrection awakens the church to life. A church faithful to the tradition that is its heritage calls it immediately to side with the weak, the sick, and suffering, the disinherited, the oppressed, yes, the impious, the immoral and the godless. "Two men owed money to a certain money-lender. . . . Your sins are forgiven." The church has nothing else to say: only the word of hope and resurrection that it has received from its Lord. To proclaim the resurrection, and to live the love that raises up, are one and the same thing: Jesus' resurrection reveals the fact that love is God's "style." Resurrection, for the church that seeks to hand on what it has received, becomes a lifestyle: to all of the disinherited, to all of the condemned, the church has the mission of speaking the words that raise the dead: "Your faith has been your salvation. Now go in peace."

■

God of infinite mercy,
God of peace,
grant us the grace of the fearless adventure of fidelity.

May our words utter your peace,
and our lives set other lives free,
that we may bear witness
to what we have received.

■

God, source of life,
teach us the movements,
the deeds that arouse life.

Day after day, may your Spirit awaken within us
the gift you have given us:
the peace born of your forgiveness.
Then shall we be the astonished witnesses
of the happiness you offer all women and men.

FRIDAY OF THE 24TH WEEK

HE LIVES!
1 Corinthians 15:12–20: Jews and pagans had different approaches to the problem of life after death. The Bible had always perceived the human entity as profoundly "one." It was impossible, then, for the soul to be separated from the body, for the soul was simply the life of the body. Indeed, the Jews had long thought that death struck down soul and body together. But when, after the Babylonian Exile, the notion of life after death had gradually worked its

way into their minds, they had begun to understand that survival as a resurrection of the whole human being.

Greek thinking was entirely different. Under the influence of dualistic philosophies, it regarded soul and body as distinct entities, and hence experienced no difficulty with the concept of an immortal soul in a mortal body. But yes, the body was doomed to destruction.

Out of respect for these pagan views, Jewish philosophers like Philo of Alexandria limited themselves to a presentation of evidence for the immortality of the soul, purposely neglecting the resurrection of the body. Paul refuses to compromise in this way. He sets forth Christian thinking in all its dimensions. In today's reading he argues from the faith he shares with the Corinthians. No one, he points out, denies the resurrection of Christ. In that case, one must hold the resurrection of everyone, for Christ's resurrection has no meaning apart from its status as firstfruits of the resurrection of all. To deny the resurrection of the dead would be to deny the Incarnation—the solidarity binding the Son of God and humanity.

Psalm 17 is a complaint. Its call for help expresses human frailty. There is no hope but in God alone.

Luke 8:1-3: (See p. 46.)

■

"We proclaim that Christ has been raised from the dead." The resurrection is the object of a proclamation, not a demonstration. It is the core of a faith, not the conclusion of an argumentation. Surely, then, believers should be less concerned with "proofs" for the resurrection than with the meaning and importance they accord that resurrection in their lives. This single event changes the destiny of the world, human destiny—and consequently our outlook on that destiny. "If Christ has not been raised, our preaching is void of content and your faith is empty too." For, when all is said and done, it is not so much a matter of showing the truth of an event as of believing in a Living one whose passage through death and resurrection is of vital importance for each of us. "If Christ was not raised, your faith is worthless. You are still in your sins. . . ."

Ours is the task of testifying to a miracle more prodigious than all others. Surely this event is out of the ordinary, to say the least. But it is bound up with a person, and concerns all other persons. And it concerns them in the whole of their humanity. While the Greeks could accept only the immortality of the soul, Paul announces the raising of the entire human person. Easter releases us from neither matter, nor the body, nor the world, nor history. Jesus' victory over death does not initiate an evasive action. It delivers us to a new relationship with self, neighbor and God. It is given to us to stand in a relationship with ourselves, the world, our neighbor and God as God stands in relationship to himself and creation.

And this is why Easter becomes our mission. "Christ has been raised from the dead, the firstfruits of those who have fallen asleep." To believe in the resurrection is to enter into the dynamism of an Easter that will be complete only when all things are recapitulated in Christ. In the meantime it is ours to wage the combat of life, to lead humanity to "come alive," in such wise that everything in our world in connivance with death may be thrown into full retreat. It is in virtue of what he has been and what he has done that Jesus is now alive. Thus he inaugurates a movement that only his return can bring to its term.

We proclaim that "Christ has been raised from the dead, the firstfruits of those who have fallen asleep." The church proclaims that Jesus is alive. Jesus has vanquished death, and no longer are we bound by unbreakable chains. God has willed for us the totally unexpected: that we should enjoy his own life. And behold we are charged to bring to light, in contradiction and conflict, what God, in the gratuity of his love, so insanely promotes: we burst through our abiding daily horizon— death! The realism of the event that is Jesus' resurrection—"If Christ was not raised, your faith is worthless"—guarantees that, as our struggles for liberation are not in vain even in history, still less are they so for the Kingdom to come.

■

For those who believe in you, Lord,
death is no more!
For those who believe in you—
never another night without Easter dawn!

Be blessed for the life
you raised up on the morn of the new day!
As we have placed our hope in Christ,
grant us to share his victory
and testify to his peace.

■

You have raised your Well-Beloved!
God our Father, from whom all life comes,
turn our hearts to the future:

may your breath give us new spirit,
  to be bearers of life,
  to give life new birth,
  until the birthday of life eternal.

SATURDAY OF THE 24TH WEEK

IN THE IMAGE OF THE RISEN ONE

1 Corinthians 15:35–37, 42–49: How are bodies to rise? In his response to this question Paul evinces, on the one hand, a solicitude for the requirement of continuity imposed by a unitary vision of the human being; and on the other, an awareness of the ineluctable breach between life and death. He does so with the help of the image of the plant that dies, only to be born anew. And to mark the difference between what is earthly and what belongs to the "heavenly" world, the world of the sky, he coins the expression, "spiritual body," a formula rooted in the contrast between the two Adams. The first Adam received life. The second, Christ, gives it.

Psalm 56, a prayer of supplication, brims with confidence: "In God I trust without fear; what can flesh do against me?"

Luke 8:4–15: (See p. 50.)

■

"A farmer went out to sow some seed." Jesus has emerged from God to hurl the Good News to the four winds. And as rain does not return to the sky without fecundating the earth, the word has germinated and grown to an abundant harvest. The grain of wheat cast to earth in the furrow of Golgotha has sprouted up and, in the train of that Risen one, a people of the saved has leapt up beside him. Suddenly those who had belonged to earth know themselves born of God! As the new Adam, Jesus raised is the firstborn of a multitude of brothers and sisters. "You will be like gods," the serpent had assured them in the garden of creation (Gen 3:5). Today it is God who accomplishes this universal human desire.

But may we never reduce the resurrection to a theory! The resurrection reaches us "where we live," in what we are. The resurrection concerns, not an idealized human being, but the human being carrying the weight of life. This, of course, is the scandalous truth that the Greeks could not bear to hear. But Paul makes sure they hear, for such is the faith of the church when it professes the resurrection of the body.

After all, is not my body the whole "I"? I do not have my body, I *am* my body. My body is simply myself. It is myself expressing myself; loving, acting. Our body is our ability to enter into a relationship with others, our faculty of acting on the world and transforming it. It is our "appearing," the opportunity to live our feelings, to "be-have ourselves," to present ourselves. Yes, the resurrection penetrates us that far—to the most fleshly fibers of our being. It is not some ideal "I" who shall live, it is I with all the dimensions of my being. In fact: the victory of the One who was raised reaches into the very dullness and sluggishness of our lives. My body is myself, then, of course—but I know that this body I am is also my heaviness, my limitation, my opacity. It hides me, and betrays me, for it is the matter of which I am, and the sin I commit. The one who will be alive again will not be some disincarnate me, but a me with the limitations of my engagements, with the clumsiness of my action on the world, with my body's betrayals of my secret being, with the sluggishness of my behavior. In fact, it is the material world itself that will be transfigured! For my body is the center of my relations with all the universe—the physical world and the human world. When Jesus' body was raised—the moment it was pierced by the divine life and transformed—at that moment the entire network of relations in the universe was transformed into God. "Just as we resemble the man from earth, so shall we bear the likeness of the man from heaven." Christ's resurrection is a renewal of the entire universe.

The farmer casts the seed, and the seed is pregnant with the coming harvest. Our faith turns us toward the days of completion. Resurrection is revelation, and the new world inaugurated by Jesus' victory is not to be imagined from a point of departure in what we are. On the contrary, it is the raised body of Jesus that tells us, in advance, what we are, or rather what we are becoming. "Just as we resemble the man from earth, so shall we bear the likeness of the man from heaven."

■

Like a grain of wheat swollen with hope,
your Son, God our Father,
> *bears us within his being.*
As he has poured out his Spirit upon us
> *for the harvest and the fruit of tomorrow,*
hasten the ripening of his promise,

that we may be like unto him,
transfigured forever and ever.

■

We have recognized the power of your promise,
God of the living.
Blessed be your name!
May the bread of life,
the surrendered body of your Son,
triumph over our deaths great and small,
that no thing or person may ever be able to snatch from us
the future that you prepare for us—
the gladness of ages without end.

FROM MONDAY TO SATURDAY

OF THE 25TH WEEK

Vocation

The gospel is vocation, calling. The light has shone in the darkness, and the darkness has not been able to quench it. Jesus says, "I am the light of the world," and Paul will tell the first Christians, still too much marked by the weakness of the world: "Now you are light in the Lord. Well, then, live as children of light" (Eph 5:8). Becoming a disciple is a question of choice, and obedience.

Becoming a disciple is a choice. The one to be a disciple will be the person who has been touched to the quick by a word too meaningful to totally comprehend. Vocation is a trial, for the call sears with its urgency, and is radical as a judgment. To be a disciple is to open oneself to a question, to allow oneself to be put to the question—without any other assurance than the grace of emerging victorious from the trial.

Becoming a disciple is an act of obedience. The one to be a disciple will be the person who has received the gift and taken it to heart. The one to join Jesus' family will be the one who will put the word into practice. The gospel is not just a lot of talk. Still less is it an "experiment." Disciples live in urgent times, and hurl themselves into the adventure with the word of grace their only knapsack. Vocation is obedience to our vocation to be human; for, since the

morning of Genesis, we are called to know God, and to live in communion
with him.

■

"But you—who do you say that I am?"
You are the Son of God,
    consecrated by the Spirit
    to lead human beings to the land of grace and freedom.

"But you—who do you say that I am?"
You are God's "Today,"
    swept away by the breath of the Spirit
    to fetch to our world
    a Reign of peace and happiness.

"But you—who do you say that I am?"
You are the Messiah, the one Sent by the Father,
    come to serve and to give yourself,
    promised to a cross on a hill,
    transfigured in glory on the mountain.

The Book of Proverbs and the Wisdom Literature
Reading the Book of Proverbs is disconcerting. What connection can there
possibly be between these "saws" and the holy word of God? Are the former
anything but the result of purely human reflection?

The question is ill-posed. Obviously the Book of Proverbs is a human
composition. But so is the rest of the Bible. This does not prevent it from
being the work of God as well. God has "taken flesh" in every age of history.

Now: what kind of persons are the wise, the sages? The Bible calls every
competent person "wise," from the cabinetmaker to the sailor. It also gives
this name to the political counselors of kings, and to the educated in general.
The wisdom literature reflects an important moment in the evolution of
Western thought. In fact, an improved understanding of the literature of the
Fertile Crescent shows not only very broad traces of Jewish influence on
surrounding civilizations, but the importance of the monarchical era as a
period of systematic compilation, as well. We may say that wisdom, which is a
mixture of experiences and traditions, was born in the classroom. It sprang
from the desire of teachers to hand on their knowledge to their young
disciples, in order to educate them and make them wise in their own turn.

Further: the wisdom literature translates an aspiration of the human mind that
can be found in the historical books of the time, as well—the wish to be free
of the all-pervasive aura of the sacred and to be able to establish the

autonomy of thought. It is interesting to compare the history of Saul and that of David's succession. The former account fairly bathes in the sacred, from start to finish. The latter seeks its explanations for the woes of the reign of David in the vicissitudes of the human heart. The sages had the same concern for emancipation from the sacred. This, among other things, explains why there is so little overt piety in the oldest sayings of the Book of Proverbs.

And yet this effort at independence did not enter into competition with faith in God. This apparent contradiction is due to the very object of wisdom's investigation. When the sage interrogates reality, he knows he interrogates a world created by God. The perceived duty of desacralization is not discharged by a rejection of the divine. On the contrary, the sage has taken care to place God in the real. The wisdom literature is an attempt to emancipate the human mind, an effort to embrace all of reality through created reason. And yet it found its place among the sacred books of the chosen people. Could there be a clearer acknowledgment of the rights of reason, a more forthright assertion that God and the human being do not stand in opposition?

MONDAY OF THE 25TH WEEK

LIGHT
Proverbs 3:27–34: Verses 27–29 deal with behavior toward one's friends, and by extension, toward one's kin and neighbors. One may neither betray them nor refuse them help. Verse 30 warns of the danger of quarrels, especially when these mutilate human relations.

Verses 31–34 contrast two groups of persons, the evil and the righteous. While "to the Lord the perverse man is an abomination," the righteous person enjoys his favor. But what is a righteous person (and hence an evil one)? For the ancient Jews, a just or righteous person was one who acted in conformity with what the natural law demanded of him.

It is characteristic of the wisdom literature never to attempt to deduce the knowledge of these demands from theoretical norms or a written law. Only with Sirach does the sage begin to take an interest in the Law. In the meantime, wisdom flows from attention to reality. The sage believes in an order revealed by God in creation. The righteous, then, are those who, in a given situation, make an effort to find the proper behavior to which to hold fast, by way of their personal experience and the tradition of the elders. This conception explains why Israel so long confused the effort to be "righteous" with material prosperity. It was thought that a comfortable existence was the natural sanction of this consistent search for truth. The one who acted thus was found, as it were, in an "aura of benediction" (von Rad).

"O Lord, who shall sojourn in your tent?" (Ps 15:1). *Psalm 15* lists the demands incumbent on one who would desire to stand in Yahweh's presence.

Luke 8:16–18: (See p. 52.)

(See p. 52.)

■

God is our Father, yes, but he blinds our gaze. He is too luminous to be beheld face to face. He can only be seen "from behind." But from all eternity, the eternal Word is born of this light. "Light of light," he has shone in the darkness, and suddenly this human night of ours is ablaze with brightness from on high. The lamp has been set on the lampstand, and suddenly the cross bestows a new meaning on our dwelling place, on our personal and collective history.

The lamp blazes, and the blackest corners of our soul see their shadows scamper for the night. Jesus has appeared, and the most secret desires of the heart are revealed and set free. Nothing has ever been sealed shut that he has not brought to light. Nothing is so tender and delicate that he fails to renew it. This Light is life and resurrection. Into the darkest crannies of the heart—the dark of despair, disgust, shame, envy, suspicion unexplored, need unsuspected, sorrow unplumbed—into our souls' folds and nooks without number, shines the pure, divine light, unabating. After all, the only reason for that lamp's existence is to light the room. Jesus has appeared for the sake of life, hope, renewal.

"You are the light of the world. . . . Your light must shine before men so that they may see goodness in your acts and give praise to your heavenly Father" (Mt 5:14–16). You have been illuminated by your baptism. Can you then escape the Spirit that calls you? Light illumines love. Without it, the cold of the void, the dark of thick, absolute night would exhale its heavy breath everywhere. But light begets gladness, and gladness melts and boils. Without gladness, life would lose its taste and meaning. Light begets day. Without day, evening would be without hope. "You are the light of the world"—its future and its gladness! Be a witness to others.

■

Lord, "your word is a lamp to my feet. . . ."
Be blessed, our Father,
    for the Brightness of your face:

his name is Jesus, and upon him you have shed
    the splendor of your countenance.
Grant that we may keep watch in faith
    till the new morn,
    when humanity will glisten with your light
    forever and ever.

■

God our Father,
    you make us a gift of light.
    How we need it to guide our steps!
May the Light of Light, Jesus your Son
    pierce our darkest depths,
that, in his brilliance,
    we may walk into your presence
    to find your face.

■

Glory to you, God our Father
    for this Eucharist,
    in which Christ lights us with his love.
We beseech you: may our eyes open
    upon the endlessness of this gift,
and may our life radiate with your light
    now and forever.

TUESDAY OF THE 25TH WEEK

A FAMILY AFFAIR

Proverbs 21:1-6, 10-13: These proverbs are part of a collection of 376
maxims attributed to Solomon. The purpose of the attribution, which is
spurious, is not so much the acknowledgment of these gifts in Solomon himself
(who may well have possessed them), as it is the proclamation of a common
conviction in the Middle East: that the king is the source of all good things.
This material is actually very old.

Although the order in which these sayings appear here does not indicate the internal logic of the original material, we are nonetheless struck by their appeal to daily experience—the principal source of the knowledge of the sages, which is then distilled in the light of a meditation on tradition.

Another passage from *Psalm 119* sings of the psalmist's attachment to the divine law.

Luke 8:19–21: (See p. 54.)

■

He glanced about him. His hearers were seated in a circle. "My mother and my brothers. . . !" To be of Jesus' family, to be Jesus' familiar, requires that we gather round him, hear him, live with him. "Blest are they who hear the word of God and keep it" (Lk 11:27). A family is a matter of the heart, a matter of adoption, a communion established and shared. To be someone's "familiar" will demand we share in that one's lot and reputation. To be of someone's family will require we connect ourselves with that person's name.

"My mother and my brothers are those who hear the word of God and act upon it." They shall bear the name of Jesus who live in their hearts that which was his reason for living: "Such as my love has been for you, so must your love be for each other. This is how all will know you for my disciples: your love for one another" (Jn 13:34–35).

The church is a family affair! To the church belong those who gather about a word to make it their own, those who hear the Good News to conform their lives to it, those whose frame of reference is what Jesus has said and done, those who take Jesus' name as their distinctive mark. The church is an affair of the heart: an affair is only a "family" one when it is taken to heart, taken as our very own.

■

We are of your family, Lord our God:
    we bear the name of your Son.
Place your Spirit within us,
and may that Spirit repeat the word of your grace:
    our adoption as your sons and daughters,
    that we may be yours for eternity.

UNINSURED

Proverbs 30:5–9: Here is another extract, this time attributed to a certain Agur. It may be borrowed from other wisdom literature of the East— theological references not withstanding, since the latter testify at the most to an accommodation of foreign proverbs to an Israelite mentality.

The series is interesting for its demonstration that the sages were capable of questioning their own knowledge. In the preceding verses, in fact, Agur explicitly confesses his ignorance, as he recognizes the truth and weight of the divine wisdom. The prayer of verses 6–9 is reminiscent of the prayer of Solomon (1 Kgs 3), where the sage asks for protection from deceivers, and a reasonable well-being: neither abundance, nor the misery that leads to vice.

Psalm 119 prolongs the sage's prayer. We hear the psalmist's horror of the lie, together, with an exaltation of the Law as a reflection of the divine word.

Luke 9:1–6: (See p. 56.)

■

"Don't leave home without one!" the ads blare. Don't be afraid—it's not scary overseas! If for any reason you should have to cut your vacation short, we'll see that you get home all right. If you have to go to the hospital while in another country, we'll take care of you. Adventure without risk! Expatriation without surprises. For your peace of mind and your pleasure, organize and program your vacation!

"He sent them forth to proclaim the reign of God and heal the afflicted. Jesus advised them: 'Take nothing for the journey' "—no bread, no bag, no money in your belt. Shoes? You may take sandals. No extra tunic! Only pilgrim's garb! Nothing but the Word, the message, the Good News. Only the breath of the Spirit, to bear the messenger along the road.

And we? We have taken out insurance. The message? Ah, we must preserve it! Codify it, then, in orthodoxy, in definitions! The Word? We must be in complete control of it. So couch it in wise, deep discourses: strangle it. The message? It must be acceptable! So sweeten it, soften it where it is too challenging, pull it back a bit from the risks of the Christian life. For the very future of the mission, we have prepared our strategies and our pedagogy most meticulously. We want a fine building, so we have taken great pains with the scaffolding.

The disciple is no better than the Master. In order to be at home among us, Jesus left his Father's house and became Word. He took a risk—the risk of incarnation in human words. Without any guarantee but the knowledge that the seed cast to the winds could not fail to bear fruit, without any certitude apart from the women and men who would hear God's word, be obedient to it, and become his relatives, Jesus became gospel—enfleshed in the deeds of these very women and men. And he himself became their path.

They set out without any other insurance but the fidelity of God, their only knapsack the promise of the one who had sent them. Happy the church that permits the Spirit to organize its mission and program its history! Happy the church with nowhere to lodge but on the open road! There is no "grant in aid" for the disciple!

∎

Lord our God,
      your Word has been accomplished in the coming of your Son.
Today it is offered to us in its eternal novelty.
Open our ears to your voice,
      and our hearts to your transforming love,
that we may welcome the glad tidings
      of Jesus' message,
and bear witness to your salvation,
      which is for everlasting.

∎

God of the word and the prophets,
your Good News has resounded in the coming of your Son,
      and its echoes ring in your church still.
Come, renew the faith of your children,
      that your word may take root in us
      and bear fruit!

∎

God, ever faithful to your promises,
you have placed your treasure in our hands.
      You have entrusted us with your word,
      you call us to raise the hopes of humanity.
Therefore we beseech you:

may your Bread be our only security
as we set off down the risky roads of history.

THURSDAY OF THE 25TH WEEK

NO ESCAPE FROM THE HUMAN

Ecclesiastes 1:2–11: Once more, Solomon's pseudonymous authorship does not mean that the book antedates the return from the Exile. Its form is comparable to that of a "royal testament," a favorite in, especially, the Egypt of the Pharoahs.

The sacred writer is an isolated individual. In the foreground of his contemplation is the cyclical movement of nature. But in the background is a soul in deep anguish. "What profit has man from all the labor which he toils at under the sun?" The lesson is harsh: not only the notion of progress, but the value of wisdom itself is relativized here. Wisdom is essentially defined as an effort to apprehend all of the real and to gain control of life. The sacred writer asserts the opacity of the world. What is evident today can be altogether questionable tomorrow. All things are vanity!

Why this pessimism? It could be explained by the ambition and intelligence of the writer. His project is surely an ambitious one. Ancient wisdom was contained in limited experiences. And this sage would pose it the ultimate question of the universe, and build a cohesive system! But he is aware of his ignorance of God's secrets. The grandeur and drama of the ecclesiast is his knowledge that he is a creature.

Psalm 90, a psalm of national supplication, acknowledges human frailty. What are we but "changing grass, which at dawn springs up anew, but by evening wilts and fades"? Yet the psalm ends with a trusting prayer.

Luke 9:7–9: (See p. 58.)

■

The hucksters of happiness have made their rounds from time immemorial. Their slogans never fail to appeal to a few, deep, instincts within us. Generation after generation, they invent their variations, racking their brains to find a way to refurbish a charm intrinsically evanescent.

254

Likewise from time immemorial, clear-sighted persons, often genuinely inspired, have reacted against this manipulation, contesting the value of the promised "happiness." In the present book, the Bible has preserved for us the testimony of an extraordinarily clear-sighted Jew. Three centuries before our era, in a period of transition between the return from exile and the explosion of the Maccabean revolt, this sage reflected on the meaning of life at a time when traditional assurances had all been shattered, and before anything of any substance had replaced them. Strangely up-to-date, this situation, and this testimony, of more than two thousand years ago!

In all of the happiness that life has to offer, the sacred writer finds nothing of ultimate value. In vain would we close our eyes to reality. Grief and gladness, health and sickness—all things lead to death. But his examination does not end here. Even so he discerns the first faint gleam of salvation. Death must be, yes, and "all things are vanity"—but then the present moment is all the more priceless! And if time flies, if moment follows moment—yet does life exist, proceeding at God's pace. "God's time is the best time," sings Johann Sebastian Bach (*Actus Tragicus*, BWV 106). The solicitude of God is revealed only in the lowly passing minute. What vanity it would be to seek distraction from the single moment that is ours, to go wandering in the mists of an uncertain future! No, blessed is "God's today"! It is in the ordinary things of every day that life is invented, and the everlasting gift of the Father received.

Seek not your happiness where it is not! Let not your life—that fragile, unique possession—be gobbled up by deceitful values! Flee not the only place where life happens—today. You are tempted to say, "What's the use?" But death itself derides all your false values, shows how deceptive they are. These values rob you of your life, cries death! Paradoxically, death, and the miniature deaths we call calamity or disappointment, are but a demonstration of the seriousness of life. Beneath every "Nothing can be done" lies a "Well, you can start over." Behind the mournful commonplace, "I must die," we hear the gladsome call (and calling—our vocation): "I must live!" Obey your human vocation, then, Hearken to the call of today. Earthly and fleshly are we. On earth, and in the flesh, are where our highest goals are achieved. There is no emigrating from the human!

■

After the rain will be more fine weather.
Then is life but an everlasting starting-over-again?

255

God, Ruler of time and history,
    for whom a thousand years are as a day,
give us this day as if it were our only day.
Grant us to receive it
    as the sign of your everlasting tenderness.

■

We give you thanks, God our Father,
that we are not alone as we grapple with our lives,
    with their decay and their hopes,
    their sufferings and their happiness.
No, to save us, you have sent your Son,
    a human being like the rest of us,
    your eternal Word,
    Light from Light.
May this bread, drawn from our earth,
    be the sacrament of your covenant:
it is you who take responsibility for this time of ours,
    and you who will guide it to its accomplishment,
    to see it swell into the ages of eternity.

FRIDAY OF THE 25TH WEEK

THE WOUND

Ecclesiastes 3:1–11: All reality has a negative aspect. The same holds for human activity. Half of existence points toward life, the other half toward death. We are so accustomed to the dark fact that we tend to ignore it.

This too serves the sacred writer as the springboard to a criticism of the ideas he has received from traditional wisdom. After all, of two opposites, we can only deal with one at a time. In other words, there is a right time for everything. But is it given to us to know that moment? The sages have always answered in the affirmative, and have even encouraged their disciples to sift through every situation and learn its proper moment. By contrast, the ecclesiast teaches that time belongs to God alone. Verse 11, especially, teaches that the faculty given us by Yahweh of perceiving the meaning of history is a limited one.

Pessimism? Actually our author is neither pessimistic nor optimistic. He is simply trying to be cold and objective. He detests extreme positions, and has a profound sense of the relativity of things. But what can we do, if we cannot recognize favorable moments when they come? Well, we can welcome life as God's gift. We can accept happiness and unhappiness with equal serenity. The sacred writer is an epicure, but he is a stoic, too.

Psalm 144 is a composite writing. Even the first verses combine thanksgiving with a reflection on the human condition: realism and moderation, in the style of the author of Ecclesiastes.

Luke 9:18–22: (See p. 61.)

■

"But you—who do you say that I am? You, not the crowd. You personally. No "canned answers." A delicate question. I should really like to know the answer. But . . . I hesitate. What will you do, lock me into facile definitions? Give me a name you scarcely comprehend? Whittle away at the mystery of my richness, a mystery whose depths I myself may not have plumbed? I know, you will answer me: Why, you are my child, the one in the manger . . . my friend . . . my "boss" . . . my love. . . . And so on. Yes, I am all of these things, surely. But I am something else, as well! How difficult it is to know another without wounding that one!

"But you—who do you say that I am?" Jesus dares ask us that question. He takes the risk. Answers abound. Books have been written. Jesus? Murdered prophet, Sacred Heart, "true God and true man," Super-Star. Jesus imposes silence. How hard it is to know God without wounding him!

Jesus asks this question when he himself is at prayer. In the truth of his being and his existence, he can say that he knows God: "Father, Abba!" Here is a name I can pronounce without wounding God! For God allows himself to be wounded by that name. "Father, your will be done!" On Calvary Jesus will show the lengths to which this answer will lead him. And in the hour of his passion he will truly be able to say: "Father . . . I have revealed your name. . . ."

To know God is passion, in both senses of the word. It is at once an immense love, and a profound suffering. To know God is to be born again. Show me your face! Peter will genuinely be able to pronounce Jesus' name only after his denial, and Easter: "Lord, you know all things, you know that I love you!" On that day, Jesus will no longer impose silence. Indeed, he will encourage Peter in his vocation to strengthen his sisters and brothers.

"Who am I?" What else, then, will tell us God's name but the wound God himself has himself engraved on our hearts with the desire to know him?

■

Then who, Lord, our Father,
    could have known your name
    had your Son not come to reveal it?
His word stirs our heart,
    and awakens in it the desire to love you.
Let this wound never be closed.
Receive our prayer:
    "Who are you, Lord, that we may give you our faith?"

■

God our Father,
increase our faith in Jesus, the One you have sent.
Open our eyes to his mystery,
    and our ears to his word,
that, in the gladness of the Holy Spirit,
we may see your magnificent deed accomplished
    in your Son, our Lord.

■

In this bread, broken for us,
    God our Father,
we acknowledge the One who gives life to the world.
May he remain our strength each day,
    and keep us one with you,
as he is the Way that leads to the communion
    of the everlasting ages.

SATURDAY OF THE 25TH WEEK

DISENCHANTMENT
Ecclesiastes 11:9–12:8: Here is a curious poem, chock-full of human
disappointment. What good is a long life, if it ends in decrepitude? The style is
highly allegorical. Old age is compared to a house still lived in, but slowly
tumbling down. Men's vigor slowly dies away, women's beauty fades. The

millwheel comes to a stop, for the servants who have turned it have died. The doors of the house are locked, for the guards are no more.

A very ancient rabbinical reading thrusts the allegory still further, attaching each image to one of our bodily parts. The trembling guardians are our arms; the hunched strong men, our legs; the women who cease their grinding, our teeth; the windows looking out onto the street, our eyes. The sound of the mill is the human voice, the almond blossoms, white hair; the locusts or grasshoppers, and the caper berries, the genitalia. (Cf. A. Chouraqui.)

Psalm 90, a song of human frailty, prolongs Qoheleth's meditation.

Luke 9:43–45: (See p. 64.)

■

Oh, come now! Very well, surely he may temper his disciples' runaway enthusiasm in private. He knew over-confident Peter very well, and surely had better try to keep him from getting carried away. What did this fisher know of the Messiah's mission? But crush the hope that the fervor of the crowds inspired in his disciples? Everyone was in admiration at what Jesus was doing—so he tells his disciples that the Son of man must be delivered up to death! Really, now.

"But you—who do you say that I am?" Faith is a judgment. It is a response to a question, but a response that can be made only at the end of a judicial proceeding. "The Son of man must . . . be put to death . . ."! The gospel can be read as the account of this trial. God is indicted and tried by his human creatures. And he receives the death sentence. Whether or not he is recognized as God has no bearing on the case.

Jesus will allow himself to be judged. This is his way of passing judgment on us. He declares that this is what he has come for! At the end of time he, the poor one who was refused bread, Caiphas' prisoner that the disciples would not come to visit, the one who died naked on a cross, will be seen to be the Supreme Judge.

The trial is ultimately concerned with a question of identity. Who are you? Who in the world do you think you are? That will be Caiphas' and Pilate's question. But it will also be the question proposed all through the gospel, and here Jesus asks it of his disciples. "But you—who do you say that I am?" And the question remains an open one even today. Any answer will necessarily be an existential commitment on the part of the one making the answer (or refusing to make it). No one can know or tell who Jesus is without implying a relationship with him. To speak of Jesus is to give testimony at a trial that has never been concluded.

He dampened the enthusiasm of the crowds. The disciples were thunderstruck. But faith is not a one-night stand. Faith is a debate, a trial. Faith is a wager, a gamble.

∎

Can we really follow your Son, Lord,
*   when he goes "the whole route"?*
And yet—could we love you
*   if you did not go "all the way"?*

As your love is our admiration,
*   may it be our strength*
*   as we set out in Jesus' footsteps.*

∎

Free and mighty God,
*   by the gospel you bring us "back to basics."*
Deliver us from all our encumbrances.
May the power of your word
*   and the breath of your Spirit*
*   make us ready, willing, and able*
*   to follow Jesus, our Lord.*

∎

God of our praise,
to whom should we go,
*   if not to your Son, Jesus Christ?*
His words become spirit and life
*   for those who communicate in his body delivered for us.*
May this bread, broken for our happiness
*   make us to dwell in him*
*   who is the food of our little faith,*
that, joined to your Son's passion,
*   we may likewise partake of his resurrection.*

And Lead Us Not into Temptation

Job: Here we have a book that echoes some of our most fundamental, most existential questions. The Book of Job is a rebellion—a revolt against the injustice of suffering and the silence of God.

Yes, Job is the person shocked by his God, and challenged to rebel. He can neither resign himself to the injustice done him, nor become an atheist. Job is the person who protests against his God. For a week, we shall plunge into the trial of faith—Job's, and ours. For, from beginning to end, the Book of Job is a parable that goes straight to our heart. It speaks to us of a human being grappling with God. Devastated in life, overwhelmed by so many sufferings, Job wages the combat of faith, like his ancestor Jacob, like the one he prefigures, Jesus. Behold the human test and trial: God treats us as enemies— and we appeal for help to . . . God.

Becoming a disciple is a test, a trial. Those who have heard the Lord's call are marked by a wound that nothing can ever heal. Like Jacob, the believer is crippled for life. This is the gospel story, and the plot thickens when Jesus goes up to Jerusalem. This is Luke's intent, especially. Faith comes into being over the course of this journey of the cross, this long debate between the unleashed powers of darkness and the humble prayer of the servant: "Lord, to whom shall we go? You have the words of eternal life" (Jn 6:68). Who awakens to faith but the one who sets out in the footsteps of Jesus and says: "I know that my Vindicator lives, and that he will at last stand forth upon the dust. . . . I shall see God . . ." (Jb 19:25–26)? O mystery hidden from the wise and revealed to the little ones whose only invocation is these clumsy words: "O God, lead us not into temptation!" O mystery accomplished in the blood of the Servant, poured out: God will fill the hungry with good things!

■

You are present to our lives,
    God most good,
and you know our human sufferings and cares.
Show us your face!
May the Good News of salvation resound this very day,
    that we may know you as our Father.

■

God, Lord of life,
    you alone can restore us to that life.
Deliver us from the fear that reduces us to silence,
that we may sing you our thankfulness,
    testifying to the grace you bestow on us
in Jesus, the Risen one.

■

On Psalm 31
Lord, have pity on me,
for I am in distress.
See the rebellion and accusation around me!
See how suffering, injustice and despair
are the daily bread of human kind.
Will the Divider carry the day?
Shall we be separated from you?
Will your renown become a laughing-stock,
and the memory of your mercy a mere tale?

■

Lord, in you we place our hope,
    for with you is our salvation.
I have placed my trust in you,
    and in my loneliness
      I proclaim you my God.
My fate is in your hands:
    save me by your love,
    and let the brightness of your face
    shine on your servant.

■

In you, Lord, I have found my refuge:
    let me never be disappointed.
In your love protect me,
    and forget not your promise
    and the obedience of your Son.
Lead us not into temptation,
    but deliver us from the evil
    that can crush us!

Be the rock of our hope,
the citadel that guards our faith.

■

Be blessed, God our Father:
those who turn to you
find a hiding place in your heart—
for they know a secret!
Yes, I can say:
this day my eyes have seen
the salvation you prepare for the earth,
the victory you accord your servants!

Love the Lord,
all you his lovers!
Love the Lord,
for he watches over his faithful ones.
Be strong, and stout of heart,
all you who wait for the Lord!

MONDAY OF THE 26TH WEEK

TRIAL
Job 1:6–22: The Book of Job originated in a piece of folklore dating from the
end of the second millenium before Christ. It shows us a wealthy property
holder living to the southeast of the Dead Sea, a person of integrity, suffering
catastrophe in his person and his goods, but demonstrating a most exemplary
patience.

The tale poses a number of questions. For example: Is there such a thing as a
disinterested piety? The answer comes in the affirmative. In the midst of the
catastrophes that rain down upon his head, Job maintains complete serenity.
"The Lord gave and the Lord has taken away; blessed be the name of the
Lord!" Job is a paragon of righteousness. Another question is that of personal
retribution: an epilogue describes the restoration of the faithful one to his
ancestral possessions.

A poet has taken up the ancient work and adapted it to the questions posed by
his age. A Jew of the second generation of the Exile, discouraged with the
confusion of his compatriots, has utilized the tale as a springboard to an

answer. First he addresses the question already asked in the story: Is there such a thing as a disinterested reverence, an unselfish fear of the Lord? The question was altogether timely for the deportees who had seen Yahweh's enemies triumph. Doubtless the Jews were not blameless. But had they merited a catastrophe of this magnitude? What was the use of their fidelity to the covenant, if the only outcome were to be their cruel abandonment by the Lord their God?

A word about Satan, the "Adversary." "By interposing a mysterious personage between God and the human being, the Book of Job has obliged the latter to consider evil and death as something transcending the individual and even the community. There is a 'surfeit of evil,' both preceding us and following each of us, whose consequences echo in us each" (*Cahiers Evangile*). At all events it is in the surfeit of suffering of the exiled chosen people that the Book of Job has posed the question of the divine justice.

In his protestations of innocence, Job often imitates the literary genre of *Psalm 17*, the complaint of the victim of a false accusation who comes to the temple to beg God to do him justice.

Luke 9:46–50: (See p. 66.)

■

A discussion has arisen among the disciples. Jesus has just announced that his mission will be a way of the cross, and tomorrow he will courageously set out for Jerusalem. But it has all gone over the disciples' heads, and here they are quarreling about the places of honor they will have in the Reign of God! They have yet to make the long ascent of Golgotha, which will show them the true face of "Jesus' family," what his real sisters and brothers "look like." Only at journey's end will they be born to faith—at the term of the trial, the battle.

A battle, a combat—all this week we shall be immersed in a most dramatic and moving parable. Before our astonished, indignant eyes, Job will rise up to confront God. He will rail against God—and yet it is he who will provide God's apologia. Job's trial is that of the believer confronted with the drama of life—confronted with his God.

Satan taunts God. Your human creatures love you because of the benefits you shower on them. Faith is "love" with ulterior motives. The book that we shall be looking at is a debate, then, a drama cast as a judicial process, with three main personages. On the one side is God. On the other is Satan the Accuser, the sower of division between God and humanity by telling God, "People will forget you!" and humanity, "God has forgotten you!" Finally, there is Job, the unhesitating arbiter of the debate.

Here is a debate for all times. The Divider, Satan, has the easy part. Everything cries out against God. How could anyone willingly choose the narrow way of the gospel, and the way of the cross? The situation of the believer, in a world of such evil and injustice, is a situation of trial and test. How will that believer behave? Become an atheist? Sink into resignation? Neither, answers the Book of Job. The believer is a protester, who never "lets God be"!

The disciples were discussing the places of honor in the coming Reign of God. They had forgotten that becoming a disciple is a challenge. Satan and God are locked in a struggle for the possession of the human heart. Job is the one who accepts the challenge, all unaware. The true disciple will know Easter, but only after an ordeal.

■

Lord our God,
be our refuge and our strength—
 you yourself personally!—
 when the time of doubting comes.

Forget not the promise of your Son!
For our peace,
 send your Spirit, our Defender.
May he sustain our faith
 in the tribunal of life,
and be the light we shall need
 to emerge victorious
 from the ordeal of our times.

TUESDAY OF THE 26TH WEEK

WHY?

Job 3:1–3, 11–17, 20–23: Job curses the day he was born, and we feel his unspeakable suffering in our bones, as we hear his cry of distress. For Job, God is the enemy now, and his complaint often has the ring of an inexorable indictment. He calls on Yahweh to show cause for his apparent injustice.

We must realize that there is more than the cry of an individual here. Job's suffering is that of a whole people, and a people in the pit of the abyss. When the poet of the generation of the Exile inserted work of his own into the primitive tale, his purpose was to suggest an answer to the enormous question raised by Israel's deportation. Why had Yahweh abandoned his own? Had he come to hate his people?

Around Job gather three of his peers (the fourth, Elihu, is a later addition). All are in agreement on one point: Job's suffering has a meaning. But no one knows what the meaning is. For his friends, who represent traditional ideas, suffering is medicinal: its purpose is to convert the sinner. But Job is not ready to accept his friends' responses. He protests his innocence. He is sure that it is God, and not he, who has severed relations.

Psalm 88 shows us a sufferer patient passing the night in one of the temple chambers and hoping, come morn, for a favorable response from Yahweh, and release from his disease.

Luke 9:51–56: (See p. 68.)

■

"Perish the day on which I was born, the night when they said, 'The child is a boy!' " Misfortune strikes, and Job sees the wisdom on which he had based his piety lying in smithereens at his feet. God has downright laid siege to him. And God has gone beyond all bounds. In the world of people, there are limits to parental correction. But here. . . . No, this is too much.

Even more than the collapse of his wisdom, it is the collapse of his religious relationship with God that devastates Job. He believes that he is abandoned by God. The good and just God of his faith seems to him no longer to exist. He no longer even dares believe that the hostile, terrifying image his sufferings force upon his brain will ever be effaced. His cry still contains a glimmer of hope for change. But his very line of questioning becomes an act of despair: Why give us life at all when there is no way out of life's agony, when God blocks every avenue of escape?

"Why?" Does this question have an echo in ourselves? Not this question . . . this accusation! In the courtroom of life, we have every right to throw this "Why?" in God's face. Else we are not human beings after all. Dostoevsky has Ivan Karamazov cry, "Oh, I understand, Alyosha, how the universe will tremble with gladness, when everything in heaven and earth blends in one hymn of praise, when the mother embraces the fiend who threw her child to the dogs, and all three cry aloud with tears, 'Thou art just, O Lord! . . . But . . . I can't accept that harmony. . . . I renounce the higher harmony altogether. It's not worth the tears of that one tortured child. . . . It's not worth it, because those tears are unatoned for. . . . I want to forgive. I want to embrace. I don't want more suffering. And if the sufferings of children go to swell the sum of sufferings which was necessary to pay for the truth, then I protest that the truth is not worth such a price. . . . I don't want harmony. From love for humanity I don't want it. . . . I would rather remain with my unavenged suffering and unsatisfied indigation, *even if I were wrong*. . . . Too high a price is asked . . . it's beyond our means. . . . And so I hasten to give back my entrance ticket, and if I am an honest man I am bound to give it back as soon as possible. . . . I most respectfully return Him the ticket." Must we not fling this excruciating accusation, this "Why?" in God's face, the moment we allow ourselves honestly, genuinely, to appreciate the catastrophe, the shambles of our human lives? Must we not "respectfully return Him the ticket"?

"As the time approached when Jesus was to be taken from this world, he firmly resolved to proceed toward Jerusalem." To our "Why?" God has no answer but a way of the cross trodden to the bitter end. Now Jesus will take Job's place, to know the utter depths of despair, to the point of crying out in anguish, "My God, my God, why have you forsaken me?" (Mk 15:34). The fact that God connives with the hubbub of the world, the fact that God makes it his own, justifies nothing. But I call to witness, in support of my accusation, God himself, hanging on the cross and joining me in my accusation: in the debate with the Prosecutor, both God and I speak for the defense.

■

God, Father of Jesus Christ and our Father,
    hear the reproach of your people.
Let the agonized screams
    of a world crushed by suffering
    mount to your throne.
Receive the prayer of your Son:
    abandon us not.
    Rise in our defense!

■

You call us, Lord our God,
    to follow your Son on his way of the cross.
May his willing humiliation become our strength,
    his death, our life.
May his body, surrendered on Calvary,
    and his blood, poured forth for us,
be the foundation of our hope

and the source of our happiness
now and forever.

WEDNESDAY OF THE 26TH WEEK

THE STRIPPING

Job 9:1–12, 14–16: Job's reply will not be a turning point. Throughout his discussion with his friends, he has sought dialogue with God. His faith demands it. After all, he knows that he is righteous, and he believes that God has always been the defender of the innocent. And so Job cannot rest content with the simple observation that the covenant has been broken. He must call God to account. But has a creature the right to hail God before a tribunal?

As is customary in the songs of complaint, the next verses of *Psalm 88* bring forward an irrefutable motive for the divine intervention. If Yahweh allows the sick to die, it is all over with their praise of him. The abode of the dead rings with no thanksgiving! Here we touch upon a constant theme in the thinking of Israel, up until the age of the Maccabees: with death we disappear utterly.

Luke 9:57–62: (See p. 70.)

■

One must advance, and resolutely broach the ascent. One must be unencumbered with any weight that would slow the march, then. Jesus has bravely taken the road for Jerusalem. The days of the great departure, the new Exodus, are upon him. "Whoever wishes to be my follower must deny his very self . . ."! Ah, here is a candidate for discipleship, ready to follow the master wherever he goes. Does he have the slightest notion how rootless is the life he is embracing? And here is another, called by the Lord and not even given the time to bury his father! The urgency of the Reign brooks no delay. To follow Christ is a perpetual passage, an ascent, a Passover. Let us be plain. The time has come to leave, to be torn away, to be uprooted. The time of the stripping is at hand. Any who have heard the call must first be cleansed and refined, at great length. "Whoever wishes to be my follower must deny his very self . . ."!

"Even though I were right, I could not answer him. . . ." Yesterday Job was a witness for the prosecution. Today he falls silent. And we see the stripping, the utter spoliation of an individual who has suffered so much that he no longer has the strength to complain. There are many such in our world!

Now that we have undergone the ordeal of faith, perhaps today we can at last ask some honest questions. But "Who can say to him, 'What are you doing?' " We have the suffering one, and we have the philosophers: Job, and his friends who come to console him. But his friends also accuse him. "Who can say to him, 'What are you doing?' " Suffering is not a question, not a problem, not a subject for a dissertation. Contrary to popular opinion, the book of Job does not attempt to solve the problem of suffering. It "disqualifies" itself, like a judge disclaiming competence. It declares that there is no "solution." In the throes of suffering, we are stripped naked, and there is no escape. And when God finally speaks to Job, God himself gives no answer. After all—there was really no question.

"Who can say to him, 'What are you doing?' " In the citadel of despair where we lie emprisoned, a tiny ray of light gleams: a word that is not an answer, but a call. "Whoever wishes to be my follower must . . . take up his cross . . . and follow in my steps" (Lk 9:23). Jesus will be stretched naked on the cross. Even his "Why have you abandoned me?" will become silence. The disciple will have to go to this extremity of spoliation. Then there will be Easter.

■

By the demanding word of your Son,
*   we are led ever further onward.*
*   Lord, be blessed.*
Permit us to follow in his steps,
*   in silence and in faith.*

■

God our Father,
you have created all things,
*   and you alone know the secret of our life.*
How could we stand before you,
*   were it not for the fact that it is you yourself*
*   who have come forth to meet us?*
As you have invited us to the table of your covenant,
*   grant that we may be faithful to your will,*
*   that we may live a life of gratitude for your grace.*

HOPING AGAINST HOPE

Job 19:21–27: Job's pilgrimage has not been in the pitch-dark. In chapter nine he formulated the hope of seeing an arbitrator appointed to conciliate the dispute between God and humanity. In chapter sixteen he asked the earth not to cover his blood until his cry of distress had traversed the skies and found an echo with a mysterious witness who could defend that humanity against God. Here, finally, Job expresses the desire that his words be carved in stone, to endure forever, for he knows that he is not without defense: his Vindicator lives!

This is a difficult passage to translate. Nor can we say that verse 26 contains an explicit profession of faith in the resurrection. Who is this "Vindicator" that will show Job his God? In the language of the Bible, the *go'el* is the relative of a murder victim who is charged with avenging the latter's blood. All that can be said here is that, amidst Job's consternation, a cry of hope has welled up—quickly stifled, to be sure, by the vision of daily reality. It is as if Job had somehow managed to preserve his profound conviction that God's main concern cannot be with crushing the human race.

Many psalms sing of Israel's faith in a God who is the protector of the poor and innocent. Such is the case with the second part of *Psalm 27* (vv. 7–14). Upon all who have passed through death but have preserved their trust in God, Easter will dawn in all its brilliance as God's response.

Luke 10:1–12: (See p. 73.)

■

On the road to Jerusalem, Jesus tells the news, and it falls like a bombshell. He declares the Reign of God inaugurated. Now it is up to each individual, and each village, to decide for or against. He chooses seventy-two disciples, and sends them out, two by two. And the brotherly teams rush into the field, two persons with the same passion. The recruiting campaign is under way. Barefoot, the messengers make haste. The harvest is near.

Once more, the road to Jerusalem. And at the end of the road, the silhouette of a cross. The harvest? There has been no harvest. The lambs? The wolves have devoured them all. Their peace had not been received. "If the people of any town you enter do not welcome you, go into its streets and say, 'We shake the dust of this town from our feet as testimony against you. But know that the reign of God is near' "!

"But know . . ."! If ever there has been a humble profession of
faith . . . ! All the evidence is against it. This Passover will be a bloody
one, and the disciples will be scattered. Suffering will have stifled the
very cry of revolt, and accusation will be mute, in the silence of the
ordeal. But hope against hope is rash. For it declares: "I know that my
Vindicator lives, and that he will at last stand forth upon the dust." The
Reign of God is near indeed, though the doors are closed. And the
harvesters have reason for joy: the Liberator will arise to stand on the
dust of the dead, the morning of the Pasch! Jesus' passion will attest
that God will deliver up his own Son, to die in utter agony and
desolation, rather than let us die by detaching himself from the human
catastrophe. The cross is not first and foremost God's plunge into human
impotence, and the woe of the world. It is first and foremost the sign
that historically, decisively, God has decided to prefer us to himself.
Yes, this is God's response to one of the most extraordinary verses in
the Old Testament—when Job, from the depths of his unhappiness,
utters this cry, presents this request, declares this certitude: "Before
God my eyes drop tears, that he may do justice for a mortal in his
presence . . ." (Jb 16:21)—that God may justify mortals to God! Jesus'
passion will be one of obstinate love, not helpless suffering. The Reign
of God is at hand the moment we set foot on the road to Jerusalem.

■

God, Father of believers,
    our lives are being tried by fire.
We know your faithfulness:
    to keep your promise,
    you have surrendered your very Son.
Grant that those who follow him in faith
    may walk with him to the end of the road,
    that they may be raised with him in glory.

FRIDAY OF THE 26TH WEEK

ACQUITTAL: GRACE ACCORDED
Job 38:1, 12–21; 40:3–5: Now God speaks. As of old on Mount Sinai, he
comes in a storm. We notice that Yahweh answers none of Job's questions.
But the divine response is not to remit the question to a lower court. God's

271

only reproach of Job is because of the latter's attempt to impose on God his own concept of righteousness. Throughout the discussion with his friends, Job has never ceased to insist on his moral integrity—as if that ought to snatch him from the human condition! Thus Job reveals himself to be as traditional as his friends: he, too, links happiness with moral perfection!

Psalm 139 is a psalm of supplication. A long treatise on the divine omniscience is counterbalanced by the supplicant's assertion of his innocence. God who sounds loins and hearts knows that he is righteous.

Luke 10:13–16: (See p. 75.)

■

From the depths of his suffering, Job has valiantly waged his battle with God. He has refused to let his resistance be softened by the idle chatter of his friends. Now Job is alone before God—to hear God's disconcerting response. That response begins with a lesson in natural history. Nor has the teacher a single word to say about Job's personal case! Far from taking up the catalog of Job's recriminations and answering them one by one, God speaks as if he still had no notion of what his interlocutor is suffering! Instead we have a fireworks display— God's creative might and power of invention. And suddenly humanity is back where it belongs. And so is God. Job must once more let himself be "trapped"—abandon himself to the One whose care is for human beings. No longer is it a question of God's recompense and retribution. Job now clings to the God of recompense and retribution.

The battle is ended. And we discover that faith is beyond justifications, indictments, or briefs for the prosecution (or the defense). True, one of faith's motives is the utter seriousness of existence. But its substance is purely gratuitous. Job now has the experience of the gift of profusion, of generosity without requital. To be sure, the heart has its reasons. But love reveals its true shape and form only when, transcending all motivation, it continues to give itself, unconditionally and unalterably. How could love ever be parsimonious, economical, reasonable? The defense will rest. And the plaintiff will withdraw the suit—in utter surrender.

■

God our Father,
creator of all things,
>   *how dare we stand in your presence?*
Reveal to us our poverty,
>   *that we may experience your overwhelming grace!*

MY EYES HAVE SEEN YOU

Job 42:1-3, 5-6, 12-17: "I had heard of you by word of mouth, but now my eye has seen you." Job's knowledge of what it means to have a personal relationship with God had been limited to whatever might have been contained in traditional wisdom. Like everyone else in Israel, he had thought that moral integrity would win a person rights against God. But one look at creation and he knew better. Now he had had a few lessons in God's greatness and freedom. Now that he has been to existential divinity school, he can say something new, something he has never before known: humbly, but joyously, he acknowledges that a personal relationship with God can only be based on trust.

And Yahweh blessed all Job's remaining years. The righteous Job, reconciled at last with himself and God, died full of days.

Job profited from his experience. And *Psalm 119* sings, "It is good for me that I have been afflicted. . . ."

Luke 10:17-24: (See p. 77.)

On Psalm 92

It is good to praise you, Lord,
to sing your name at every moment,
to proclaim your love and faithfulness.

You fill the hungry with good things
and send the rich away empty.
You trample in the dust
the accusation weighing upon us,
and you raise up the ones you have justified by your love.

How grand are your deeds, O Lord—
how infinitely deep, your thoughts!
The blasé cannot know them.
Only the child, with empty hands, can receive them!
Be blessed forever and ever!

■

Job's old solutions are bankrupt. Now the sufferer leaves God's rewards and punishments behind, to embrace the God of rewards and

punishments. Then that sufferer finds God no longer through the sole intermediary of a received tradition, but in the embrace of a lived experience: "I had heard of you by word of mouth, but now my eye has seen you." The suffering had thought they knew God. Now they realize that, in comparison with what they have known before, their present knowledge is like seeing something with their own eyes after hearing about it second-hand. The Book of Job offers no response to the dramatic questions we ask. It makes no attempt to justify this God indicted by the scandal of our distress. It shows us a human being like ourselves set free, at peace, because he has had, in despoilment and gratuity, the experience of God. It has been a crucifying encounter, as we had the occasion to observe yesterday. Standing at the cross, before a Lord stripped and naked as Job—and ourselves stripped as he—we grasp at last that the only relationship that can arise between this Lord and ourselves is love. "Now my eye has seen you"!

Well may the disciples return from their mission all aglow. The paschal victory is already at work! "I watched Satan fall from the sky like lightning." Well may Job fill himself with days—in Jesus' ordeal, victory is ours. In him we have lost all and gained all, even now. And well may the Book of Revelation declare, alluding to the book on which we have meditated this week: "The accuser of our brothers is cast out, who night and day accused them before our God. They defeated him by the blood of the Lamb and by the word of their testimony . . ." (Rv 12:10-11). By the blood of the Lamb, and not by their own blood, by the ordeal of the only Son of the Father, and not by their own ordeal, believers enter the Reign of love. Throughout the earth, the blood of the suffering Righteous one, the blood of Jesus, trumpets the defeat of Satan and the triumph of the Servant of Yahweh. But this victory is given to those alone who show their empty hands. "O Father, Lord of heaven and earth . . . what you have hidden from the learned and the clever you have revealed to the merest children . . ." (Lk 10:21). And turning to his disciples, Jesus adds, "Blest are the eyes that see what you see!" (Lk 10:23) By consenting to be saved by naught but Love, we are rescued from our frailty once and for all. Hope is possible. God fills the hungry with good things.

■

Now do you discharge your servant, Lord, in peace—
for our eyes have seen the salvation
*   that you prepare for the earth:*
a piece of bread,

bespeaking today
the paschal victory of tomorrow,
and flowing blood
proclaiming the triumph
of those your Servant has saved.
Glory to you for all eternity!

FROM MONDAY OF THE 27TH WEEK

TO WEDNESDAY OF THE 28TH WEEK

Reversal

The gospel is life in reverse. One would think that the way to live would surely be right-side-out. The trouble is, we do not know how to define right-side-out. Our false perspectives stand in continual need of revision. Christ is on the road. Those who follow him learn to redirect their lives.

"Who is my neighbor?" Law delimits, organizes, codifies. After all, love must be reasonable! "Martha, you are anxious and upset . . ."—anxious to do well, anxious to give God, his demands, his law, a good reception. A religion of law is certainly active. But it has no heart. It would have faith be a duty for each and every believer. "Teach us to pray. . . ." Prayer is taken for a religious exercise, a special time devoted to religion. Prayer would be the fruit of a human effort to reach a useful God. "Blest is the womb that bore you . . . !"—either you have faith or not, depending on your birth and upbringing. A religion of law demands signs in the form of proofs: it codifies God's call in laws to observe and rites to perform. And so on. This is what people think when they think "religion."

Which of these was his neighbor? "The one who treated him with compassion." Charity is active, then. It starts in the heart, and knows no limits. "Mary has chosen the better portion. . . ." To welcome God means to be seduced, and one thing alone is necessary: to listen to the word, in prayer and service. Your heavenly Father will "give the Holy Spirit to those who ask him." But the Spirit is life, renewal, fire and peace: the response outstrips the request, and prayer becomes the art of living according to the Breath of God. "Blest are they who hear the word of God and keep it." Faith is the acceptance of a promise, and the fertility of a response to that promise: for the believer is a child of Abraham, and the certificate attesting to that child's birth is the adoptive word. There is no other sign to receive—only Jesus himself, and consecration by the Holy Spirit, which sets one free. This is how genuine life is built. And it is called Gospel.

God, Father of Jesus and our Father,
you call us to be free,
     to become persons,
     to reflect the image and spirit of Jesus.
And so we pray:
Give us the strength by which he lived.
Fill us to overflowing
     with the Spirit that makes all things new.

MONDAY OF THE 27TH WEEK

ONLY LOVE TO SHARE

Galatians 1:6–12: It is unusual for the lectionary to omit the beginning of a letter, but it leaves out Paul's salutation to the Galatians and immediately launches into his vehement reproach to this community in the vicinity of Ancyra (today's Ankara), in Asia Minor. The Galatians, he says, have deserted him.

Why this fiery language? "I am amazed," writes Paul "that you are so soon deserting him who called you in accord with his gracious design in Christ, and are going over to another gospel." Had we no other sentence to read but this one, we should know at once that something has gone terribly wrong in Galatia. The gospel itself hangs in the balance.

What is the meaning of the term, "gospel," of which Paul and Mark speak in such absolute tones? The Good News, of course. But this says relatively little. The circumstances surrounding the composition of Galatians help us grasp what the bare words leave unsaid. In his letter to the Galatians, Paul is reacting against attacks by "Judaizers," as we call them today—Jews converted to Christianity without a sufficient appreciation of the importance of the breach implied in such a conversion. In the minds of these Christians, Christ had abolished no jot or tittle of the Old Covenant. On the contrary, he had confirmed Jewish law and practices, especially circumcision. These Christians are a real danger to the church. They want their rules imposed on everyone. This, says Paul, would not only block the conversion of the pagans for all practical purposes, but would void the cross of Christ: a return to Jewish practice would belittle the salvific value of the cross, and hence of Christian baptism. The question was clear. Which is the true source of salvation, the Law or the Faith?

276

Usually classified as a hymn, *Psalm 111* follows an alphabetical structure. Like many similar psalms, it formulates certain wisdom principles, and invites the community to return thanks to the Lord for his mighty deeds. Christians praying this psalm will think of the mightiest deed of all: the cross.

Luke 10:25–37: (See p. 79.)

■

"I did not receive it from any man. . . . It came by revelation from Jesus Christ"! Surely anyone who would maintain that the possibility of a future, anyone who would dare to deny the foolishness of hoping against hope—and yet would refuse to admit that this hope is revealed, that it is attested by someone we know, someone who has already experienced it—would soon hear the questioning and accusation of their fellow human beings turn to derision. My gospel comes from Jesus Christ. It is his word, it is his person.

It is his word. "There was a man going down from Jerusalem to Jericho. . . ." We have left Jerusalem behind, the proud city on the heights, safe behind its walls. We have left charming little Bethany. We are on our way to Jericho, the city all surrounded with red and violet hamlets. We fall into the hands of a band of brigands. The road is deserted, and we are defenseless.

Along comes a priest. He sees the human heap along the roadside; apparently someone dying. Or even dead? The priest passes by. He has a perfectly "valid" excuse. The law forbade a priest to have contact with a corpse. Besides . . . well, for some days now he has been mounting to the altar, offering sacrifice, singing psalms, reciting the Law, and . . . his heart is full of all this. Might it be this that prevents him from being seized with pity? Along comes a Levite. He too is in haste to complete the mission he has received from the temple today. Along comes a Samaritan—reprobate, traitor and schismatic. And it is the outcast, the good-for-nothing, who stoops down over the thing in the ditch. The excommunicate becomes the person of communion, the heretic the one after God's own heart. For he bends down over a fellow human being. God loves the one with a heart.

Jesus recounts this parable in response to a lawyer's question. "Who is my neighbor?" Love my neighbor as myself? How far does the Law force me to go? Jesus replies: How close will love thrust you to your fellow human beings? The answer actually parries the question rather than answering it. It is the wrong question.

277

There are setbacks in life that teach us to redirect our lives. The priest and Levite are not evil persons. They are simply religious people. They are following the rules. They are ourselves—the side of us not yet evangelized. "Who is my neighbor?" Law delimits, law organizes love, so that it will be reasonable. The gospel sets this narrow logic on its ear. Love is without limit, or it is not love! For God is love. And he has nothing but love to share.

"There was a man going down from Jerusalem to Jericho. . . ." My gospel "came by revelation from Jesus Christ." My gospel is his word. It is also his person. Soon Jesus will be walking this same road. Only, he will be taking it in the opposite direction. He will be headed for Jerusalem. And it will be he who is the rejected one, ridiculed, covered with blood, hanged along the roadside and left for dead. Law and order, good sense and good conscience, will be reestablished at last. God will be silenced. For God has only love to share. "No one has ever seen God. Yet if we love one another God dwells in us." (1 Jn 4:12)

Were I still capable of modeling what I say on reasonable human discourse, "I would surely not be serving Christ!" No, brothers and sisters, "the gospel I proclaimed to you is no mere human invention."

■

God, Father of tenderness,
* you are near all those who invoke you.*
Pour forth your love into our hearts,
* that we may become neighbor*
* to those you place along our path.*

TUESDAY OF THE 27TH WEEK

THE SERVICE OF GOD

Galatians 1:13-24: The Judaizers were reminding Paul that he had not known the Jesus of history; they were raising the question of the source of his apostolic authority. For Paul there was only one possible response. He has his gospel from Christ Jesus himself.

The apostle's defense is remarkable in every way. First of all he reminds his adversaries that his education had scarcely prepared him to become the champion of a doctrine calculated to replace Jewish law. The choice that God had made of his person must therefore have been God's utterly free and spontaneous act. From his mother's womb, then, he had been chosen, exactly as the prophets—who had also been the object of their compatriots' snarling persecution, and had had no other protector than the One who had sent them. God "chose to reveal his Son to me, that I might spread among the Gentiles the good tidings concerning him." This revelation is Paul's gospel—the gospel of universal grace.

Pointing out that he had begun his missionary activity immediately upon being converted, Paul emphasizes that he had not applied to the other apostles for his commission, or received any mission from the mother church in Jerusalem. He had acted entirely on his own initiative—on the strength of his conviction of having been chosen by God. It was three years before he had gone up to Jerusalem to make the acquaintance of Peter.

We have seen *Psalm 139* before, echoing the words of Job. It is a supplication, whose disquisition on the divine omniscience functions as an affidavit of the psalmist's innocence.

Luke 10:38–42: (See p. 81.)

■

Jesus has set out now, but he pauses along the road that will take him to Jerusalem at the end of his mission. He is in Bethany, for a moment of peace in the house of a friend, Lazarus. Lazarus' two sisters, Martha and Mary, receive him.

Mary sits at the Lord's feet. The attentive disciple awaits the Master's word. Mary hears his word, savors it, meditates on it and is seduced by it, like God's people in its youth.

Martha, for her part, is busy—overwhelmed by the manifold tasks of serving a guest. She is a generous, devoted woman, like the Samaritan whose charity Jesus has just praised so highly.

Martha and Mary both prefigure the church. Martha's zeal symbolizes the many services required by the life of the community. The church must attend to others, and exercise the ministry of charity. Indeed, was this not the point of yesterday's parable? The ones who belong to Jesus' family are the ones who do the will of his Father. But to hear the word of the Lord of the community is likewise an essential, primary task. This is the task Mary has chosen—that of adoration, which is service of God, the age-old discipleship of Israel.

The sisters are two prefigurations of the church, then. But why is Martha reproached? She has only done what the centurion did for his slave, or what the Samaritan did who stopped along the lonely road to Jericho.

She symbolizes the mission of the church—to reveal to the pagans the deeper meaning of what they were already doing. Might it be the fact that she seeks to turn Mary aside from her "portion," impose on her her own way of hearing the word? Martha and Mary—two ways of hearing the word—are complementary. Then stop complaining, Martha! One thing alone is necessary: to embrace the service of God in the silence of the heart, and in a ready charity that knows its source and origin.

■

We pray to you, Lord,
    on behalf of those who stand before you in praise:
grant them the joy of the one thing required.

We pray to you for all those who give you glory
    by their lives lived for their sisters and brothers:
may they discover you in that service.

And we pray to you for your church:
may the many different pathways its members take
    converge in one and the same love.

Eternal God, our Father,
    deign to turn your heart to us
that we may be altogether at your service
    in the quest for the one thing necessary.

■

God of goodness, our Friend,
you bestow on us the Word of life and the bread of your Reign,
    and this is the better portion for us.
Grant that we may seek, day by day
    the one thing required, Jesus Christ,
    who lives forever.

AS OUR ELDER BROTHER

Galatians 2:1-2, 7-14: Paul's awareness of his mandate from Christ has never led him to fracture the unity of the church. On the contrary, after four years of an apostolate, he had gone up to Jerusalem to meet the local community, and the ones he calls the "pillars of the Church"—James, Peter and John. And the apostle had not only been treated as an equal there, but had been assigned the role among the pagans that Peter performed for the benefit of the Jews. An accord had been struck, provisionally delineating two distinct apostolic fields, and Paul had had a heart large enough to concretize his communion by maintaining among the pagan Christian churches the principle of financial aid to the mother church.

But the accord had not diminished Peter's universal role: immediately thereafter, we find him in Antioch. In fact, his prestige is already such that his behavior has the force of example. Paul reacts violently, then, when Peter, under pressure from Christians of Jewish origin, wishes to abandon a communion of life and table with the pagan Christians. Peter's attitude is an assault on the truth of the gospel. It threatens the principles of the universality of salvation and the exclusive salvific value of the cross.

Despite its brevity, *Psalm 117* has both of the primary characteristics of a hymn: the invitation to universal praise, and the motive for this praise.

Luke 11:1-4: (See p. 83.)

■

"Lord, teach us to pray . . ."! A humble request in the spirit of the human heart suddenly steeped in the truth of its being. The prayer of the poor who know themselves to be sinners. The prayer of those who cannot speak, and the prayer of those whom doubt will not leave in peace. The prayer of folk too hurried, and a prayer murmured in the silence of the night. The prayer of happy people, and the lament of those who suffer. "Lord, teach us to pray . . ."!

"Our Father. . . ." Lord, teach us to be your children. Behold the secret of the women and men of God. Not many well-turned phrases, but . . . being daughters and sons. While the Our Father is certainly the school of prayer, it is even more a school of life. "Hallowed be your name . . ."! —the Our Father invites us to emerge from ourselves. Saturated with our desires, overwhelmed with our concerns, devastated by our questions, here we are, called to be interested in God. "Your kingdom come"! Love is our vocation, and the call draws us forward.

Can we really say, "Our Father"? Can we manifest this bond, this intimacy, this familiarity? "We dare to say . . ."! Yes, praying the Our Father is risky. To pray in this way is to take the risk of God. It means risking the presence of fire, risking universal love. What can we say? We can only babble—we can only take the risk of saying someone else's words, as a child will repeat what her big brother has said, without too much understanding of what it means. Jesus prayed in this way. "Abba!" Daddy. Not "Father," in an adult's confident way, but in the hesitant syllables of a tot: "Daddy!" The words of the Our Father are words no one can say except in the Spirit. And it is the Spirit who prays, within us, "Our Father. . . ."

■

God our Father,
*   Jesus shows us the path of prayer.*
Then receive us as your children.

Teach us to do your will.
May our prayer be the school
*   of the life that comes from you.*

■

God most high,
*   yet so near to us,*
you invite us to pray to you in all confidence,
*   in the name of your Son*
*   and in the liberty of your Spirit.*
Grant us the courage
*   to ask in order to receive,*
*   to search in order to find.*
Transform all our desires into one only:
*   Thy kingdom come!*
*   Yes, now and forever.*

■

God our Father,
*   you have given us the bread we require.*
May this communion in the body of Christ

instill in us his life's breath—
the Holy Spirit, who alone can send up from within our hearts
the prayer that you will hear.

THURSDAY OF THE 27TH WEEK

A DOOR CANNOT BE BOTH OPEN AND CLOSED . . .

Galatians 3:1–5: Having shown that his gospel has received the approval of
the other apostles, Paul will insist that it is in conformity with the promises of
the Old Covenant, as well. But first he shows the Galatians their stupidity.
Their own personal contact with the Christian experience has failed to open
their eyes. A few Judaizing speeches and their minds are troubled. What is the
gospel that Paul has preached to them—the cross of Christ or the Jewish law?
By what have the Galatians been saved? Certainly not by the Law, of which
they have never heard. When all is said and done, the attitude of the Galatians
is eminently illogical: first they received the Spirit, and now they would like to
regulate their lives according to Jewish practice. Paul is obliged to send them
a stern warning: to act in this way is to deny their baptismal profession of faith.

The Canticle of the *Benedictus* reasserts the principle that salvation is found
in Jesus Christ, heir of David according to the flesh. By him we are released
from the constraints of the Law, to live by the Spirit.

Luke 11:5–13: (See p. 86.)

■

The door is closed—closed by catastrophe. There seems to be no escape
—through the closed door of death, through which none return, or the
closed door of unheard prayers, which leave the believer in trial and doubt.

The door had been closed since Friday evening. The sealed tomb
imprisoned the body of God's well-beloved Son. So many hopes, so many
foolish expectations pounded upon that cold, hard rock of a door. For
three days the faithful had watched, in helplessness, doubt, and yes,
despair. They were weak, but stubborn—stubborn as a flickering candle
flame that refuses to die. "I tell you, even though he does not get up and
take care of the man because of friendship, he will find himself doing so

---

because of his persistence. . . ." God has heard the heavy cry of so much hope. And Easter morning the rock explodes.

That morning, the women and the other disciples understood that death would never have the last word. The mournful pilgrimage is at an end, and they have found victory in love. The door opens, and there stands the risen Christ. In him there is an escape from suffering. The door is flung wide, and behold, life: hope is possible. The door opens, and behold, the prayer of the Son: from this moment forward, our requests will find, in him, the right words to say—the words of the Spirit.

This is why the thing for us to do is to keep asking, never stop asking. Why? Not in order to discharge a duty, nor in the naive intent of making a miracle happen. No, the words of our intercession are deeds of life. Our words are the engagement of love. What we ask is only to be allowed to follow the path of Jesus, only to live in the breath of the Spirit. Together with all believers of all times, we stand erect before the door. With tenacity we intercede in behalf of the world's soul, lest it be lost. With Christ, we pray in the words of his love that bring us to say, "Father."

■

Father of all goodness,
*   we stand before you, our heads erect,*
*   in stubborn invocation.*
Hear our prayer,
*   which Jesus himself has taught us:*
May your Kingdom come
*   today, and forever.*

■

God our Father,
*   your word is at work in the hearts of those who receive it.*
In the freedom of your Spirit,
*   give us to desire what you wish,*
*   and to will what you ask,*
that our prayer may be to do your will,
*   and your hope may be our joy forever.*

■

God, source of all good things,
*   we bless you for your gift:*

the bread that is our life,
and the wine that gives us gladness.
May the Holy Spirit give us the gift
of asking for the very boon you already prepare
for all ages to come.

OUR FATHER ABRAHAM

Galatians 3:7–14: The Galatians vaunt their practice of the Law. Very well, then, let them hear the lessons of the Law. Salvation history, Paul explains, is couched in two contradictory regimes: that of the Law, and that of grace. The former shuts us up in a curse, for the Law calls for the observance of all the commandments which, experience attests, is totally impossible. The Law, then, is shown to be incapable of saving us.

The other regime is that of grace. We are saved not by virtue of our merits, which are always insufficient, but by the divine favor. This is the regime of the promise—which, for that matter, is antecedent to that of the Law, since Yahweh made his commitment to Abraham before he was circumcised.

Christ has set us free from the curse weighing upon us—becoming himself the object of a curse. Paul uses very strong terms here, to set in relief the consequences of the crucifixion. On the one hand, Deuteronomy 21:23 declared that anyone hanged on a tree was cursed by God. And so the torture to which Jesus has been subjected could only make him hateful in the eyes of the Jews, including his dismayed disciples. On the other hand, the expression, "delivered us back," meaning "ransomed" ("redeemed" in the literal sense of the word), suggests the price payed by Jesus to set us free from the slavery of sin. Just as the Jewish people had been delivered from their servitude in Egypt to enter the service of Yahweh, so we have been delivered from sin to be at the service of good.

Psalm 111 recalls the Lord's tenderness and faithfulness toward humanity.

Luke 11:15–26: (See p. 90.)

■

With all of the violence of a disappointed, anguished love, Paul addresses the Galatians tossed by the storm that has broken over their

---

heads. They have tasted the matchless liberty of the gospel, and then fallen back into observances and rites. They have had the testimony of the humiliation of Christ and his limitless love, they have believed in the Word who proclaims to them this stupefying novelty. Then how can they go back to the scrupulous, pseudo-meritorious observance of the Law? "Who has cast a spell over you . . . ?" asked the apostle in yesterday's reading. "How could you be so stupid?"

Can the Galatians have forgotten the logic of the covenant and the pedagogy of God, manifested to Israel over all these centuries? Did Abraham become the father of believers because he observed the law? "Abraham believed God, and it was accredited to him as justice" (Rom 4:3). It was his faith and fidelity, against all the evidence, that won Abraham his blessing. The "righteous" in God's eyes are those who trust him, those who believe the word of grace, and acknowledge it, discover it in thanksgiving. Abraham would be blessed in a multitude of daughters and sons as extensive as the stars of the heavens, because he accepted as a fact, against all reason and experience, that the word that creates the world and its history also set his own whole existence in motion. As vehicle of the promise, Abraham became the witness of this great blessing—the witness of this unfailing love, this magnificent "Yes" to which the only answer can be "Amen."

"If you belong to Christ you are the descendants of Abraham" (Gal 3:29), and justified by faith. Therefore you are delivered from the fear engendered by law, and from your guilt, generated by religion. But if you ascribe to the signs Jesus gives of his mercy a meaning contrary to the love they reveal, if you claim that they are the work of Beelzebul, then you are rejecting the light. And suddenly your justification serves for nothing, for you are surrendering to the curse of the forces that seek your perdition. Your state is worse than before: your new imprisonment is perpetual. Stupid Galatians, come to your senses! The curse that hangs over you? Christ has redeemed you from it, ransomed you, by making himself wicked in the eyes of the Law! Are you believers? Then Christ is the Righteous one of God, the cause of your blessing. Really, it is high time you came to your senses!

■

God of Abraham and God of Jesus Christ,
God of the promise and God of grace,
    we beseech you:
Deliver us from whatever holds us still in our shackles,
    that we may surrender to your mercy.
Confirm us in faith,

286

that we may know the blessing of your love
for all eternity.

■

God, Father of our forebears in faith,
blessed be your name!
Your grace makes us righteous
and your mercy is our succor.
Do not allow us to return to our false certitudes,
to abandon ourselves once more
to our deceptive assurances.
May our merits not blind us;
rather let your tenderness be our only strength,
and the pledge of our hope.

SATURDAY OF THE 27TH WEEK

ADOPTION

Galatians 3:22–29: The monitor (*paidagōgós*, "pedagogue") was the slave entrusted with the upbringing and education of a son of an upper-class family. This is precisely what the Law was for the Jews under the Old Covenant. The existence of a law permits us to take a position with regard to that law. Now we can know whether we have applied it correctly or, on the contrary have transgressed it, "broken" it. But once the Jews had become conscious of their sin, and thus of their guilt, the Law could do no more for them. After all, of itself it was not a source of salvation. Thus it shut human beings up in their malediction. Therefore its regime could only be transitory.

Psalm 105: You, the race of Abraham, you, believers saved by grace—learn to return thanks!

Luke 11:27–28: (See p. 92.)

■

There are children who think that they may do whatever they may wish because, as they say, "This is my house." They think that the simple fact that they have been born into the family permits them to act as the ones in charge. After all, is what their parents have not theirs as well? Will they not be "left" whatever their parents own, as their inheritance?

287

Everything is owed them. There is nothing to wait for. Their prideful claim is their smug assurance. "Blest is the womb that bore you . . ."! You have certain rights, and "that's all there is to it."

"Rather," he replied "blest are they who hear the word of God and keep it." Birth is never the work of the flesh. Birth is a gift to be accepted, to be thankful for, to be confirmed. Is genuine birth not an adoption? After all, a parent says, "You are my child," and the child responds, "Mother!" Membership in a family is woven of bonds of mutual adoption.

"Each one of you is a son of God because of your faith in Christ Jesus"! Faith is adoption. In Jesus, God has acknowledged us as his daughters and sons. In Jesus, we recognize the image of the invisible God, and then we see it in ourselves. And we can use the words of God's Son and say, "Our Father."

Children may think the house is theirs, but it actually is not. After all, they have not really lived in it! They have reduced it to a legacy, a museum. The family dwelling is a house that has been adapted, remodeled in accordance with today's needs. It is a house alive. "Rather," he replied, "blest are they who hear the word of God and keep it." As C. Péguy says: "The words Jesus has given us are not canned preserves to be stashed on a shelf. The words Jesus has given us are alive. They have to be fed." Do you finally understand? "If you belong to Christ you are the descendants of Abraham. . . ." Abraham? Abraham began his journey on the strength of his faith in a word!

MONDAY OF THE 28TH WEEK

FREEDOM

Galatians 4:22–24, 26–27, 31–5:1: Hagar represents the life of the Law, a life of incredulity and activism. When Sarah's sterility seemed to present an obstacle to the realization of the divine promise, Abraham had assumed that he would have to cope with the problem alone. But the child conceived in unbelief could never become heir to the promise. Abraham and Hagar had produced an offspring for servitude (Gen 16; 21:8–21). By contrast, Isaac was the child of gratuity. He alone was free, and he received the divine promise as his inheritance.

In Paul's eyes pagans and Jews had been slaves, the former of their dissolute morals, the latter of the Law (cf. Rom 1–3). But Christ, the child of the promise, had freely delivered them. They must not return to a new slavery, then—like the Galatians, if the latter were to adopt the practices of the Law. They are born not of Hagar, but of Sarah!

Psalm 113 invites us to praise the God of the promise and its faithful fulfillment.

Luke 11:29–32: (See p. 95.)

■

No sign will be given but Jesus! They demand proofs and demonstrations. But only the living word of a human being like his brothers and sisters, and the power of the Spirit who calls us to go beyond the evidence, will be accorded them. Faith is lived in a regime of freedom. Demonstration locks up and imprisons the mind. Evidence reduces us to servitude. With evidence, there is no discussion. But faith, like love, lives by encounter and engagement, by sharing and communion. In other words, faith is a victory over indifference. We take ourselves and our false certitudes in hand. No sign will be given us but a person we will meet. Faith is tied to the hazards of an encounter!

"Each one of you is a son of God because of your faith in Christ Jesus," Saint Paul declared in yesterday's reading. To be daughters and sons, contrary to so many contemporary slogans, is to be free. Law and religion lock you up in the pillory of their evidence, their dogmas and their rules. But love—love awakens you to freedom. The new relation with God inaugurated by Jesus culminates in the prayer of children who adopt their parent: "Abba." This "Abba" given by Jesus to his disciples as the first word of their prayer and their faith brings Christians directly into the dialogue that is the secret of the obedience of the children of God. We can understand Luther's triumphant assertion: "The Christian is a free lord of all things, and subject to no one!" "We are not children of a slave girl. . . ." We can likewise understand the anguish, and also the fury, that seizes Paul when he observes that those he has awakened to this freedom wish to fall back under the yoke of pseudo-disciplines and practices. Could they so quickly forget that they are members of a community that, as Calvin put it, is "a mother whose Father is God," and who has won the beautiful title of the "free woman"?

"It was for liberty that Christ freed us." The gospel, founded on the sole sign of Jesus, outstrips all the expectations of the religious mind. No wonder then, if, even among those who accept him in faith, the temptation creeps back to add "another gospel" (Gal 1:6) alongside the first, a gospel of human dimensions. Filter the light, outfit a Christianity that will finally be reasonable, practicable, politically viable. Seek your personal assurances behind the protective shield of practices, discharge your duties, rely on definitions and concepts! No, the church must be the place of incarnation of the one gospel, the gospel of freedom. Doubtless it will be embodied in a tradition, a doctrine, a liturgy, an institutional form. To guarantee the divine tradition, the church installs human traditions. To protect the divine teaching, the church imposes its formulas. To preserve order in the community, it insists on its authority. But all of these necessary measures are accompanied by the constant danger of "another gospel." Human traditions may cover over the divine tradition, the institution may chain the Spirit, honor may supplant service. Happy the church that, in the living reality of its faith, organization and mission, will succeed in showing the world that it is the servant of one gospel, a gospel textured of grace and invitation, freedom and calling. That church will be called the mother of the living, the new Eve. Sprung from the side of the new Adam, it will have given birth to the freedom that is life's loveliest gift.

■

To you, God our Savior and our Father,
to you we offer our thanksgiving,
through Jesus Christ.
Through him you lead us out of the house of slavery,
to receive us in your own dwelling.

Your love for us has been madness.
For your Son has experienced in his body
the death of a slave
that we may live as your daughters and sons.

And we believe in that Easter sign.
For you have given us a new birth of freedom—
the freedom of your own children—
to offer, with your Christ,
the praise of a redeemed creation.

TUESDAY OF THE 28TH WEEK

FROM SERVITUDE TO SERVICE

Galatians 5:1-6: Paul will soon be concluding his letter. But before he does, he is determined to point out all of the consequences of the Galatians' behavior. He knows that it has been mainly utilitarian. They wish to have circumcision as a supplementary means of salvation!

But then there are two things they should know. First, if they receive circumcision, they must adopt the Mosaic law in its entirety. (Have the Judaizers glossed over this point?) Next, placing their trust in the Law will cut

---

them off from Christ. For if Christ is the sole source of salvation, to expect this salvation elsewhere will be equivalent to voiding Jesus' resurrection of its salvific value. Christians are those who place their hope in Christ and receive the Spirit. These persons may confidently look forward to the benefits of God's Reign. Their faith is a faith that acts, a faith expressed by love, which is the true life of the Spirit.

Paradoxically, the responsorial psalm chosen for today, *Psalm 119,* is a hymn to the law. Thus we are reminded not only of Paul's warning, but of the fact that all women and men of good will, at the term of their quest, will find God.

Luke 11:37–41: (See p. 97.)

"Do not take on yourselves the yoke of slavery a second time!" What is the use of the freedom granted by Christ and unmerited by the believer? From slavery to freedom, from servitude to service: behold the Christian exodus. In the imitation of Christ, it is the commandment of love that is the shape, the breath, the incarnation of a rediscovered freedom. It is love that makes the heart pure—not the practices of a slavery of old! Our covetousness, our conquering, seductive ambition—these have been crucified with Christ. A new law appears. But this law is no longer a law of constraint and bad conscience. This law is the regime, the very rhythm, of freedom.

Freedom is a passage, a passover, a conquest. It is a daily conquest: for it is in time, in the pain of beginning again, everlastingly, day after day, that we assert our freedom. Ours is a difficult freedom, for the Christian remains a being tempted to servitude. Like the Hebrews after the crossing of the sea, we long for the onions of Egypt, and have little taste for this trek through the desert, this road to liberation. And so we are ceaselessly obliged to tame a "fleshly" reason and will, which lust against their nascent liberty. Our conquest is the welcome of Another at the very heart of the thrust of our freedom, and this quality waxes with the passage of time. On condition that we allow the Holy Spirit to act within us, to lead us, we pass to the new world, to resurrection and rebirth. It is the paradox of Christian freedom that its full possession coincides with total surrender. Only in total surrender is full communion realized. It is in the hour that Jesus cries, "Father . . . not my will but yours be done," that he enters into the total liberty of his being. The hour of the Son and his glorification is the hour of his passion and stripping.

"Do not take on yourselves the yoke of slavery a second time." Do not return to Egypt. March bravely forward, to the desert, plunge into your stripping and spoliation, surrender to the word that lifts you up.

Freedom is the other side of the coin of love. Nothing counts any longer but "faith, which expresses itself through love."

■

"Do not take on yourselves the yoke of slavery a second time" . . .
　　Deliver us from our false certitudes!
　　Lord, have mercy.

"Do not take on yourselves the yoke of slavery a second time" . . .
　　Deliver us from our parching moralism!
　　Show us your grace, and have mercy.

"Do not take on yourselves the yoke of slavery a second time" . . .
　　Deliver us from our illusory holiness!
　　Let your mercy be our salvation.
　　Lord, have mercy.

■

God of liberation and salvation,
by the power of your Spirit
　　grant us passage to the new world.

And if we return once more to our chains,
grant us the wisdom to know that the word of your Son
　　will lead us to eternal communion.

■

You have chosen us, God our Father,
　　to become your children
　　and co-heirs with your Christ.
Grant us your Spirit in superabundance,
that your church,
　　utterly taken with the love of your Well-Beloved,
　　may tremble with all its being
　　to know the grace of its deliverance.

SPIRITUALIZATION

Galatians 5:18-25: If Christ has delivered us from the burden of the Law, are we not free to do what the Law forbids? The question will be a frequent one. Paul's answer is that liberty and libertinism are not the same thing. In fact, a misunderstanding of the notion of freedom can lead to another slavery—that of the flesh.

In Paul, the word "flesh" denotes frail human nature, especially the selfish desires that wage war against our genuine calling. The real question of freedom is why—to what end—we are free. To this question there is only one answer: we are free in order to love more. The sum and substance of the Law is fulfilled in this single observance: "You shall love your neighbor as yourself" (Gal 5:14; Lev 19:18). But only those who live by the Spirit of Jesus can accomplish this. "You should live in accord with the spirit and you will not yield to the cravings of the flesh" (Gal 5:16). The flesh is opposed to genuine love, as we see from the list of its works, which appears in other letters as well. The flesh is human love run amuck, the lusts that rule the pagan world. Perversions of worship, unloving activity and the excesses of table convey the degradation of the human person.

By contrast, the fruit of the Spirit is one: love, viewed successively in its signs (joy and peace), its manifestations (patience, kindness, benevolence) and its conditions (faith and humility, which make it possible to receive grace and gain self-control).

Psalm 1 is a lyrical contrast of the condition of the righteous one, who lives according to the Spirit, with that of the wicked slave of the flesh.

Luke 11:42-46: (See p. 99.)

■

"If you are guided by the spirit, you are not under the law." Behold the mystery of our freedom in faith, which consists in a deliverance—in a grace, and in a liberated life, guided by the Spirit.

Freedom is a mystery of deliverance, of liberation. To be free in the Spirit is to discover ourselves to be loved by God—and loved with an insane love, so that we can feel altogether free to disarm, to dispossess ourselves. We are to be the yeast of communion and transfiguration, the artisans of liberation, in the history of humanity. For this, we must ever be the witnesses of Mystery, of the Living one, of this God who bestows meaning and a correct perspective on all things. We must be able to hear the mysterious sigh of a creation, and the loud cry of its birthgiving; and we must bear our witness even now, in order to prepare the universe and its history for participation in the glorious freedom of those whom God has ransomed from their slavery through the Passover of eternity.

Freedom is the mystery of a life delivered. Saint Paul opened Romans 8 with a cry of triumph: "There is no condemnation now for those who are in Christ Jesus. The law of the spirit, the spirit of life in Christ Jesus, has freed you from the law of sin and death" (Rom 8:1-2). The Spirit is already at work in our world, and the new Law, the Law of Easter, is identified with the very person of that Spirit, who consists of his very Activity in us. Now the law we are under is no longer a code—not even a code laid down by the Holy Spirit—but a law accomplished within us by that Spirit. The law that rules us is no longer a simple norm of activity, an external yardstick but—and obviously no legislation as such can be this—an interior principle of action, an interior dynamism.

Mystery of liberation, vocation of a life delivered! "I will place my law within them, and write it upon their hearts" (Jer 31:33). Saint Thomas was right: "The Holy Spirit himself is the New Covenant, in that he works in us love, which is the fullness of the law." No longer do we belong to the world of the flesh. The Spirit has given us new birth.

■

You consecrate us, Lord, by your Spirit,
    who accomplishes in us the work of Easter.
Deliver us
    from all that is not ourselves,
    from all that is not yourself,
that we may one day be surprised to see
    that the fruit born in freedom,
    with unstinting effort,
    abides forever.

■

Lord, our Father,
    our peace and our faithfulness
    are gifts of your Spirit.
Here at the table of your mercy,
    we have tasted these gifts.
Grant that we may live them day by day.

A Long Voyage

From the very day of his calling, Paul has burned with the community dimension of Christ. In his interior life and missionary activity alike, he has experienced Christ's universality. Paul has matured. The answer he must give to the questions asked by the people of Asia Minor lead him to contemplate the place of the church in God's project for all history and all time.

Where are we headed? All about us, prophets would have us hope this or fear that. Students of the future abound, all bringing forward their facts and figures as they sketch the profile of the new society. Activists devote their lives, at times even giving up those lives, to the materialization of the old dreams of justice and fellowship. All about us we perceive a slow childbirth, charged with pain and crisis.

In this patient maturation, the church is the vessel of an incredible promise. "God chose us in him before the world began . . . to be his adopted sons. . . ." We are made for something else than for the sarcophagi of history, for bootless wanderings from one crippled civilization to another. To the bar of history's tribunal the church carries its testimony, for it has been charged with the mission of pointing to the signs of the Reign of God and investing them with meaning.

We are made for something else. . . . Perhaps this is not really the right way to put it. Salvation history is not really "something else." It is simply human history—but human history seen in a light from elsewhere. The coming of the new age depends on the patient human quest for an . . . "otherwise." The history of salvation and redemption are identical with, simply, history. "Through love, God takes the initiative of proposing to man a participation in his own life. In the very act of creation, God enters the interplay of the laws of love, which would have the 'other' condition my love. In order to realize this communion with man, God becomes man. That is to say: this life in common is organized according to the structures of man, structures that are physical and mental, individual and collective, historical and prospective."[1] Despite the contradictions of its history, the blindness, the sad inadequacies that burden its witness, the church remains a people redeemed, and the sign of a world that has received salvation. The heavenly Jerusalem is not a dream of the future, a myth forever. The heavenly Jerusalem is founded today, and also in throughout history. And the chronicles of all believers, from Abraham to present-day peoples, is the story of a long voyage in the direction of the haven toward which we have set sail. Indeed, the first of the line, the Head of the Body, the Shepherd, has already achieved his Passover, and in him history has already succeeded. Let humankind rejoice.

■

O God,
Savior of the world and Ruler of history,
    you take up our cause with all your heart.
Blessed be your name!

Be conqueror of the powers
    that threaten our life.
Give us hope,
    for love of the One who has vanquished death,
    your Son Jesus Christ.
May he guide us toward the new world.

■

Be blessed, Father of Jesus and our Father!
You destine us to receive the heritage of your Well-Beloved.
    You have called us,
    your word has created us
    and you gather us in the Body of your Son.

May your Spirit come to our aid,
that, together, we may be a new beginning
    of hope and peace,
and the witnesses
    that the endless ages are upon us.

■

Be blessed, Father most holy,
eternal God of all goodness and bounty!

In Jesus Christ, your Well-Beloved,
you reveal the mystery
    of your presence and our glory.

Be blessed for the one thing needed
    to fill our poor hearts to overflowing with gladness.
Be praised too

*for the hope that burns within us
at the sound of your Word!*

*Therefore in anticipation of everlasting joy,
we sing our thanks to you
for your faithfulness to your promise,
and for the grace of our one history,
yours and ours.*

THURSDAY OF THE 28TH WEEK

AT THE TRIBUNAL OF HISTORY

Ephesians 1:1–10: To celebrate the accomplishment of God's salvation, the Letter to the Ephesians opens with a lengthy blessing in the style of Jewish tradition. In fact, some authors claim that its writer maintains this style throughout the first three chapters. The church is at the center of this benediction, for it is the only reality in which the whole universe can contemplate the magnificent mystery of the will of God—his salvific designs upon his creation.

This torrent of divine grace, which finds its goal in the church, sweeps along in the patterns of a project whose outcome has been fixed from the outset. What God has projected is to fill all humanity with his spiritual benediction— that is, to associate us all with the triumph of Christ over the powers of death. Election and predestination are for one purpose only: our adoption, and the reunification of all things under one head, Christ.

The Letter to the Ephesians raises many questions. Its Pauline authenticity is contested. The Ephesians do not seem actually to have been its addressees. Many scholars think the letter is a composition of the generation that came after the apostles, the product of a community so deeply marked by Paul that it has been universally attributed to him. Thus in this respect it would be like the "pastoral" letters.

New creation? Then sing a new song! *Psalm 98* prolongs the praise of a God who has "revealed his justice in the sight of the nations."

Luke 11:47–54: (See p. 101.)

■

Crises, modifications, uncertainties, hesitations. . . . The image is far too much an image of our everyday lives to surprise us any longer. Our world is not doing well! The physicians all have their heads together, and their prescriptions are endless. Meanwhile evil reigns, and the great fears of the heralds of doom not only cram the shelves of our bookstores, but touch the inmost fibers of our hearts. What is the future of our world?

Is it in the free life, of which we say with such admiration, "Now, that's living"? We seek it unflaggingly, and unflaggingly it eludes us, whether in the oppressive personal or social conditions of our life, or in the bottomless gully of a desire that yawns ever wider until one day we must admit the difficulty—the impossibility?—of filling it!

How can we justify this hope? We dream of a life no longer merely endured but created, no longer imposed but invented, no longer coveted but shared, no longer feared but loved. And we continue to experience a life that is limited and conditioned. Our hands, called to open, stay closed. Our hearts remain frozen with fear. No, our road leads not to the penetrating sweep of the light of day, but to choking, stifling night.

The danger of this moment is that we may see the mirage of hope—a false hope—rise up before our eyes. We may seem to discern, beyond time, the wonderful thing we are denied today. In history, this fundamental rhythm is election to grace: God has predestined us to be his sons and daughters. Today in the uncertainties of our lives we glimpse as through a glass, darkly, what, in tomorrow's gape-mouthed astonishment of the face-to-face vision of God, will appear in all its explosive, brilliant light. The sparks of that first inspiration with which the whole human adventure is shot through, the glimmers of that divine election, have flashed here and there down all the centuries: God prefers what is small, what is nothing. God prefers the love that is still secret. This is the divine melody of history, and it will find voice the day Mary sings: "He has deposed the mighty from their thrones and raised the lowly to high places. The hungry he has given every good thing, while the rich he has sent empty away" (Lk 1:52–53). God has predestined us from all eternity to become his daughters and sons, engendered and adopted. From this first inspiration has welled a series of mysterious reversals, a series of paradoxical substitutions of younger sons for elder, little persons for great; sterile women for fertile. We see Jacob preferred to Esau, Joseph excelling his brothers, sterile Sarah called to be the mother of the child of promise. We have Mary, the servant flooded with grace. Finally, we have the church—poor, and without any wealth but a word to proclaim, and yet called to become the mother of humanity to come.

God's plan was "to bring all things in the heavens and on earth into one under Christ's headship." The church has nothing else to say at the bar of history!

■

God, Ruler of time and history,
as we await the hour of manifestation of your project
in an eternal covenant,
raise up among us
witnesses of the age to come.

■

In this Eucharist, God our Father,
you renew your covenant
and confirm our hope.
As you have chosen us
to manifest your benevolence,
grant that we may be the witnesses of so great a mystery.
Blessed be your name, now and forever!

FRIDAY OF THE 28TH WEEK

CHILDREN OF LIGHT

Ephesians 1:11-14: Unfortunately we should never be able to guess from the lectionary that these verses are still part of the solemn benediction with which our letter opened. This is the case, however. And yet their interpretation is a delicate matter. We may discern two stages in the salvation process. First there are those whom God has "predestined to praise his glory by being the first to hope in Christ"—that is, historical Israel. Then there are the addressees of the letter—"you too were chosen. . . ."—and through them, the converted pagans. Finally, of the latter it is said that, after having heard the word of God and become believers, they received the mark of the Spirit, with this Spirit constituting a kind of first installment on the heritage of the end of days.

But our translation does not make this distinction explicit, and allows us, alternatively, to understand a bond between the Jews and the pagans from the very outset. It is not a matter of the chosen people as God's legacy, but of a people who await their legacy in the celestial heritage (the new Land of Promise), of which the Spirit constitutes the first installment. In either case, the church is seen from two sides as the culmination of the divine work.

299

Hymnic in its structure, *Psalm 33* invites us to praise God for the constancy with which he has brought his work of salvation to term. The response refers to the holy community of Israel.

Luke 12:1–7: (See p. 103.)

∎

"There is nothing concealed that will not be revealed"! The church's calling is revelation. "We were predestined to . . . [be] the first to hope in Christ." Surely a doubt arises here. With so much non-sense, so much absurdity, so many miscarriages of the efforts we bend to give a meaning to our personal and collective history—how can we continue to believe in the promise that will come to light, the hidden face of all things? And yet the fact is that the church has been entrusted with the mission of pointing out the signs of the Reign of God and making them meaningful. "We were predestined. . . ."

"You heard . . . the word of truth. . . ." What joy—is the church not a kind of prototype on earth of the city to come? The first Christians rightly regarded themselves as entrusted with an immense blessing for the whole of humanity. What joy—"The Holy Spirit who had been promised . . . is the pledge of our inheritance, the first payment against the full redemption of a people God has made his own. . . ." Fire needs no other proof of its presence and vitality than the heat it radiates. Can those to whom grace has been shown be anything but grace and benevolence for others? Can those who have received forgiveness have any rule of conduct but mercy? Can those whom truth has set free have any ambition but to extend liberation in an unbroken chain? "There is nothing hidden that will not be made known." God has nowhere to manifest the mystery of his covenant but in the people of believers he has called to his light. The church—what joy!

But we should not be telling the whole truth if we refused to recall that the church is an occasion of tears as well. The church has not always been on its guard against the yeast of the Pharisees. Instead of being apprentices of a new breed of humanity, believers sometimes present a veritable showcase, a downright caricature, of the defects of a sordid humanity. What jealousy and strife, what vanity and foolishness, what arrogance and pretentiousness, what despair and neglect of duty! Yes, the church is still "worldly." The church is still immersed in a world whose salt, whose light and yeast, nevertheless, it remains by calling.

A point for God, a point for the "world". . . . What is the score in this period? Is the church pretty much a tie between God and the world? No, God's promise abides: "Fear nothing, then. You are worth more than a flock of sparrows"! Christ has been raised, and he will raise the dough of a new humanity. The yeast of the Pharisees is all worn out. For "in the decree of God . . . we were predestined to . . . [be] the first to hope in Christ."

■

We beseech you, most good Father,
    keep us faithful to the word of your Son.
Send us your Spirit:
    may he be the living memory within us
    of everything Jesus has told us,
for he has been your word from the beginning,
    and your word he remains
    forever and ever.

■

Lord our God,
    by the Body of your Son,
    delivered for us,
you have made us the people sanctified by your love.
We pray to you for the church you have chosen:
    may your Spirit animate us who have received your word.

Teach us to recognize in the church of your love
    the eternal company of your son,
    the vanguard of the new age.

SATURDAY OF THE 28TH WEEK

SUCCESS
Ephesians 1:15–23: "I have never stopped thanking God for you and recommending you in my prayers." This prayer is not just an expression of the writer's admiration for his addressees. More than anything else it is the result of his contemplation of the church, this church he proclaims "the fullness of him who fills the universe in all its parts." The church, then, is God's most perfect work, his reflection in creation. We are close to Johannine ideas here,

where the Father is in the Son, the Son in the disciples, and the disciples in the world.

The divine work is at the heart of the sacred writer's prayer. Again and again he beseeches the Father to enlighten Christians that they may perceive the depths of what God has accomplished. But nowhere else does the mighty work of God burst forth as magnificently as in the resurrection and exaltation of Christ, now constituted the pinnacle of the universe and the head of the church. Paul's prayer becomes christology: the principalities, powers and so on, of which he speaks, denoted, in the pre-Christian world, intermediate entities (angels or stars) regarded as God's vicarious instruments in the governance of the world.

Psalm 8 should be interpreted within the liturgy as addressing the person of Christ, the pinnacle of the universe, from whom the church cannot be dissociated.

Luke 12:8–12: (See p. 105.)

■

We have reduced Christianity to an individual affair, a personal salvation enterprise. We have reduced Christianity to a matter of sentiment, devotions and good conscience. Obviously our faith concerns each of us, and we have known since the days of the prophets that God touches the heart of each of us. It is there, if anywhere, that his covenant is written in letters of blood. Our salvation would be in vain if it did not involve our deepest being.

But Christianity would likewise be in vain if it did not mean something for the history of all human beings, for humanity *in globo*. The risen Jesus is established as Lord—placed above all things. His Easter victory involves all of the history of all time. History has succeeded. In Jesus it has come to full bloom. History is not an everlasting recommencement. We are not locked into some infernal cycle, where tomorrow is fated to be like today. Jesus, established as Lord of all things, bursts the circle of our imprisonment. Christian history is a dynamism, a movement that opens out on an Elsewhere, an Otherwise, a Future. A breach has been opened in the revolution of the centuries, through which we contemplate what our earth is promised to. Jesus the Lord is the Shepherd who leads his people to the Dwelling Place.

In the victory of its Head, the church, which is now the Body of Christ, already beholds the successful conclusion of its journey. The history of this people, a history of risk and hazard, of the comings and goings of a humanity in search of itself, is fulfilled, even now, in the victory of its

Shepherd. It already has the assurance that it will arrive safely in port. The new age is born where, knowingly or unknowingly, men and women become gospel—that is, where they take up the defense of the human being. The church is the "fullness of him, who fills the universe. . . ." We are guaranteed that history will end well, regardless of our fears and apprehensions. With the Resurrection, a new world is already born. We are the witnesses and guarantors to the world that this is the truth.

■

God our Father,
in the name of all who live on earth,
        united to Jesus Christ, our Lord,
we commend to you our world—
the women and men who seek the meaning of their lives,
        and those who seek it not,
those who wish to cement the great body of humanity,
        and those who seek to shatter it.

In our prayer, we recall
all those who have lived before us,
        such treasure, and such ruination,
        so much love, and so much affliction.
We thank you
        for those who have made and fashioned us,
        those who have given us a habitable world,
        a humane world, a world of communion.

We pray to you in behalf of the women and men of today,
        for those we know,
        and those who are strangers to us,
for those we acknowledge as sisters and brothers,
        and those we would like to see wiped off the face of the earth.

We beseech you on behalf of the men and women
        who will come after us:
may we leave them a world
        that is more nearly what you desire.

■

God our Father,
        in the resurrection of your Son,
        you have guaranteed our hope against all failure.
Grant that your church, the living Body of the Lord,

*may be the sign of the promise
to be fulfilled in eternity.*

MONDAY OF THE 29TH WEEK

TO LIVE

Ephesians 2:1–10: This rather difficult passage calls for a closer examination, as it is of prime importance for an understanding of all of the dimensions of the divine act of salvation. First of all, we must not detach it from what precedes it—the imposing fresco of the blessing "to the praise of the divine glory." In other words, we must connect the following propositions: (1) God has set his strength, his power and his vigor to work in Christ "in raising Christ from the dead and seating him at his right hand in heaven" (Eph 1:20). (2) "With and in Christ Jesus he raised us up and gave us a place in the heavens . . ." (Eph 2:6). Making this connection allows us to see that everything God has done for his Son, he has done also for us, his adopted children. Having subjected all things to Christ, God "has made him, thus exalted, head of the church, which is his body," and which is thereby "the fullness of him who fills the universe in all its parts" (Eph 1:22–23).

We come upon other landmarks in the contrasts we encounter in the course of the pericope. For example, there is a contrast between: "You were *dead* because of your sins and offenses" and "he brought us to *life* with Christ." We have: "By *nature* [we] deserved God's wrath like the rest" and "By this *favor* [grace] you were saved." This twofold opposition gives full weight, on the one side, to our personal sins, which lead us to death, and on the other, to a salvation that comes not from ourselves but from the divine beneficence.

Verse 10 is simply the consequence of this assertion as applied to human activity. "We are truly his handiwork, created in Christ Jesus to lead the life of good deeds for which God has prepared us in advance." But the actual point of departure for this assertion is to be found several verses earlier: "We were dead in sin" (v. 5). While this proposition asserts that sin slew human nature in its very roots, verse 10 explains that human activity, too, has been purified by God's salvific act. Thus we have an authentic "predestination" by God. We have been created to pulsate with the divine. We can do this in virtue of the confluence of our activity with that of Christ, the perfect person. And the locus of this "synergy" is the church.

Psalm 100 invites us once more to offer our praise.

Luke 12:13–21: (See p. 108.)

I do not like paying visits of condolence, nor do I enjoy the odor of decaying carnations. But today I really must stop by the casket of the rich gentleman in the parable. What a big, fat person. And only yesterday he was dreaming of bigger grain bins! Poor ninny. But let me out of here. His heirs are already coming in the door, and they are just as fat and sleek as he was.

None of these persons are actually evil. They are just beef-witted. It is the idiocy and inanity of their lives that we must denounce. Money? You have to have money to live. But our hero, instead of investing his goods for the welfare of everyone, buried it! Yes, here is an addlepated individual indeed He shuts his harvest up in his silos, as if grain were not for bread, and for the seed that will sow the hymn to life once more. Let us face the fact: he did not deserve to live any longer. By the way he behaved, he blocked life.

And this was his great sin. Blocking life. Money is only a symbol here. This person had thought he could buy life, fence it in, and dominate it. He had thought he "had" life. But it got away! His is the conduct of the Pharisees, and it has led Jesus to recount his parable. Pharisees enclosed people in rules so strict that they could no longer breathe. You were dead, says the writer of Ephesians, when you lived at the level of the flesh, following every whim and fancy. This is the evil that would gulp down every last one of us, and Paul denounces it. He rails against the hellish circle of having, the intoxication of power, the conceit of learning. Regardless of the specific nature of the sin, the result is identical: life is chained. "You fool! This very night your life shall be required of you." Grain is for bread and seed, religion is for the human being—the gift of life is for living.

"Seek the things that are above!" What the gospel is proposing to us is . . . well, a fresh-air cure. When all is said and done, neither capital nor labor will ever be the last word on the human being. Neither of the two has any answer to death, and death is the greatest question pursuing us. "You were dead. . . . But God is rich in mercy . . . he brought us to life with Christ . . ."! You are risen, and the first thing to do is live. "This is not your own doing, it is God's gift. . . ." "You are anxious and upset . . ." Jesus objected, seeing Martha so busy. "One thing only is required" (Lk 10:41–42). And: "Seek first the Kingdom of God, and the rest will be added unto you." As for your money, regard it with humor. It is made for life. Spend it when appropriate, share it, make it fructify for the happiness of all. You were dead. Now you are alive. Then take a fresh-air cure, sisters and brothers. Breathe more deeply in the open air

of God, which is his Spirit—the Spirit of a new world, a world
inside-out, a world from above!

■

God of life,
do not allow us to live a life of the earthly commonplace.
We should only go to our ruin.
Bring us to life again in Christ,
that we may know happiness for all eternity!

TUESDAY OF THE 29TH WEEK

THE LIVERY

Ephesians 2:12–22: "My house shall be called a house of prayer for all
peoples" (Is 56:7). Thus begins Third Isaiah. To the question of the admission
of foreigners and eunuchs into the Israelite community, the prophet had
pointed out that "any member of the human race can come to faith in the true
God and enter into his covenant, if he observes the religious and moral
prescriptions."

For the author of Ephesians, the church is the place where Jews and pagans
are reconciled. He expresses his admiration of such a church, after having
insisted on God's free initiative in the order of salvation. He seems to have
been guided by the image of the barrier that prohibited pagans, under pain of
death, from entering the Jerusalem temple. Here he sees a symbol of the
isolationism in which the prescriptions of the Mosaic law (notably those
concerning what was clean and unclean) had held Israel. But Jesus, "in his
own flesh," a crucified flesh, has destroyed this barrier, this erstwhile source
of hatred. Henceforward pagan and Jew alike live a new life, and have access
to the presence of God.

Images of the church fairly tumble from our author's pen. He has already
identified the church with the body of Christ. The church is Christ's absolute
fulfillment. Now he speaks of it as the "new man," and a "dwelling place for
God"—both of these including all men and women living under the auspices of
the Spirit, without any distinction. Old Isaiah's prophecy has been fulfilled.
The law governing relationships among us is now the law of the Spirit.

Echoing the contemplation of Ephesians, *Psalm 85* portrays the reconciliation
of the universe, of which the unification of the Jews and pagans is a
prefiguration.

Luke 12:35–38: (See p. 111.)

306

■

In Jean Giraudoux's *Electra*, a woman asks: "What is it called when the day begins, all cold, and everything looks ruined, devastated—and yet the air is fresh and sweet?" Electra sends her to the beggar, for it is the poor who know these things. And the beggar replies, "Ah, this has a very beautiful name, a woman's name. It is called 'Aurora'—Dawn."

Remember your pagan days, when "you had no part in Christ"! In those days "you were without hope. . . ." These cold morns of an endless night, the invitation resounds like a cry of hope: "Let your belts be fastened around your waists. . . ." Don the livery of service! The air is fresh, your breathing less labored. Yes, you can believe in life again! And you can smile at the one who awakens from the night at your side. "It is [Christ] who is our peace. . . . He came and 'announced the good news of peace to you who were far off, and to those who were near'. . . ." Certain promises have been made to us. Let us help one another not to waste them! Let us help one another to cast off whatever burden impedes the circulation of love and light! We had been overcome with lassitude, and we wallowed in our resignation. But with this breeze that presages the dawn, why not try, together, to shake off those illusions, those paralyzing dreams? Why not try to render one another the service of the love of life? Together, let us choose a better life! For we have all been reconciled in one body, and have been transported to the dwelling place that God is building himself in this world.

"They call it 'Aurora'—Dawn"! The church would be an enchanted castle, the tale of a make-believe world, were it not for its invitation to peer into the night. And this invitation is its life. Countless times, a sudden wind from nowhere has blown out our lamp. Tirelessly we have relighted the light that thrusts back the night. We keep on the watch, we toil, we do the best that in us lies. It is in the dead of night, when night stands stock-still, that we must arouse the dawn! Vested in our livery, watchful for the slightest sign of hope, with our lamps ceaselessly relighted to serve notice on night that its death ruses avail it nothing, we stride forth to greet the dawn. Christ is risen from the dead, creating in himself a single New Human Being. The Master has struggled with the dark even as we, the dark that had held him prisoner in the night of the tomb. Now he puts on an apron—for us. He has set the table, and broken the bread, for us—to give us access to the presence of God. Sister, brother, don your livery once more. Be for those still afar the lamp that makes night recoil into its own shadows.

■

Lord, you are our never-failing light,
brought to patient birth by the night:
Lord, have mercy.

You come to inaugurate your peace,
to join us together in a single act of
thanksgiving:
Christ, have mercy.

You call us to watch through the night,
and to keep your hope alive in our hearts:
Lord, have mercy.

■

Blessed shall we be if you find us at our posts!
Lord, stir up our faith anew,
for the day of your coming.

What would become of us
were sleep to make off with us?
Grant that we may be faithful to your service,
for the salvation of our brothers and sisters,
and for your own joy
forever and ever.

WEDNESDAY OF THE 29TH WEEK

THE WARNING

Ephesians 3:2–12: The first two chapters of Ephesians have been devoted, respectively, to the salvific work of God (chap. 1), and to Christ's role in that salvation (chap. 2). Narrowing his purview once more, with chapter three the sacred writer now comes down to his own role, that of the "least of all believers." He has been a toiler for the unification of Jews and pagans, extending to the latter the opportunity to approach God directly.

The church continues to be at the center of the sacred writer's reflection. Since the church represents the culmination of what he calls God's "mystery"—that is, God's eternal salvific design—it follows that this mystery must be clearly manifest today. The church is God's revelation, then, or sacrament. "Now therefore, through the church, God's manifold wisdom is made known to the principalities and powers of heaven"—that is, to the powers responsible for the pre-Christian religious world, the powers of which we have heard in chapter 1, verse 21. As we know, one of the high themes of the wisdom literature (for example, of Prov 8) is the function of Wisdom to Yahweh's work of creation. And so the Letter to the Ephesians can look on the church as a personification of Wisdom, for the church is precisely the locus of universal reconciliation. By means of the sacraments, the church is the locus and font of a new world.

"You will draw water joyfully from the springs of salvation"! The refrain of today's responsorial psalm is a fine expression of the role of the church in God's work of salvation. Today's responsorial psalm, taken from *Is 12*, is often regarded as the conclusion of a collection of hymns to Emmanuel, God-with-us, whose manifestation today is precisely the task of the church.

Luke 12:39–48: (See p. 113.)

■

"The Son of man will come when you least expect him." Certain personages in the history of the church are famous for their most tendentious dramatization of the Lord's visitation, the subject of today's gospel. They presented Jesus as a kind of hobgoblin or bogey-man, swooping down on the scene to catch his followers in the act of wrongdoing. Fear, they insisted, was the beginning of wisdom. But this was in total contradiction of the tenor of today's gospel. The Second Coming was the object of earnest longing in the primitive church! We need only recall Christians' constant prayer, the cry of the Book of Revelation, "Come, Lord Jesus!" And now that Parousia is to be the object of fear and terror? Has the Master gone on a journey so that he can come back when least expected and find his stewards lolling about and neglecting their task? Does he hope to find something to judge and punish, then?

Love banishes fear. How can the gospel have been so poorly read? All are now "co-heirs . . . members of the same body and sharers of the promise"! The gospel is Good News. After all, it is grace! The gospel is an invitation to offer thanks for freedom received, for liberty granted as a gift. "In Christ and through faith in him we can speak freely to God, drawing near him in confidence." The gospel warning is our commission to watch the Master's house. Staying awake, staying ready, comes to be part of the disciple's responsibility because disciples have discovered, in astonishment and wonder, the grace of light. Can you abide the night when you see the first dawn glowing in the East? Can you neglect the house when you belong to the family?

"Be on guard . . ."! The One to come will surprise you in the midst of your work. He will come when there are so many things left to do! Or . . . he may come instead when you have fallen asleep like a child who has played her heart out and finally put down her toys the way warriors finally lay down their arms. But never fear, for then he will lift you up carefully in his arms and gently carry you up the stair, to rouse you in the land of New Day. For he is the Sentry who has watched through the night that he may be reborn in the Morning. He is the Easter Victor.

■

Lord God of tenderness,
 you have called us to share in your promise.
You have made us the heirs of your grace,
 beneficiaries of your loving kindness.

Grant that we may not wander off in the night!
For your Spirit sweeps us up
 to the encounter with the One to come,
 Jesus the Christ, our Lord.

■

We are called your church,
 a people on a journey.
 open to us
 a new future.

At your call, may we emerge from our past,
 and these snug certitudes of ours
 that keep us safe and captive.
With free hands,
 and without a knapsack on our backs,
 we shall leave for the new land.
Sure of your fidelity,
 we shall toil in faith,
for we believe that what you promise will truly come to be,
 and abide forever.

FIRE!

Ephesians 3:14–21: "To him be glory in the church . . ."! Even in his prayer the writer maintains his theme: the church manifests the work of God.

What does this prayer ask for Christians? That God the Father may grant them power in the Spirit, thus strengthening them "inwardly." The theme of the "inner person," a person's heart, is taken from popular Greek philosophy. It is not to be confused, then—at least not usually—with the "new man" of the "old man/new man" antithesis characteristic of Jewish thought.

Ephesians expresses a hope that Christ may dwell in Christians' hearts by faith. They will then "attain to the fullness of God himself." Here we find the expressions of chapter one, so reminiscent of the gospel of John: believers participate in the fullness that Christ receives from the Father and communicates to his body.

The conclusion of part 1 of Ephesians finds an echo in *Psalm 33,* which sings of God's constancy in bringing his salvific deed to its full accomplishment.

Luke 12:49–53: (See p. 115.)

■

Jesus the firebrand, then? "I have come to light a fire on the earth. How I wish the blaze were ignited!" Fire is seductive. Yes, but do not play with it. When you set fire to a field of grass or brush, how quickly everything is gone! And yet country folk actually scorch the earth to renew it.

"I have come to light a fire on the earth." Kindle love in your heart, and it becomes all-devouring. Who can tell the height, the breadth, the depth of the tenderness that has seared us? We are on fire! Love is a passion. We are aflame! Love is all-consuming. The church is a passionate bride. Yes, she has love on her mind!

"How I wish the blaze were ignited! Jesus sets out for Jerusalem, for the trial by fire. Love is passion. Scorched in the fire of love, the church will be baptized in death, to attain to resurrection. There is no room for half-measures in the gospel. Once the fire is lighted, you have to take the risk of seeing it blow out of control. After all, a wind may come up. The church which, along with its Lord, has known the baptism of fire, simply cannot keep its footing in the glowing blast of the Spirit. The church is possessed by a word that reveals the prodigality of love. "Thus you will be able to grasp fully . . . Christ's love, and experience this love which surpasses all knowledge," all things knowable!

Fire divides. It purifies the gold of its dross. "Do you think I have come to establish peace on the earth?" Taken seriously, love divides. The church is in the world without being of the world. Purified by fire, it lives the hour of witness and contradiction. Ever since those glowing days when the word of fire kindled an unquenchable furnace, ever since the days that opened a new epoch in history, the Christian wedge has never ceased to penetrate our world. And the church, burning with desire, addresses its prayer to the Father, in the name of all the ages: "How I wish the blaze were ignited!"

■

That your church may be the fire
to consume every dried branch
and rekindle the smoldering ash,
Lord, hear our prayer.

That the baptized may not forget
the Spirit in whom they have been new created,
Lord, hear our prayer.

■

God our Father,
you enrich us with your own life.
Grant that the cares of this earth
may not keep us from living.
Keep our hearts and our minds
turned toward the realities that are from above,
and may your Spirit enable us
to confront the life of every day in hope.

BOND OF MISSION

Ephesians 4:1–6: The first part of the letter is followed by an urgent exhortation in the form of a blessing: "I plead with you . . . to live a life worthy of the calling you have received. . . ."

What would the writer have his addressees do? Very simply, he would have them concretize, wherever they stand, the "mystery of God," and thus live in concord and peace. For when he invites them to "preserve the unity which has the Spirit as its origin and peace as its binding force," it is a matter not of platonic words, but of a disabused view of the reality of the church. Divisions are to be found in the church as in any social body. But with the church, it is a matter of utmost urgency to surmount them, inasmuch as the sole *raison d'être* of the church is the manifestation of the divine design of universal reconciliation already initiated by the incorporation of the Jews and pagans into the one people of God, the incorporation of which the great Paul has been the special instrument.

Psalm 24 was sung to welcome pilgrims to the temple. Today's liturgy retains only the list of requirements for entry to the sanctuary, together with a few verses of a processional hymn used for the Ark of the covenant, suggesting the march of the entire people toward its God.

Luke 12:54–59: (See p. 117.)

■

"Make every effort to preserve the unity which has the Spirit as its origin and peace as its binding force. . . ." On the eve of his death, Jesus will pray that his disciples may be one, that the world may believe (Jn 17:21, 23)! Thus he will leave a fiery testament in the conscience of the church. "When you see a cloud rising in the west, you say immediately that rain is coming. . . . If you can interpret the portents of earth and sky, why can you not interpret the present time?" Peace will be established by the death of the Shepherd, and the sign of unity will be two arms stretched out over the world in the form of a cross. Will you be able to read God's deed? Unity is a passion, and peace a judgment. Unity is a testament, and peace a vocation. "Make every effort to preserve the unity . . ."!

"There is but one body and one Spirit, just as there is but one hope given all of you by your call." Unity is not an end in itself. Unity is not bestowed for the purpose of getting along better, or being stronger. It is bestowed for the purpose of lending credibility to the gospel proclamation. There should be one body, since we are called to a common hope. The oneness that is the church's calling is born of its mission.

And what is that mission but to unveil, in every age, the one sign, Jesus Christ? Like our contemporaries, we question ourselves about the meaning of the world that we are in the process of making. We live the same fears and the same incertitudes, the same aspirations and the same hopes, when we consider the face of humanity tomorrow. But we are in our fiery youth, the everlasting youthfulness of our faith, and we insist that, where women and men are derided, crushed, diminished, ignored and crucified, where peace is abused, God too is outraged, in the only sign that he has given of himself. And we make an effort to look at the world with critical perceptivity, in the light of the mystery of Christ. With all respect, we really must say that there are those in the church who would be tempted to succumb to fear and retreat into the ghetto of the righteous remnant, the "faithful little flock." They would condemn other Christians, the ones who seek to enflesh the gospel in the concrete reality of our culture. But it is precisely in that concrete cultural reality that the church finds its vocation! It is the task of the church to scrutinize our times, for the purpose of reading, in those times, news of the advent of Hope.

■

God our Father, Father of all men and women,
    you have called us to one hope.
Pour forth your Spirit upon us!
May that Spirit enlighten our minds,
    that they may discern the signs of your Reign.
And may that Spirit warm our hearts,
    that we may begin to build, even today,
        the peace offered in Jesus Christ forever.

■

Father most holy,
    hallowed be thy name!
Be blessed for the faithfulness of your church:

you have given it to your Son,
and to the keeping of your Spirit today.

You have initiated us into the revelation of your name.
    For this be blessed!
And as you instill in our hearts
    a desire to preserve our unity in the Spirit
    by the bond of peace,
may we sing your praise with one voice,
    O Father who calls us to be one body!
One with the praise of all who have preceded us in faith,
may our song become a song of the universe,
    that we may bless you for such great love.
May it be at once a song of acclamation
    and of thanksgiving!

SATURDAY OF THE 29TH WEEK

CHURCH OF PATIENCE

Ephesians 4:7–16: Pursuing his discourse on the edification, the upbuilding, of the body of Christ, the sacred writer now makes two crucial assertions. On the one hand, he emphasizes Christ's initiative. At the same time, he underscores the responsibility of the faithful.

The initiative of Christ is brought out in his exegesis of Psalm 67:19. Certain Targums had applied this verse to the ascent of a Moses struggling up the slopes of Sinai. Our author applies it to the Paschal exaltation of Christ. Enthroned at the right hand of the Father, the Risen One bestows the Spirit (at Pentecost, the Jewish feast of the giving of the Law). Instead of actually naming the Spirit, the author lists the various ministries bestowed by Christ on the church for the purpose of its edification and upbuilding. The perfect Human Being bestows a gift that will make the human being perfect.

Secondly, the author underscores Christian responsibility in the matter of this growth. The holy people of God are organized "in roles of service," he writes, that it may "build up the body of Christ. . . ." And further on: "The whole body grows, and with the proper functioning of the members joined firmly together by each supporting ligament, builds itself up. . . ." Each Christian in his or her place has a contribution to make to the construction of the church. Ephesians represents a veritable revolution vis-à-vis the earlier letters of the New Testament. The expectation of Christ's imminent return has given place to that of the construction of his body, the church.

315

Psalm 122 is one of the canticles of ascent, and thus is easily accommodated to the march of the peoples toward the new Jerusalem.

Luke 13:1–9: (See p. 119.)

Luke 13:1–9: (See p. 119.)

■

What must those stupid Siloamites have done, to have a tower fall on them? And the Galileans that were massacred while they were offering sacrifice—what awful deed must they have committed? How the tongues wagged! How people wondered! Ah, they must have deserved it! One would have thought the deaths had been thunderbolts of judgment from heaven. After all, where there's smoke, there's fire! If those people provoked an accident like that, and those Galileans had a massacre like that happen to them, well, they must have gotten mixed up in a pretty crooked affair. Virtuous people will even explain to you that God did well to punish the likes of them. It is safer for a religion to venerate a policeman-God or a judge-God than to imagine the terrifying absurdity of tragedy that strikes blindly.

"Do you think they were more guilty than anyone else who lived in Jerusalem?" Do you think that they were any more guilty than yourselves? "Certainly not! . . . You will all come to the same end unless you reform"! Do you think you can secure a "good conscience" for yourself by thinking that, since you were spared, you are without sin? Well, I have news for you. The sinners—the next to go!—are yourselves, all of you! Did you think God was judging others? God is judging you!

Is it all over, then? Are we simply doomed, now that we have been flushed out of our nice, peaceful "good conscience"? But "Jesus spoke this parable. . . ." The judgment that God pronounces is a judgment of grace, a decision in our favor. Who is God, then? A gardener who intercedes in favor of a sterile fig tree! Perhaps it will bear fruit next year. To the people of Israel, God's beloved vine that yields pure verjuice, to every one of us who bears no fruit, Jesus proclaims God's patience. Who is God? Not a judge or a police officer, but the holy God who reveals to us our deep misery without crushing us on account of it, a God of tenderness and forgiveness, a God of mercy and boundless love.

"Each of us has received God's favor in the measure in which Christ bestows it. . . . Through him the whole body," the church, "grows . . . in love"! The church will never have any other mission than that of bearing witness to the patience of God. Confronted with our stonyheartedness, God only adopts the attitude of persevering love—the sole antidote for the scandal of suffering and the absurdity of evil. Love alone can remedy despair.

316

What should we be, were we not your work?
How should we live,
    were you to abandon us to our wickedness and our despair?

God of infinite patience,
never tire of reminding us
    of your love and mercy.
By your grace, the day will surely come
    when we shall profess your name in faith.

The time will surely come,
    when we shall live for you
    throughout eternity.

MONDAY OF THE 30TH WEEK

THE SEVENTH DAY OF CREATION

Ephesians 4:32–5:8: The exhortation contained in the second part of Ephesians alludes to traditional themes of the primitive baptismal catechesis. And so we hear of a change of garments (vv. 22–25), the imitation of God, and the contrast between light and darkness.

As we know, the contrast between light and darkness is characteristic of the Qumran theology. On the other hand, the importance ascribed to baptism is typically Pauline. Ephesians' meditation on the church could only culminate in a theology identifying baptism as the hour of decision for a Christian participation in the upbuilding of the Reign of God.

Indications like the borrowings from Qumran have forced most scholars to propose a later date for the letter than is generally attributed to the Pauline epistles as a group. But while the letter to the Ephesians may be more typical of the post-apostolic generation, it comes from a milieu mightily impregnated with the thinking of the apostle.

The contrast between the respective destinies of the just and the wicked, so important in *Psalm 1*, was an equally important theme of the primitive Christian catechesis.

Luke 13:10–17: (See p. 122.)

■

"There are six days for working. Come on those days to be cured, not on the sabbath." At the close of the first week of the world, God rested. And he exclaimed, upon the termination of his six days' work: "All this is good!" How God had admired the work emerging from his hands: a human being, kneaded of clay and spirit, free and filled, pinnacle of creation! Israel will remember this, and consecrate the seventh day to returning him thanks for so many marvels.

Jesus performs a cure on the sabbath day. Why would not the day consecrated to God be the ideal day of deliverance? How could one sing the wonders of God and not bend low over this afflicted one—over sick humanity? And Jesus rehearses the divine deed of creation. He bends down, reaches out his hand to poverty, and touches it—as God had once bent low over a lifeless Adam to flood him with his Spirit. Jesus lifts up the sufferer, and humanity is raised again in its pristine beauty. "Everyone else rejoiced. . . ." A new sabbath exploded, in gladness and thanksgiving.

"There was a time when you were darkness. . . ." In the first days of the universe, God had separated the darkness from the light. On the first day of the new week, Light will burst forth in a Paschal celebration: the darkness will have been powerless to hold It in the night of the tomb. "Now you are light in the Lord." We have come back to the beginning, and the risen Jesus inaugurates a new creation. "Well, then, live as children of light (Eph 5:8b). Christians will have no other task than that of manifesting what they already are. Their mission is to become by grace what they are by character. The church will have no other task in this world but to live what has been given it. The history of the world will be the patient incarnation of creation, proclaimed one sabbath day when a human being found herself on her feet again, free and filled.

■

At the dawn of the world, God our creator,
you made light to appear,
    and the sun to warm the earth.
Be blessed for the work of your hands,
    kneaded of such love and tenderness!

On the first day of the week,
you raised your Son,
    Light sprung from Light,
    Sun risen on those who had lain
    in the shadow of death!

Be blessed for the new world,
    delivered from all servitude.

Each day, Father of all goodness,
you make to shine upon us
    the victory of the One you raised,
    and we become children of the light.
Grant us to be faithful to such a grand vocation.
Make us live as children of the day,
    until the time when we shall be transfigured
    for everlasting ages.

■

In this Eucharist—
    the bread of our earth, transfigured by your grace—
God of light and life,
even now the resurrection of your Son
    germinates in us.
Remove every obstacle to its growth within us,
    until the day when we shall bathe in your light
    for all eternity.

TUESDAY OF THE 30TH WEEK

PARABLE OF LOVE

Ephesians 5:21–33: This passage, so discredited today (wedding liturgies tend to prefer Kahlil Gibran's *The Prophet*), is yet one of the most perfect of all the biblical texts on the church and Christian marriage. Taking his point of departure in a universal phenomenon of the age—the unconditional authority of the father of the family—the writer executes an in-depth revision of the prevailing concept of the human couple. For him, the paternal authority of his culture must be an authority of service. The husband must love his wife as his own body, a body he nourishes and cares for as Christ feeds and cares for the church.

The union of woman and man, this oneness of such tenderness and love, is the sacrament, the efficacious sign, of the unity of Christ and the church. Of old the Prophet Hosea, in the deep feeling he bore his faithless bride, had seen a reflection of God's love for humankind. And marriage, with its joys and its sorrows, its betrayal and its forgiveness, was destined one day to become the purest symbol of the everlasting covenant God had struck with that humanity.

Looking the mystery of the cross full in the face, the sacred writer engages in a meditation on the church. The church is born of Christ's supreme sacrifice, his overflowing love. The espousal of the church and the Lamb is no cortege of little boys escorting into the presence of her groom a bride bathed and adorned in the fashion of the East! The wedding of the Lamb is the wedding of the church to a Christ who has himself bathed his spouse in the laver of baptism, that she might come to him "immaculate, without stain or wrinkle. . . ." The bride of his youth!

The image of the believer at the heart of the family has led to the selection of *Psalm 128*. But is it the best choice for prolonging the meditation in Ephesians? As it stands, it is a psalm of congratulation, a mnemonic for priests in charge of welcoming pilgrims.

Luke 13:18–21: (See p. 125.)

■

Parallels between our love for one another and the love we bear God can be distasteful. In order to succeed, these hazardous operations must distort both terms of the comparison. How frequently we must listen to idyllic, luminous descriptions of human love bearing precious little resemblance to the vicissitudes of the ordinary life of lovers and spouses! Not a word about frustration, neglect, disappointment, and yes, the basic absence of the other at the very heart of a love that has come to seem nothing but emptiness. And still we are told that love embodies God. Do not everyday experience and encounter evince a more ambiguous truth? Surely love stands on its own merits, or lack of same.

We must take another route. Wives, love your husbands. Husbands, love your wives. After all, Christ loves the church: God's love sheds its light on human love. No longer do we move from human love to God. We move from God to human love. The parable of human loves is God's love, not vice versa. "Love one another as I have loved you" (Jn 15:12). What a powerful "as"! We are accorded the essence of the life of God. We are capable of God! If marriage is a sacrament of God, surely it is because its tenderness and its commitment say something of God's own tenderness and fidelity. Perhaps it is especially because it sets before us God's love as a project that will take a lifetime to accomplish. "Love . . . as. . . ." The yardstick of love is—God!

"What does the reign of God resemble?" The mustard seed is the smallest in the garden, but it will grow into a tree in which birds will come and build their nests. God has sown sufficient love in us for us to become capable of him. Marriage is a sacrament of the church. It says something of the espousal of Christ with the creature whom God gives him as his Body—an espousal in unfailing love, a betrothal in a love that forgives and saves. Our poor human loves are but its distant image. But in the ambiguity of our world, they afford a glimmer today of the fecundity of the promise tomorrow. The Reign of God "is like yeast. . . ."

■

God, source of all love,
we thank you
    for your church, beautiful and holy,
    for your covenant with it
    in Jesus, its Spouse, its Savior.

He has given it everything—
    his heart, opened on the cross,
    his blood, his love,
    the bread that is the yeast of God's Reign
    and the new wine of the wedding feast.

Father, who call us to grow in love,
instill within us the Spirit of your Well-Beloved,
    that we may become his Body in this world.
Pour forth upon us his mercy,
    that your Christ may present his bride to you
    resplendent,
    without stain or wrinkle.

God our Father,
bless your children,
    that they may bless you
    forever and ever.

NO SPECIAL FAVORS!

Ephesians 6:1–9: The precepts listed here were current moral prescriptions of the author's age and time. But in his continual reference to Christ, our author profoundly modifies these prescriptions—thereby calling attention to the fact that membership in the church should modify relationships among human beings. Still more remarkable is the notion (also to be found in the third chapter of Colossians) of reciprocity of obligation between the stronger members of the community (parents and teachers, just as, previously, husbands) and the weaker (children, slaves, wives). Not content with preaching the obedience of children and slaves, the sacred writer demands that parents and slave owners practice patience, and abandon their reliance on threat and force.

Psalm 145 sings of a new humanity in Christ, to the glory of God the Father.

Luke 13:22–30: (See p. 127.)

■

"Lord, are they few in number who are to be saved?" Hypocrites! You only want to know whether you and yours are saved! Not for one moment do you care about the salvation of others! Ah, how you love your spiritual ledgers, your comforting tradition, the education that proves you right, a membership that saves. How you are going to be scandalized, when unbelievers, sinners and pagans enter the Reign of God! "Lord, are they few in number who are to be saved?" You think that you are going to "be in that number," do you not? After all, you can tell me, "We ate and drank in your company." Oh, we have received Holy Communion so often! Well, I tell you, I don't know you from Adam.

"Try to come in through the narrow door." A certificate of a good life and morals will not do as a ticket. When it comes to entering the Reign —no special favors! There is only one condition for entry there. Come in through the door. The name of the door is Jesus. Oh, you want the password? That is the password. Jesus. The password is a person, not a word. Still less a theory. You ride in on love, not a system.

"I am the gate" (Jn 10:9), and this gate opens not onto a private courtyard, the domain of a few privileged persons, the jealously guarded preserve of a few righteous individuals and groups—but onto the world of God and our world. The door opens upon lush, green countryside, a land of the open air. On the horizon we descry foreign caravans approaching, to hear the Good News of their deliverance proclaimed, and proclaimed in their own language. "I am the gate," Jesus says, and I bring the narrow parapets of fear and guilt down to dust. Like the church of Saint Paul near Rome, God is "outside the walls." And if we do not know this now, we need only watch for the day he is raised on a cross at the gates of the city, outside the city walls.

"I am the gate." Jesus speaks, and the walls come tumbling down. The city gate is where everyone comes, on the way to everywhere. Here is the gathering place. The people stream through. Or come to sit and talk. Either way they are part of a community in which the internal bonds of acquaintanceship, love and sharing are stronger than any constraint or prescription. A whole people crowd into the banquet hall. Innumerable, unexpected, here they are! Look at them: poor, despoiled, disarmed. And they are so many! But the Master attires them in his robe of mercy, and the door is closed. Then those who live hunched up in the shell of their "rights," or draped in the ludicrous mantle of their purse-lipped justice, are left outside, to raise their indignant cries.

"I am the gate." This gate strains out the camel, and shuts out the smug, sleek rich. This gate is a demanding one, for it leads to a steep ascent indeed—the way of the cross. Jesus is on his way to Jerusalem. The city is already on the horizon. For Jesus it will be the city of prison, torture and death. Woe to those who will not have left all for the gospel! Once recognized, love becomes even more demanding. The gate swings wide. Behold the way of the cross.

Yes, there is Jerusalem, on the horizon. Relying on their law, human beings will think to hold fast to the key of the Reign by silencing the one who has come to open their city to the masses of the deprived. But God himself has opened the sealed tomb. In the days of sin, God posted two angels to stand guard at the entryway to a paradise lost. Today and forever, God himself becomes that gate and the passage. For those who set their feet in the footsteps of Christ, the Narrow Door has become the threshold of the Reign of God.

■

God our Father,
    come,
      open our sealed doors.
Send our certitudes scurrying.
Denounce our false justice.
Steep us in the breath of your Spirit.

And may your Son be the breach
>   *through which we may emerge from our impasses,*
>   *the Gate that opens out on freedom and life.*

■

Gate of heaven, Jesus Christ, be blessed!
Happy are those who advance toward you
>   *and persevere in love.*
As we have communicated in your body delivered up for us,
>   *grant that wherever you lead,*
>   *we may follow.*

THURSDAY OF THE 30TH WEEK

NEXT YEAR IN JERUSALEM!

Ephesians 6:10–20: Let us return to these invisible "principalities and powers," the powers of darkness and spirits of evil, that rule the world. The forces they represent are elements of a worldview inspired by Gnosticism. Gnosticism was a speculative movement that reached its apogee around the second century before Christ, when it had spread throughout pagan and Jewish worlds alike (as we see in Qumran). The root notion of this current of thought was that of a dualistic governance of the created world, in terms of an antagonism between a good God and evil spirits. The Gnostics denied that matter, being essentially evil, could have been created by God. Matter had been created, and continued to be governed, by certain intermediate powers, customarily localized in the stars. The Pauline letters make frequent allusion to the angels, who were thought to play a particularly key role in the striking of the Old Covenant and hence in the imposition of the divine law on human beings. In Gnostic thinking, these powers were generally hostile to humanity.

And so the writer is concerned to make a systematic presentation of the supremacy of Christ over these invisible forces (cf. Eph 1:20–23). From this point of view, our redemption appears as the liberation of the created world from the slavery in which these forces had bound it. The exhortation of the Letter to the Ephesians explodes in a battle cry, in terms of the thematic combat (again, as we find in Qumran) of the sons of light and the sons of darkness. But this battle cry resounds further in Ephesians, being a call both to those who had mounted a resistance to the Judaizers and a Mosaic law obligatory on pagans (cf. Galatians), and to those who resisted the debauchery that ruled the contemporary pagan world.

Psalm 144 is a composite writing, drawn from several sources. The verses sung at today's liturgy have been inspired by a royal act of thanksgiving, and invite us to acknowledge the security and strength represented by Yahweh's protection of his faithful.

Luke 13:31–35: (See p. 129.)

■

"Go on your way!" some said. "Leave this place!" Jesus will go on his way. He will leave for Jerusalem.

"Next year in Jerusalem!" The people turned their hope toward the Holy City. "If I forget you, Jerusalem, may my right hand be forgotten! May my tongue cleave to my palate if I remember you not . . . !" (Ps 137:6) The temple, standing in the southern quarter of the city, manifested God's presence and fidelity to his covenant. To authenticate their message, prophets must bear that message to Jerusalem.

"Next year in Jerusalem!" Jesus had chanted the psalms of ascent that an impatient people sang with all their might at the time of the great festivals of pilgrimage. He had turned his eyes toward "God's bride." How often he had reminded his disciples that he must go up to Jerusalem! He "must." It was a necessity of obedience! He must ascend to Jerusalem, that the glory of God, dwelling in the temple, might truly be manifested. His decision had been taken in the first days of his mission in Galilee. "No one esteems a prophet in his own country" (Jn 4:44).

"In Jerusalem"! For it was there, Jesus understood, that his destiny would be sealed. At the end of the road loomed the silhouette of death. Death would be his, not only because he questioned conformism, authority and false absolutes, but because the fate of the prophets had always been consummated in blood. In these latter days, tombs had been erected to the prophets. By their murderers, in expiation! Now perhaps it would be easier to continue to ignore their words of fire. Jesus had repeatedly presented himself as the last of these great persons of God, whose martyrdom had seemed to punctuate the rhythm of sacred history down through the ages. John the Baptist had come to a bloody end now, and Jesus knew what fate would be his own, in the holy city of God.

"In Jerusalem"! Jesus will leave this place. He will pursue his route, and continue to open a new way for those who take up their cross and follow him. In Jerusalem, the prophet will be killed, but God will raise him up.

The temple will be destroyed, but it will be rebuilt in three days. And Jerusalem, where the ancients situated the juncture between heaven and earth, will become a symbol of the resurrection. "I also saw a new Jerusalem, the holy city, coming down out of heaven from God, beautiful as a bride prepared to meet her husband" (Rev 21:2).

"In Jerusalem"! The church will turn its heart toward its birthplace, the city of the Paschal mystery. For one must pass by way of death in order to reach the new world. The time of the church will be the time of trial and combat. The church will have to "put on the armor of God" if it is to "resist on the evil day. . . ." But it will also be the time of its birth, in the faith of the resurrection. For on the horizon, Jerusalem like a sunburst, calls. The eternal city beckons.

"In Jerusalem"! We must take the road again. "We can only build if we have death to lean our backs against. We can only build if we are attuned to tomorrow" (André Chedid).

■

Father, the hour approaches.
Glorify your Son!
For he is on his way to the cross
and Easter morn.

Call us to follow the Prophet of your Reign.
Clothe us with your strength,
that we may be once more on the road
that leads to the new world.

FROM FRIDAY OF THE 30TH WEEK

TO TUESDAY OF THE 32ND WEEK

Servants of Grace

What has Jesus been attempting to do? A glance at the gospel gives the answer. Jesus has come to defend the cause of the human being, and thereby to take sides with God. May what God wills come to pass! This is the message proclaiming the coming of the Reign. "Thy will be done"!

To do God's will is to immerse ourselves in the word that is grace, and to be altogether at home in that word. To do God's will is to follow in the footsteps of the one who has humbled himself to be exalted in the glory of the cross. Of course, the journey requires a certain behavior. But this is only because it has been charted by someone. Liberality, gift and grace come before norm, ethics, exigency and precept. Each one of us is called. To each of us is offered salvation, without any antecedent demand. And even the exhortations only emerge from a love for the Reign of God.

To be the servant of such a reign means accepting its dynamism. The road becomes journey and promise. Reflect before you build a tower. But do not forget: "Unless the Lord build the house, they labor in vain who build it" (Ps 127:1).

Finally, entry into this Reign, this regime of grace, means allowing ourselves to be carried off by the word that inaugurates it. God demands all. Because God is love, he wants our heart. God is not satisfied with good fruit. He wants a good tree.

God grant that grace work its power in us! Then the impossible will come to pass: trees growing in the sea, stewards that dare to risk the decisions that must be taken, and men and women with the courage to believe in God's gracious mercy.

■

It is good to bless you, Lord,
*   at all times,*
but especially on this day
*   when your Son comes to revive our fervor in his following.*
In his passion to do your will,
*   he will manifest your grace and your love*
*   to the point of giving up his life*
*   as a ransom for the many.*

Raised to the right hand of your glory,
*   he bestows on the church*
*   the Spirit of strength and freedom.*
And that Spirit sends us to proclaim the coming of your Reign.

God, our hope,
*   together with all those begotten of your mercy,*
*   we praise you!*

IMMEDIATELY

Philippians 1:1-11: Along with his brief message to Philemon, Paul's letter to the Philippians is one of the two most personal and cordial writings of the Pauline corpus. Most commentators no longer range it among the letters from captivity, although it is not altogether clear what ought to be done with it instead. If Paul is actually dictating his letter from prison, then it must not be his Roman captivity, but probably an imprisonment at Ephesus. Thus the letter would be from A.D. 57.

Philippians is written in a kind of rambling style altogether different from that of the other letters. Were there several redactions? Or several letters? At all events, our epistle is unified in its main thrust, for its great themes, like that of joy, run through the letter from beginning to end.

That the Christians of Philippi were particularly dear to Paul's heart may be deduced from our letter's exordium. Ever since their conversion, writes the apostle, they have given him material assistance. Indeed, theirs is the only community from which he has accepted such assistance.

Paul begins his missive, then, by giving thanks for the divine fidelity: what God has so well begun at Philippi, he will surely bring to its perfection. Then, altogether naturally, Paul's thanksgiving blends into a celebration of God's design: may the love experienced by the Philippians increase their clear-sightedness and sensitivity, that they may ever accomplish what is pleasing to God and thus be justified by Christ on the day of judgment.

Psalm 111, an alphabetical psalm, prolongs Paul's thanksgiving.

Luke 14:1-6: (See p. 134.)

■

It is the sabbath day. Jesus is invited to the home of a leader of the Pharisees. As usual, he will denounce the practices of these oh! so religious gentlemen. And he will denounce the substance of their corrupt behavior rather than its details. Is the soul of religion a list of permissions and prohibitions? Or a subtle alloy of rights and duties? "If one of you has a son or an ox and he falls into a pit, will he not immediately rescue him on the sabbath day?" Jesus recenters our relationship with God on the true nature of God: love.

Christianity was only emerging from its infancy when Origen cried out, "It is a dangerous thing to speak of God!" Jesus experienced this danger in his flesh. He leaves for Jerusalem, and he will promptly die there, for he has spoken of God in a different way. "It is a dangerous thing to speak of God!" Yes indeed, for God is not pure austerity, devoid of intelligible content, or the sham prestige of an idol. God is the disarming —because disarmed—presence of love. "If one of you has a son . . . and he falls into a pit, will he not immediately rescue him . . . ?" Jesus bends over the dropsy victim. Some irrepressible force in the prophet from Nazareth wrests a saving act from him whenever he comes in contact with suffering. Misery lies before him and he cannot allow it to continue. He heals it. And herein lies a revelation. Jesus is testifying to a secret known to him alone: the Reign to come is . . . God's mercy.

■

A poor sufferer cries out,
*   and immediately*
*   Jesus rises and heals that sufferer.*
The Reign of God is grace,
*   for God has a heart.*

For the sick, the chronically ill, the isolated,
for those whose every day is hard,
*   let us pray to the Lord of the poor.*

For the lowly, the voiceless,
for those crushed by a law that should have defended them,
for the victims of "law and order,"
*   let us pray to the God of mercy.*

For all of the lost sheep of the flock,
for those whose poverty is their poverty of virtue,
for those to whom no hand is willing to reach out
*   in compassion and solidarity,*
*   let us pray to the Lord of tenderness.*

God our Father,
rescue us from the claustrophobia of our rights.
May our faith become an anticipating love,
*   a love that flies to the rescue before the need.*

TABLE TALK

Philippians 1:18–26: Paul is not one to be guided by self-interest. He cites the anxiety that causes certain jealous preachers, caught up in their selfish interests, to enter into intrigues against him, "thinking that it will make my imprisonment even harsher" (Phil 1:17).

But why all the fuss, if, by one means or another, the gospel is proclaimed? Here is the mission to which Paul has consecrated his life. That mission is an urgent one, and the apostle has no intention of letting anything interfere with it. Even his most personal, most intense desires (the Greek text uses the word for "lust") must fall silent before it. Like Christ, the apostle has given his all. Forevermore, he knows, he has been absorbed into the mystery of his Master, for better and for worse—in suffering and joy, in death as in life.

The complaint of *Psalm 42* voices Paul's deep desire. He seeks his Lord earnestly, as the thirsting stag seeks the spring.

Luke 14:1, 7–11: (See p. 136.)

■

It was the sabbath, God's own day, a feast day the Jews loved to solemnize with a meal to which relatives, friends and acquaintances would be invited. On this particular sabbath day, at the home of one of the leaders of the Pharisees, a special attraction was on the bill. The young prophet from Nazareth—yes, the one who was all the rage these days—would put in an appearance. Surely before the meal was over he would recount one of the parables that came so easily to his lips.

"When you are invited by someone to a wedding. . . ." Make no mistake. Jesus is speaking of the world of God, and the kind of life incumbent on those who look for its impending appearance. ". . . Do not sit in the place of honor. . . ." Jesus is not merely doing some finger-wagging at the prideful Pharisee: Mind your manners, now! Jesus is not preaching modesty. No, Jesus intervenes in this way because God "tears down the mighty from their thrones and exalts the lowly" (cf. Lk 1:12). And on that day the divine Host will say to the guest reclining at the foot of the table, "My friend, come up higher"!

Presently Jesus will go to the foot of the table himself, there to kneel at the feet of his disciples. And the whole order of things will be reversed. Behold the revolution of the Reign! God reveals what he is by what he does. Seeing Jesus at his disciples' feet, I see God himself mysteriously the Servant, and this forever. Dumfounding revelation! God, our God, the God of Jesus, is a God in an apron! Zacchaeus, Mary Magdalene, the good thief, will recline at the table of the Wedding Banquet. Sinners, all who count for nothing, will celebrate. Peter, who will have denied the Master, and the disciples who will have abandoned him, will be welcomed back, and will sit at the table where the One who has been raised will break bread! All will proclaim the wild, insane news: God has taken his seat in the lowest place of all!

God in an apron. No, Jesus is not playing "Let's Pretend." He really does prefer the lowliest. Even if their poverty is a want of virtue! God's love is not a condescending love. God is infinitely rich, yes. But he is rich in love, not in having; and he certainly cannot be "had," be possessed. In the matter of love, wealth and poverty are synonymous. God is sovereignly free. But therefore he is free to love, and to love to the limit. A love that "goes all the way" is a renunciation of independence. God is measurelessly mighty, yes. But his greatness is to be able to do all that love can, to the point of being riveted by a look, a glance.

God in an apron! Otherwise how could we say, with Paul, "To me, 'life' means Christ"? It is not enough to say that God is a Father. We all know that being a son or daughter can be too much to bear! We must say more. We must say that God is the Father of this particular Son who, to manifest the quality of parenthood of the one who engendered him, kneels before his disciples. Jesus reveals a God in an apron. For us, then, "life" means to be willing to be daughters and sons—to be willing to receive, to be dependent, and to be glad of the grace of this gift and dependency.

"He who humbles himself shall be exalted." Soon Jesus will be living this parable in his own flesh, and the promise will become reality. Humbling himself even unto death, the Servant will be raised to the right hand of God. Surely this God is upside-down and backwards. And his Reign belongs to those who live by this "madness."

■

Lord our God,
    you never cease to astonish us.
Your Son had to take the lowest place
    to enter into his glory.
May your Spirit initiate us into this new world
    that you inaugurate through Jesus
    in our times and forever.

■

We have no right to a place at this banquet table.
But you have led us to your house,
  and made us to enter there,
  God our Father.

Be blessed for your love,
  which re-creates the face of the earth!
We were nothing,
  and you have made us your holy people.

May the banquet to which you have invited us
  be for everlasting!

MONDAY OF THE 31ST WEEK

REIGN OF HUMILITY

Philippians 2:1–4: At Philippi as elsewhere, divisions and cliques prevail. Thus Paul exhorts his addressees to preserve their unity, a profound oneness of unselfishness, humility and mutual concern. Obviously this passage is to be read in the context of the verses that follow it, which set Christians before their living model, Jesus, the Christ.

Psalm 131, composed for private use, belongs to the complaint genre. The psalmist wishes to forestall Yahweh's reproaches, and so protests that his life is pure.

Luke 14:12–14: (See p. 138.)

■

"He who humbles himself shall be exalted"! We can imagine the heavy silence around the table that provided the occasion of a like revelation. Jesus goes on: "Whenever you give a lunch or dinner, do not invite your friends or brothers or relatives or wealthy neighbors"—in other words, everyone the leader of the Pharisees has invited to table. This is the way of the world, yes. Reciprocal guarantees of a society where no one owes anyone anything. "No, . . . invite beggars and the crippled, the lame and the blind," the marginalized of Israel. Once more, everything is set topsy-turvy. The mores of the Reign are the opposite of those of our world. Before long Jesus himself will be the excluded one, the condemned, kneeling at the feet of his disciples. Today is a sabbath day. The celebrity invited to table today knows the meaning of things, and dreams dreams of the messianic Great Sabbath, the banquet of the Reign of God.

"As I have done," I your "Teacher and Lord," Jesus will say, "so you must do." His testament? This he will make in a servant's apron. God in an apron! A glance at this scandalous tableau is all we need in order to appreciate the immense failure of Christianity when it attempts to replace the gospel with the good manners of the world. You have said very little about our God when you have recited the platitude that he rewards the just and punishes the wicked. The gods of morality do that! The resurrection that will flash forth on the morn of the new sabbath will set the world on its ear, and found the reign of humility.

Humility is such a misunderstood virtue! Real humility has the savor of earth, of soil, the taste of a patiently developed truth. Only God can practice it perfectly. God is almighty, and that is mighty enough to invent forgiveness and love. Only those of us who "have a heart" can enter the Reign. When God calls us together for the wedding banquet of his Son, he alone knows why we resemble one another so much: we wear on our faces the traits of his Son. And thanks to this resemblance, God can seat us all in a row and begin to wash our feet. Decidedly, the church of God bears very little resemblance to the world!

■

We have put on the new human being:
> *in Jesus Christ we have become daughters and sons of light.*
May our prayer be the humble invocation
> *that will convert us to the mores of the Reign.*

May those who engage in the affairs of the world
> *tend to those affairs as good stewards—*
> *as servants of others,*
> *servants of life.*

May the poor find in our hands
> *whatever they require to live without anxiety,*
> *in the dignity that is their right.*

May the problems of an underdeveloped world
> *never find us cynical or resigned.*

May our faith in Jesus,
> *who delivered himself to manifest his Father's love,*
> *be the mainstay of our charity:*

may the happiness of all men and women
   be our very reason for living.

God of love,
   grant that the word of your Son not be sterile in us.
May his call rouse us to his following.
Yes, the path he calls us to walk
   is the way of his passion.
But it is also the road to Easter.

■

When you send your invitations,
   Lord our God,
you do so so delicately
   that we all but believe ourselves worthy of them.

As you have given us to share
   in the common table you set for us,
grant us the humility
   of those who are saved by grace,
that our life may be the glad reflection
   in which women and men may know
   with what great love they are loved
   for all eternity.

TUESDAY OF THE 31ST WEEK

NATURALIZED CITIZENS

Philippians 2:5-11: In order to confirm Christians in the unselfish attitude he has just recommended, Paul recalls the example of Christ himself. The pre-Christian hymn here modified and handed on by the apostle must therefore be read against the backdrop of his moral exhortation.

The hymn is constructed on the fundamental antithesis of Christ's voluntary abasement and his exaltation by God. But—and this reinforces the exhortation—we must by all means observe that Christ has brought the being of God into view by way of his own earthly conduct. He was despoiled not of his divine nature, but of the glory naturally attaching to that nature, which of itself ought to have flashed forth in his humanity. It is probable that Paul was thinking of the comparison, so familiar to his addressees, between Christ, the new Adam, and the first Adam. The latter had appeared in the universe as a model of pride and rebellion. But Jesus' only concern was to do his Father's will. The point of departure for Paul's contrasting diptych is Genesis 1:27, where human beings are said to have been created in the "image of God." Christ, the true image of God, is the "visible figure manifesting [God's] inmost being" and essence.

Before we proceed, let us consider another point of Christ's obedience. Obviously a question arises about his Father's will. Did the Father then desire the death of his Son? By no means. Events, and events alone, led to Jesus' ignominious death on the cross. The will of the Father was only the salvation of humanity, nothing more. In order to secure that salvation, of course, Jesus must assume all of the risks of his prophetic preaching—all of the risks of incarnation.

The hymn in Philippians is actually a rereading, applied to Jesus' destiny, of the Fourth Song of the Suffering Servant (Is 52–53). Instead of insisting on his right to be treated as equal to God, Jesus humbled himself. Therefore he has been exalted over all things. Thus the hymn appears as the culmination of a reflection that spans the Bible from covenant to covenant. It likewise reflects the thinking of the primitive church, which saw in the self-abasement of the Son the necessary condition of his glorification.

By way of a response to the hymn, the liturgy cites the finale of *Psalm 22*, which, in a lamentation (vv. 2–7) and a hymn of its own (vv. 28–32), expresses the certainty that the persecuted of all times will one day sing the praise of the faithful God who will have delivered them from their enemies.

Luke 14:15–24: (See p. 141.)

■

Here is a page from the heart. No theological discussion, no moral recommendation, but the apostle simply becomes a supplicant: "Your attitude must be Christ's"! Join the race of Christ. Become naturalized in the gospel!

"Though he was in the form of God, he did not deem equality with God something to be grasped at"! Adam had been created in the image of God, but had sought equality with God, and that was his downfall. Another reflection of God's being, Christ, chose humility and obedience on earth. And so he received the title of Lord, which the Old Testament had reserved to God alone. What the first Adam had sought to plunder, Christ was freely given. Jesus exchanged his divine state for the condition of a slave. But God consecrated his Servant: he made all Plenitude to dwell in Christ. Now the name that is God's is his as well.

Become naturalized citizens of the gospel! The Christian's rule is the behavior of Jesus. Love makes itself service. And our church, this heap of deformed, miserable, mediocre cripples, yes, even the church shares in its Master's abasement. But it knows, too, that it receives grace: we are made for communion with God. When, in humility and obedience, we strive for all we are worth to have the attitude and dispositions of the only-begotten Son of God, then, we know, we already have a share in the victory of Easter. For the church knows God, and knows his name. After all, we live on Love!

Become naturalized in the gospel. We must come to a strange land. We have been living in the town streets and squares, the back alleys and the dead-end streets. Then, lame and blind, we are suddenly invited to the wedding feast. The celebration is a bloody one, for the meal we share is the farewell supper of the Suffering Servant. The sacrament we celebrate is that of the hour when, under the guise of a repast, the Master gives himself to his disciples in this same attitude of trustful surrender. It is the hour when, along with death, Jesus accepts all that goes with it—all that belongs to human weakness. "Though he was in the form of God . . ." he whose being, unlike ours, was altogether innocent of that mysterious congenital complicity that drives us to our own ruin, has seized the cup of his life with both hands. He has surrendered to God, and publicly. Death has been vanquished, and the old cup has been exchanged for a new one—for the chalice of the New Covenant, in blood poured out for the redemption of the multitude. The table we share is even now the table of the Reign, our communion with the one every tongue proclaims as Lord. "Be naturalized in the gospel." Invited to the table of the Eucharist, behold, we are led to a dwelling place that from this moment forth is our own: Christ has reared us, "brought us up"—snatched us from our mediocrity and educated us in the uses of the Reign of God.

■

We praise you,
*   God of the Name above every name.*
For you have glorified your Servant,
*   and established him as Lord,*
that you may love in us
*   what you have loved in him.*
By his self-abasement,
*   he has raised us to your very heights,*
and you have invited us to the Supper of the Reign.
Blessed be the name of Jesus!

May his life be our life,
 and, one day, his glory our own.

WEDNESDAY OF THE 31ST WEEK

PLEDGED TO PASSION

Philippians 2:12–18: After recalling the example of Christ, Paul comes down
to the matter of the Christian task, which he defines in terms of God's salvific
will. God, the source of all movement, secures for human beings a free will. It
is up to them to open themselves to the activity of the Spirit. They have a
twofold task: to toil at their own sanctification, and to bear witness to the
world. These two activities are actually identical; and this helps us understand
why obedience in Paul is so nearly identical with faith. Paul is dealing with a
relationship of trust between God and a human being, which ought to issue in
a common deed. The foundation of the church at Philippi is the part of this
work, this deed, that falls to Paul; and if the Christians of that city do what he
asks of them, he will not have run his race in vain. If necessary, he will not
hesitate to lay down his life for them. Thus the Christian task, of which Paul's
apostolate is one facet, becomes part of the "new worship," the worship "in
spirit and truth."

Psalm 27 as we have it in its final redaction is actually a splicing of two
poems. The first (vv. 1–6) is a song of trust, suitable for the lips of a king. The
second (vv. 7–14) is a complaint, of which the liturgy has retained only the
verses expressing confidence.

Luke 14:25–33: (See p. 143.)

■

Jesus' call is most abrupt. He demands we put our lives on the line for
him, and with the most radical priority. Jesus has set out for Jerusalem.
On the horizon, we can already make out the silhouette of a cross. He
will drink the cup of his passion to the dregs. The one who had said,
"Say, 'Yes' when you mean 'Yes' and 'No' when you mean 'No' " (Mt
5:37) has been the first to live up to the "Yes" he gave to the calling
received from God. There are not two gospels that fall from Jesus' lips
—the one a very human, somewhat flower-child, "Now, you be nice,"
gospel, fashioned by him in moments of that beaming indulgence of his,
and the other a rigoristic, fanatical doctrine proclaimed in moments of

anger and exasperation. No, very simply, "Anyone who does not take up his cross and follow me cannot be my disciple."

". . . Take up his cross. . . ." Jesus is not enunciating some kind of metaphor for the trials, the strivings, the burdens of life; he is speaking of a pair of planks to which Romans used to nail living human beings. For Jesus, the "cross" is very simply the reality of a life surrendered to love and not taken back. Anyone willing to follow Jesus must be willing to share his life and death.

"If one of you decides to build a tower, will he not first sit down . . . ?" We are pledged to all the passions of Christ, his human passion and his divine, his passion of love and his passion of the gift. Jesus' cry is a cry of the urgency of God's Reign. He is talking about this entity so intensely awaited, this world turned topsy-turvy by God, at hand, imminent, here for the asking.

"Whoever wishes to be my follower . . ." (Lk 9:23). What does it mean to "follow" Jesus today? Some have a ready answer: since they own Christ, they may of course permit themselves to make use of Jesus to stabilize and consecrate their way of life. Others simply deny that the question has a great deal of relevance, as if they had assimilated all there is to assimilate in the message of the meek utopian of Nazareth. But would being Jesus' follower not mean rather that we would allow him to surprise us, to "drop in" on us—just when he is the most "bother"—with his inexhaustible being and novelty? Would it not be to be willing to let him come and "punch holes" in our well-being and self-assurance, our theories and our practices?

"That man began to build what he could not finish." Once God begins to speak to us, there is nothing he cannot do with us. We should have to despair only if the living Word of God were to be extinguished. But in every age of the church women and men have risen up to say, "We have put aside everything to follow you!" (Mk 10:28). My sisters and brothers, if you have said this to him, are you willing to "put your money where your mouth is"? If we love him, we shall follow him. I leave you with this invitation. But I do not leave you alone, for the Spirit of Jesus, which you have received, is with you today as always.

∎

Lord, you call us to follow your Son,
    and to set out on the path to your Reign
    with high resolve.

We beseech you:
by your Spirit, set our hearts free,
     and fix our gaze on the goal.
For the time has come to set out
     on the long road
     to everlasting communion.

■

The road is so very long
     that leads to you!
Lord, come to meet us on the way.
Be yourself our way!

The call to follow you
     holds so many trials!
Lord, come to meet us on the way.
Be yourself our strength!

How hazardous the life we build!
Lord, come to join us at our task.
Be yourself our future!

THURSDAY OF THE 31ST WEEK

GOD INSIDE OUT

Philippians 3:3–8: Some scholars regard the warning against the Judaizers (3:1–4:9) as adventitious to this letter, spliced into it from another epistle to the Philippians. This third section reprimands its addressees, affording the apostle the opportunity of emphasizing both the gratuity of justification (vv. 2–11), and the duty to lead a holy life (vv. 12–16) and to aspire to the life that comes from above (vv. 17–21).

Against the claims of the Judaizers Paul, like the Old Testament prophets, proposes the circumcision of the heart. The true people of God are those who offer worship to God in spirit, who place their trust in Christ rather than in personal privileges and merits. Privileges and merits? Paul has a few of those! Nor are they inconsiderable, as for example his membership in one of the most venerated of the tribes, that of Benjamin, which gave Israel its first king. But in the presence of Christ, these privileges are as dust and sweepings, and should be relegated to the refuse bin.

Psalm 105 has the structure of a hymn. It appeals to the tribes never to cease repeating the wonders of God.

Luke 15:1–10: (See p. 145.)

■

When will we ever get God right-side-out? We seek to avenge an insult, and so we think of God as vindictive. We cannot forget an offense, and so we think of God as rigorous in our own prosecution. The only thing we do well is sin, and so we think of God as only being able to damn. For two thousand years, Christians have spoken of God in a way that can only make one wonder how they could have failed to suspect themselves of fabricating an illusion: a creator God to explain our feeling of dependence, a God of justice to put law and order in our lives, a paternalistic, and all-powerful, God to justify our guilt!

God is God, and that is all! It is not our despair that he wishes to arouse, but our conversion. It is not our fear that he seeks, but our love. When will we no longer think of God as just the opposite of the way he really is? God is a shepherd looking for a missing sheep until he finds it, abandoning the ones that are safe in the fold in order to search for the one he has lost. God is a woman turning the house upside-down for a coin that has gone astray. Under trite historical appearances, the most astonishing secrets of the heart of God are revealed. God undertakes all things to find his human creature. God spends his life saving us! A bird in the hand is worth two in the bush, human wisdom says. But the wisdom of God is human foolishness. Who else would walk off leaving ninety-nine sheep and go looking for one he might or might not find? God is the opposite of all that we think. He is the God whose bowels tremble with emotion. Why? Because he has become a human being—that human being that he has always dreamed of as so beautiful and great!

God inside out—the God who does not despair of us. God inside out, the God who annihilates himself to exalt us. Only Jesus, and Jesus Christ crucified, a heap of wreckage erected at the navel of the world, could make us suspect how much God loves us.

It is a dangerous affair to speak of a God like that—a God who asks everything! Love cannot but demand all, under penalty of not being love. It is a dangerous matter to speak of a God like that—for the relationship he sets in motion is founded on a mutual faith, on a reciprocal, total trust. And the life he stirs up is synonymous with risk and adventure: On his account I have lost all, Paul cries. All else is rubbish! Faith in a God like that is a passion, and love makes people do crazy things.

And this is why faith is also a source of joy. "Rejoice with me!" In each of the two parables, the motive force of history is the thing lost and then found again. But the essential element in these parables is the attitude of the figure who, because of the thing found, calls together servants, friends and neighbors, to celebrate and rejoice.

God has created us for joy—his own joy. And if our heart is restless until it rests in him, the heart of God is still more restless, until it has found us. With us, sadness is a habit. Not with God! God is just the opposite. The joy of forgiving is God's greatest joy. Would you deprive God of his one joy—the joy of loving? The God of Jesus Christ sits at table with sinners. He simply says, "Please. . . ."

■

God of tenderness and mercy,
let heaven rejoice and earth be glad,
for you rejoice to welcome us to your house!

Father of longsuffering,
you set out to look for us,
*   and even now you invite the whole universe*
*   to share the joy of our finding.*
Be blessed, Shepherd of our lives.
Grant that we may dare believe in such a caring,
*   which nothing will ever exhaust,*
*   through all the ages.*

FRIDAY OF THE 31ST WEEK

HELP WANTED: CAPABLE MANAGER

Philippians 3:17–4:1: "May I never boast of anything but the cross of our Lord Jesus Christ!" (Gal 6:14). For Paul, the cross is the clearest sign of God's gratuitous love. And so he lets the Judaizers know how he feels about them and the pride they take in their unavailing practices. "Belly" and "shame" seem to refer to the Jewish dietary laws and circumcision. Christians must not let themselves be turned aside from the goal for which they strive—the Reign of God. Let them remain firm in their expectation of the return of Christ, who will transform all things.

"We have our citizenship in heaven," says Paul. *Psalm 122* is a beautiful specimen of the genre known as the song or canticle of ascents. Pilgrims sang it to encourage one another on their ascent to the holy city and the temple. In adopting it themselves, Christians celebrate the heavenly Jerusalem, the goal of their entire lives.

Luke 16:1–8: (See p. 148.)

■

The town is abuzz with excitement. "Have you heard? So-and-so got caught embezzling his boss's pile!" Tongues are wagging. Everybody is chattering at once. How will the rascal get out of this one?

Panic never solved anything. Stay cool, be smart. Take a chance—don't worry, it'll pay off. And our swindler makes the most of the few days' grace he has obtained from his employer. One debtor sees fifty jars of oil stricken from his account. Another, twenty sacks of wheat. These are astronomical sums—more than a year's wages for a laborer.

And on top of it all, Jesus says the old boy did a great job! What's going on here, anyway? For that matter, has anyone ever understood "what's going on" with Jesus? Had Jesus preached a morality of expediency for people of respectable rearing, you can be sure that he would have been allowed to preach away! But Jesus is proclaiming a revolution: Happy the poor! Happy you who weep now! It is a topsy-turvy world he undertakes to build, where the last will be first and the first last. What a crafty old boy, that manager! He made the decisions he had to, he had the courage to invent the way of life that circumstances demanded. With his world teetering on the brink, the sly old steward keeps his wits about him.

Jesus appears, and the world teeters on the brink. But will the children of light be as skillful as the children of this world? Jesus speaks, and the world starts spinning in the other direction. But will Jesus' disciples make the decisions they have to? All through Jesus' life, his deeds and his words proclaim a God of gratuity. There simply must be a reaction! A shepherd gathers his friends simply because he has found one sheep. An impoverished woman holds a celebration because she has uncovered a little money she had lost. A father slaughters his fatted calf because one of his children is home again. There. That's God. God's love is grace, without any conditions. Shall we follow him in his regime of gratuity?

■

Lord our God, you call us
    to enter into your Reign.
The times are accomplished:
    the hour of faith is come.

We beseech you:
    by your Spirit, set our hearts free,
    and confirm our decision.
The time has come to set our feet
    in the footsteps of your Son,
    who opens to us the everlasting ages.

■

Lord our God, Ruler of heaven and earth,
    through your messenger, Jesus Christ,
    you reveal our future to us,
    and you call us to make an irrevocable decision.
Keep our faithfulness from becoming routine.
Place in our hearts the daring
    to make a commitment of our entire lives
    on the strength of your promise.
This we ask through your Son,
    the Witness of the astounding newness of your Reign.

■

God of love and tenderness,
    in Jesus Christ you have given us all.
In him we are citizens of heaven,
    and his body, delivered for us, keeps us steadfast in faith.

We beseech you:
    may he be the treasure of our life.
May he acquaint us with the Reign
    where all is grace.

DEVALUATION

Philippians 4:10-19: Now Paul's pen becomes more personal. He speaks of the friendship that binds him to the Christians of Philippi. From them alone has he accepted material aid, and he expresses his gratitude. At the same time the apostle delicately safeguards his independence: for he has placed his trust in the one "who is the source of my strength," and this has equipped him to cope with life's vicissitudes. And so Paul has carried the gospel to the Philippians, but the Philippians have helped Paul with all their might. This exchange demonstrates how effectively the Spirit is at work, in the apostle as in his converts.

Psalm 112, alphabetical in structure, served to welcome pilgrims to the temple. It lists the conditions for admittance to the sanctuary, which is open only to those who have already offered God the worship of their entire life.

Luke 16:9-15: (See p. 151.)

■

There is a striking expression in the gospel: "elusive wealth." But wealth does more than elude. It deceives. It pretends to be true happiness. It begins as a necessary means of exchange—then suddenly it leads these same human beings into relationships of domination and subjection. It deceives them. It becomes the justification for so many things! When money reduces us to slavery, it devaluates us. It devaluates love by buying it. Fools alone will exchange the humanness of persons for gold. Only a fool will bribe, corrupt, devour—purchasing empty air! Fools alone will build on their gold—building on air! Fools alone will bend their necks to the yoke of gold, with its retinue of war and blood, exploitation and injustice—serving the wind! You are marrying money. You are clinging to a plank that cannot save you. You are so sure of the power it gives you! And all the while what you are really doing is entrusting yourself to something that devaluates you. For you are a human being!

"No servant can serve two masters." How unintelligent, to harvest the grain and then put it under lock and key. Grain is for bread, and for next season's sowing. Greed is ridiculous! Money is to be spent, shared. Life is made for rebirth, invention, germination. Money imprisons you, locks you up in the vicious circle of its allure. Money is insidious as a snake.

"Make friends for yourselves through your use of this world's goods. . . ." Money is at your service. It is not your owner. Live for a society of quality, and not quantity. Restore money to its function of exchange, work for the coming of a world built on solidarity, and not on monopolies, domination and exploitation.

Jesus speaks, and the world collapses. Will the children of light be perceptive enough to grasp the urgency of the decision to be made? Will they be astute enough to invent the necessary reaction? Tomorrow will be too late. A choice hangs in the balance. We should like to be able to escape that choice, but it is inescapable. Either we shall serve God and neighbor, or we shall serve money and ourselves.

■

Let us pray that God may turn human hearts toward genuine values.

Let us pray for all who have political, financial, or economic responsibilities.

That justice and the common good may guide their decisions and their actions, we pray to the Lord.

Lord, hear our prayer.

Let us pray for the intellectual community—our scientists, our scholars, our thinkers, our spiritual leaders.

That truth, and the happiness of all men and women, may direct their decisions and actions, we pray to the Lord.

Lord, hear our prayer.

Let us remember too those who live lives of bare subsistence—all the forgotten, all who are excluded from the common welfare.

That a more equal distribution of goods and a more just recompense for their labor may be the reward of their toil, we pray to the Lord.

Lord, hear our prayer.

Finally, let us pray for the church that God wishes to have poor, and a servant.

That the church in the world may be a parable of sharing, let us pray to the Lord.

Lord, hear our prayer.

■

Lord, our Father,
you give your gifts superabundantly,
in all extravagance.

In giving us the life of your Son
in this eucharist,
you commit us to live by the same love as he.
Grant that we may be the faithful stewards
of whatever part of your Reign you entrust to us,
that, one day, we may enter into possession
of the heritage you have promised.

MONDAY OF THE 32ND WEEK

ON GUARD!

Titus 1:1-9: Like the other pastoral epistles, the Letter to Titus reflects the situation of the church at the close of the first century. Most of the apostles were gone now, and the threat represented by the teachings of the Gnostics had occasioned the need for a more highly developed church organization.

Titus is in charge of the church of Crete. Here he receives instructions for appointing "presbyters"—"elders"—in each locality. As we know, Moses appointed seventy lieutenants to assist him in his task, and the Old Testament presents the institution of the "elders" as the prolongation of their role. Thus each Jewish community was headed by a group of men chosen because of their knowledge of the Torah. And so we see why the letter stresses the presbyters' teaching role: they must be attached to the teaching they have received, and honor it by leading a worthy life. Like the bishop, an elder must be "married only once"—literally, "a man [husband?] of one woman [wife?]," an expression destined for a wild odyssey at the hands of the exegetes. Is the author insisting on conjugal fidelity, or is he forbidding second marriages? Opinions are divided here. To complicate the question still further, Jewish and pagan inscriptions understand the expression in the sense of a particularly ardent married love.

Like Psalm 112, *Psalm 24* lists the conditions for admittance into the temple.

Luke 17:1-6: (See p. 153.)

■

"Be on your guard . . ."! Who made faith the dreary repetition of a rote lesson, an insipid compliance with a set of rules? Faith is a battle. It is a battle with ourselves, and hope wins out over a fatalism that is trying to get us to say, "What's the use? I'm not going to change." Faith is a battle with human wisdom: our welcome of God's word gives us the strength to proclaim, in the face of the pessimism of our age: "The earth is in travail. . . ." "En garde!" cried the heroes of the novels of cape and sword. It was their cry of defense, a cry of vigilance and enthusiasm, the cry of a life threatened but sure to conquer.

"En garde!" To maintain a watchful faith is to confront the common thinking that makes God an idol, an image rigidly fixed once and for all. To maintain a watchful faith means abandoning the limits of our imagination and discovering the God who steps out of his eternity to create something genuinely new. To maintain a watchful faith means to smash to smithereens the futile nostalgia of a paradise lost, and dare to believe in the possible, dare allow ourselves to be drawn toward the unforeseeable. To maintain a watchful faith is to cast far from us the burdensome mantle of a specious holiness built by our own efforts and accomplishments. It means presenting ourselves to God stripped of every assurance, that God may first of all erase the nightmares of our guilt. To maintain a watchful faith is to refuse to be distracted by the slogans of a world that thinks it can build fellowship by its own resources. It means fixing our gaze on the new day in whose first faint glimmers we see God creating on the horizon of our struggles.

"En garde!" With a bit of faith, we could revolutionize our relationship with God, discover our future, accept the holiness offered us, build a genuine fellowship, a true communion of sisters and brothers! "If you had faith the size of a mustard seed. . . ."

■

God our Father,
watch over our little faith
    lest our hope fail.
By your Spirit, come,
    rekindle the flame our eagerness
    spent in the quest of other wealth than you.
May your word, sown in our hearts,
    spring up and bear fruit,
to set our world spinning the other way,
    and inaugurate eternity.

■

Behold the seed of eternity in our hearts, Lord:
    the Body of your Son!

May the power of your Spirit steep our lives,
snatching them from the limits of our time
        and expanding them to endless ages.

∎

Be praised, God our Father.
for entrusting us with the body and blood of your Son,
        the sign of your approaching Reign.
Fruit of the earth and the work of human hands,
        these are the firstfruits in our own times
        of the age to come.

May they be our food and drink
        all along the way that leads
        to everlasting ages.

TUESDAY OF THE 32ND WEEK

THE "MORE" OF FAITH

Titus 2:1–8, 11–14: It is a certainty of faith that Christ gave himself for the church. Upon this certainty must be built the community witness, which emerges from the testimony of an exemplary life. We note the insistence on family virtues, and the role in the broader family of the "elder," who bears the responsibility of binding all into one by means of his teaching.

Psalm 37, alphabetical in its composition, is a collation of disparate pieces on the theme of the just and the wicked.

Luke 17:7–10: (See p. 155.)

∎

"Lord, increase our faith" (Lk 17:5). They have asked for more faith as someone might apply for supplemental security income. They have spoken of faith like laborers demanding better working conditions. Jesus' response is a reproach, and a challenge: "If you had faith the size of a mustard seed, you could say to this sycamore, 'Be uprooted and transplanted into the sea,' and it would obey you"!

348

Jesus dumfounds his disciples. He is determined to eradicate the mistaken notion they have of faith. Believing may not be what they think it is. Faith is not primarily a conviction that can be lost or strengthened. Faith is more than a trust, a fidelity to be maintained come hell or high water. "When you have done all you have been commanded to do, say, 'We are useless servants. We have done no more than our duty.' "

Faith is welcoming the gift that God makes of himself. This is why it is always a beginning, always creation. The faithfulness of the believer is not the loyalty of the beast of burden, which simply plods ahead in the general direction of its nose, with nary a new thought in its mind. Faith is birth. It overthrows the order, the regime of things to which the astonished disciples are accustomed.

The servant will be invited to recline at table. The Master will wash the feet of his astonished disciples. After all, faith is more than respect for a duty which would only confirm the order of things. Faith has the power to inaugurate a new world. God is no longer a potentate to be respected, but a friend to be loved. Religion is no more a code of rules to be observed, but a communion to be invented. Law is no longer a list of precepts to be kept and prohibitions to be observed, but the blueprint for a new way of life, which is always a step ahead of anything that can be said. Prayer is more than merchandise; it is thanksgiving for gifts received, and the consecration of a life bestowed in return. By faith an order is instituted that must nevertheless be continually sought, in the expectation of the coming of what will be established forever: the Reign of God.

FROM WEDNESDAY OF THE 32ND WEEK

TO WEDNESDAY OF THE 33RD WEEK

Face to Face with the Coming Reign
God, Friend of humanity, Father of the poor,
God whom no one has ever seen or contemplated,
be blessed for Jesus Christ—
for the fascinating glance that heals our leprosy,
and the breath with which he gives body to our flesh.
He has walked the pathways of humanity,

---

his hands lifting the legions of the paralyzed
    that they might walk on to the land of freedom.
Be blessed for the words of grace you have uttered,
    the echo of your mercy,
    the secret revealed, the good news proclaimed.
Be blessed for the One who has become your face,
    your compassion for us,
    and, for you, our face and our suffering.
By him you inaugurate a festive celebration without end,
    you who consecrate us in him:
upon us you place his mark,
    you who make his Spirit to dwell in our hearts.

Be blessed, God who loves us!
In your Son, we are dead to sin
    and alive for you.
In him our old world has departed,
    and from the refuse heap of ourselves
    you raise up a new land.

The table of the covenant is set.
Publicans feast,
    the lame leap for joy,
    and lepers, their fresh faces all aglow, join in the dance!

Father of Jesus Christ and our Father,
with Christ we offer you our world,
such as our eyes behold it still—
    unfinished, disfigured by fear,
    torn by discord,
    sick of their despair.
Be mindful of those who toil to rebuild its beauty!
May the hour come, for them and for us,
    when we can give you thanks eternally
    through Jesus Christ,
    who is your tenderness
    and our love.

LESSON FROM A HERETIC

Titus 3:1-7: Titus 3:3–8 is regarded by some as a prayer echoing the liturgical life of the primitive church. In any case the passage extols God's work of salvation: Has he not freely saved us, pouring out his Spirit upon us in superabundance in our baptism?

Psalm 23 is well chosen. The church has always regarded it as the baptismal psalm par excellence.

Luke 17:11–19: (See p. 158.)

■

A leper! The very word struck fear into the hearts of the people. To the affliction of the illness, culture must add the oppression of social exclusion. Protect the cities and villages! The Dantesque illness had been erected into a symbol of the wrath of God. The leprosy of the body was regarded as the reflection of a heart rotten with sin, and the ban of the human community was simply the acknowledgement of the divine excommunication.

The pitiful little group that called to Jesus from a distance was made up of nine Jews and a Samaritan. For centuries, a fierce hatred had kept these two peoples apart. But in the case at hand, a common distress had united the abandoned. An outcast is an outcast.

Ten lepers cleansed! Of shapeless refuse, Jesus re-creates beauty, and of towering hatred, love. He obliterates humiliating labels, and refashions distorted faces and disfigured hearts.

Now occurs the most astonishing scene in the drama. Suddenly the Samaritan is alone again. The Jews have left him. Healed, they are on their way to the priests for the long ceremonies that will permit them to reclaim their place in Jewish society. And the Samaritan is once more the outcast. But he "came back praising God in a loud voice." The stranger par excellence, the lowest of the detested, the arch-heretic, has penetrated the secret of the Good News. The one who had seemed most estranged from God has uncovered the mystery of the gospel. The most decayed of all human beings sees himself regarded, respected and loved. No more will a twisted, terror-stricken body prevent him from growing tame, sociable. He stands erect again. Ashamed of his wounds, depressed at the hatred of his brothers, isolated at the door of a society

351

of "saved," the Samaritan has felt the tenderness of a glance, the welcome of open arms, the knowing wink of a God who is a friend. With a bound he returns to the wellspring of his resurrection, exploding with gratitude and singing his thanksgiving at the top of his lungs—totally ignoring the scandalized fervor of his nine companions, the hostile astonishment of the priests or the guffaws of the bystanders.

The foreigner, the excluded one, the "no account"—has he any right to salvation? Luke loved the Samaritans. They had welcomed the Good News of Jesus in the years of Christianity's first expansion. The history of the young church bears the same testimony as Jesus' preaching: all can be cleansed and be grateful for it, even those who are told that they have been denied the right to enter the Reign of God. The gospel does not surprise us when it shows us Jesus welcoming ten human beings who have been excommunicated for their leprosy. It flabbergasts us when it places us before the logic of the Reign. No longer in Jerusalem, nor on Mount Gerizim, is God to be worshiped! The hour has come to "worship in Spirit and truth" (Jn 4:24). No, the place and locus of thanksgiving to God is henceforth . . . Jesus himself.

Jesus departs for Jerusalem. There he will be crucified, in disfigurement beyond any leprosy. The Samaritan leper has already recognized God's glory in this face. And suddenly God will raise his Messenger, "so that at Jesus' name every knee must bend in the heavens, on the earth, and under the earth" (Phil 2:10). You who think you are a stranger, you who feel rejected, forget not the lesson of the gospel. Prostitutes will lead the just into the Reign of God, and the first of us to burst through the door of the new world will be a crucified insurrectionist.

■

One thing you may rely on. The Lord's love is from everlasting to everlasting. He restores the universe, and makes all things new.

For those disfigured by selfishness, that they may rediscover the joy of love, we pray to the Lord.

Lord, hear our prayer.

For those consumed with a thirst for power or a concern for appearances, we pray to the Lord.

Lord, hear our prayer.

For those who toil for a more beautiful, a greater human being: for physicians and social workers, for scientists and political leaders, and for all who struggle, humbly and day by day, for justice and peace, we pray to the Lord.

Lord, hear our prayer.

Let us not forget, in God's sight, those who suffer from illness, or are under

suspicion, or who must live with the pressure of insinuation or calumnies.
We pray to the Lord.

Lord, hear our prayer.

For those whose confidence is undermined by the hardheartedness of others,
for all who find neither understanding nor words of healing, we pray to
the Lord.

Lord, hear our prayer.

God our Father,
you are the God of deliverance and salvation.
Grant that we may follow your Son.
For if we die with him, with him we shall live,
and a new world will be born,
to endure forever.

THURSDAY OF THE 32ND WEEK

HARNESSING OUR TIME

Philemon 7–20: The letter to Philemon is intended not only for its addressee
but for the "church that meets in your house" (v. 2)—probably the church of
Colossae, of which Philemon seems to have been an eminent member. It was
customary in the primitive church for individuals to make their homes
available for the liturgical assemblies, and Philemon was one of the ones who
did so.

Like the rest of the ancient church, the apostle is frequently the target of
criticism today for his alleged myopia with regard to the social evil of slavery.
But this is not only to forget the economic foundations of antiquity, it ignores
the message of the Letter to Philemon—precisely one which must have
sounded strange indeed in the ancient world—concerning relationships
between Christian slaves and slaveowners. "Welcome him as you would me,"
Paul writes. To the apostle, this slave is a brother, as he hopes he will be for
Philemon as well. We are dealing with a direct application of the reflection
addressed by Paul to the Galatians: "There does not exist among you . . .
slave or freeman. . . . All are one in Christ Jesus" (Gal 3:28).

Psalm 146 is regarded as an individual hymn, made up of elements long
independent. The verses retained by the liturgy form a psalm of congratulation
addressed to the faithful who had come to take part in the temple liturgy. That
Yahweh is on the side of the oppressed is a certainty of long standing with the

Jews, dating from their liberation from slavery in Egypt. Thus it is an evangelical certainty as well. Christians, bear witness!

Luke 17:20–25: (See p. 161.)

■

"Make your day to appear, and the time of grace!" How very impatient we are! How insistent our prayer! And how strong, too, is the temptation to designate the day before its time, and imprison this grace. We are ever ready to cry out, "It is 'here' or 'there.' " We should like to be able to fix a term to history, we should like to be able to describe with certitude the signs of the coming of the Reign of God. And suddenly we are told that the Reign of God does not come in a visible manner. We are sent back to our "today"—precisely to the becoming of the Reign. We are returned to the ambiguity of its coming in everyday life, its growth in human history. No one can tell the day or the hour. We are condemned to harness our own time, for it is here and now that the term of salvation history, its completion and its meaning, actually come.

We must "tame" the history of salvation. It takes time to make a human being, it takes time for the day to pierce the night. We share this human waiting, this human "disappointment." With the rest of humanity, we must experience our weakness. "You will long to see one day of the Son of man but will not see it"! We know all the barriers that we erect against despair. We try, with the rest of our race, to conjure forth the stars that presage the day. We want to keep on living. We search, invent, love, listen, cry out and discover. Our hope is fashioned of no other flesh than that of the hopes of all human kind. Harnessing time, taming our present moment, begins with making humanity's long journey to a better future our own.

But it also means allowing the light of another time to reach us—the light that "will be like the lightning that flashes from one end of the sky to the other." We have a hymn: "This day we feel the dawn—let not the winds of night quench in us the fire that gleams as that night departs!" And here is the password that tells why we were made: "Today." We have no faintest idea of the trembling that will come upon humanity when it enters God's glory. And yet we feel something of that palpitation even now. For, from the depths of our paths of night, we perceive the reflection of that glory: in an occasional love stronger than discord, in a justice that vanquishes selfishness, in a peace more vibrant than disunion, in a joy that erases anguish.

And suddenly the questioning of women and men joins our own supplication, in the lisping of faith: The day of God, the day that will renew heaven and earth . . . will come, yes, it will come!

■

In a world weary of injustice,
    Lord, may we not give in to sleep.
Raise us up,
keep us watchful
    to see the dawn of the day of your Christ:
for he comes today,
as he shall come tomorrow and forever.

■

Lord our God, we bring you our prayer,
    the token of our watchfulness.
As you have divided among us
    the bread that upholds our hope,
hold us erect, keep us ever on our feet,
    watchful for the coming of your Reign,
    the new world of the everlasting ages.

FRIDAY OF THE 32ND WEEK

THE BREACH
2 John 4–9: The scope of the shorter Johannine letters is identical with that of the first: to reinforce the bond of Christians in the face of heresies that threaten the unity of the church by attacking the incarnation of God's Son. Indeed, the First Letter of John may actually be a later composition than these little epistles, which are addressed only to a local church and testify to the appearance of a new heresy. First John is addressed to all of the churches of Asia, where the new infection has become a veritable gangrene. Second John seems to anticipate the themes that will govern the great letter: the urgency of mutual love, and the profession of the creed of the church.

Psalm 119 proclaims blessed all those who cling to the word of the Lord.

Luke 17:26–37: (See p. 163.)

■

They were eating, drinking, marrying. . . . Well, what do you expect? Isn't that what life's all about? And we shrug the whole thing off. "No, no, nothing has changed," goes the old ditty (still up-to-date!).

They were eating, drinking, marrying. . . . The world kept on turning, more or less well—around and around, without a future. Until the day Noah boarded the ark. He had been specially chosen by God, he had obeyed—and the shock waves of the breach he wrought are still reverberating. In a world closed in on itself, appeared the utter novelty of a brand-new beginning. God would remake the face of the earth! Once more he would divide the dry land from the waters, and cause to appear in a pacified sky an arc of light to divide the day from the dark.

God cleaves the hellish circle of human history, this history of ours ever folded back upon itself, this history bereft of either desire or novelty. God calls Noah, and behold, the ark shapes a new humanity. Here on the carousel of our daily existence, we hear God's call, and suddenly the future is upon us. Salvation history occurs today where we refuse to side with "fate," wherever any one of us, hoping against hope, stays on the alert for an opportunity to take one step forward. There will be men in the fields, women at the grindstone. Some will be taken, others left. Some will hear the word, others will already be dead.

They were eating, they were drinking, they were marrying. . . . Stop the merry-go-round! Do not be swept away in the current. You are women and men raised from the dead. Up, sisters and brothers, for the day of God dawns!

■

Our world turns on.
Come, God our Father,
break the circle
of our futureless histories!
Open them to a new life
here and hereafter.

SATURDAY OF THE 32ND WEEK

SHE'LL BE THE DEATH OF ME!
3 John 5–8: These few verses simply register the zeal with which Gaius has assisted the itinerant missionaries. The rest of the letter consists in sparks

from the polemics between its author, who was in charge of various local communities, and the head of one of these communities, a certain Diotrephes, who was demonstrating insubordination and opposing the young church's mission.

Psalm 112, one of the alphabetical psalms, was used in receiving pilgrims who had come to the temple, and lists the conditions for admittance to the sanctuary.

Luke 18:1–8: (See p. 165.)

■

Everyone knows a woman who refuses to give up. In fact, the French have a saying, "What woman wishes, God wishes." Hear the decision of the judge. "I am going to settle in her favor or she will end by doing me violence." She'll downright do me in! To the Christians of the first communities, surprised and puzzled to see God's judgment delayed, Luke declares: Stay on guard! Do not tire of waiting! Never fear, God will bring his work to its conclusion.

The longsuffering of the church is in the image of God's longsuffering, God's patience. The Reign of God is already coming to light, but, as we say, "Don't hold your breath." True, that Reign is even now God's eternal "today." Still, God has all eternity before him to fashion the face of our earth!

"Will not God then do justice to his chosen . . . ?" Jesus' parables are most creative. In recounting this parable, Jesus carries his hearers immeasurably beyond the bare details of the story. The judge will "settle in her favor," merely; while God will "do justice." By the time Jesus gets to the point, the decision of the unjust judge is forgotten. When the Bible says that God "does justice," it is proclaiming that God restores order, renews, makes-just. Far from suggesting raw, arbitrary power, so prone to oppressing, "justice" in the Bible means fulfillment, perfection, righteousness and right in full bloom. "I tell you," Jesus says —God will keep his promise! Watch in hope. Turn history around! Make it face the future!

Sisters and brothers, when we commemorate the happening that is Jesus Christ, when we celebrate the event of Easter, we give meaning and significance both to human history as a whole and to our own personal history. We focus them both. No longer are they headed just "somewhere." Now they are moving toward their fulfillment. We are not locked into a pseudo-history that consists only in starting over again— and again and again, ever in the same way. We are caught up in a living adventure, and it moves from start to start. Ours is the task of stopping history from going around in circles.

"Will not God then do justice to his chosen . . . ?" Our loves are still stained by selfishness, even today. We know this. But in faith, every deed of love becomes the vehicle of eternal life. Our efforts on behalf of justice and peace, fellowship and freedom, are as yet only paltry tokens of God's project for humanity. But they are being performed on the construction site of the new world.

"Will not God then do justice to his chosen who call out to him . . . ?" Brothers and sisters, be vigilant. Wait in hope. You glimpse this new world in your prayer even now. Even now you turn history around till it faces its future. Those who do not grow weary in their call for a new universe in their prayer and in their lives, God will justify, make to be righteous, and fulfill as human beings. The world is full of impossibilities. We can so easily say, "What's the use?" There is more than enough distress, injustice and violence in the world for us to lose heart. But prayer sends us straight down the road to God's fulfillments. Prayer magnetizes us, pulling us around till we face God. Pregnant with the future, prayer makes that which will be, germinate in us. Surely we do not wish to succumb to some manner of spiritual confinement. God is determined to swell this human life and human world beyond measure!

"Will not God then do justice to his chosen who call out to him . . . ?" When Jesus points us in the direction of God's fulfillments, he knows perfectly well that our existence will be split in two. "Wake up, and pray that you may not be subjected to the trial" (Lk 22:46). Prayer shows us God's horizon, and stirs our lives to the activity that will realize our happy presentiment. Prayer will always revive, reanimate, a person of the future. For prayer is the Easter song. Prayer protests, grows impatient, goads, builds. To pray is to create, in the mute, humble expectancy of the universe. To pray is to create life by shaping it anew. Yes, at the very heart of our burdens.

■

We call on you, Lord.
For we know you can hear and answer.
Hear us! Listen to what we say!
Keep us as the apple of your eye.
Be our refuge.
Protect us.
And may your grace be upon us.

■

God of the faithful promise,
by this communion
    you grant us a participation in the Spirit of Christ.
Therefore we beseech you:
when we are weighed down by fatigue,
    and discouragement crouches in wait for our step,
come, revive our strength:
    increase our faith.

MONDAY OF THE 33RD WEEK

TOWARD THE LIGHT

Revelation 1:1–5, 2:1–5: The Apocalypse of Saint John, or Book of
Revelation, is the last book of the Bible. The Greek word *apokalypsis* means
an "unveiling," a "revelation." Hence the interchangeability of the titles,
"Revelation," and "Apocalypse."

What is being "unveiled" in this book, this particular piece of apocalyptic
literature? This book reveals the heavenly world, the things known to God
alone, especially the end of days. But we must not be misled by expressions
like, ". . . must happen very soon." In the Book of Revelation such
expressions express an urgency, or a depth of meaning, rather than referring
to the future. Christian apocalyptic had an altogether different tenor from that
of its Jewish counterpart. In Christian apocalyptic, the expected "end time"
had already begun, for Christ had risen. In other words, Christian apocalyptic
expresses the eschatological tension of the time of the church. On the one
hand, the Reign of God is already present, and the church appears as the
fulfillment of the prophecies. On the other hand, this Reign has not yet
achieved its full realization, and the church is as a "bridgehead, a colony" of
the coming age. But if it is not yet fully realized, then the Reign can be the
object of revelation. What the Christian visionaries are concerned with, then,
is not the elucidation of the future, since that future has already begun, but a
contemplation of the "sacramental" realities of that Reign.

The intent of the author of Revelation is to occasion a "spiritual awakening."
Not only is the church experiencing persecutions, but certain communities
have lost their first fervor, as we may surmise from the letter addressed "to
the seven churches in the province of Asia. . . ."

First the author cites the three divine persons, one by one. The formula, "who is and who was and who is to come," expanding the "I am" of the Book of Exodus, denotes the Father. Here the emphasis is on the eschatological nature of the Lord's coming. Christ is likewise designated by a ternary formula, recalling his passion (his testimony), resurrection and exaltation. The Spirit is viewed in the fullness of the "seven spirits."

But the interest of the letters goes beyond that of their designated addressees. These letters are intended for the whole Christian people. They convey both praise and blame, and are addressed to the churches by a Christ appearing under traits borrowed from various apocalyptical sources. The seven stars, like the seven lampstands of gold, may stand for the seven churches. The stars precisely as held in the hand of Christ would symbolize his sovereignty.

The first letter is addressed to Ephesus, the metropolis of Asia, and reproaches it with a cooling of its fervor that could cost it its rank.

Psalm 1 is a paraphrase of a song of congratulation. It was later reworked by a scribe as a piece of wisdom literature, through the introduction of the classic antithesis of the "two ways."

Luke 18:35–43: (See p. 167.)

■

Jesus draws near Jericho, the city of palms, the oasis amidst the desert. Here, in ancestral times, the people had entered the Land of Promise. But today Jericho is the city of the promise become reality, the place of the covenant become tangible. As Jesus draws near Jericho, someone calls out: "Jesus . . . have pity on me!" Here is the figure of our distress, here is the cry of our waiting.

For—is it not true?—I think I know where I am going, and yet, when all is said and done, I am a road leading nowhere. Blinded by mirages and loud advertising, I live by slogans. Blinded by desires I cannot govern, I am simply swept along by my fancies. Blinded by the fear that I shall not fully exist, I try to squeeze the last drop out of life. And I am alone, like someone blind, lost in a crowd of persons unconcerned with my existence. Others surround me, yes, but their visages remain closed to me. I look them straight in the eye—and see only the reflection of my own indifference. Why this veil of night before my eyes? Why this darkness in my heart?

And yet I should surely like to see the light! I should surely like to know who I truly am, who others truly are. I should like to be certain that a great black hole will not suddenly open up in my path and swallow me. "Lord . . . I want to see. . . . Receive your sight. Your faith has healed you." Jesus heals because he is the definitive covenant of God with the earth. "The light shines on in darkness, a darkness that did not overcome it" (Jn 1:5). The blind one becomes the enlightened one. Because Jesus touches us, we know that life does not go down to dust. No, a new light shows all things in their newness. Because Jesus looks upon us as we are, without excusing and without condemning, we can look at ourselves: we can see our sin without false justifications, and see the road that opens before us, with its pitfalls and hopes.

We call out from the roadside. Jesus is passing by, on his way to Jericho. The reversal of our existence, the passage to the world of light, our conversion, begins with this cry. God alone knows the ways that lead to him from deep within us. Our cry is not the cry of one day, it spans our lifetime, for the whole of our existence would not be enough for the accomplishment of this passage. But today, hear God calling to you, begging to touch you along the side of the road. "Do not become discouraged," he seems to say. "I do hold this against you, though: you have turned aside from your early love. Keep firmly in mind the heights from which you have fallen. Repent, and return to your former deeds."

■

Along our dark pathway,
Lord our God, you come
to find us wandering along a road leading nowhere.
Hear our avowal of frailty.
Transfigure our countenance with splendor.
Lift us up again,
that we may begin anew.
Then lead us to the light
of ages everlasting.

TUESDAY OF THE 33RD WEEK

FESTIVAL
Revelation 3:1–6, 14–22: We observe a progression in the words addressed by Christ to the churches. In the letter to the church of Ephesus, compliments precede reproaches. In that to the community of Sardis, the order is the opposite. And the letter to Laodicea voices nothing but reproaches. And so we

have some idea of the relative degree of fervor maintained in the various communities.

The church of Sardis had begun the Christian journey all enthusiastic. Now it finds itself poised at the edge of the abyss. For Sardis God's Reign may come as a bitter surprise! Christ encourages the community, promising eternal life to those who are victorious.

The community of Laodicea is one rung lower on the ladder of fervor. What delusions of grandeur, in a church that is only lukewarm. Christ's letter to his followers contrasts the material prosperity of their mighty banking center with its spiritual impoverishment. It is high time this city recalled where the true light is to be found! For, if converted, Christians there will share once more in the Christ's victory.

Psalm 15 was used in the liturgies of entry into the temple. The pilgrim requested admittance (v. 1), and the priest responded with a list of the requirements for presenting oneself to God in his holy sanctuary.

Luke 19:1–10: (See p. 169.)

■

The scorned, the misjudged, the "good for nothing," are so often the stars of the theater of the gospel! Today the spotlight is on a tax collector. Now, here is someone who will gouge you out of house and home if he can! Curse of all "respectable" hearts, object of the sneering contempt of all society, Zacchaeus is a "publican." People don't care for publicans. Publicans aren't very savory company. Labeled, judged, rejected by "good society"—especially by the passionate devotees of the law of Moses—little Zacchaeus could very well banish any fantasy he may have had of somehow getting to the front of the crowd to catch a glimpse of the celebrated prophet. For the believing elite, Zacchaeus was unworthy of Jesus, and that was that!

"Zacchaeus, hurry down. I mean to stay at your house today"! We readily imagine the wonder-worker's fans squabbling over who might touch him, vying to catch his eye, jockeying for position in the hope of having some word, some deed addressed to themselves personally. Ah, there were plenty of "good" people to receive the Master; it went without saying that he would presently be flashily welcomed in the home of one of the "righteous." Then would the feast begin! So there would surely be a banquet, with the attendant parlor patter and artificial hilarity, all soon to be forgotten. . . . "Zacchaeus, hurry down. I mean to stay at your house today"!

The episode is simply . . . astounding reality. And the secrets of encounter are revealed. Yes, a feast there will be—to put it mildly! The feast to be celebrated today will be the festival of a God who has encountered a human heart, a poor heart, poor enough to receive the astonishing News! The tireless Pilgrim has found a depository for his secret. "Here I stand, knocking at the door. If anyone hears me calling and opens the door, I will enter his house and have supper with him, and he with me." Yes, there will be a festival, but it will be the festival of a human creature who has discovered the truth of his being. For a new Zacchaeus has just been born. He is still short, still a tax-collector, still the practitioner of a despised profession. But now he can open himself to the insane norms of the gospel: not to renounce his superfluities, but to give away half of everything he owns!

Festival? Indeed! But the soulless banquet of paltry human anticipation will be replaced by an impromptu supper at which each guest will partake of what the others have brought. The diners will have the strange experience of the absence of wealth at their table, together with a superabundance of love freely offered. The one the righteous have excommunicated will become their friend and neighbor. "This is what it means," Jesus says, "to be a son of Abraham." He too is one of the family!

"Today salvation has come to this house. . . ." The time of promise gives way to the time of salvation. At Jericho, gateway to the Land of Promise, the covenant between God and human beings becomes reality. The gladness of the end-time becomes the gift of today. What has always been evident for God begins to be perceptible to us. How can we doubt, when Jesus goes in search of the outcast, the excluded—whoever no longer dare to hope even in themselves?

The moment of encounter is the moment of discovery. We discover ourselves in the glance, the regard of others. The judgments of our neighbor are so many mirrors reflecting our image. And Zacchaeus has experienced this truth in an electrifying manner today. Someone had looked at him, regarded him, without contempt or reproach! And he was awakened to himself. Could it be possible? Could he be lovable to someone? "I mean to stay at your house today!" Behold the moment of faith, the moment of encounter—the moment we discover what we are for God.

Brothers and sisters, know this: God sees right through us. And this is why he can never again look upon us without seeing his well-beloved Son. Quick, open the door! He wants to live right here—with you! In his glance, you will read the truth of life. "Today salvation has come to this house . . ."!

■

When love seduces us
    like a rush of wildfire,
    Lord, come dwell with us.

When love frightens us
    like too strong a wind,
    Lord, come dwell with us.

When love prunes us
    like an attentive vinedresser,
    Lord, come dwell with us.

Today love has awakened us
    like a fragile hope.
    Lord may we dwell with you
    forever and ever.

WEDNESDAY OF THE 33RD WEEK

FIDELITY

Revelation 4:1–11: The style of chapter 4 is more overtly apocalyptic. In fact, we may regard chapters 4 through 11 as a kind of preparation for the account of the great and final battle, in which the antagonists will be God and Satan (beginning in chapter 12). Thus the sacred writer invites us to join him, after a vision by way of a prelude, in a celestial liturgy, doubtless a transposition to heaven of a contemporary earthly one.

Carefully selected prophetic reminders (from Ez 1 and 10) recall the creative power of the One seated on the throne. The four living creatures, identified by Irenaeus of Lyon as representing the evangelists, symbolize the created world. Like the seraphim of the vision of Isaiah, they have six wings, and they extol in song the divine holiness. As always in the Bible, the "elders" will be those responsible for the people of God. Beyond this it is difficult to identify them. Might they represent the twenty-four priestly classes of 1 Chronicles 24? Or might they symbolize the Old and New Testaments (representing twelve prophets and twelve apostles)? At all events, they pledge their allegiance to God the creator by casting their crowns at the foot of his throne.

Psalm 150, the last of the Psalter, is a grand invitation to praise.

Luke 19:11–28: (See p. 172.)

■

Bury your money six feet under—and what do you think will grow, a money tree? Unproductive money promptly loses its value—inflation aside! But the parable, which speaks of God and his Reign, asserts that we have received something a great deal more important than money. God has entrusted us with his Word, his grace, his sacraments, his love.

Now, if you bury love or grace, when the time comes to restore them to one who has the right to them, what will they be worth? Unproductive love is worthless. And honoring the memory of Jesus Christ does not mean raising a monument to his glory! Our fidelity bears no resemblance to the preservation of a legacy—even a religious one!

What the Lord expects from us is that we return him grace for grace. But notice, grace is not an object, a museum piece, an insurance policy. Grace is life, God's life in us, God's Spirit. God has entrusted us with the best he has. He expects us to give him our best in return. What is a faithful love but a love capable of inventing life, instead of freezing with fear?

"I was afraid . . ." say useless servants. This is their excuse. This too is their fault, their sin. They are afraid. They are stubborn, they are tenacious, but their brand of steadfastness is worthless, for it must avow its utter incapacity to invent pathways of grace to the world to come. Fidelity is altogether different from what people say it is. We must not reduce it to the equivalent of keeping watch with the dead, or decorating tombs with flowers. Our fidelity is faithfulness in a movement and a risk. It is a fidelity on its feet.

Be faithful as God is faithful. Ceaselessly he is the creative God: "By your will [all things] came to be and were made!" God maintains all things in life and being, and by him all things awaken to a renewed future. God takes the risk of life. And you who have delivered yourself over to the Spirit without a very clear notion of where he would lead you, you shall hear the word of your Lord that will cause your everlasting life: "You are an industrious and reliable servant. . . . Come, share your master's joy!" (Mt 25:21)

■

Lord, grant that we may find our joy
    in our fidelity;
for it is lasting, profound happiness
    to serve with boldness
    the Creator of every good thing.

■

God, who places your trust in your human creatures,
    blessed be your name!
In our clumsy hands
    you have placed the earth and the skies,
    to design there the traits of your countenance.
Then place in our hearts, wounded with fear,
    your superabundant grace
    and the revelation of your love!

Be blessed! For your spirit releases our fears,
that in boldness and timidity alike
    we may return you grace for grace:
    our life, with our gratitude.

FROM THURSDAY OF THE 33RD WEEK

TO SATURDAY OF THE 34TH WEEK

He Comes!

The Book of Revelation is not a collection of prophecies a la Nostradamus.
Nor has a Christian reading of this book ever mistaken it for such, throughout
twenty centuries of history. It is not a book of enigmas, then. It is a
"revelation," precisely. True, it is filled with images. But so is the rest of the
Bible. After all, God can perfectly well speak to us in images rather than in
abstract concepts or juridical definitions. The seer of Revelation is attempting
to make us understand the history of the world and the church not inside-out
and backwards, as we have it, but as that history really is—the way God sees
it. We are invited to contemplate our living experience—what we regard as
the truth of history—as something far more than that: as the visible flowering

of a deeper reality. We go behind the appearance of the passing world to discover the face of new heavens and a new earth.

In the Book of Revelation, then, we behold the world to come, the object of Jesus' so-called eschatological teachings. The latter may be obscure in many of its details, but they are crystal clear on two points: that Jesus is Lord of the future, and that, at the proper moment, the entire content of human history will find its fulfillment and meaning. At the moment he sees the destiny of his people sealed, at the moment of his leaving his own in the midst of this people, Jesus opens to them a future. Thus Jesus engenders the church that will pursue his mission after his death. And he knows that this is the church he will find again when he returns as the Son of man.

Behold the church, God's sign for today's times: a church poor, deprived, so cruelly treated by history's uncertainties—and yet decked in the marvellous mantle of the heavenly Jerusalem! It is the church amidst its battles—but it is nearing the end, its term and goal. The line that extends from Alpha to Omega tells the meaning of the history of the world in the church and the church in the world. Then behold the epic of Christian hope. Enter into this history: "The Spirit and the Bride say, 'Come!' " (Rev 22:17). Enter the fray! Join the action, and know, even now, the joy that will last an eternity.

■

Living God, you have not made life this wondrous wellspring
to drain to the bowels of the earth
and be lost forever!
Fecundate by your Spirit
our too burdensome humanity.
Make life explode
in these hearts of stone,
that, deep within us, its fantastic spring may steep
the germ that will bear its fruit tomorrow.

■

Father of heaven and earth,
it is good for us to praise you on this day—
the day that brings us ever nearer the eternal morn!
For you will not allow to sink back into the night
the universe you created
to gleam with the radiance of your light!

Yes, be blessed, God of hope,
    Creator of the future,
    Father of the world to come,
    Dayspring of peace in this world's night!
As the shy spring wells up in the hollow of the hill,
    so do we desire you.
    Come quench our thirst!
As the friend recognizes a presence
    that speaks heart to heart,
    so we stammer:
Come, Lord Jesus!

And as the hour draws near,
and we take our stations
    to watch for the One who has come, who comes,
    and who is to come on the clouds of heaven
    to sweep over the face of the earth
    and be its passage to the age of tomorrow—
revive our memory,
that we may celebrate the Passover of the Lord
before we set out once more
    down the long route of this age.

In a night dark as death,
    resounds a cry:
the cry of your Son
    calling to you for life!
Like the first morning,
    like the gleaming nimbus of the first sunrise,
a hope has arisen:
    the Son of man, raised to life!
Before his passage from this world to you,
    he promised to keep his church
    in faith and in love.
Hear, then, most Good Father,
    the cry of your people,
    for it is a cry from their whole heart.
Array the spouse of your Son
    for the eternal banquet.
May she be radiant as a bride
    coming to meet the bridegroom.
May she find the place of her birth,
    which is in your heaven.
Make away with whatever might tarnish her beauty.
Be with the tempted,

gather the lost,
welcome those who come in search of you.
Guide your people:
give them courageous shepherds,
who will walk with gaze fixed on the goal—
the day of your judgment.
Hear the prayer of those you have chosen from out of the world
to be your inheritance.
Thy kingdom come!
For a cry of supplication rises to you
from our earth:
"Come, Lord Jesus!"

THURSDAY OF THE 33RD WEEK

KEY OF HISTORY

Revelation 5:1–10: We are shown a book, with writing both inside and on its cover. The book is sealed. We are likewise shown a lamb, the victim of a sacrifice, but on its feet in the midst of the heavenly assembly. Our curiosity is piqued to the quick. We should like to penetrate both the symbolism of the animal and the secret of the book. And we find that they are interconnected. As the sequel will tell, it is the lamb who will open the seven seals that lock the scroll. For the lamb knows a secret. And this secret, like the book containing it, is in the hands of God.

What is the role of the lamb, then? The lamb stands for a Christ who has died and who has been raised again. Standing erect in the midst of the celestial court, he is Christ Victor, the vanquisher of death.

It was long customary to see in the opening of the seals simply a series of woes to fall upon the earth and presage the imminence of judgment. But this interpretation does not tell the whole story. For when the lamb opens the fifth seal, the visionary sees "under the altar the spirits of those who had been martyred because of the witness they bore to the word of God" (Rev 6:9). These martyrs receive white robes, symbolizing their everlasting share in the life of God himself.

By contrast, when the sixth seal is opened (Rev 6:12–17), a cosmic catastrophe ensues, and the population of the earth flees to hills and caves. In other words, the action of the lamb occasions the formation of two different groups of persons, the first benefitting from the revelation of the secret, the second suffering from it. The latter are plunged in terror. The former, who have testified to God's word, pass from death to life. Must this not be something of an echo of Jesus' declaration, "Whoever acknowledges me before men—the Son of man will acknowledge him before the angels of God" (Lk 12:8)?

Psalm 149 invites us to join our voices to those of the four living creatures and the twenty-four elders to render homage to the Lamb that was slain in sacrifice.

Luke 19:41–44: (See p. 175.)

■

Those who have followed Jesus along the highways and byways of Palestine have shared a unique experience with him, in which God, life, death, human beings and things appear in a new light. His miracles of healing and resurrection, followed by his own resurrection, change the meaning of death, and bestow on life and human activity an undreamed-of dimension. Jesus' followers have gradually discovered that Jesus is "God with us."

Who can open the book of history and read what is written there? Jesus alone, the One who died and was raised again, is the witness of what must come to pass, for he alone is God's last Word on human history. And he is a word of salvation and grace. Christians have no other testimony to give: Jesus is the term of history. Here is the source of the fundamental hope and optimism of our word to the rest of human kind.

Surely, discouragement dogs our steps, as it did those of the first communities. How could these folk hope to resist this raging, implacable persecution at the hands of an empire so high and mighty, so immensely successful? But it was precisely in the moment of that terror, the moment of the threat of total despair, that the hope of the first Christians grew pure and strong. The Book of Revelation presents us with a lightning survey of time present and to come; whereupon the seer, in the light of his faith, declares that Jesus is the Living One, by whose blood all things are redeemed for God. Contemplating Jesus established in his glory, the seer is thunderstruck by his Master's exaltation and sovereignty. Never again shall Christianity be able to tolerate the image of a Jesus shrunken to the measure of our routine, the dimensions of our slender faith.

With Jesus, our hope consists neither in an earthly messianism, nor in the expectation of a Reign of God bereft of any bond with our human history. Our hope immerses us in all of our tasks, but it allows the light of revelation to shine on them and illuminate them. Salvation history is woven of no other tissue than the flesh of our daily adventure. The scroll opened by the Lamb speaks a human language: standing in God's presence now, Jesus is mindful for all eternity of the waiting, the hopes, the words and deeds, the sorrows and joys, that made up his human life.

■

God, Ruler of history,
    open to us the scroll of our worth.
Reveal to us the sense of our life.

May our efforts to build a more humane world
    be inscribed in the project of your everlasting covenant,
and inaugurate, for the women and men of our own times,
    the Reign to last for all eternity.

■

No one will ever lock up your Word
    in the pages of a book.
Lord Jesus, from now till the end of time,
    make your church the open book
    in which humanity will read the unheard of story
    of your endless love—
the Good News of indefatigable hope
    forever and ever!

FRIDAY OF THE 33RD WEEK

YOU MUST PROPHESY!

Revelation 10:8–11: The scrolls we are shown by the Book of Revelation are very different from each other. The first is held shut by seven seals, and when the lamb opens it is revealed the precariousness of a Christian existence caught up in the merciless struggle of Good and Evil. The scroll in chapter ten, by contrast, is small, and lies open, suggesting a more limited, more immediate revelation.

The "assimilation" of the smaller scroll by the visionary accentuates the paradox of the prophetic mission, as enunciated long ago by Jeremiah and Ezekiel. The scroll turns out to be sweet as honey, and the prophet is to consume it, thereby assimilating a content to be shared with his sisters and brothers. But once in his bowels the scroll turns bitter—apparently an allusion to the judgment contained in its pages.

Taken from the great *Psalm 119*, the verses of today's responsorial psalm center on the prophet's search for truth.

Luke 19:45–48: (See p. 177.)

■

"Here, take it and eat it!" We must "digest" the word of God, at length, that it may bear its fruit in us and become the wellspring of a new word for us to speak to the world.

"You must prophesy. . . ." But before you do so, you must hear what you shall have to say. The reason why we seek to contact the word addressed to human beings of bygone centuries is that we wish that word to have its effect on us today. After all, unless God speaks to us today, what do we care whether he spoke in the past? What we so passionately seek in the Bible is how God is accustomed to speak to humanity—how he did so yesterday, and how he does so today. "Take it and eat it!" The experience of revelation is the experience of communion. God's word becomes our word, engendered in the innermost recesses of our being.

"You must prophesy. . . ." You shall utter what you have consumed. We are not alone or abandoned. The Eternal Word has become a living book—living, fleshly testimony of both the creator's solicitude, and ongoing solicitation. Promoted to the status of God's privileged conversation partner, humanity has rediscovered its eminent dignity. We have been healed of our deafness, delivered from its dumbness. The Bible, that alpha and the omega of our anguish and our hopes, is the "miracle book" that speaks to all of us at once while addressing each person individually. And since it is not only the book of human destiny, but a manifestation of God's destiny as well, we believe, with all our faith, that God lives for us, as long as his word lives for us. "You must prophesy . . ."! For revelation abides in the words of women and men possessed by the one Word—digested, and become our Christian substance.

NEW WORLD

Revelation 11:4–12: The vision of the smaller scroll is accompanied by the entry of two witnesses charged with the task of prophesying. Their description is inspired by the famous vision of Zechariah 4:2–14, in the course of which the prophet had contemplated a lampstand—symbol of the divine presence in the temple—and two olive trees—representing the high priest Joshua and the scion of David, Zerubbabel. Both of these personages had been charged, after the return from the Exile, with the immediate reconstruction of the temple, with a view to the restoration of Yahweh's legitimate worship. And Zechariah's vision had become a celebrated messianic prophecy. The author of Revelation has modified the image by introducing a second lampstand. Scholars tend to see, in the twin chandeliers, the image of a church "recapitulating the testimony of Moses and Elias (v. 6), and that of the Christ who died and was raised at Jerusalem." But while verse 5 underscores the power of the testimony, the conclusion of the vision recalls that this witness must sometimes go all the way to martyrdom.

Here we must point out that the Book of Revelation is contemporaneous with the first persecutions unleashed by the Roman Empire. The beast emerging from the abyss (v. 7) can be identified with the persecutor, the state. More generally, along with the dragon and the other beast, it symbolizes the demonic powers. It is called a "false prophet" (Rev 16:13), and its task is to organize societies hostile to God, seducing Christians by its spirit of prevarication. The great city called " 'Sodom' or 'Egypt' " for its idolatry and shamelessness is Jerusalem, the city that murders prophets (Mt 23:37). At the same time it is the capital of the Empire, Rome. Finally, we notice that, after depicting so much persecution, the sacred writer proclaims the victory of the martyrs, in terms reminiscent of the resurrection of the "dry bones" of Ezekiel 37.

Psalm 144 is a composite of pre-existing material. The verses used in today's liturgy sing of the protection with which God has surrounded the Jewish king during his battle with the enemies of his people. Today they celebrate the victory of the faithful witnesses of the gospel.

Luke 20:27–40: (See p. 180.)

■

The Sadducees refused to believe in the resurrection of the dead. For them this dogma was a new invention lacking any basis in tradition.

With the example drawn from the law of Moses—which, good traditionalists that they are, they respect—they hope to set a trap for Jesus. But Jesus puts a damper on their riotous imaginations! The world established by God has nothing whatever to do with the old norms, neither confirming nor contradicting them. What God promises is not the prolongated perfection of a limited world. God's world transcends our categories. Indeed, it is for this reason that this world must be revealed in order to be known at all. It is given. It is gift.

Does this mean that our present world is of no importance in the eyes of God? Then what is the use of our struggling to be faithful in our present lives? Shall we not live altogether differently in the world to come? Why spend our strength and exert our efforts to build a better world today when that world is to be annihilated and replaced tomorrow? Ought we not simply adopt the attitude of the early Christians who looked for the Lord's return in watchfulness and prayer and cared not a whit for the present time? Ought we not simply turn to tomorrow, and reject our earth, this vale of tears? No, in the light of faith, our world is of extraordinary value. It is our parable of tomorrow. Surely there will be a breach between what we build today and what will then be revealed. But the communion of the future will be built according to the blueprint we create in our communions of the present. Peace at the last—which we call reconciliation with God and justice among human beings—is being born on earth, this very minute, in the pangs of someone's courageous labor to change the face of the earth. Tomorrow will be new, yes. But the amazing novelty will be the discovery of the hidden, secret value of the present time. As tomorrow's adult is already entirely present in the child today, even though that child will be radically other by tomorrow, a radically new person—so also the land of God, bestowed in seed in our very "today," will only be the expansion and fulfillment of God's single project for our salvation.

■

God our hope,
*   you gather us together*
*   and your Word reveals the meaning of our existence.*
Open our eyes and our hearts,
*   that we may see beyond the concerns and limitations*
*   of our everyday lives.*
Grant that we may recognize in Jesus
*   the source of all life*
*   now and forever.*

Lord, Ruler of time and history,
    your Reign is not of this world.
You offer it to those
    who persevere to the end in faith.

May your Spirit of love be our daily strength,
that we may await in peace
    the coming of the future age—
    our own world, rebuilt from end to end
    in the ages to come.

MONDAY OF THE 34TH WEEK

SONG OF THE SAVED

Revelation 14:1–3, 4–5: The vision of the lamb in chapter fourteen follows the description of the dragon's two ministers, and precedes the proclamation of the judgment. In this vision the seer shows us a heavenly liturgy, celebrated by one hundred forty-four thousand persons whose state of innocence is the occasion of the author's paean. They are men who have never been defiled by women (v. 4a), and "on their lips no deceit has been found." This biblical language means that the saved have refused to commit idolatry—virginity standing for the opposite of the prostitution of those who embraced the false cults, especially that of the reigning Caesar.

This is a vision of the age of the church. We have seen the lamb, immolated but erect, the figure of a Christ sacrificed and raised again. He is "on Mount Zion"—the locus of encounter between earth and heaven. Thus the lamb is the equivalent of the high priest of the Letter to the Hebrews, at once "accredited with God" and "capable of understanding" where human beings are concerned. He is the norm and standard of all who follow him—these one hundred forty-four thousand marked with the divine seal, but who, living in time, undergo persecution. The martyrs are immolated even as the lamb, but the liturgy that appears in the heavens anticipates their victory. Like the lamb, they belong to the heavenly sphere, and for them the judgment to come will be their passage from death to life. And so the function of the lamb is more profound than we have suspected: the opening of the seals has the further consequence of the constitution of a living community under his sign.

375

Psalm 24 is a lyrical celebration of the devotion of those who "follow the Lamb wherever he goes."

Luke 21:1–4: (See p. 185.)

■

Long has Jesus walked with his disciples, experiencing in his very flesh the opposition his presence constantly provoked. He has confronted evil in all its forms. Now he is in the temple. The time of controversy is over. The rift between Jesus and the captains of established religion is complete, consummated. Presently Jesus will announce the destruction of the temple. At that moment the validity of the legal observances of a corrupt world will perish. The "last times" are upon him, and his adversaries will collapse in rhythm with the world they represent.

Now within the temple area itself, Jesus watches a poor woman cast into the money chest the last penny she had to live on. She has kept nothing for herself. In being widowed she has already lost all human support. Like the foreigner and the orphan, she is the living symbol of the defenseless oppressed. She despoils herself. She is now without anything at all—without material goods, indeed without any special religious qualities to recommend her. She can only crouch behind a pillar and pray, "Lord, I am not worthy to come forward." In the church square, the rich dispense their lavish, showy "generosity," and the scribes push to the front rows. But the widow has nothing more to give.

"Whoever would save his life will lose it . . ." (Lk 9:24). Jesus feels his life ebbing away. He will strip himself, he will keep nothing back. His tunic will be taken from him, and all his garments will be divided among his torturers. Even his death will be stolen from him! He who has sought to speak in the name of God will be sentenced to die as a common insurrectionist. Meanwhile the rest of human beings will continue as they were, secure in their wealth and smug in their good conscience, still believing in a salvation for which they take credit themselves.

But the poor woman Jesus has watched has given all—every penny she had to live on. And in her Jesus sees . . . his own image! She has given all because of her passionate love. Just so, Jesus will give his all that we may recognize the passion God has for us. Only those will enter the Reign who will have learned from the Lamb the song of the saved, the song of those who have followed the Son to the limit of love: one hundred forty-four thousand, a countless multitude. They are the crowd of the poor and the little who have naught to offer in sacrifice but their poor lives—lives surrendered, in the humdrum of every day, to love and mercy. They are the multitude of the poor and the little who think that they have done nothing extraordinary when they have been faithful to the extraordinary regime of God. They have learned the song of the Lamb. In communion with him, they can pass to the world of God. In the deed of this poverty, in the life of all those who are like unto him, Jesus has seen his own destiny.

■

Lord, behold the immense people
of those who have sought you!
Poor in virtue, rich in your mercy,
they abandon themselves to your judgment.
Do not forget—
they have renounced every assurance
but the kindly glance of your Son.
Receive them into your Reign.
For even now, in their self-offering,
they are learning, from your Well-Beloved Son,
the song of triumph.

TUESDAY OF THE 34TH WEEK

TO TRAVERSE HISTORY IN HOPE
Revelation 14:14–19:

Let the nations bestir themselves and come up
to the Valley of Jehoshaphat;
For there I will sit in judgment
upon all the neighboring nations.

Apply the sickle,
for the harvest is ripe;
Come and tread,
for the wine press is full;
The vats overflow,
for great is their malice. [Joel 4:12–13]

It is doubtless these verses of the Old Testament that the author of Revelation has used as his inspiration for his altogether traditional description of the eschatological judgment. Both the Old and the New Testaments frequently depict this judgment in images of harvest and vintage. The case is the same with the figure of the Son of man: while the lamb suggests rather the protection enjoyed by the community of the elect, the Son of man, here as in the letters to the churches, is portrayed with the attributes of royalty and justice.

Hymnic in its style, *Psalm 96* makes use of theophanic elements calculated to underscore Yahweh's royal sovereignty.

Luke 21:5–11: (See p. 187.)

■

"Nation will rise against nation. . . . There will be great earth-quakes . . . and in the sky fearful omens and great signs." The doomsayers have always been glib, and fear and anxiety will always be able to find some place in our hearts where they can strike root. Are not fear and apprehension among the mighty movers of history? For the prophets of doom, times of crisis are times of grace!

At the moment the evangelist Luke is consigning the faith witness of his Christian communities to writing, the temple lies in ruins. Of this sanctuary, pride of the Jewish people, not a stone remains upon a stone. Nothing! How solid, nay, indestructible, that edifice had been thought to be! What storms it could surely withstand! Yes, Herod had wanted this temple more beautiful than Solomon's. Its mighty walls had reached nearly to the sky, and believers' faith was confirmed. Now suddenly, only a few years after it had been completed, war had razed it to the ground. And the world around had collapsed as well.

Would this not be the hour of judgment? For the first Christian generation, will not the destruction of the temple be the sign of the end of all?

No. "Take care not to be misled. Many will come in my name saying . . . 'The time is at hand.' " Do not listen to the prophets of doom! They are impostors. Filled with faith, the evangelist lifts his head. The gospel is a proclamation of grace and blessing. The last days shall not be a moment of cataclysm. No, the day of the Lord had dawned when a certain Friday night exploded in everlasting daybreak. God's judgment had been pronounced the morning the sealed tomb had opened and gave forth a Life that cannot be exhausted. The times are accomplished. The end of days is here. In the Passover of the Lord, the world has accomplished its final passage. For the world is now the land of God. The balance of history has swung for good and all, tipped to the side of salvation. Now neither signs in the sky nor the terrors of our world can ever call this inversion, this transposition, into question. How ever can we have sung, "Dies irae, dies illa"—O day of wrath, that awful day!—as if everything were to end in panic and pandemonium?

The times are accomplished. The end of days is here. With the resurrection of Jesus Christ, all has changed. But we do not enter the new land through a gate simply swinging carelessly ajar. Hope is a daily event, history is ever to be created anew. There is a battle to be waged —the battle of a faith persecuted by such overwhelming evidence against it, mistreated by so many slammed doors and disappointed hopes, assaulted by such a profusion of failures and catastrophes. The day of the Lord is upon us! The Lord is ever coming, ever more near, ever at hand. The end of days is continuous Easter, Passover forever: a passage and an invitation to perseverance, an invitation to enter into history and live on the yeast of the gospel.

Brothers and sisters, were all the walls of our too human assurances to come tumbling down, were everything we hold most sacred to plunge to its ruin—yet close your ears to the prophets of doom! They are not telling you the truth. God's benevolence will have the last word. Believe me: we have hope with us, and that fragile bark will weather the storm and come safely into port. We have the hope to traverse history!

■

God our Father,
Lord of the ages, Ruler of all history,
the times of your promise are accomplished,
and your Word judges the world.
The old world now passes away—
      then let us see the new land!

By the power of the Spirit received in our baptism,
      grant us safe passage to your Reign,
that, together with all the blessed,
      we may sing the canticle of the saved.

TESTIMONY

Revelation 15:1–4: The end approaches, and with it the destruction of the enemies of God. The victory of the elect is assured. They have triumphed over the beast. They already live in the Land of Promise, where they sing the hymn of the Lamb—here doubtless a liturgical hymn inspired by the psalms. The image of the sea suggests the scope and nature of the battle they have had to wage. As we know, in biblical symbolism the sea is the refuge of the powers of hell. Here it suggests the pagan world and its perpetual struggle against the church of the witnesses.

But this sea is hard and transparent as crystal, and the vanquishers of the beast have crossed it as the Hebrews crossed the sea in their escape from Egypt under the leadership of Moses and the protection of Yahweh. The new people of the rescued too, may thank God, just as the people snatched from the hand of Pharaoh had sung their own gratitude (cf. Ex 15).

Psalm 98 invites us to sing the praises of the One who has never ceased to surround his people with such special protection.

Luke 21:12–19: (See p. 189.)

■

With faith persecuted by such overwhelming evidence against it, with hope mistreated by so many slammed doors and disappointed hopes, with our will to follow Jesus assaulted by such a profusion of failures and catastrophes, we have but one recourse: to cling not to any stammering words of our own, but to the faithfulness of a testimony; to rely not on our wavering little hopes, but on a love that transcends the vicissitudes of time; to gain our assurance not from a failed obedience, but from a seduction great with forgiveness. If we persevere, it will only be because the faith, hope and love of the church have come to the rescue of our hesitations, our cringing and our tepidity. Only the perseverance of the church is our assurance in these difficult times.

We stand before the church like children listening to their mother's reminiscences of her departed spouse. We shall never more know our Father but through her. Her memory bears the deep imprint of her faith and love, of course, and we suspect it may be colored by them. But we know that she would not intentionally deceive us. And then . . . whom could we believe if not his life companion, who has assimilated in his presence not only history, but history's heart—the heart of that spouse? If we persevere in faith, it will only be because our mother has taught us how to penetrate the secrets of our Lord.

We stand before the church like children who clutch their mother's hand to take a new step, to cross a new threshold. All our confidence in the face of life's challenges and questions has been learned from her steady guidance. If we persevere in hope, it will only be because our mother has taught us how to confront the unknown, how to take the necessary risks. We hope because she has brought us up in such a way that we really grow up, and dare to invent tomorrow.

We stand before the church like children who run to the mother who alone can console us in our failures, acting as our compassionate interpreter and advocate with our Father. From her we learn his parental mercy. By her we have been initiated into the secrets of life, and guided in our first steps. To her we return when assailed by doubt, error and disappointment. If we persevere in charity, it will only be because our mother has taught us how to live an ideal. Thanks to her loving support, our project has substance and consistency.

When your faith, your hope or your charity fall on hard times, brothers and sisters, run back to your mother. And by her perseverance, you shall have life.

■

God our Father,
ever faithful to your promise,
    you support us by your Spirit
    in the trials of these times.
Preserve us in faith, hope and charity,
that our perseverance may win us life.

■

In the hour of discouragement,
    Lord, be our strength.
In the hour of distress,
    be our peace;
in the hour of denial,
    our forgiveness.

At each and every moment
grant us the bread of your mercy:
that we may not find it too hard
to persevere to the term of history.

ON THAT DAY

Revelation 18:1–2, 21–23; 19:1–3, 9: "Babylon Station. Trains Stop Here." A station stop amidst an endless desert. Just a century ago, nothing beside remained of Babylon. In 539 B.C. the city of Babylon, so prideful that it had inspired the story of the tower of Babel, had fallen to the assaults of Cyrus. We can readily imagine the repercussions on the exiles. The oracles of Jeremiah 50–51 had already drawn lessons from the mighty catastrophe: the fall of Babylon was the beginning of the end for whatever imperialisms might attempt to impose their law at the expense of human rights.

The author of the Book of Revelation hands down the same judgment. The new Babylon, the "great harlot who sits by the waters of the deep" (Rev 17:1), the Rome of the Caesars, that blasphemes the God of the Christians, will know decline and fall. Yes, even mighty Rome. Once more the frailty of the powers of earth will be revealed!

"Happy are they who have been invited to the wedding feast of the Lamb"!— all those who have been marked by God's sign, all who have "washed their robes and made them white in the blood of the Lamb" (Rev 7:14). And it is these who are invited by *Psalm 100* to celebrate the victory of God over the dragon of hell.

Luke 21:20–28: (See p. 191.)

■

We may as well be straightforward about it. This sort of thing is not very much to our liking today. We find it disconcerting. The language of this proclamation has a strange ring in our ears, and its wild visions strike us as unrealistic. We find the violence distasteful or artificial. And enigmatic visions like these, these not altogether coherent images, these flashy, thunderous, simplistic abridgments of history's finale not only serve to sketch out, in the spirit of Jesus, the final event of the world, the last day—they embrace the whole future, the world's and ours. These passages may be obscure, but the fact remains that they attest that Jesus is Lord of the future, and that the ages will be completed by his coming—that, in this hour, the whole content of human history will find its meaning and fulfillment. The future is not cut from whole cloth. It is the product of a present that is heavy with meaning.

On that day, "men will die of fright. . . ." But you, "stand up straight and raise your heads, for your ransom is near at hand"! In the fate that tosses us about like corks in a typhoon, a call comes to our ears, reverberating like a thunderclap. No, we are not caught up in the hellish circle! Daily we tremble with fear, "dying of fright in anticipation of what is coming upon the earth." Are the horrors of starvation and civil war, the agony of other peoples today, our destiny tomorrow? Are we doomed to economic underdevelopment—or the development of chains of gulags? No, lift up your heads! You are not spinning in circles, you are striding toward the Day of the Lord! And if it takes another hundred thousand years, this world—this broken old world of ours, from which justice and love have flown, this world of people condemned to rotate in one spot because they have excommunicated love—this world will perish! On that day, "justice shall flower . . . and profound peace" (Ps 72:7), justice and peace for everlasting! Then shall the blind see the almond tree in bloom, and the imprisoned their night coming to an end. Yes, that time will come! We are not characters in a mad tale whose end is ever its beginning. No, God tells you, and tells you today: Keep awake, stay on the watch, examine the signs! Keep moving. And, hang it all . . . live!

That day will come! History is moving toward its fulfillment. That day will come. Life is not destined for destruction. But take the time to live, really to live, and a thousand years will be as one day, for you as for God. For God, the end has already begun. Eternity is already under way. "Alleluia! Salvation, glory, and might belong to our God, for his judgments are true and just!"

■

God, our Providence,
deliver us from fear,
and grant us peace in our days.
By your love release us from our fears.
In your mercy raise us up.
Grant us to see your promise,
your salvation, become ours
for ages without end.

■

Happy are they who have been invited to the wedding feast of the Lamb!

Be blessed, our Father.
Salvation and power are yours!

Pronounce your judgment upon us:
let our world see
> *the time of grace and divine espousal,*
> *the fulfillment of your covenant.*

FRIDAY OF THE 34TH WEEK

SPRING BUDS

Revelation 20:1–4, 11–21:2: The proclamation of the fall of Rome is followed by news of Satan's temporary imprisonment (vv. 1–6), a judgment scene (vv. 11–15) and the passage on the wedding of the Lamb (21:9–22:5). A great deal of ink has been spilled over the thousand-year chaining of the dragon. Let us return for a moment to the symbolism of the dragon and the beasts. First we note that God's rival, the dragon, never attacks God himself. Its assaults are reserved for his representatives on earth, as the messianic child and the offspring of the woman (chap. 12). And the dragon seems doomed to failure in all its undertakings. In chapter twelve it has been cast down to earth by Michael's heavenly armies (Rev 12:9), and with deadly consequences. True, having lost its place in heaven, it has taken up its abode by the shore of the sea (12:17) and conjured up from the deep two great beasts, to assist it in its satanic task (chap. 13). For, as we see, the dragon represents a pseudo-god from the nether world who, with the assistance of his lieutenants, seeks to deceive humankind. He is the god of the lie; but his chaining, like the liquidation of the beasts, prevents him from achieving his design.

The thousand years suggest contemporary speculation on Adam's sojourn in Paradise. With the coming of Christ and the imprisonment of Satan, believers once more have access to the life of Paradise. And indeed the incapacitation of the dragon is followed by a return to life of "those who had been beheaded for their witness to Jesus." The last judgment is concretized by the successive opening of a number of scrolls or books, one of which is the book of life. The saved are those whom God has chosen (listed in the book of life) and who have performed good deeds (recorded on the other scrolls). Physical death is then destroyed, and suffers the dragon's fate as it is cast into the abyss. As in all the apocalyptic frescos, the primordial creation is eliminated, to make room for a new world, in which the sea—Satan's refuge—is no more. And so we have the great vision of the heavenly Jerusalem, the church of the victorious.

Psalm 84 is drawn from sources originating in a number of different genres. Its core component is a song in which the pilgrims express to the temple functionaries their joy at finding themselves in the courts of the Lord.

Luke 21:29–33: (See p. 195.)

■

Jesus ascends the Mount of Olives. He contemplates Jerusalem. Yes, the city is still in the throes of death. The Pharisees are attacking him. The priests are obstinate, the Romans are moving into position. Jesus ascends the Mount of Olives and contemplates our world. He sees a world exploded, a society in full decomposition, religion itself on the point of collapse. Everyone is in search of points of orientation, planks to cling to in the storm—signs. And there are no signs! Our world is tumbling to its ruin, and everyone is still hanging on—all slogging away, the old regimes still in place, the church still beating its breast over the past. A world is born, and no one is there to watch!

Be ruled by the parable of the fig tree! Suddenly a dead tree blooms. Even now the cross explodes in resurrection. The seed cast to earth yields its fruit. One must die if one would live. "The book of the living was opened. . . . Death and the nether world gave up their dead. . . . Then I saw new heavens and a new earth. The former heavens and the former earth had passed away. . . ." The prophets of doom will have one more swaggering day—but do not believe them! Those who say that the world is not all right—they forget that God is at the bar of history. Do you see the fig tree in bud? Then let the old world die, for the new one is already here!

"The heavens and the earth will pass away, but my words will not pass." Then our hope can hold fast—this absurd act of trust we make in persons who have told us that they have received the Word of God, and that this Word is living, active, utterly revolutionary! Hope is what we experience when we see this word still uttered—still springing up, still decisive, even today. And this hope of ours is more than a mere expectancy on our part—more, even, than a sure, certain expectancy. It is our demand, as well. We insist that God keep his word. We will not permit God to make himself a liar! For God has told us: "My words will not pass." When God seems no longer to be at the helm of history, he must be compelled to take that helm once more, or to show that he has never abandoned it. We may compel him with a cry of anguish, or a reproach, or lamentation or contrition. We may force him with boldness, protestation, accusation. Our hope is neither smug confidence, then, nor affrighted rejection of the future nor sterile, pollyannish optimism. It is the full, vigorous response of a woman or man firm and decided: God must be held to his word. Our hope is an intentional provocation, and will not brook God's word dwindling away to a thing of the past. Our hope calls God to account if he fails to act as he has said he would act, or if he has not given evidence that he is acting. Hope is a defensive thrust when failure moves too close—"freedom's parry of death" (Neher). "Then death and the nether world were hurled into the pool of fire. . . ." Hope is a kind of blasphemy, in that it compels God to take the stand in his own prosecution. Our future, our history, cannot go down to destruction. No, the new land, the new earth, the Jerusalem from above, will descend from heaven, lovely as a bride arrayed for her groom. The word of God is true, and will gain the victory!

■

Time flies, and the world passes.
But the fig is already in bloom,
*   and the cross sprouts buds of green.*
Be blessed, God our Father,
*   For our history is moving toward you!*
We beseech you:
*   let not our hope fail!*
May it afford us, even now,
*   a glimpse of the joy of your salvation.*

SATURDAY OF THE 34TH WEEK

ON THE WATCH FOR TOMORROW
Revelation 22:1-7: "The angel showed me, John, the river of life-giving water, clear as crystal, which issued from the throne of God and of the Lamb. . . ." The river of Revelation recalls the river of Genesis, which issued from the earth to drench the Garden of Eden. It likewise suggests the torrent of Ezekiel's vision, which flowed from the right side of the temple to decontaminate the Dead Sea. The symbolism is clear: life comes directly from God and the Lamb. And now the vision of the river blends with that of the tree of life, with its medicinal virtues and its specifically eschatological fertility. Life and light, then—these are the special marks of the heavenly Jerusalem, for "the glory of God gave it light, and its lamp was the Lamb" (Rev 21:23).

We could wish that today's liturgy had included the closing verses of the Book of Revelation, especially those describing the encounter of the bride and the Lamb (Rev 22:17). These verses are of capital importance for the scope of this Johannine book, which does not recount "a simple return to the primitive golden age, but rather the fulfillment of a plan prophetically proclaimed by the history of our beginnings" (P. Pringent). The Book of Revelation centers on Christ. It is he who opens paradise. (Rev 22:3 explains that the ancient curse has been lifted.) And so we wonder when and how access is won to this paradise. In other words, is the Book of Revelation wholly and entirely orientated to the future?

The millenarian theme, as we have observed, stresses our present share in the life of Christ, for the Reign comes even now. On the day of Christ's resurrection, our expectation of the Reign was fulfilled. Christ is already here, in the sacraments, especially in baptism and the eucharist. (This is the obvious sense of the water of life, as well as of the *Marana tha*). Thus the Book of Revelation does not escape the eschatological tension that characterizes the "meantime," the time of the church. On the contrary, it makes every effort to express both the "already" and the "not yet." Through and through, the Book of Revelation is sacramental.

Of *Psalm 95* the liturgy has retained only the psalm of pilgrimage. Today we sing this song as Christians, as we go forth to meet the Lamb, slain and erect on God's holy mountain.

Luke 21:34–36: (See p. 198.)

■

At the dawn of the universe, in a garden of delights, was a tree of life. Humanity had been forbidden its fruit, and Satan the Divider had whispered that, were human creatures to eat of it, they would become God. At the end of history, a marvelous city, the great citadel of all human kind, descends from heaven, emerging from the presence of God, and beautiful as a bride arrayed for her husband. In the center of the city stands a tree, which bears its fruit twelve times a year, symbolizing life bestowed in superabundance: upon all of us, forever. The curse has been lifted! Life will be endless now, for it is the Lord himself who becomes the lamp and the light of the new city.

You will tell me: Yes, this is promised us. But the promise still remains a dream. Here we are today at the end of the road—the end of the last book of the Bible and the conclusion of our continuous reading of the Gospel of Luke—and what do we find? That we must begin again. "Be on guard . . ."! Have we been going around in circles, then? No, we have been travelling an ascending spiral. We are to walk the same road, ceaselessly, yes—but in a new way each time. "Be on guard . . ."! Naturally we remember the things that have happened in our lives. But this does not mean that we must repeat them. No, we are not in thrall to the dream of the past. And when we have taken our refreshment by the side of the road, it has been with a bit of bread that has both calmed our appetite, and whetted it. We have walked until very late tonight. But we have reached our destination. We await the dawn.

We watch for tomorrow, but we are not befogged by it. Fix your eye obstinately on one point and you will see nothing around it. The future, the new city, are on the horizon, but the route thither has yet to be charted. The passages of that route must be prepared, in a thousand ways. And the very horizon will withdraw at our approach.

"Be on guard . . ."! Remain awake! Has our waiting become too toilsome for us, the night too deep at times? But listen: God is coming. And he never ceases to come. The day is sure to dawn: therefore the new city is a-building even now. Therefore, too, our present history has an eternal dimension. Well does Péguy admonish me to believe that "I am human history, I am temporal history, I have a certain importance. I am history, and in my long history all that I do, all that I engage, involves—physically and naturally, as it were—Jesus, God. All that I do temporally inserts me quasi-physically into the very body of God. This is Christianity. Else earth and man would not be. There would be only heaven and the angels. . . . Else it would not have been worth the trouble to do so many things, to conduct so much business." Because we are on our guard, the age of God is born—today. Heed the word of the Lord: "Remember, I am coming soon! Happy the man who heeds the prophetic message of this book!"

∎

Lord our God,
you have placed all things
*   in the hands of your well-beloved Son.*
Grant us this grace: that we may hold fast in faith
*   and live by its light.*
May the time of your grace come—
*   the day of an eternity ever new.*

For a Continuous Commentary on the Gospel of Luke

Readers who prefer to center their meditation entirely on the Gospel of Luke may use the following table to locate the reflections ranged variously under odd and even years. (The missing pericopes are those on which we have not been inspired to compose a commentary!)

THE MINISTRY IN GALILEE

22 Monday	4:16–30	Beginning of Preaching
Tuesday	31–37	Jesus at Capharnaum
Thursday	5:1–11	Call of the First Disciples
Friday	33–39	The Question of Fasting
Saturday	6:1–5	Plucking Grain on the Sabbath
23 Monday	6:6–11	Jesus Heals on the Sabbath
Tuesday	12–19	Choice of the Twelve
Wednesday	20–26	The Great Discourse
Thursday	27–38	Love of One's Enemy
Friday	39–42	The Eye and the Plank
24 Monday	7:1–10	Cure of the Centurion's Servant
Tuesday	11–17	The Widow's Son
Wednesday	31–35	Christ's Verdict
Thursday	36–50	The Penitent Woman
Friday	8:1–3	The Women Who Served
Saturday	4–15	Parable of the Sower
25 Monday	8:16–18	Parable of the Lamp
Tuesday	19–21	True Kindred of Jesus
Wednesday	9:1–6	Mission of the Twelve
Thursday	7–9	Herod Learns of Jesus
Friday	18–22	Peter's Profession of Faith
Saturday	43–45	Second Prediction of the Passion
26 Monday	9:46–50	Against Ambition

THE ASCENT TO JERUSALEM

26 Wednesday	9:57–62	The Apostles' Requirements
Thursday	10:1–12	Mission of the Seventy-Two
Saturday	17:24	True Object of Rejoicing
27 Monday	10:25–37	The Good Samaritan
Tuesday	38–42	Martha and Mary
Wednesday	11:1–4	The Our Father

Thursday	5–13	Two Parables on Prayer
Friday	15–26	Jesus and Beelzebul
Saturday	27–28	True Happiness
28 Monday	11:29–32	The Sign of Jonah
Wednesday	42–46	Hypocrisy of Pharisees and Lawyers
29 Monday	12:13–21	Trust in God, Not in Possessions
Tuesday	35–38	Preparedness for the Master's Return
Wednesday	39–48	Preparedness for the Master's Return
Thursday	49–53	I Have Come to Light a Fire
Saturday	13:1–9	Patience
30 Monday	13:10–17	A Sabbath Cure
Wednesday	22–30	The Narrow Door
Thursday	31–35	Jesus and Jerusalem
Friday	14:1–6	Cure of a Dropsy Victim
Saturday	7–11	Lesson in Humility
31 Monday	14:12–14	Places at Table
Tuesday	15–24	Wedding Invitation
Wednesday	25–33	To Follow Jesus
Thursday	15:1–10	Parables of Divine Mercy
Friday	16:1–8	The Wily Manager
Saturday	9–15	Right Use of Money
32 Monday	17:1–6	Appeal for Faith
Tuesday	7–10	To Serve with Humility
Wednesday	11–19	Ten Lepers
Thursday	20–25	Coming of the Reign of God
Friday	26–37	Days of the Son of Man
Saturday	18:1–8	The Corrupt Judge
33 Monday	18:35–43	Cure of a Blind Person
Tuesday	19:1–10	Zacchaeus the Tax Collector
Wednesday	11–28	Parable of the Sums of Money

JESUS' MINISTRY AT JERUSALEM

33 Friday	19:45–48	The Traders Expelled
Saturday	20:27–40	Resurrection of the Dead
34 Monday	21:1–4	The Widow's Mite
Tuesday	5–11	Signs of the Reign to Come
Wednesday	12–19	Signs of the Reign to Come
Thursday	20–28	Coming of the Son of man
Friday	29–33	Parable of the Fig Tree
Saturday	34–36	Be on the Watch!